TREACHEROUS WEATHER

&

EARTHQUAKES

'I think that I shall eventually go to the North Island to stay & risk being swallowed up by an earthquake for this island has a treacherous climate. It is predicted that the whole of the North Island will disappear & also some of the South. The North Island has received plenty of warnings like San Francisco.' – Letter from Eleanor CHALMERS in Otekaike to sister Clara in London, December 16, 1906.

A

CHALMERS FAMILY

FROM

DUNDEE

LORRAINE BERRY

Published by Lindsay R Watson

36 Reid Crescent

Ashburton 7700

New Zealand

ISBN-13: 9781724112996

A catalogue record for this book is available from the National Library of New Zealand.

Printed by CreateSpace, an Amazon.com company

Charts were created with *Reunion 11.0.10*

Cover: Oil painting 'Macetown' by Barbara Smith, great-grandaughter of John and Eleanor CHALMERS

Dedication

This book is dedicated to our CHALMERS ancestors who left their homes and families in Scotland. After enduring a three month sea journey they settled in an untamed country on the other side of the world to fulfil their dream of a better quality of life.

Contents

Dedication iii
Acknowledgements vii
Preface ix
PART 1: The Dundee Connection 1
  1 Dundee Scotland 3
PART 2: Tauranga 11
  2 Bay Of Plenty 13
PART 3: Otago 23
  Otago-Southland Map 24
  3 Waitaki River Basin 25
  4 Beaumont and Gibbston Part 1 49
  5 Beaumont and Gibbston Part 2 63
PART 4: Southland 87
  Mataura Map 88
  6 Mataura 89
  7 Waiarikiki, Balfour, Gore and Hokonui 105
PART 5: The Next Generation 117
  8 Donald Rolls CHALMERS and Amelia Maribel PEART 119
  9 Malcolm Shaw CHALMERS and Nellie HASTIE 141
  10 David George CHALMERS and Betson Margaret
  CUNNINGHAM and Muriel Sophia Florence DANE 157
  11 Douglas Gollan CHALMERS and Violet Dina NATHAN 173
  12 John (Jack) Charles CHALMERS and Frances Louisa Beaven
  MITCHELL 191
  13 Gertrude Elizabeth CHALMERS and Philip BOYLEN 225
  14 Constance Eleanor CHALMERS and James McKIBBIN 245
  15 Gordon Rupert CHALMERS and Janet ANDERSON 257
  16 Norman Chamberlin CHALMERS and Elizabeth Mary
  MARSHALL 269
  17 Dora Grace CHALMERS and Arnold Henry McLeod GRUBB 281
PART 6: Early Scotland 307
  18 Early CHALMERS Families 309
PART 7: Leaving Dundee 343
  19 John BAXTER CHALMERS & Isabella FYFE 345
  20 Elizabeth CHALMERS and Charles STRACHAN 349
  21 George CHALMERS and Mary McQueen HUNTER 363
  Index 377
  About the Author 403

Acknowledgements

The material in this book has been collected over several decades and most of the people acknowledged have passed on.

Dora GRUBB (née CHALMERS) for an extensive collection of documents, photographs and letters on the John and Eleanor CHALMERS family, also for her personal knowledge.

Jessie KIEL (née CHALMERS), Raymond and Kenneth CHALMERS for information on and photographs of the Donald and Maribel CHALMERS, Malcolm and Nellie CHALMERS and John and Frances CHALMERS families. Jessie also provided information on William CHALMERS and Raymond on Norman and Elizabeth (Betty) CHALMERS.

Rosalie BLANCHARD (née CHALMERS), Neville and Martin CHALMERS for memories of the John and Frances CHALMERS family of Greenhills.

Lloyd CHALMERS for information about the family of David CHALMERS and Betson CUNNINGHAM.

Thelma GEARY (née BOYLEN) for information about the Philip and Gertrude BOYLEN and Constance and James McKIBBIN families, also for the Rupert and Janet CHALMERS family and William CHALMERS. Stephen GEARY and Barbara SOUNESS (née GEARY) for photographs and information about the Philip and Gertrude BOYLEN family.

Eleanor (May) EVANS (née CHALMERS) for information about the Rupert and Janet CHALMERS family, also Arnold and Dora GRUBB.

Agnes FRASER for a letter about John Charles CHALMERS.

Elizabeth COLE for letters and information about the John and Frances CHALMERS family.

Mervan MACARTNEY for information about the John and Frances CHALMERS family.

Jocelyn CHALMERS (née KERSE) for a taped account by Jessie KIEL (née CHALMERS).

Barbara SMITH (née CHALMERS) for providing the cover picture 'Macetown' and a black and white version of her work 'Gibbston'.

Special thanks to Lindsay WATSON, grand nephew of John and Frances CHALMERS, who made this publication possible and for meticulous preparation, adaptation and placement of maps, charts and photographs. Also much appreciated is his time-consuming work in the compilation of notes and indexes as well as assistance with editing. His suggestions and support have been invaluable.

National Library of New Zealand for maintaining the Papers Past website.

Preface

Family historians face many problems in their research. One of the frustrations is that the task is endless, since there is always the possibility that a new piece of evidence will turn up. However, genealogists eventually have to decide that their research is more or less complete and there is enough material to publish or/and deposit in an archive.

Today family historians can avail themselves of self-publishing and print-on-demand technology. This book was printed only after it had been purchased. This system allows the author to revise the text file easily, so the next print will be consistent with the latest research.

CHALMERS family descendants are invited to contact the author with omissions or corrections.

Lorraine Berry
No 6 Aqua Way
Paraparumu 5032
New Zealand
lorraine-berry@hotmail.com

More copies of this book are available from Amazon.com.

PART 1: The Dundee Connection

1 Dundee Scotland

This is an account of the family of John Howe CHALMERS and Eleanor Rebecca TIMS, their children and grandchildren. John Howe CHALMERS emigrated from Aberdeenshire in Scotland and arrived in New Zealand around 1878. The CHALMERS ancestors of John Howe are shown in Figure 1.2. The early Scottish ancestors and CHALMERS relations are covered in Chapter 18.

The name CHALMERS is thought to be a Scottish variant of the English occupational name CHAMBERS, used for someone who worked in the private living quarters of the aristocracy and is derived from the old French word 'cha(u)mbre,' meaning 'chamber'. CHALMERS had been traced back to the sixteenth century in Scotland.[1]

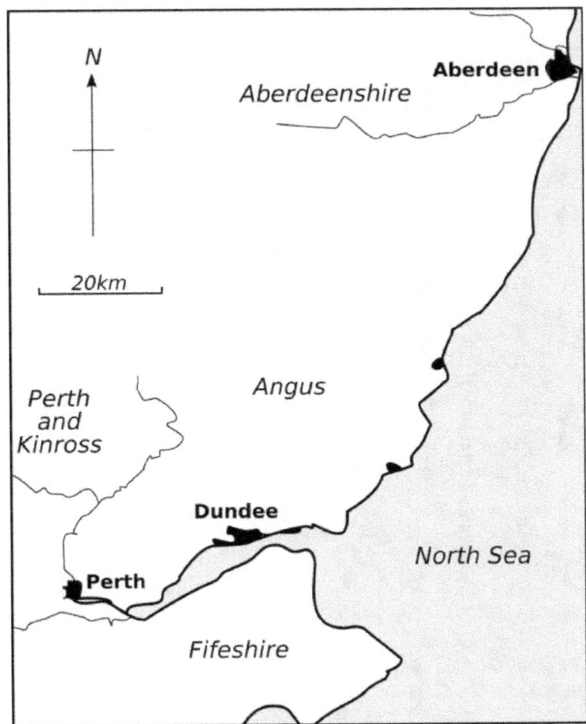

Figure 1.1. Part of the east coast of Scotland showing the places occupied by early members of the CHALMERS family.

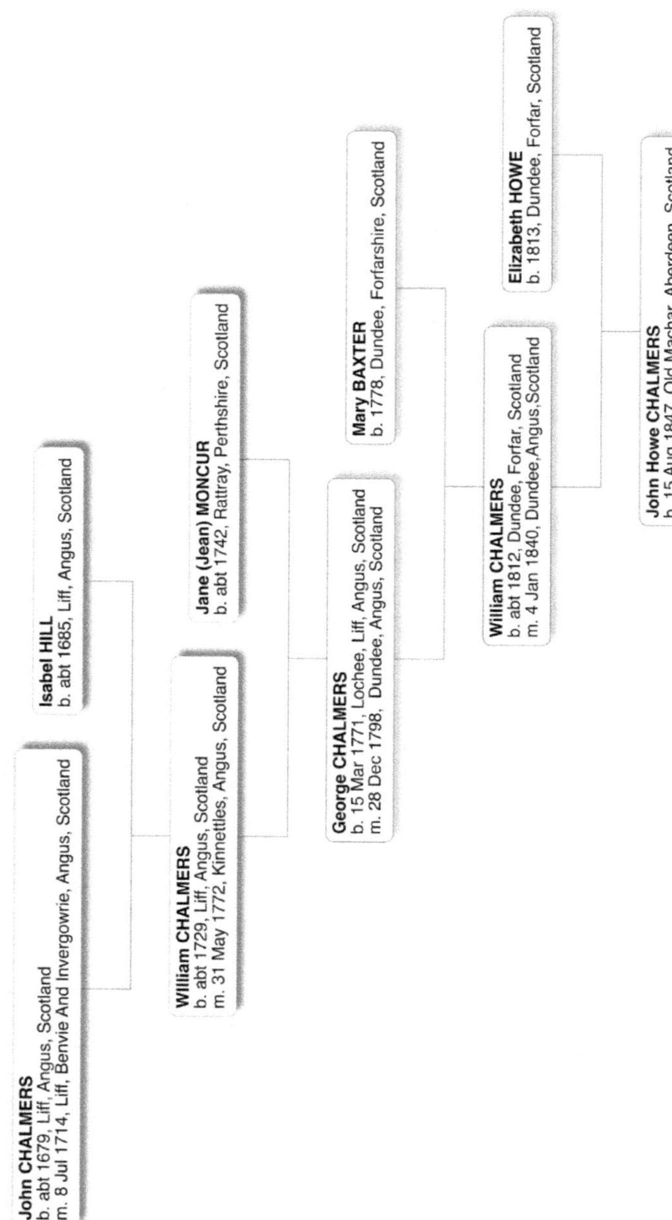

Figure 1.2. The CHALMERS ancestors of John Howe CHALMERS

William CHALMERS and Elizabeth HOWE

John Howe CHALMERS' parents were William CHALMERS and Elizabeth HOWE who married on 4 January 1840 at Dundee.[2] Elizabeth HOWE was born at Dundee in 1813, the daughter of David HOWE, leather merchant, and Ellen (maiden name unknown).[3] William and Elizabeth had five children. The first three were all born at Dundee. Their second child, David was born about 1840. He died at Dundee on 26 February 1842.[4]

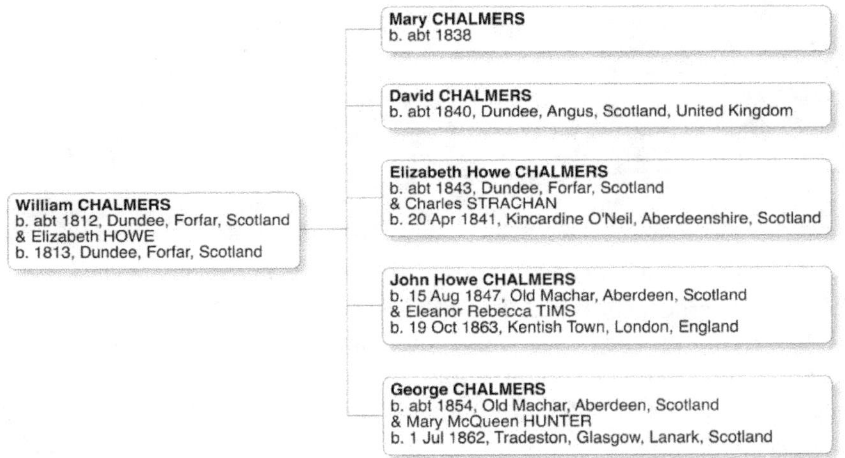

Figure 1.3. The family of William CHALMERS and Elizabeth HOWE

William CHALMERS was a mariner, probably on a whaling vessel. He changed his career later. In 1841 he was living with his wife Elizabeth HOWE and their three children at Norze Land, Dundee.[5]

Dundee was a major centre of the whaling industry in Victorian times and whale oil was used in jute production to soften the jute fibres before weaving. This became less viable by the late 19th century when excessive hunting exhausted the Arctic whale stocks.[6]

The family did not remain in Dundee for long and went to seek greener pastures in other burghs of Scotland. The fourth child of William CHALMERS and Elizabeth HOWE was born at Old Machar, Aberdeenshire on 15 August 1847.[7] He was named John Howe CHALMERS.

Figure 1.4. Shipping at Dundee, 1836. Source: author's collection

In 1750 Aberdeenshire had a population of almost 120,000, with about 16,000 living in Aberdeen. Thus more than 85% of the population lived in 85 rural parishes with populations varying from about 300 to 3000. A century later (about 1850) the population was almost 200,000 – 42,000 families living in 32,000 homes. About a third of these were living in Aberdeen city. About a third of the land was under cultivation, mainly for oats, and sheep and cattle were grazed. Most of the rural population lived in small towns and farm hamlets.[8]

In 1851 the family was living at Love Lane, Spittal, Old Machar. William had become a flesher, otherwise known as butcher. He is listed as one of 77 fleshers in Old Aberdeen.[9]

The Seven Incorporated Trades of Aberdeen came to pass when the Fleshers were added to the membership in 1657 to entitle them to use the first Trinity Hall following its establishment in the city centre. The six preceding trades were: Hammermen, Bakers, Wrights and Coopers, Tailors, Shoemakers and Weavers. The Fleshers as skilled men from butcheries, businesses and slaughterhouses in the burgh had first been incorporated as a trade in 1534. It became custom for new entrants to provide a lavish banquet as part of their acceptance, making use of their renowned produce. Still today, their social function has shared responsibility with each of the Seven Incorporated Trades of Aberdeen for organising a range of social activities to open the doors of Trinity Hall to members and guests alike.[10]

Figure 1.5. Flesher Arms. Source: author's collection

Figure 1.6. John Knox Churchyard, Aberdeen. Source: Lorraine BERRY

A fifth and final child was added to the CHALMERS family with the arrival of George in 1854. William died on 14 July 1860 at Old Machar, the cause of death being given as 'aneurism of the aorta opening into trachea for weeks'. His death certificate gives his occupation as Master Flesher. Elizabeth CHALMERS his daughter was the informant. William was buried at John Knox Churchyard, Aberdeen. (See Figure 1.6.)

Elizabeth initially stayed on at 3 Love Lane during 1861 with children Elizabeth, John and George. The family was still living there at the time of daughter Elizabeth's marriage to Charles STRACHAN on 24 December 1863 at Old Machar, Aberdeenshire. Charles was born at Kincardine O'Neil, Aberdeenshire. He was a son of Charles STRACHAN, farmer and Henrietta COOPER. At the time of his marriage he was a provision merchant. (See Chapter 20.)

By 1871 Elizabeth, cattle dealer's widow, and youngest son George were living at Mitchells Land, Bishopbriggs, Lanarkshire, probably to be with or near Elizabeth and Charles STRACHAN. In 1881 Elizabeth and son George were living with the STRACHAN family at 49 Tillie Street, Glasgow.

Figure 1.7. Elizabeth HOWE. Source: author's collection

Later that year Elizabeth STRACHAN and children sailed for New Zealand to join Charles who had already left Scotland to prepare the way for his family.

The 1961 obituary for a daughter, Miss H.C. STRACHAN states that 'she came to New Zealand in 1881 at the age of 14 with her mother, sister and two brothers to join her father who had migrated here two years earlier.' (See Chapter 20.)

Elizabeth died in 1886. Her death certificate records: 'Elizabeth CHALMERS, widow of William CHALMERS, daughter of David HOWE Leather Merchant (decd) and Ellen HOWE (decd) ms … (decd) died on 2 March 1886 at Kimberly Villa in Mary Street, Dunoon, County Argyll. She died after suffering from liver cancer for six months. Informant: George CHALMERS Son Present.'[11]

Elizabeth's estate was given as:

> CHALMERS Elizabeth 23/03/1886 or HOWE, residing in Dunoon, d. 02/03/1886 at Dunoon, testate Dunoon Sheriff Court SC51/32/33. Value of personal property £142.75.[12]

Nothing further is known for certain of Elizabeth's daughter Mary CHALMERS after 1851. She had been born about 1838 in Dundee.

John Howe CHALMERS born 15 August 1847 does not show on any later Scotland records revealed to date. His last known event there was in 1863 when, as a sixteen year old, he was witness to the marriage of his sister Elizabeth in Old Machar, Aberdeenshire. His next appearance is in 1879 in Tauranga, New Zealand where he is listed as a settler and farmer.

NOTES

---

[1] House of Names, 2018, https://www.houseofnames.com/chalmers-family-crest/English; Surname Database, 2017, http://www.surnamedb.com/Surname/Chalmers

[2] William CHALMERS, seaman, and Elizabeth HOW, both this parish, married 4 January 1840, Old Parish Registers, Marriage 282/220 400, Dundee, Page 400 of 434, National Records of Scotland.

[3] General Registers Office for Scotland, *Census Scotland 1851* Online database, Parish: Old Machar; ED: 2; Line: 4; Year: 1851; Death certificate of Elizabeth CHALMERS.

[4] CHALMERS David WM CHALMERS 1 M 26/02/1842 282/270 287 Dundee.

[5] 1841 Scotland Census.

[6] "The Victorian Achievement History Trail Victorian Dundee Jute, Jam and Journalism", last modified 19 September 2014, http://www.bbc.co.uk/history/scottishhistory /victorian/trails_victorian_dundee.shtml

[7] Index to Baptisms for Old Machar, 1820-1854 Film no 0991251.

[8] "Life in Aberdeenshire, 18th & 19th centuries Geography and history", no date, https://mcnaughtonfamilyhistory.wordpress.com/info/life-in-aberdeenshire-18th-19th-centuries/

[9] CHALMERS, William, flesher, Love-lane, Spittal, Basement-floor, New-market (spelling as given). Cornwall's New Aberdeen Directory for 1853-54 Aberdeen: Printed and Published by Geo. Cornwall, 54, Castle Street. 1853.

[10] "Seven Incorporated Trades of Aberdeen/Fleshers", modified 2016, www.seventradesofaberdeen.co.uk/2013/04/fleshers/

[11] General Registers Office for Scotland, Death certificate of Elizabeth CHALMERS.

[12] Scotland, National Probate Index (Calendar of Confirmations and Inventories), 1876-1936; www.scotlandspeople.gov.uk.

PART 2: Tauranga

2 Bay Of Plenty

The last knowledge of John Howe CHALMERS prior to 1879 was his attendance at the marriage of his sister Elizabeth at Aberdeen, Scotland on 24 December 1863.[1] His whereabouts in the intervening years is unknown. A later neighbour knew he was much travelled. Family tradition has it that he joined the navy which accounted for the tattoo on one arm, also that he spent time practising his trade as a draper at a warehouse in Ceylon, currently known as Sri Lanka.[2]

Figure 2.1. John Howe CHALMERS, 1870s.
Source: author's collection

A record of his migration to New Zealand has not been found and it can be assumed that he would have sailed on a merchant vessel and jumped ship or have been accommodated in the steerage part of a passenger ship along with other single men. He arrived in New Zealand in about 1878.[3]

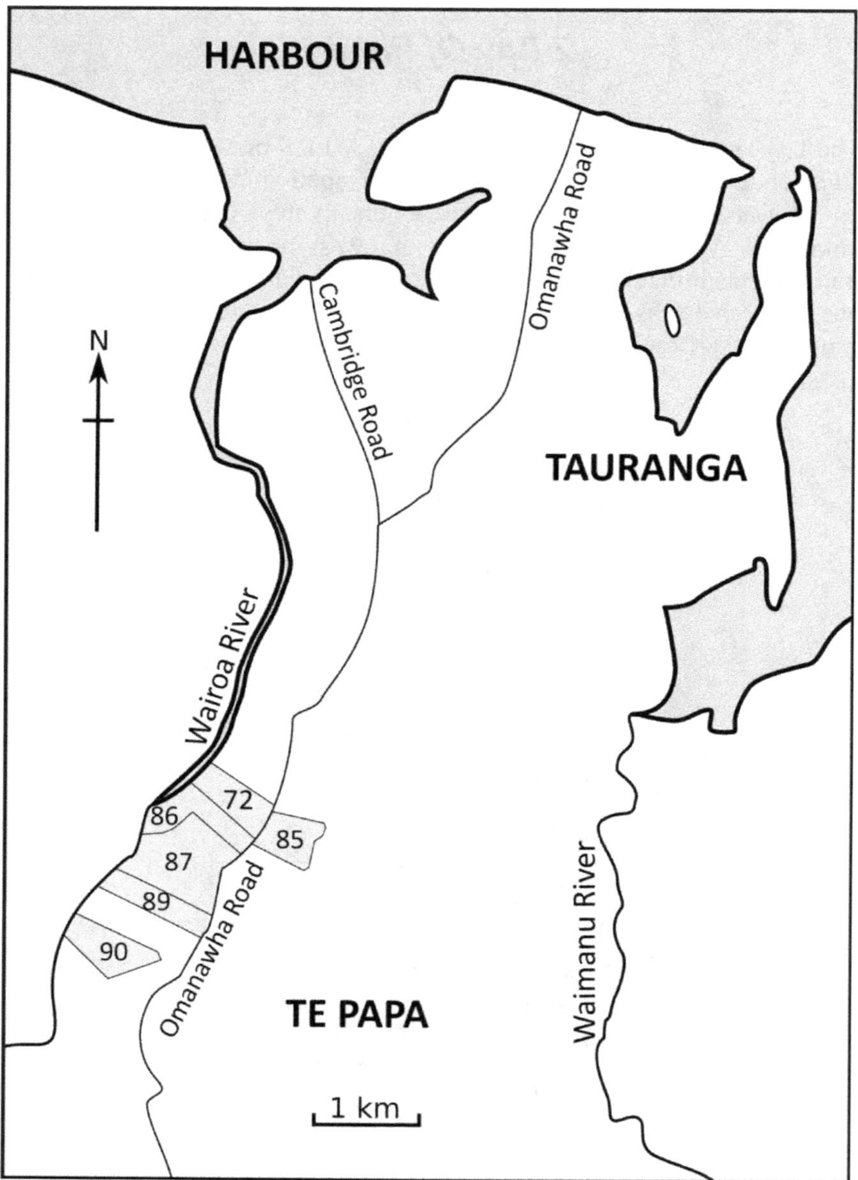

Fig 2.2. Map showing the sections belonging to John CHALMERS (85,), John CHALMERS and George SHAW (89), George SHAW (90) and Rupert STEVENSON (72, 86 and 87). Source: Based on Tauranga County Index Map 1889 held at Tauranga Public Library

Figure 2.3. Rupert STEVENSON and his wife, c.1885. Source: author's collection

Whatever the means, John must have been in a position to save a reasonable amount of money. In 1879 he is listed as a resident of Tauranga and as a settler in Tauranga as of September 1880.[4] By 1880–1881 John was the owner of freehold property (Lots 85 and 89) in the Parish of Te Papa. Te Papa is now a suburb of Tauranga.[5] Rupert STEVENSON and his wife owned property, Lots 72, 86 and 87 next to John CHALMERS near the Omanawha Road, Te Papa.[6]

Also next to John's property, Lots 80a and 90 were owned by a Mr George SHAW. John and George SHAW owned Lot 89.[7] (See Figure 2.2.) By November 1881 the two men had become partners in the dairy industry with success at cheese-making at 'Sauchie', their farm. 'Sauchie' was probably named after a village in the Central Lowlands of Scotland. It lies north of the River Forth and south of the Ochil Hills within the council area of Clackmannanshire. It was likely George's birthplace.[8] A newspaper report of that time reads:

We have to thank Messrs SHAW and CHALMERS for a sample cheese made on their farm at 'Sauchie'. Judging from this specimen of local production, we should say that our Tauranga settlers should be able to compete successfully in the manufacture with any part of the colony. In two or three days, when we get rid of the pressure on our space, caused by election excitement, we shall refer more fully to this matter. At present we content ourselves with saying that the cheese is well-flavoured, and appears to possess all the qualities for which some of the favourite English cheeses are famous.[9]

15

True to its word, the Tauranga-based newspaper published an in-depth article on the progress in and plans for an increase in locally manufactured goods for domestic use with less reliance on importation. Using George and John as examples, it went on to expound their successful endeavour:

> There is always a prejudice, somehow, against a local article, but in the latest development of our local industry the article produced is of so satisfactory a quality that it will rapidly become popular. We allude to the cheese manufacture by Messrs SHAW and CHALMERS, and which we have inspected, and can say is a first-class article. Although only a commencement, the article produced is of most excellent manufacture, tempting to look at, and quite equal in every respect to the best imported from the South. The only thing it wants is what it is gaining day by day, and that is age. It is very gratifying to find the maiden attempt here of Messrs SHAW and CHALMERS such a thorough success, and we trust the public of Tauranga will thoroughly appreciate their enterprise and so patronise the local article as to enable it to become soundly and firmly established in the market in preference to the imported article.[10]

Coincidentally, on the same day the newspaper reported an event taking place that John would be unaware of but that was to profoundly affect his future.

> A report was spread this morning that a square rigged vessel was seen out beyond Mayor Island, and it at once became the talk of the town that the ship *May Queen* was in sight.' Despite enquiries to several reliable sources that refuted the claim, many people gathered on the Victoria and Town Wharves to see something like the top-masts of a vessel appear between the pilot station and the Mount. The hopeful crowd was to be gratified on 16 December when the *May Queen* dropped anchor at Tauranga Harbour.[11]

Figure 2.4. Tauranga Harbour, 1880s. Source: Tauranga City Council, 'Tauranga Street Directory 1880. As published in the Bay of Plenty Times July to September 1880

16

On board was the TIMS family who had sailed from London on 26 August.

> MAY QUEEN
> LONDON TO TAURANGA
> 26 AUGUST 1881 - 16 DECEMBER 1881
> Passengers marked * were for Tauranga. Captain Best.
> CABIN
> TIMS *T. H., Clara, Thomas C
> SECOND CLASS
> TIMS *J, Mrs, Eleanor (Nelly), Martha (Dolly)[12]

Eleanor had travelled with her father, John Rolls TIMS, her mother, Caroline Elizabeth MEYER and younger sister Martha. Their intention in travelling to New Zealand is unknown, but son and brother, John Chamberlin TIMS had arrived aboard the *Oxford* on 2 April 1881 to settle in the Bay of Plenty. They were still there on 24 January 1882 when Caroline wrote a letter to a company in England acknowledging receipt of fifty-three pounds, fifteen shillings and fourpence (£53 15s 4d) that she wished to be lodged in the Tauranga branch of the Bank of New Zealand. In her letter she expressed pleasure at New Zealand's climate and mentioned the engagement of her daughter Eleanor and her marriage that was to take place the following month.[13]

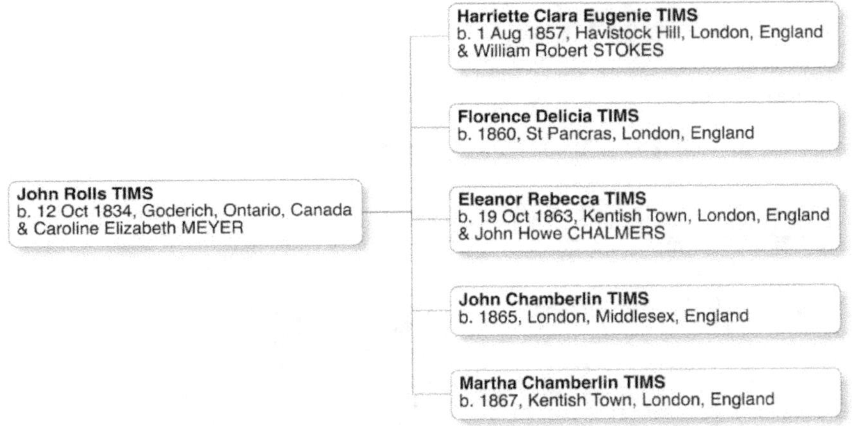

Figure 2.5. The children of John Rolls and Caroline Elizabeth TIMS

Eleanor had taken up work as a governess. Although considerably older than herself John Howe CHALMERS appealed to her on account of his good looks and fine dress sense. She especially liked his white, silk belltopper. Her parents were devastated at the news of her forthcoming marriage of their minor daughter to him, however Eleanor's mother Caroline gave her permission. The couple was married at Tauranga on 20 February 1882.[14]

John and Eleanor had met at Rotorua where they were said to be entertainers. They shared musical talents, John as a concert singer and Eleanor an accompanist on the piano.[15] Eleanor had learned to play the piano from the age of four. She also sang in public.[16]

The route between Tauranga and Rotorua was a very rough one.

> Despite difficulties of access, the area has long drawn visitors. Travelling by foot or horseback, intrepid European adventurers arrived at the heart of the Hot Lake District from as early as 1830. The end of the Land Wars in the 1870s brought an immediate boom to tourism. Visitors travelled to see the wonders of the Pink and White Terraces, to investigate the powers of the curative waters and to see the unique thermal activity. Travelling by ship to Tauranga, they completed the journey by wagon, coach, horseback or foot to a frontier town with unpaved roads, accompanied by dust in the summer and mud in the winter the journey was not for the faint-hearted.[17]

Figure 2.6. Advertisement for E. Robertson & Co.'s Coach Service that ran between Tauranga and Rotorua. Source: Tauranga Street Directory 1893

Figure 2.7. Eleanor Rebecca CHALMERS (née TIMS), 1906. Source: author's collection

On 17 May 1882 John Howe, along with forty-five other signatories, requisitioned the Mayor of Tauranga and Chairman of the Tauranga County Council, George Vesey STEWART, urging him to consider certain pressing requests of the district, and in particular the construction of a railway line between Tauranga and the Hot Lakes District.[18]

> The Government took over the Rotorua Railway Company operations in 1886. From this time onwards, the Public Works Department undertook construction of the line. At the time of the Mount Tarawera eruption (21 June 1886) George Vesey STEWART proposed a railway route between Tauranga and Rotorua, but this did not eventuate.[19]

Three of John and Eleanor's children were born at Tauranga. The first two were twin boys:

> CHALMERS At Tauranga, on the 30th inst, the wife of J.H. CHALMERS, of Sauchie, of twins, both sons,[20]

Named Donald Rolls and Malcolm Shaw, the boys were born prematurely and wrapped in cotton wool. Their father would walk the floor at nights with both babies in his arms.[21]

In 1882 the first meeting of the Tauranga, Butter, Cheese and Bacon Factory Company (Limited) was held and 'very largely attended – the neighbourhood being well represented – and the leading farmers in the district were present, and entered heartily into the projects.' The name of CHALMERS was listed amongst nineteen others with several more, unnamed. 'Mr CHALMERS proposed that there should be a cheese, butter and bacon factory started. Seconded by FARRER and carried.'

The Chairman then said that as a matter of experience it was far more satisfactory to work with a liberal number of dairy cattle than in a small way, and this to him was the great advantage in the Company. The Chairman then called upon the secretary, W. de R. BARCLAY, to read the prospectus and explain the proposed scheme of operations, This was complied with, and it was then resolved that the Company should be formed under the Companies Act, 1882.

It was further resolved, on the proposition of Mr LOUCH, seconded by Mr CHALMERS, that the prospectus as read be approved of. This was carried unanimously.'

J.H. CHALMERS was one of fourteen men proposed, seconded and duly elected as provisional directors. They agreed to take shares in the Company to the amount of £480.

> The Provisional Directors held a meeting immediately after, and appointed a working Committee to take the outside district limits, and ascertain how many cows can be relied upon from the farmers to insure the required milk supply.
> The Secretary was authorised to canvass the district and take the necessary steps for the formation of the Company.[22]

A daughter was added to the family with the arrival of Violet Hoppner on 11 February 1884 at Tauranga.

> CHALMERS on Monday, 11th inst, at 'Sauchie' Omanua [Omanawha], the wife of John Howe Chalmers, of a daughter.[23]

It is difficult to know the reason why the CHALMERS family decided to move to the South Island when there were accounts of successful enterprises in the Bay of Plenty with more on the horizon.

NOTES

---

[1] Marriage Certificate, Elizabeth CHALMERS, 24 December 1863, Aberdeen, Scotland, Scotland Statutory Records.

[2] Dora GRUBB (née CHALMERS), pers. com.

[3] Register of Marriage for the District of Tauranga from 1 January 1882 to 31 March 1882.

[4] *Bay of Plenty Times*. September 2, 1879; *Bay of Plenty Times*. "Tauranga, Ptitiki, Rotorua and Katikati Directory." September 25, 1880.

[5] CHALMERS, John, Hawke's Bay, Bay of Plenty, East Cape Electoral Rolls, 1880-1881.

[6] *Bay of Plenty Times*. December 12, 1881.

[7] George SHAW and John Howe CHALMERS. Allotment 89, Parish of Te Papa, Cook County, 80 acres, *The New Zealand Gazette*, 1884, No.109, p.1422.

[8] 1851 Scotland Census.

[9] *Bay of Plenty Times*. November 30, 1881.

[10] *Bay of Plenty Times*. December 7, 1881.

[11] *Ibid.*

[12] *Bay of Plenty Times*. December 17, 1881; "New Zealand Yesteryears: Passenger Lists 1800-1900", no date, www.yesteryears.co.nz/shipping/passlists/ mayqueen.html

[13] Letter in possession of the author.

[14] Thelma GEARY, daughter of Gertrude CHALMERS, pers. com.; Marriage Certificate, John Howe CHALMERS and Eleanor Rebecca TIMS, Tauranga, 20 February 1882 in possession of the author; *Bay of Plenty Times*. February 24, 1882.

[15] Dora GRUBB (née CHALMERS), pers. com.

[16] Jessie KIEL (née CHALMERS), daughter of Donald CHALMERS, pers. com.

[17] D.M. Stafford, *The New Century in Rotorua* (Ray Richards and Rotorua District Council: Rotorua, 1988).

[18] *Bay of Plenty Times*. June 3, 1882.

[19] "Rotorua Branch", last modified 2018, https://en.wikipedia.org/wiki/Rotorua_Branch

[20] *Bay of Plenty Times*. October 31, 1882; *Bay of Plenty Times*. November 1, 1881; NZRG, Birth Register, 1882/14246, CHALMERS, Donald Rolls, Eleanor Rebecca, John Howe; NZRG, Birth Register, 1882/14247 CHALMERS Malcolm Shaw, Eleanor Rebecca, John Howe.

[21] Dora GRUBB (née CHALMERS), pers. com.

[22] *Bay of Plenty Times*. "Tauranga Butter." September 1, 1883.

[23] *Bay of Plenty Times*. February 12, 1884.

PART 3: Otago

Otago-Southland Map

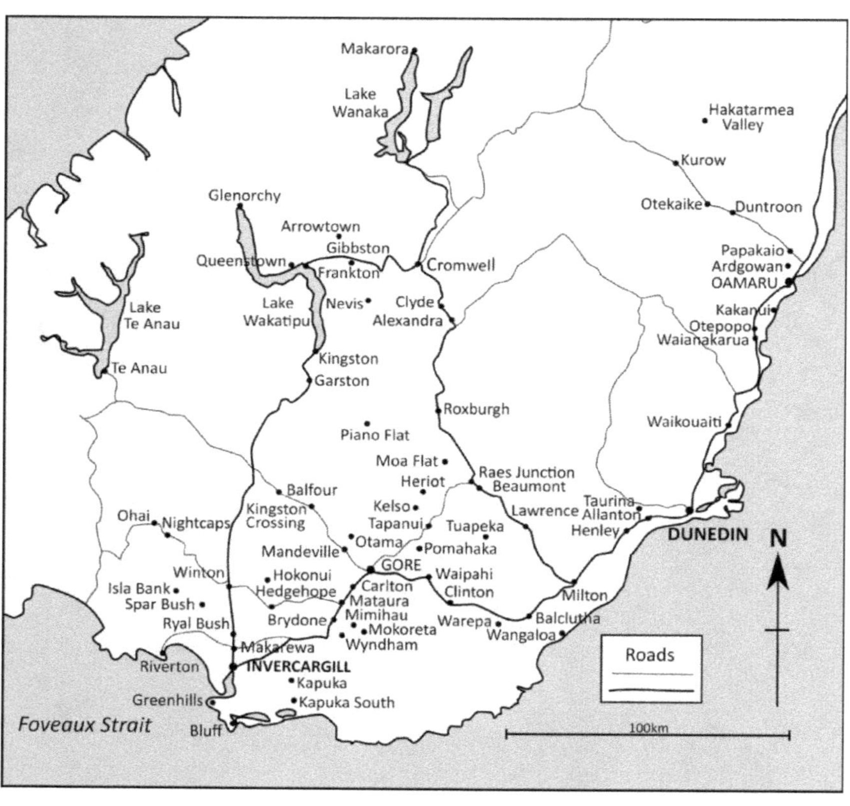

3 Waitaki River Basin

Although by 1885 John and Eleanor CHALMERS were living in Duntroon in the Waitaki region of North Otago, in the 1885-1886 Electoral Roll John Howe was still listed as a farmer of Freehold Lots 85 and 89 Parish of Te Rapa.[1] In July of 1885 Eleanor's brother John Chamberlin TIMS was staying with them at Duntroon.[2]

By October 1885 John Howe's business partner George SHAW had joined with a man by the name of MILLER at 'Sauchie'. They received two pure-bred Berkshire brood sows with the intention of improving the breed of pigs in the district.[3]

Figure 3.1. John Howe CHALMERS,
1880s. Source: author's collection

George appears to have maintained his farming business at Te Rapa. The 1885-1886 Electoral Roll also has him listed as freehold owner of a warehouse at Christchurch. The contents are unknown. It can be surmised that both George and John Howe shared an earlier interest in drapery. At some stage their partnership had taken a new form as storekeepers at Duntroon. The business did not last.

An advertisement appeared in the *North Otago Times* on 14 September and another on the 27 September, 1886.

WE have this day sold our Grocery Business at Duntroon to Mr GEO. PERRY, for whom we solicit a continuance of the favcrs extended to us.

SHAW AND CHALMERS.

WITH reference to the above, I would respectfully inform the Public of Duntroon and Surrounding Districts, that no eff rt will be spared by me to merit a continuance cf their suport.

srl4   GEORGE PERRY.

Figure 3.2. Advertisement. Source: North Otago Times. September 14, 1886

THE PARTNERSHIP existing between GEO. SHAW and JOHN HOWE CHALMERS, trading as Storekeepers in Duntroon under the names of SHAW and CHALMERS since 17TH January last, has this day been DISSOLVED by mutual consent.

ALL ACCOUNTS owing by the late firm will be paid by Geo. Shaw. All accounts owing to the late firm will be received by Geo. Shaw.

GEO. SHAW,
JOHN HOWE CHALMERS.

Figure 3.3. Advertisement announcing the dissolution of the partnership between George SHAW and John Howe CHALMERS. Source: Oamaru Mail. September 27, 1886

George moved to Christchurch where, by 1890, he had become firmly established as a draper.[4]

It is difficult to understand why the general store and drapery business was abandoned and why John and Eleanor then chose sheep and crop farming over dairying. Perhaps land availability and the 1884 Married Women's Property Act, allowing women to hold property in their own right, had something to do with it. Previously it was the right of widows only.

Following the sale of the business the CHALMERS family's focus returned to rural life and over the following twenty years there were numerous dealings with the Otago Land Board. In 1885 decisions were being made about whether or not to throw open land known as the 'Kurow Run' for settlement at Kurow and Otekaike. Settlers were ready to purchase for agricultural purposes without delay. They requested an inspection by the Land Commission to ascertain the land's quality and suitability. There was discussion about the merits of local settlement compared with company profits being sent Home (to the United Kingdom). The size of the sections was debated and also whether the settlers would prefer the land to be opened up under the deferred payment system or by perpetual lease.[5]

Figure 3.4. Photo of William Howe CHALMERS as a toddler, b. 28 December 1886 at Duntroon. Photographer Martin, Thames Street Oamaru. Source: author's collection

Figure 3.5. Photo of David George CHALMERS as a baby born 30 August 1887 at Kurow. Source: author's collection

While William Howe was born at Duntroon (b. 28 December 1886), David George (b. 30 August 1887) and Douglas Gollan (b. 18 September 1889) were born at Kurow.

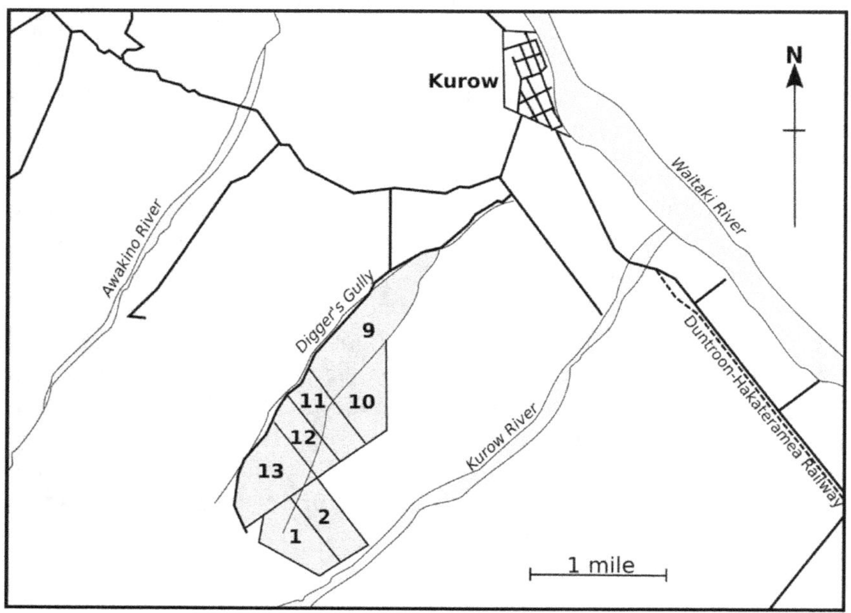

Figure 3.6. The CHALMERS' land holdings at Kurow 1887-1906: Block 8, Sections 1 and 2; Block 10 Sections 9, 10, 11, 12 and 13. Source: based on New Zealand. Department of Lands and Survey, Saunders, A. H. Series: NZMS 13 (Online); OT 53, 1922

It took several years and dealings with the Land Board before the CHALMERS family finally acquired their land. They considered various sections in Blocks 1, 4 and 9, but due to poor land quality or cost John and Eleanor eventually settled for Block 8, Sections 1 and 2 and Block 10, Sections 9 to 13. (See Figure 3.6.)

In September 1886 John Howe applied to lease rural land Section 6, Block 4 in the Kurow district on deferred payments.[6] After a personal inspection of the land, six weeks later he asked that his deferred payment of Section 6, Block 4 in the Kurow district be revalued as he considered it to be only fit for pastoral purposes on account of its stony nature. His request was referred to Ranger Hughan for report.[7]

By 1887 John Howe CHALMERS had leased land and was farming at

Kurow in the Waitaki River Basin.[8] However, on 14 August the *North Otago Times* published the new price per acre for perpetual lease holdings and the rate for the CHALMERS' property was increased. (See Table 3.1.)

Table 3.1. Deferred Payment and Perpetual Lease Holdings[9]

Name of Selector	District	Lease or License No.	Area A.R.P.	Original Upset Price per Acre £.s.d.	Price agreed to be paid per Acre £.s.d.
John H. CHALMERS	Kurow	5057	302.2.15	1.5.0	3.0.0

Through 1890 to 1896 John Howe and Eleanor Rebecca CHALMERS continued to farm at Kurow.[10] By the middle of 1890 Kurow settlers were still finding it difficult to make ends meet and secure their property rights. They placed an objection to the rentals they were expected to pay for Crown lands. The Board needed to reconsider previous valuations of sections. Regarding Section 6, Block 9, Kurow, containing 302 acres 2 roods 15 perches, it considered the present rate of 60s to be fair and well worth the money. This was in accordance with the opinion of the ranger and negated John Howe's proposed price of 25s. The Board could not see their way to make any further reduction.[11]

Eleanor Rebecca CHALMERS applied for rural land on perpetual lease for Sections 10 and 11, Block 10, Kurow district from James STRACHAN. Approval was given by the Board subject to payment due.[12]

The Receiver of Land Revenue had given notice some months previously to relectors whose sections had been revalued, requiring payment of adjusted amounts (due by them on 30 June last) before the approval of the Minister could be obtained in revaluation. He had received no replies. Relectors referred to included J.H. CHALMERS. The meeting agreed that if payments were not paid within a month the revaluation would have no effect. The Board would then have to take proceedings to forfeit for non-payment of the original arrears.[13]

The application of J.H. CHALMERS Section 6, Block 4, Kurow district, to capitalise, was approved by the Lands Board in October.[14]

Eleanor CHALMERS responded to Edward STRINGER's non-compliance with conditions of his perpetual lease. She wrote stating that he had put in twice the required amount of improvements, and for that reason was exempt from residence. Referred to Ranger HUGHES for correctness of statements.[15]

In February the following year Eleanor CHALMERS was asked to show why her license of sections 10 and 11 on perpetual lease should not be forfeited. The case of Mr CHALMERS was allowed to stand for a week.[16]

About two weeks later applications were approved for Eleanor Rebecca CHALMERS to transfer Sections 10 and 11, Block 10, Kurow to her husband John Howe CHALMERS.[17]

Notice was given by way of advertisement with regard to having Deferred Payment Licence No. 5066 transferred. Joseph GREEN of Kurow applied under Section 117 of The Land Act 1855 to have John Howe CHALMERS also of Kurow, farmer, accepted instead of himself as the licensee of Section 1 Block 8, Kurow Survey District; and that such application would be considered by the Land Board at a Meeting to be held on Wednesday, 16 day September 1891. The advertisement had been placed by J.P. Maitland Commissioner of Crown Lands, Crown Land Office Dunedin on 10 August 1891.[18]

Consideration of an application by Joseph GREEN to transfer deferred payment Section 1, Block 8, Kurow district to John Howe CHALMERS was deferred for a ranger's report concerning improvements to the property.[19] In 1892

> The Waitaki Basin was seriously affected by a flood that took down bridges at Kurow and Duntroon. The railway line was badly damaged and many farms were submerged. 'Several settlers had narrow escapes from drowning and were rescued from their houses by ropes.'[20]

Part of the CHALMERS property was in the low-lying section of Diggers Gully and may well have been subjected to flooding.

The Board approved transfer of the perpetual lease of Section 2, Block 8 Kurow district from John HARWOOD to Mrs Eleanor CHALMERS in March 1892.[21]

Another application made by Eleanor was approved six weeks later for Section 12, Block 10 from Mary MULVENIA.[22] However, there was a dispute over the deal when Mrs Mary MULVENIA wrote requesting the board to rescind the approval of the transfer of perpetual lease of Section 12, Block 10, Kurow. The Chief Commissioner could see no reason for rescinding the approval that had gone through once the title to the section acquired by transfer was complete.

Mr HISLOP (Perpetual Trustees, Estate and Agency Company), who represented Eleanor, said that Mrs MULVENIA could not have completed her title without making a payment of rent. This she had done and the money was deposited with a third party by Mrs CHALMERS until the transfer should be effected. While Mrs MULVENIA could not be compelled to sign a transfer to Mrs CHALMERS, the Chief Commissioner said that, of course, Mrs CHALMERS had a remedy at law. After some further discussion it was agreed to defer consideration of the application for a fortnight, to afford an opportunity for the parties to come, if possible, to an amicable agreement.'[23] The board approved of the transfer of perpetual lease Section 12, Block 10, Kurow, from Mary MULVENIA to Eleanor Robecca CHALMERS.[24]

Figure 3.7. 'Waitaki Homestead Mr and Mrs John CHALMERS'. Source: author's collection

The transfer of perpetual lease Section 9, Block 10, Kurow district, from George PHILPOT to John Howe CHALMERS was approved. Approval was also given to the transfer of Section 13 Block 10 from George STRINGER to Eleanor Rebecca CHALMERS.[25]

In 1893 Eleanor was listed as a voter in a national election:

Eleanor Rebecca CHALMERS resident of Kurow. 1893 Electoral Roll for Women No. 507 Waitaki.[26]

The law allowing women the vote had just been passed. Many years later during the English women's suffrage movement Eleanor opined to her sister Clara, 'I think they must be horribly coarse women when they would mask windows like larrikins to try to gain their ends. I am glad that they are put in gaol & sentenced to hard labour. However, I do not see why N.Z. women are allowed to vote & not those in the Old Country. I am sure that the greater part of the women here do not know what they are voting for, unless when they are voting for "no-license" (meaning prohibition of alcohol).'

Financial woes continued when the holdings of settlers J.H. CHALMERS, Kurow; Edwin (means 'Eleanor') R. CHALMERS, Kurow were declared forfeited for non-payment of rent in 1894.[27]

There were times when settlers needed the support of one another to secure their property rights. Neighbour A.H. CHAPMAN sought reassurance that he was not to lose his occupation of a 20 acre reserve held rent free. The reserve in question was a long narrow strip of land in the bottom of the gully. It was only three chains wide and no more than a mile long. His land was on one side of it, and Mr John CHALMERS' land was on the other side. By permission of the Land Board the boundary fence was erected partly on one side of the reserve, and partly on the other, and partly upon it, the object being to allow stock on both sides to get access to the water, which is very scarce in summertime.'[28] Future dealings with A. CHAPMAN were less amicable.

Desperate for money, John and Eleanor had no choice but to allow their properties to be forfeited. The following leases and licences were forfeited for non-payment of rent: 'J.H. CHALMERS, Sections 9, 10 and 11 Block 10, Kurow district; Eleanor R. CHALMERS, Sections 12 and 13 Block 10 and E.R. CHALMERS Section 2, Block 8, Kurow district'.[29]

Luckily for them, government intervention saved the day and forfeitures of pastoral leases were rescinded, the lessees having obtained relief under the provisions of "The Pastoral Tenants' Relief Act 1895": J.H. CHALMERS Sections 9, 10 and 11 Block 10, Kurow district; E.R. CHALMERS Sections 12 and 13 Block 10 and Section 2, Block 8, Kurow district.[30] (See Figure 3.6.)

In the closing years of the nineteenth century the basis of the New Zealand welfare system was formed. It began in Kurow following a period of unusually severe economic depression and environmental difficulties. The welfare services established had been concerned largely with, first, the overseeing of the consequences of poverty; second, preventing future poverty; and third, the progressive removal of economic impediments to the general social welfare of families and individuals.[31] John Howe and Eleanor Rebecca CHALMERS were able to benefit from this financial support.

It must have come as a huge relief when the announcement was made that J.H. CHALMERS' applications to exchange perpetual leases of Sections 9, 10 and 11, Block 10 Kurow district for leases in perpetuity were granted.[32] (See Figure 3.6.)

These were hard times that the family had to face. The nation-wide economic depression lasted until the mid-1890s. Added to the ongoing threat of snowstorm and drought was the rabbit problem that plagued the area. By 1888 it was found that rabbits had begun making their way from Otago into Canterbury across the Waitaki River by means of the Kurow bridge that was unprotected against their approach.[33] Introduced as a food source and for game, rabbits had come from established populations in the coastal sandhills between Invercargill and Riverton in the 1860s. Moving by rivers onto plains they had covered Southland and Otago by the early 1880s.[34]

By 1897 the control of rabbits had become an important industry in the Kurow area, with some 15 to 20 hands employed in trapping and preparing the rabbits for export. Up to 12 tons of the rodents, numbering 10,000 to 20,000 were shipped from the Kurow district weekly.[35] Frozen rabbit was being exported from Port Chalmers from 1882.[36]

The locals were opposed to poisoning the rabbits.[37] At the same time the Minister for Lands was anxious to strictly enforce other measures to eradicate the pests to ultimate extinction.[38] A network of public and private fences was instrumental in checking the advance of rabbits. Later it was deemed that the whole state should bear the burden of eradication costs and not the impoverished squatters of the south alone.[39]

J.H. and E.R. CHALMERS applied for the issue of licences over the portions of the mining reserve fronting their holdings in Block 10 and which were included in their respective boundary fences. The application was referred to the ranger for report.[40]

By 1901 the family of John and Eleanor was complete, but for one late arrival, Dora Grace CHALMERS, in 1909. (See Figure 3.8.)

- John Charles (Jack) was born on 18 February 1892 at Kurow

- Twins Gertrude Elizabeth and Constance Eleanor were born on 21 November 1894 at Kurow
- Gordon Rupert was born on 28 November 1899 at Kurow
- Norman Chamberlin was born on 30 May 1901 at Kurow

Figure 3.8. The children of John and Eleanor CHALMERS

Schools were well established in the area by the time the CHALMERS family arrived. However, not all students were able to enjoy a full education, especially the older ones in the family. Donald and Malcolm had left school at an early age after completion only as far as standard two.[41] They were required to drive a team of farm horses when barely in their teens.[42] Violet would be required to stay at home and help look after the younger children. On December 17 1896 William was presented with third prize for general work in standard three while attending Kurow School.[43]

Douglas also attended Kurow School.[44] Sports events were always popular and Douglas was a successful participant. The local schools combined for a sports event in 1900. The school children of Otekaike, Kurow and Duntroon mustered and competed in various races after a provided lunch. Douglas took part in races for boys under twelve years and was successful in a number of events: Sprint 2; High Jump 1 (4ft 3ins); Wheelbarrow Race COLLINS and CHALMERS 2 and Three-legged Race CHALMERS and GARD 3. The racing provided a great deal of amusement, and, besides such games as rounders, Kiss-in-the-Ring 'Tiggy' were provided.[45]

On 28 April 1902 a vote was taken in support of Dr STEVENS' efforts in having the school thoroughly cleaned and supplied with up-to-date ventilators. Two members, including John CHALMERS were unsuccessful in opposing Dr STEVENS and supported Mr KELLY.[46] The following year John sought election on the Kurow School Committee for the management of the school. He was nominated but not elected.[47]

In 1901 John had sought permission to occupy land adjoining their property: 'Licenses were granted to the following applicants for the right to occupy portions of the Kurow riverbed fronting their holdings in Blocks 1 and 8, Kurow district at 20s per annum: J.H. CHALMERS and four others.'[48]

It was followed by a request lodged by son Donald: 'Ranger ATKINSON reported on the application by Donald CHALMERS for a licence to occupy the small portion of the mining reserve in Block 10, Kurow district. CHALMERS' application held over.'[49]

By 1903 the family was in a position to increase its flock of sheep. (See Fig 3.9.) At the annual Otekaike Sale, John Howe bought 100 merino ewes of the 3,000 brought from Benmore Station.[50] However, this does not explain the enormous increase in his flock numbers shown in the annual returns when the number of sheep at 2,828 in 1903 dropped to 40 in 1904. At the same time neighbours experienced dramatic changes, one dropping from 2,379 to 400 and another rising from 0 to 396 in 1903. Perhaps there was trading amongst themselves.

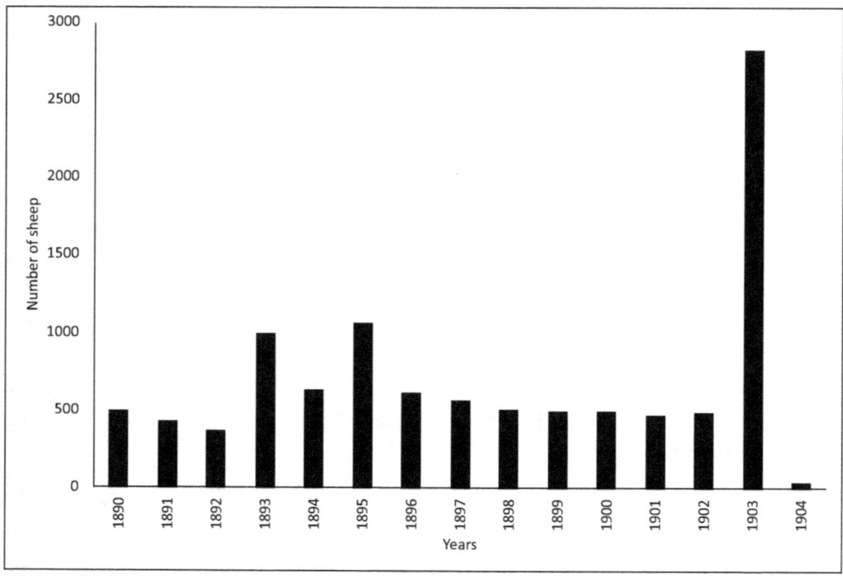

Figure 3.9. Sheep returns for J.H. CHALMERS, Kurow, Waitaki, 1890-1904. Source: Appendices to the House of Representatives: H-15a, 1890-1; H-32, 1892-3; H-23, 1895-1905

A major reason for the reduction in stock numbers in the 1903-1904 season was the severe snowstorm of July-August 1903, in which the snow lingered for weeks due to frost. In Arrowtown the kerosene froze.[51] Newspaper reports from Kurow noted:

> There are heart-breaking reports of the loss of sheep on most of the stations here, and on many of them it is estimated that fifty per cent, or over of the stock will have perished.[52]

> The losses in stock have been very heavy. One gentleman from the back country declares that he will only save 500 sheep out of a flock which before the snow numbered 10,000. Happily all runs have not suffered so much as this one, but still they all have suffered more or less.[53]

However, on the positive side the snowstorm 'brought about a huge reduction in rabbit nuisances'.[54]

At about the same time John was looking to have the road to their property upgraded by the Waitaki County Council. After an inspection the road was deemed to be unsuitable to be made safe for even light traffic because of the cost.[55]

Mr A. CHAPMAN wrote to the Waitaki County Council complaining that the road to Diggers Gully, Kurow, was impeded by a milking station, and that it obstructed the way to his land. He stated that 'he purposed initiating his solicitor to bring an action against the Council, claiming for loss, damage, and delay of work if the nuisance is allowed to continue. It was resolved that the clerk write to Mr CHALMERS, who was supposed to be the defender, requiring him to remove the complained of obstruction forthwith.[56] A more serious complaint against John by disgruntled neighbour A. CHAPMAN was looming.

By 25 March 1904 John and Eleanor had decided to put their property up for sale by public auction.

FRIDAY, 25th MARCH.

At Kurow.

Immediately after Mr Hille's Sale. NORTH OTAGO FARMERS' CO-OPERATIVE ASSOCIATION, Ltd., have received instructions from Mr J. H. Chalmers to sell by public auction—

His Valuable Lease in Perpetuity, being Sections '9, 10, 11, 12, and 13, Block X., and 1 and 2, Block VIII., Kurow Survey District, containing 900 acres (more or less), together with improvements, viz., Good Six-roomed Dwelling House, Cowshed, and Yards.

The property is well fenced and divided into 11 paddocks. 300 acres have been cultivated and sown down with English grass, 300 have been surface sown, and the balance is in tussock. The property is well watered, and is very conveniently situated, being about half a mile from the Kurow Railway Station.

The rental of £40 per annum is remarkably reasonable, and the auctioneers confidently recommend the property to anyone in search of a really good cheap grazing farm.

For further particulars apply to
Mr R. C. GILLIES,
Kurow;

Or

THE AUCTIONEERS.

Figure 3.10. Advertisement. Source: Oamaru Mail. March 21, 1904

A day later it was reported by the same newspaper that the sale had been withdrawn in the meantime. No explanation was given.[57]

Mr Tertius MUNRO wrote to the Waitaki County Council stating that he had leased a portion of Mr J.H. CHALMERS' farm, Kurow, and asked permission to erect a gate across the road leading to Diggers Gully which was seldom used. 'Mr A.H. CHAPMAN wrote at length objecting to the gate, as a road bordered on his freehold and lead to his leasehold, and Mr

MUNRO was only a tenant for three months, the real applicant being Mr CHALMERS.'[58]

At about the same time, neighbour CHAPMAN laid a serious charge against John CHALMERS. On 16 August 1904 a charge of stealing two crossbred sheep was brought against John Howard (means Howe) CHALMERS in the Supreme Court by his neighbour A.H. CHAPMAN. The case was to be tried by a grand jury of sixteen in the Oamaru Courthouse and reported in detail in the *Oamaru Mail*.

Figure 3.11. The Court House, Oamaru, c.1884, where John Howe CHALMERS' sheep stealing case was heard. Dunedin, Burton Brothers studio. Te Papa (C.012750), no known copyright restrictions

The witness, W. WILLS reported it as a breach of the Slaughtering and Inspection Act. Two of John's sons, Malcolm (aged 22) and Jack (12), gave evidence in favour of their father.

J. H. CHALMERS, the accused, said he remembered Inspector WILLS coming to his house on July 2nd and calling his attention to one of the skins. He said that one ear appeared to have been recently marked … He had marked the ears of hand-fed lambs when they were being killed, if they had not been previously marked. He thought that was usual. He had no experience of sheep until going onto the farm. He had been a storekeeper … He questioned WILLS' authority of taking away the skins. There was another skin – a merino – witness handed to WILLS, saying that he might take that also. He did this because he did not understand why WILLS was taking the skins, and remarked that it was some of CHAPMAN's work … .WILLS made out that the penalty under the Inspection Act was £50 … the witness went on to explain how CHAPMAN had been persecuting him, and told WILLS what a trouble CHAPMAN's sheep were to him. They were destroying his crop so much that he asked CHAPMAN to take his sheep away. He told him that CHAPMAN had informed the Council about his yards and gates, and showed WILLS a letter he had received from CHAPMAN's solicitor threatening action for libel. He told him the history of the persecutions he had received at CHAPMAN's hands. WILLS said, "If CHAPMAN got you in a corner he would never let you go."[59]

John was very distressed over the conflict and unable to sleep. He rose from bed in the early hours of the morning and tried to sort matters out with CHAPMAN, but to no avail. CHAPMAN told him to plead guilty. After detailed presentation of conditions that might have come to play in the case, on the third day the judge asked the jury not to convict the accused, but to go further than acquitting him and that he leave the Court without a stain on his character. After deliberating for thirty-five minutes, the jury returned a verdict of not guilty, and accused was discharged.[60]

Two months later, despite strong opposition by J.H. CHAPMAN, John Howe was granted permission by the Waitaki County Council to erect a swing-gate across the road at Block 10, Kurow.[61]

> John H. CHALMERS, farmer, of Kurow district, said he had 885 acres lease in perpetuity, held in two blocks at 1s and 16d respectively. It was a portion of the old Kurow Run, pastoral country, but would grow turnips. The land would carry 600 sheep and a few cattle and horses. Had tried grass surface sowing with great success. His difficulty was that he was paying too much, so he got the ranger to value the land, which he did at 6d an acre. There were extensive improvements on the land – fencing, six-roomed house, grass etc. As good land was held in the district at 4½d and 9d. he wished to surrender, as the value was too high, but could not, being lease in perpetuity. He would like now to retain the holding at a reduced rent, and transfer it to his family.[62]

On 1 April 1905 the family reconsidered the state of affairs. Since the property was unable to be sold it was decided to rent at a reduced rate and have it transferred to the family.

By the end of May 1905 'Kurow westwards had been experiencing drought with only scanty rainfall for some months past'.[63] This may well have been the reason for John's decision to sell stock:

STUDHOLME JUNCTION SALEYARDS.
PRELIMINARY NOTICE.
AT AN EARLY DATE. NORTH OTAGO FARMERS' COOPERATIVE
ASSOCIATION
In conjunction with MESSES GUINNESS &. Le CREN, will sell by public
auction, On account of Mr J. H. Chalmers – 300 2 and 3-ycar-old STEERS[64]

John and Eleanor had changed their minds about selling the farm. Rather
than sell they decided to lease the property.

Application was made by J.H. CHALMERS to sub-lease Sections 1 and 2
Block 8 and Sections 9, 10, 11, 12 and 13 Block 10, Kurow district, to
William SIMPSON for a term of five years – sub-lease granted, subject to
the payment of rent and on the understanding that Mrs CHALMERS sign the
agreement and become a party to the lease.[65]
Leases in perpetuity 309, 517 ex and 519 ex were granted J. H.
CHALMERS.[66]

Eleanor was not happy with the agreement. On 24 January, 1906 she
wrote to her sister Clara in London: 'Our old farm is leased for five years,
lease counting from May last. It is leased for £90 per annum – it is
supposed to be far too little but the business was settled in too great a
hurry. We had previously been offered £110 and had funded it. Of course
all taxes and rates are paid by the lessee.'[67]

At the time of the 1905-1906 electoral roll compilation John Howe
CHALMERS, farmer was living with Eleanor Rebecca, Donald Rolls and
Malcolm Shaw, contractors and Violet Hoppner, spinster at Otekaike in
the Mount Ida District. John and Eleanor were renting a property, so far
unidentified, and the younger children attended Duntroon School.
Donald and Malcolm had become independent by 1905, working as
contractors in the Hakataramea Valley.[68] They applied for a licence to
occupy the Ferry Reserve Sections 2 and 3, Block 7, Papakaio District
under the name of Chalmers Bros. Their application was declined.[69]

In her January 1906 letter Eleanor wrote, 'Jack is entitled to a scholarship
for two years and is going to the high school at Oamaru after the holidays.
Both the Kurow and Duntroon schoolmasters speak highly of his
abilities.' Jack attended Waitaki Boys' High School where records show
he was quite athletic. (See Figure 3.12.) He is recorded as having been
placed third in the high jump, first in the high jump to a height of 4'8"
(1.42 m) and was second in the heats of 100 yards. Jack remained at
Waitaki Boys for one year only.[70]

By this time David George had left home. Eleanor wrote: 'Davy is at
Oamaru now doing very well – he is in a similar position to that in which
40

he was when at Kurow. He studies in any spare time that he can get and intends attending some technical classes in the winter time.'

Figure 3.12. Waitaki Boys' High School. Source: author

Eleanor went on to tell that before he left Kurow his employers gave him solid gold cuff links and a sovereign case. Other presents were also forthcoming from his many Kurow friends. Members of the Presbyterian Church held a social for him. They took the opportunity to present him with a writing desk and gold pencil. David had been a regular attender at church and taught in the Sunday School.

By the end of the year Eleanor wrote that she had not heard from David since August. David married Betson Margaret CUNNINGHAM at Oamaru in 1908.[71] 'As regards the children, some of them are busy with their farming operation and others are hard at work studying. I have one idle boy – the baby – 5 years and 7 months (Norman Chamberlin). Donald and Malcolm are doing well and will be applying for some land within the next twelve months.'[72]

Last summer's drought (i.e. 1906-7) continued into the middle of the following year.[73] Having experienced flood, snowstorm and drought, Eleanor wrote: 'I think that I shall eventually go to the North Island to stay and risk being swallowed up by an earthquake for this island has a treacherous climate.'[74] Following the 1906 San Francisco earthquake New Zealand newspapers predicted a catastrophic seismic event that would affect all of New Zealand, particularly the North Island.

1906 had promised to be a productive one but Eleanor said she could not have any idea 'until the grain is in the bags.' She went on to say: 'My life is such a very busy one that I have very little leisure but I take that all as a matter of course now. With the exceptions of sometimes Saturday and Sunday I am up at 6 o'clock in the morning both during the summer and winter months.' [75]

John's niece Henrietta STRACHAN, who had immigrated to New Zealand with her family in 1881 and settled in Timaru, echoed Eleanor's words when she recounted spending a holiday with the family at Hakataramea Valley near the Waitaki River. (See Chapter 20.) She said that Eleanor had been up all night baking bread and preparing for harvesters and shearers coming and needing to be fed. [76] An old resident of the area, Mrs A. COWAN, later living in Oamaru, wrote: "It was all hard work. My husband always grew about 1,000 bags of grain and it all had to be stooked." She went on to say that she remembered 'Malcolm bringing your mother (Dora's) one Sunday and it was a lovely sing-song. Your mother played the piano … and sang too but she was a very busy woman too. We often saw Malcolm."[77]

Money problems were plaguing the family again and rents were behind. The Receiver of Land Revenue of the Otago Land Board reported that holders of miscellaneous licences and leases have not paid their rent and they included J.H. CHALMERS (Otekaike) If the rent was not paid within a month it was to be declared lapsed. [78]

There were no options left but to be relieved of the lease. The transfer of Sections 9 to 11, Block 10, Kurow District licensed by John Howe CHALMERS to John KELLY was approved. At the same time, Section 2 Block 8 licensed by Eleanor R. CHALMERS to John KELLY was approved. The application to transfer miscellaneous licences by J.H. CHALMERS to John KELLY part Block 10, Kurow District were granted. [79]

As a result of the engineer's report Mr J.H. CHALMERS, Kurow asked for permission 'to make a small water race across [the] road line at his place'. This was agreed to by the Waitaki County Council at the end of 1907. [80]

Licence No 1053 was granted and held in the name of J.H. CHALMERS until the warden caught up with and recommended to cancel the licence on 14 May 1909, by which time John was no longer the owner of the Kurow property. [81]

After failing in their application as landowners, Donald and Malcolm advertised for outside work.

WANTED
Contract ploughing or cropping for one to four teams
Apply to CHALMERS Brothers Otekaike[82]

Having begun farmwork at an early age, Donald and Malcolm were experienced teamsters. Years later, Donald explained the working conditions where 'under runners' are found. These are fissures caused by erosion of limestone or earthquakes and later covered by vegetation. 'They are noticed by a hollow sound when walking on the surface. The horses notice this and it is most difficult to persuade them across such places.' Donald worked as a teamster for the LEONARD family in the Hakataramea Valley, on the Canterbury side of the Waitaki River.[83]

Figure 3.13. Early postcard photo of the Hakataramea Valley. Source: author's collection

He also told the story of a lady who was an organist for the Church of England at Duntroon who 'went out one Sunday afternoon alone. She was reading a book and walking through long grass when unexpectedly she fell down one of the crevices. During the evening service she was missed and at once they called for a search party and traced her tracks through the long grass leading to the spot where she had fallen. The fact of her book lying by indicated the exact spot where she had disappeared. They immediately secured a long rope and let it down to a depth of 80ft where they rescued her on a ledge of limestone.'[84]

There was great public excitement about and enthusiasm for the newly purchased Otekaike Estate by the Land Purchase Board that had so many options on offer and would 'prove one of the most successful in the district … as a fair portion of it is good wheat-growing land, and the bulk of the remainder admirably suited for small grazing purposes.'[85] However, the people of the district became disappointed at the delays in taking up the Otekaike estate as promised by the Premier during his visit to Duntroon. Added to this, a satisfactory arrangement with regard to payment could not be reached.[86]

By December of 1907 good crops of wheat were expected.[87] However, along with other uncertainties and their own financial problems, it seemed John and Eleanor were not interested in further investments or could not afford to lease more land there. John probably yearned for his store keeping days. Their next request to the Otago Land Board was in a different part of the province, much further south. John Howe applied for a licence to occupy the Reserve in Block 22, Town of Dunkeld.[88] The yearly licence rate of 18s per annum was granted.[89]

Figure 2.14. CHALMERS Family, 1906. From left: John Howe, Violet Hoppner, Norman Chamberlin, Gordon Rupert, Eleanor Rebecca, Constance Eleanor and Gertrude Elizabeth. Source: author's collection

NOTES

---

[1] CHALMERS, John Howe, freehold, Tauranga, Farmer, Lots 85 and 89 Te Papa, Bay of Plenty Electoral Roll, 1885-1886

[2] Letter from John C. TIMS to his parents in possession of the author.

[3] *Bay of Plenty Times.* October 8, 1885.

[4] CHALMERS, George Shaw, Onslow Street, Christchurch, residential, Canterbury Electoral Roll, 1890.

[5] *Otago Daily Times.* January 8, 1855.

[6] *Evening Star.* September 30, 1886.

[7] *Evening Star.* November 15, 1888.

[8] CHALMERS, John Howe, farmer, Kurow, Waitaki Supplementary Electoral Roll, 1887.

[9] *North Otago Times.* August 14, 1889.

[10] CHALMERS, John Howe, farmer, residential, Kurow, Waitaki Electoral Roll, 1890; CHALMERS, John Howe, farmer, residential, Kurow, Waitaki Electoral Roll, 1896.

[11] *North Otago Times.* June 30, 1890.

[12] *Evening Star.* September 17, 1890.

[13] *Otago Witness.* September 18, 1890.

[14] *Otago Witness.* October 16, 1890.

[15] *Evening Star.* December 10, 1890.

[16] *Otago Daily Times.* February 5, 1891.

[17] *Evening Star.* February 18, 1891.

[18] *Otago Witness.* August 27, 1891.

[19] *Otago Witness.* September 17, 1891.

[20] *Auckland Star.* February 25, 1892.

[21] *Otago Witness.* March 10, 1892.

[22] *Evening Star.* April 27, 1892.

[23] *Otago Witness.* May 12, 1892.

[24] *Otago Witness.* "Land Board." April 28, 1892.

[25] *Otago Witness.* August 4, 1892.

[26] No. 507, CHALMERS, Eleanor Rebecca, resident, Kurow. Waitaki.Electoral Roll for Women, 1893.

[27] *Otago Witness.* March 8, 1894.

[28] *Oamaru Mail.* June 25, 1894.

[29] *Evening Star.* October 31, 1895.

[30] *Otago Witness.* February 13, 1896.

31 "Welfare Services", from An Encyclopaedia of New Zealand, edited by A. H. McLintock, originally published in 1966. Te Ara – the Encyclopedia of New Zealand URL: http://www.TeAra.govt.nz/en/1966/welfare-services

32 *Evening Star*. February 27, 1896.

33 *Wairarapa Daily Times*. "Rabbits and Rabies." February 17, 1888.

34 Robert Peden, "Rabbits:The spread of rabbits in New Zealand", Te Ara: The Encyclopedia of New Zealand, last modified 2008, http://www.TeAra.govt.nz/en/rabbits/page-1

35 *Auckland Star*. May 6, 1897; *Wairarapa Daily Times*. May 22, 1897.

36 Otago Daily Times, "History on our doorstep,"last modified 2018, https://www.odt.co. nz/ lifestyle/magazine/history-our-doorstep

37 *Evening* Post. March 5, 1898.

38 *New Zealand Times*. March 2, 1898.

39 *Evening Post*. June 4, 1904.

40 *Otago Witness*. November 25, 1897.

41 Raymond CHALMERS, pers. com.

42 Dora GRUBB (née CHALMERS), pers. com.

43 William's book prize, in possession of the author.

44 Ibid.

45 *Oamaru Mail*. December 28, 1900.

46 *Otago Daily Times*. June 2, 1902.

47 *North Otago Times*. June 25, 1903.

48 *Otago Witness*. August 21, 1901.

49 *Evening Star*. August 21, 1902.

50 *Oamaru Mail*. March 13, 1903.

51 *Southern Cross*. August 1, 1903.

52 *Oamaru Mail*. August 17, 1903.

53 *North Otago Times*. August 18, 1903.

54 *Evening Post*. September 5, 1903.

55 *North Otago Times*. June 25, 1903.

56 *Oamaru Mail*. March 21, 1904.

57 *Oamaru Mail*. March 22, 1904.

58 *Oamaru Mail*. July 28, 1904.

59 *Ibid.*

60 *Ibid.*

61 *Oamaru Mail*. October 26, 1904.

62 *Oamaru Mail*. April 1, 1905.

63 *Evening Post*. May 27, 1905.

64 *North Otago Times*. "Advertisements." April 26, 1905.

65 *North Otago Times*. August 1, 1905.

66 *Oamaru Mail*. September 1, 1905.

[67] Letter from Eleanor CHALMERS (24 January 1906 Otekaike, Oamaru) to Clara STOKES, in possession of the author.

[68] CHALMERS, Donald Rolls, contractor, Otekaike, Mount Ida Electoral Roll, 1905-1906; CHALMERS, Eleanor Rebecca, married, Otekaike, Mount Ida Electoral Roll, 1905-1906;
CHALMERS, John Howe, farmer, Otekaike, Mount Ida Electoral Roll, 1905-1906; CHALMERS, Malcolm Shaw, contractor, Otekaike, Mount Ida Electoral Roll, 1905-1906;
CHALMERS, Violet Hoppner, spinster, Otekaike, Mount Ida Electoral Roll, 1905-1906.

[69] *North Otago Times*. June 5, 1906.

[70] Letter from Rory GOLLOP, Rector of Waitaki Boys' High School (26 May 1993), in possession of the author.

[71] Bride and Groom Collection Oamaru Folio, No. 7824, Genealogical Society New Zealand Society of Genealogists.

[72] Letter from Eleanor CHALMERS (24 January 1906 Otekaike, Oamaru) to Clara STOKES, in possession of the author.

[73] *New Zealand Herald.* 5 June 5, 1907.

[74] Letter from Eleanor (16 December 1906 from Otekaike, Oamaru) to her sister Clara in London, in possession of the athor.

[75] Ibid.

[76] Account of Henrietta STRACHAN as told to Dora GRUBB (née CHALMERS).

[77] Account of Mrs COWAN as told to Dora GRUBB (née CHALMERS).

[78] *Otago Witness.* July 17, 1907.

[79] *North Otago Times.* August 16, 1907.

[80] *North Otago Times.* December 25, 1907.

[81] *North Otago Times.* May 14, 1909.

[82] *Oamaru Mail.* February 8, 1908.

[83] Kenneth CHALMERS, pers. com.

[84] Letter from Donald CHALMERS (23 September 1935, Kelso) to cousin Margaret.

[85] *Oamaru Mail.* November 15, 1905.

[86] *Oamaru Mail.* February 3, 1906; *Oamaru Mail.* 5 February 5, 1906..

[87] *New Zealand Times.* December 27, 1907.

[88] *Oamaru Mail.* November 15, 1905.

[89] *Otago Daily Times.* May 14, 1908.

4 Beaumont and Gibbston Part 1

Beaumont, a small inland Otago town is surrounded by high hills. It is located on the Clutha River six kilometres southeast of Raes Junction, between Roxburgh and Balclutha. The Beaumont River is a tributary of the Clutha River, merging with it just upstream of Beaumont.[1] (See Map p.24.)

Surveyor John Turnbull THOMSON originally named Beaumont Dunkeld, a Gaelic name from Perthshire, Scotland, meaning Fort of the Caledonians. Early maps showed Dunkeld. However, locals who were familiar with the nearby Beaumont Burn and the Beaumont Ferry preferred the name Beaumont, being French for 'beautiful mountain'.[2]

Figure 4.1. Early Beaumont. Source: Hands Off Beaumont, http://handsoffbeaumont. blogspot.com/2009/11/our-history.html (Permission applied for)

Table 4.1. CHALMERS children in the Beaumont School Admission, Progress and Withdrawal Register[3]

Admitted	Pupil	Previous	Date Left	Destination
15 Jul 1907	[Gertrude] Elizabeth	Duntroon	15 Feb 1909	-
15 Jul 1907	[Constance] Eleanor	Duntroon	11 Jun 1908	-
15 Jul 1907	Rupert Gordon	Duntroon	20 Dec 1912	Work at home
15 Jul 1907	Norman Chamberlin	Duntroon	-	-

On 15 July 1907 twins Gertrude and Constance as well as Rupert Gordon and Norman Chamberlin CHALMERS were enrolled at Beaumont

School. While living at Otekaike the younger children had been attending Duntroon School before moving to Beaumont.

Other children had left school and become employed, while those who remained at home were able to work in the newly acquired family business at Beaumont. Eleanor owned both the general store and bakehouse that were connected to one another and the house where they lived. John Charles, William Howe and Douglas Gollan worked in the bakehouse while the daughters Violet Hoppner, Constance Eleanor and Gertrude Elizabeth worked in the store. Eleanor did the book-keeping. (See Figures 4.2. and 4.3.)

A general store in those days sold anything from 'an anchor to a needle' as it were. Goods were delivered for miles around the countryside. The family lived in Beaumont in the days before the railway line was pushed through from Lawrence. John Howe delivered goods in Beaumont and to the farms nearby by horse and open cart where the driver was exposed to all kinds of weather. The local minstrels sang this little ditty at a concert:

'John Howe is quite well read,
He's on the road when you're in bed'[4]

Figure 4.2. Family members outside their Bakery and Grocery Store. Missing ripped section, bottom left. Partially restored. Source: author's collection

While the CHALMERS family lived at Beaumont there was a large settlement of Chinese residing at nearby Chinaman Flat. Like many others they had come seeking gold. John Howe and other family members delivered groceries to the community.[5] Old Mousey was the head man. Many found work in orchards, market gardening and laying poison for rabbits. On one occasion Rupert made arrangements to have one of them help dig potatoes.[6]

Figure 4.3. The bakers William Howe CHALMERS, Douglas Gollan CHALMERS and Jack CHALMERS, c.1914. Source: author's collection

The family wasted no time in becoming involved in community affairs and activities. On 23 August 1907 Eleanor, 'already recognised as a past master of the instrument', assisted another pianist in the performance. She opened the second part of the concert at the Beaumont schoolhouse with a solo performance and was followed later by the Misses CHALMERS who 'sang a duet very charmingly'. John Howe, who had become a member of the Beaumont Public Library gave a humorous reading at a valedictory social.[7]

In a Service of Song concert, 'probably the gem of the evening was a duet "Passing Away" by the Misses [Gertrude and Constance] CHALMERS'.[8] The Beaumont Sports Club held a concert on 25 October at which the CHALMERS family shared its talents in song, readings and recitations, along with other locals. Mrs CHALMERS played the accompaniments. 'The climax was reached when the chairman (Mr N. DEMPSEY) called on the Misses CHALMERS to sing the flower song which they did most beautifully. The young ladies came on to the stage with garlands of beautiful flowers, and small bouquets of roses, heather, shamrock, and fern, representing England, Scotland, Ireland and New Zealand.'[9]

Another Service of Song programme entitled "Promoted, A Tale of the Zulu War" included readings by Mr J.H. CHALMERS.[10] A concert and dance given by the Beaumont Sports Committee opened with an overture played by Mrs CHALMERS (piano) followed by individual vocal items and musical selections by Mrs CHALMERS. She provided the accompaniments throughout. Donald CHALMERS, paired with another resident, presented a humorous dialogue. He was also part of the band that provided music for the dance that followed. Donald played the cornet while Rupert played the trombone.[11]

The CHALMERS family took leadership roles within the community. By 1909 Donald had become chairman of the Beaumont Sports Club.

On 25 March 1909 Dora Grace CHALMERS was born into the family, at Beaumont. She was the last of twelve children with an eight year gap between her and the next youngest.[12]

Picnics were part of the annual social calendar. A Beaumont resident, Mrs DORSEY told of an incident one year when a man, who didn't approve of the picnic being held where it was, chopped down a tree, making it fall across the road. It had to be cut up and removed before the picnickers could return home.[13] In 1912 the Presbyterian Sunday School picnic was held at the Beaumont Racecourse where teachers entertained their scholars and were ably supported by Messrs CROCKETT and J.H. CHALMERS.[14]

One of the neighbours, a Mrs DORSEY, supplied the family with eggs and butter. Many years later she was able to share her memories of the family members who lived at Beaumont. She identified all those who had attended the 1910 Beaumont School Picnic. (See Figure 4.4.). Eleanor was a piano tutor who had given Mrs DORSEY lessons as a child. Mrs DORSEY said that Eleanor was a reserved, refined lady who was not unapproachable.[15]

Figure 4.4. The 1910 Beaumont School Picnic. Chalmers family members pictured include John Howe, Eleanor Rebecca, Violet, Jack, Gertrude and Constance. Source: author's collection.

Figure 4.5. Detail of John and Eleanor CHALMERS from Figure 4.4.

For the two remaining schoolchildren of the family 1910 was a successful year. Rupert and Norman received prizes at the Beaumont School end-of-year break-up, as shown in these extracts from the newspaper report. (See Figure 4.6.)

BEAUMONT SCHOOL.
CONCERT AND BREAK-UP CEREMONY.
On Friday evening, the 16th inst., the annual break-up and distribution of prizes took place in the schoolroom, the distribution being preceded by a short concert by the pupils. The schoolroom was packed to overflowing and financially and otherwise the concert proved a unique success. The programme was greatly appreciated in every item, and words of high praise were heard from various quarters. The teachers and pupils have every reason to be satisfied with the quota of approval meted out to their efforts. The programme included:
'Pushed it through the Window,' Masters J. DEMPSEY, R. WOOD, A. WATSON, N. and R. CHALMERS; duet, 'Japanese Love Song,' Miss R. WOOD and Master R. CHALMERS; song, 'Tin Can Band,' seniors; song, 'I'll tell you a story,' Stds. I. and II.; club swinging, Miss R. WOOD and Masters A. WATSON and R. CHALMERS.
Each child was presented with a book; the names of prize-winners are given below, five first-class and four second class attendance certificates were also presented and the proficiency certificates won by the Std. VI. pupils were distributed.
   Specials. – Attendance (donors, School Committee): First-class: Rupert Gordon CHALMERS
   Class Prizes:
   Std. IV – First. Rupert CHALMERS
   Std. I. – First. Norman CHALMERS.[16]

When 'Kawarau' Station at Gibbston was subdivided in 1910 and it became available to the public by ballot, Eleanor drew the smallest of the sixteen blocks of land offered, the selection being 5,450 acres or 2206 hectares in area.[17] Run No. 345E was to be leased at an annual rent of £80.0.0., effective from 1 March 1910. As suggested, she named the property 'Mt Rosa' after one of the highest points on the hills to the south.[18] It was situated between Arrowtown and Cromwell. The Nevis Bluff was beyond. (See Figures: 4.9, 5.3, 5.11.)

In December 1866, the *Otago Witness* described the setting: 'This is a beautiful piece of grass country and second to none in Otago. The scenery is highly romantic, with mountains and precipices on every side. Looking down from the track to the left hand, many hundred of feet below, is the Kawarau River, churning itself into white foam as it rushes madly along its rock-bound courses. After getting well round the Annie and looking to the opposite side of the Kawarau are the Nevis Bluffs, which rocky projections have formed the chief obstacle to the opening up of the main trunk road from Dunedin to Wakatip.'[19] 'The Annie' refers to the Gentle Annie Creek. (See Figure 4.9.)

Figure 4.6. Beaumont School 1909. Source: Beaumont Primary School Centennial History 1872-1972 by Dorothy M. Coburn

Figure 4.7. The cave in the schist rock where the CHALMERS boys lived. Source: author's collection

The family retained its business interests at Beaumont whilst developing the new property at Gibbston. John Howe CHALMERS was listed in 1911 as a storekeeper with Eleanor Rebecca, Donald Rolls, farmer, William Howe, baker and Violet Hoppner at Beaumont.[20]

When acquired, the Gibbston property had no house on it. The men were baching and living in an old cave behind where the house was eventually built. (See Figure 4.7.) William found some Maori curios in the cave.[21] The original portion of the eventual house came from Macetown where it was dismantled and taken to Mt Rosa by wagon. (See cover painting.) It was rebuilt on its present site 21km along the Gibbston Back Road.[22] (See Figure 4.8.)

When the CHALMERS family arrived their new property had only one fence that ran up and over the Antimony

55

Saddle, cutting off the small corner that extended down to the mouth of the Nevis River. This is where the old wethers were run to provide station mutton. Fencing was a priority and Malcolm CHALMERS put up the fence to divide the dark side (Doolans Creek)) from the sunny side (Gibbston). (See Figure 4.9.) He won much acclaim for the amount of material he lugged up the hill each trip – half a hundredweight (25 kg) of wire and 10 standards! A further fence at the foot of the hill enabled the crops to be grown on the flats. A third cut off the Victoria Bridge flat that had been surveyed into the 'Wentworth' run. Sheep yards and a dip were built beside the newly erected woolshed. (See Figure 5.5) The first crops were sufficiently productive to finance new machinery. A portable Blackstone engine replaced the horse power driving the chaffcutter.[23] The old yellow buggy was cast aside for a new Ford car.[24]

In May of 1911 Ranger LEONARD of the Land Board reported on the small grazing run of 345 acres at Kawarau, held by Eleanor R. CHALMERS, that he had valued the improvements effected. He also stated that the lessee needed to explain before the next meeting of the Board why she was not residing on the Run.[25]

Eleanor wrote to her sister Clara in London later in the year explaining her position on the matter:

> The Land Board expect me to reside on the run before the end of the year so I shall, as far as I know at present, leave Beaumont for a time. I regret this for one reason, for Jack says that he thinks I shall not like the change unless for health reasons – Kawarau is healthier than this little spot.[26]

Figure 4.8. The original portion of the Mt Rosa Run house. Source: author's collection

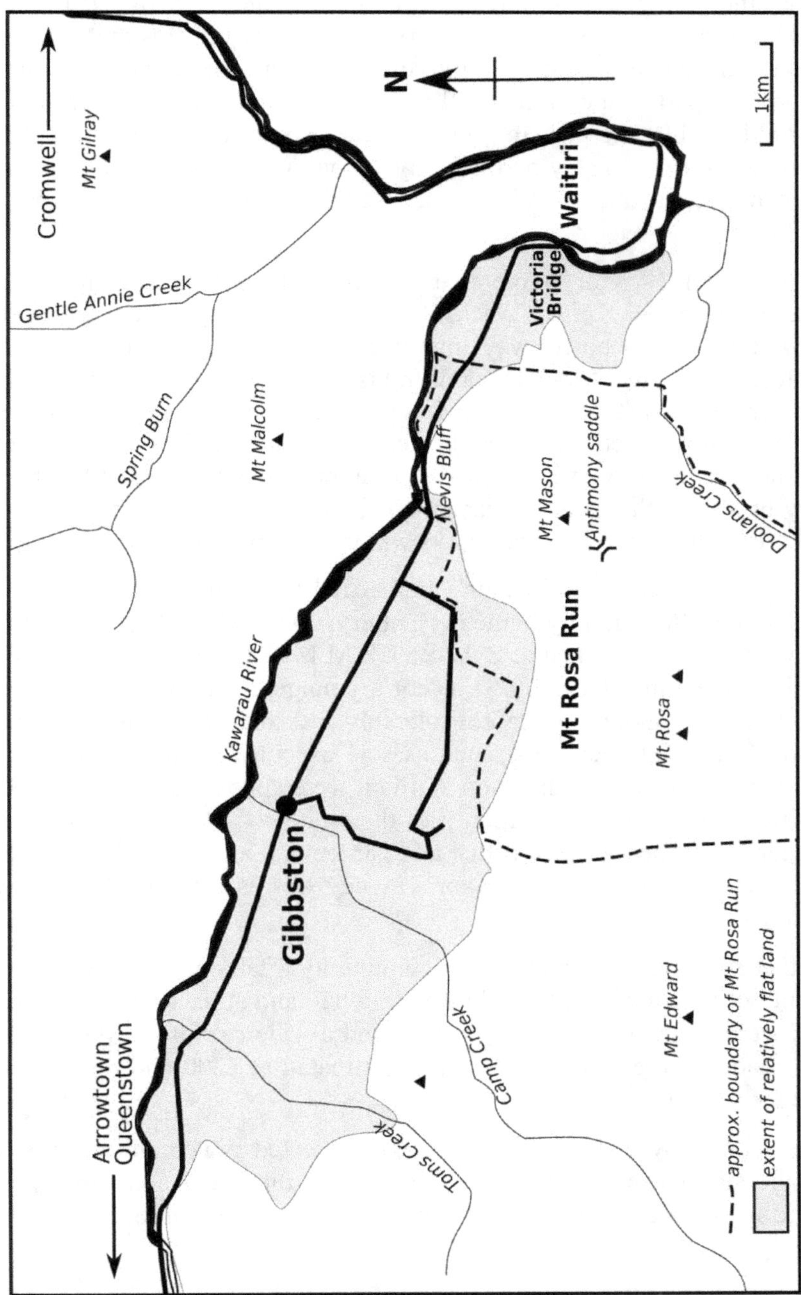

Figure 4.9. Map of the Mount Rosa and the Gibbston area.

'For other reasons it is advisable to go for the sake of Willie and Malcolm; they are both working very hard & Jack informs me that they find it very inconvenient having to do their own cooking etc. Of course the greater part of the family will remain in Beaumont with their father. I would not like the girls to go to the Run. Some say that it will not be necessary for me to stay permanently so that my first visit will only last three months probably. We are situated fourteen miles away from a doctor.'[27]

In her letter Eleanor wrote that Donald was expected to return to Beaumont in five or six weeks for a short holiday before going to Kawarau. He had been away involved in what seems to have been a venture of his own. 'Poor Donald. In his last letter to me he said that he had buried the past misfortune & was living for the future – he is thankful that he is not in debt.' No details were given of Donald's 'misfortune'. Eleanor went on: 'Gertie has had the mumps for a week. She has been very bilious at the same time; perhaps biliousness is a symptom of the disease – I have two medical works which I am tired of looking up.'

On 2 September 1911 Eleanor's unmarried aunt, Eleanor Anne TIMS died at the TIMS' family home in Banbury, Oxfordshire. Her will stated: 'I give to my Niece Eleanor Rebecca CHALMERS now residing in New Zealand the sum of £1,000.' Eleanor's younger sister Martha received £500. These amounts were considerably less than their sister Clara's share. Clara had been designated as sole executrix, while her husband William STOKES and their son William were appointed executors. The STOKES family received the rest of the estate comprising two freehold residential properties with office and garden and a freehold farm, along with all of the contents.[28] Eleanor's money was used to develop the Mt Rosa Run.

Further family involvement in the community affairs of Beaumont came about with the decision to build a district hall and athenaeum. The local folk were in earnest about the project and a wide canvass of the district was made. The cost of erection was estimated at £200 and of that £92 was soon found.[29]

The following year J.H. CHALMERS was elected as a committee trustee for the site and building of the Beaumont Public Hall and Library. A working bee was arranged and carried out to gravel approaches to the hall.[30]

During the year the committee was informed that two trucks of timber for the building was at the Big Hill and was expected to be on site later in the week.

The opening ceremony of the Coronation Hall and Library was reported by the *Otago Witness*: 'a grand affair that will be long remembered by the residents of that district, for it brought together one of the largest and most enthusiastic gatherings that has ever assembled in that rising little town.' The cost of the 40' x 24' x 14' 'fairly substantial building and furnishings' amounted to £218. Being the year of the Coronation of King George V a £50 grant was available that added to subscriptions by residents. Outstanding costs were to be met by hall rentals as well.

> Speeches followed the opening overture 'tastefully played by Misses WOOD and CHALMERS'. A speech of patriotic fervour and loyalty to Britain was made and the hall, described as 'commodious and substantial' declared officially open. A verse of 'God Save the King' was sung. A gift of the Union Jack flag was presented on behalf of Raes Junction while other communities offered their congratulations.[31]

Figure 4.10. Sorting potatoes outside the Beaumont Hall. Source: Otago Witness. August 10, 1920.

John Howe was called upon from time to time to give speeches. When the post office assistant, who was a native of Beaumont, left the district John Howe spoke in complimentary terms of Miss CUMMINGS' amiable qualities.[32]

A social was held to help clear the debt of £63 still owing for the erection of a manse for the Beaumont Presbyterian Home Mission. The church was well filled. The choir, including Mr CHALMERS as a member 'rendered satisfactorily four items'. 'Mr CHALMERS, snr., is deserving of a special vote of praise and bids fair to gain fame by his rendering of [a] Scottish song. The musical part of the programme having been brought to a close, Mr CROCKETT called upon Mr A. MILNE who in a short speech asked the Rev. ALLAN's acceptance of a handsome travelling rug and silver mounted umbrella.' Mr J.H. CHALMERS supplemented the remarks of the previous speaker and claimed an acquaintance of some 20 years with the recipient who was then in the Waitaki district. He wished to add his testimony of the many good qualities possessed by Mr ALLAN both as a man and as a preacher.'[33]

At the farewell to Mr and Mrs DEMPSEY, the recipients' of a silver teapot and sovereign purse, John Howe spoke highly of their obliging habits and many good qualities. He wished them every success in their yeoman undertakings in the bush settlement of the King Country.[34]

Jack's name would appear in the newspaper for sporting achievements. He was elected as committee member of the cricket club in 1911. Jack enjoyed successful games of cricket for Beaumont, one example being the time he bowled the opposition for a duck and scored fourteen runs not out.[35] He was selected for a combined football match in 1913.[36] John Howe and Eleanor Rebecca had supported the club in May by playing the piano for the opening overture 'Blaze Away'. She 'played the accompaniments in her usual tasteful manner' while Mr CHALMERS made his debut as a singer. His rendering of a Burns' Scottish song was greatly appreciated.[37]

The Beaumont Horticultural and Industrial Society's activities interested the young women of the family. Gertrude was a committee member. She was also a stallholder at the Beaumont Presbyterian sale of work. She sold sweets while her twin sister Constance managed the fishing pond.

At the same time, John Howe's financial support was shown in yet another account for payment owing him being approved by the School Committee. These were ongoing. He was also a creditor in a bankruptcy case, with £6 due him.[38]

Eleanor assured her sister Clara in England, that the family had not left 'Mt Rosa' as far as she was aware, although she needed to reside in it occasionally. She wrote that Malcolm, Willy and Donald were managing it. Eleanor was concerned that the men needed some refinement in their lives. At the same time Violet was involved with keeping the household running. She and Eleanor took a trip to Dunedin together and sent a postcard to Clara.

Rupert Gordon gained his proficiency certificate at Beaumont School at the end of 1912 and left school to work at home.[39]

BEAUMONT ANNUAL CONCERT AND BREAKUP.
On Friday the 20th inst. Mr BENNET took occasion to call for cheers for the teachers. Chairman, and Mr BATES, Master R. CHALMERS calling for a similar compliment to Mr BONNET from his fellow pupils. As usual the cheers were given with much vim.
Special prizes: Drawing: Seniors – Rupert CHALMERS
Certificates gained 1 . – Std. VI ; Proficiency, Rupert Gordon CHALMERS[40]

NOTES

[1] "Beaumont River", last modified March 2008, https://en.wikipedia.org/wiki/Beaumont_River

[2] "Hands Off Beaumont", last modified 2012.
http://handsoffbeaumont.blogspot.com/2009 /11/our-history.html

[3] Beaumont School Admission, Progress and Withdrawal Register, New Zealand Society of Genealogists.

[4] Dora GRUBB (née CHALMERS), pers. com.

[5] Ibid.

[6] "Hands Off Beaumont", last modified 2012.
http://handsoffbeaumont.blogspot.com/2009 /11/our-history.html; Account of Dora GRUBB (née CHALMERS).

[7] *Tuapeka Times*. August 28, 1907; *Tuapeka Times*. October 12, 1907.

[8] *Tuapeka Times*. October 21, 1908.

[9] *Tuapeka Times*. October 30, 1907.

[10] *Tuapeka Times*. September 16, 1908.

[11] *Tuapeka Times*. October 14, 1908.

[12] Certified copy of Entry in the Register-Book of Births in the District of Gabriels Riding; NZRGO, Birth Register, 1909/22308 CHALMERS, Dora Grace, Eleanor Rebecca, John Howe.

[13] Account of Mrs Dorsey, as told to Dora GRUBB (née CHALMERS).

[14] *Tuapeka Times*. February 7, 1912.

[15] Account of Mrs Dorsey, as told to Dora GRUBB (née CHALMERS), 1982.

[16] *Tuapeka Times*. December 21, 1910.

[17] Deed No.613 concerning Lease of Small Grazing-Run. Under "The Land Act, 1908." Copy in possession of the author.

[18] Anne Cook, *The Gibbston Story* (Dunedin: Otago Heritage Books, 1985).

[19] *Otago Witness.* "A Visit To The Lakes." December 1, 1866.

[20] CHALMERS, Donald Rolls, farmer, Beaumont, Bruce Electoral Roll, 1911; CHALMERS, Eleanor Rebecca, married, Beaumont, Bruce Electoral Roll, 1911; CHALMERS, John Howe, storekeeper, Beaumont, Bruce Electoral Roll, 1911; CHALMERS, Violet Hoppner, spinster, Beaumont, Bruce Electoral Roll, 1911. CHALMERS, William Howe, baker, Beaumont, Bruce Electoral Roll, 1911.

[21] Letter from Eleanor CHALMERS to her family in England.

[22] Anne Cook.

[23] As of 1985 the engine was on display at the Lakes District Centennial Museum.

[24] Ibid.

[25] *Otago Witness.* May 17, 1911.

[26] Letter from Eleanor CHALMERS (18 September 1911) to her sister Clara STOKES in London.

[27] Ibid.

[28] Eleanor Anne TIMS, signed will, 5 October 1911, copy in possession of the author.

[29] *Taupeka Times.* September 27, 1911.

[30] *Taupeka Times.* August 17, 1912.

[31] *Mt Benger Mail.* May 1, 1912.

[32] *Tuapeka Times.* March 3, 1909.

[33] *Tuapeka Times.* July 19, 1911.

[34] *Tuapeka Times.* October 21, 1911.

[35] *Tuapeka Times.* November 15, 1911.

[36] *Tuapeka Times.* August 6, 1913.

[37] *Tuapeka Times.* May 31, 1911.

[38] *Mataura Ensign.* January 16, 1912.

[39] Beaumont School APW Register: admitted 15 July 1907, born 28 November 1898, last school Duntroon, last day 20 December 1912, destination 'work at home', NZ Society of Genealogists, HKN Ag438/1/292.

[40] *Tuapeka Times.* December 25, 1912.

5 Beaumont and Gibbston Part 2

The youngest CHALMERS boy, Norman stayed at Gibbston with his mother and attended the Gibbston School for most of a year. Eleanor had said she 'would miss him and worry a little when he didn't accompany her to Gibbston'.[1]

Figure 5.1. Gibbston School. Source: author's collection

Figure 5.2. Gibbston School pupils, c.1916. Dora middle row, third from left. Source: author's collection

Table 5.1. CHALMERS children at Gibbston School 1912-1916. Source: Education Department, Index Gibbston School, Admission, Progress and Withdrawal Register, Invercargill Public Library

Registration Number	Year	Pupil	Parent
175	1912	Norman	Mrs CHALMERS
177	1913	Norman C.	J. CHALMERS
193	1916	Dora Grace	-

Travelling to and from Gibbston was a challenge. As a teenager, Norman Chamberlin rode the distance from Beaumont by horse-drawn gig. He took a supply of food for himself and chaff for the horse to last the three days' journey.[2]

In March of 1912 John Howe and Eleanor made the trip to Gibbston by Ford car. They were the second in the district to own a car. Eleanor wrote from Gibbston: 'The first part of the journey that we undertook when driving here was very enjoyable, but towards the end, it was the reverse. We drove seventeen miles through the Kawarau Gorge – it was a sultry day & seeing mountains (you fancy could reach the sky) on either side, I felt suffocated. I don't think I will ever go that way again. There is only the road and the Molyneux River down below to look at. I don't know how many feet down the river is, but I know, I don't like thinking about it.'

Figure 5.3. Nevis Bluff and Kawarau River. Source: author's collection

'No motor cars are allowed through the gorge – that is one consolation. Howe said that he would never take me that journey again – I was quite shaky after I arrived at Gibbston & that was an unusual experience to me. Of course we could have travelled by train but we did not wish to cause the boys inconvenience by having to meet us when they were busy with their harvest.' John Howe stayed for just four days before driving back to Beaumont to look after affairs there.[3]

After about two years life at Gibbston had become more settled, although the house needed to be put in better order. In making comparisons with Beaumont, Eleanor noted: 'The climate here is very much nicer than that of Beaumont. There is plenty of sunshine & the house has a splendid aspect. Gibbston is much higher than Beaumont the latter is a valley & gets a tremendous amount of rain.' (See Figure 4.1.) She hated having to contend with all the mud which she described as 'shocking'.[4]

'Our house there is situated under a big hill – we did not build it or it would not have been built there. In some part of July, the sun does not reach the Beaumont house until 11:15 a.m. I feel very much inclined to stay at Gibbston for the winter.' Eleanor found the people there to be very 'countrified' but extremely good-natured. She had received several cases of fruit from different people: cases of apricots, peaches, plums and apples. She found a quick way of making marmalade by mincing the peel of oranges and lemons and cutting the pulp as finely as possible by knife and fork.[5]

Figure 5.4. Beaumont Race Meeting, 1915. Cars L to R: Ford, Mr Benjamin HART seated in Sunbeam, Ford. Rugs are spread over the tyres to protect them from the sun. Source: Hands Off Beaumont, http://handsoffbeaumont. blogspot.com/2009/11/our-history.html (Permisson applied for.)

Figure 5.5. The woolshed on the Mt Rosa property, 1950s. The old portion is at the rear. Source:author's collection

In the new year of 1913 Eleanor was able to send reports of bounteous produce at the run, having been able to get plenty of gooseberries for jam, although peaches were scarce. The vegetable garden was a great success with a quantity of tomatoes. About 160 acres of seeds had been sown, 100 acres of which was in barley. Eleanor was of the belief that there were only three districts in New Zealand where barley would grow. Shearing was about to take place at the shearing shed two miles away from the house. At Kurow Eleanor had needed to work to provide meals for the shearers, by herself. At this stage a man cook was employed and so she was relieved of extra work at the house.

By 1914 the run at Gibbston had become established as a working concern and home to several family members.[6] The run was prospering.

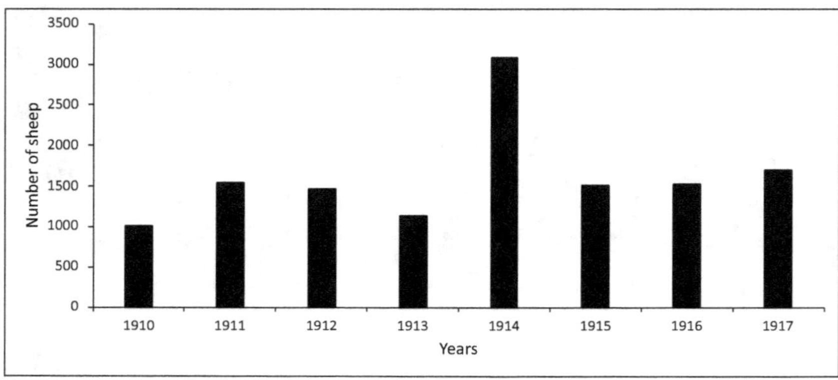

Figure 5.6. Sheep returns for Eleanor CHALMERS, Gibbston, Lake County, 1910-1917. Source: Appendices to the House of Representatives: H-23, 1911-1917.

Having received a copy of the magazine *Lady's Pictorial* from England, Eleanor hastened to say that the fashions there were becoming worse, to the point of being ridiculous. New Zealand was no exception, as the girls in Wellington had been wearing bracelets on their ankles.[7]

In August she expressed concern to her sister Clara, over the misfortune her Aunt Harriette had in losing two of her long-time servants, particularly when her health was in decline.[8] On 11 December 1913 Eleanor's remaining maiden aunt, Harriette Anne TIMS, died at Banbury. She, too, left £1,000 to Eleanor and it was decided to invest it in properties for the oldest sons, twins Donald and Malcolm.

The Gore paper reported: 'The Government is losing no time in making an effort to bring several recently purchased Southland estates to the market. Already surveyors are in possession of the Knowsley Park, Ardlussa and Fortification estates. A gang of surveyors under Mr OTWAY is at present surveying Knowsley Park and is laying off suitably sized sections for closer settlement.'[9] Donald Rolls CHALMERS, farmer of Gibbston became lessee of Section 4, Block 6 in the Tuturau Survey

District, known as Knowsley Park. Its area covered 570 acres, 3 roods and 14 perches. The capital value of the allotment, apart from buildings, was £3,600 and the clear annual rent was £162. The settlement date was 20 March 1914.[10] (See Figure 5.10.)

Figure 5.7. Donald driving a team of horses pulling a reaper-binder during the oat harvest near the CHALMERS property at Beaumont, c.1910. Source: author's collection

Donald was an experienced teamster and he had good quality machinery, including a 17-coulter drill, used for sowing grain, particularly oats and wheat. (See Figure 5.7.) It had eight more drills than the norm. Made of cast iron, it would cut into the ground and allow seed and manure to spread at the correct depth. It was a new machine, of which Donald was very proud.[11]

Malcolm's investment was not as successful. About 1913-14 Mrs Mammy JOHNSTONE, who had retired to Arrowtown at nearly 100 years of age, put the hotel at Victoria Bridge by the Kawarau River up for sale. Malcolm took out a mortgage and bought the property.[12] He was unable to acquire the license to sell alcohol but he did live there for a time. When he went to give war service in WWI the hotel was leased but the license had been allowed to lapse. There were no guests to cover the costs and business naturally died. The building itself was eventually destroyed by fire. It had been sited on a reserve and the land was not owned by Malcolm.[13] (See Figure 5.8 and 5.9.)

Figure 5.8. Old Victoria Bridge across the Kawarau River between Cromwell and Arrowtown, c.1875. Victoria Bridge Hotel on the right. Source: author's collection

Figure 5.9. Victoria Bridge Hotel, 1901. Muir and Moody Photography. Source: author's collection

The death of Clara on 11 January 1915 must have been a painful loss to Eleanor. Harriette Clara, her older sister, had been her closest link with the Home Country and they had corresponded regularly expressing their deepest concerns. Whenever illness came about Eleanor would refer to her medical books for advice to share. They were always supportive of one another, regardless of the situation. Being so far from family must have been difficult for her. She once wrote in a letter: 'I wish it were possible to visit England in an aeroplane so that I could have a long conversation with you all and save all this writing.' Of her mother, Constance Eleanor wrote to an English cousin: 'Aunt Clara's death was a terrible shock to her. I really don't think she ever got over it.'

On 25 February 1915 John Howe applied for a renewable lease of mixed agricultural and pastoral land containing 912 acres and 5 perches, also as part of the Knowsley Park Settlement. It was an adjacent property at the back of Donald's land. This farm did not have any dwellings on it. It was Section 11 of Block 7 in the survey district of Tuturau, Southland. The capital value was £2,990 with a clear annual rent of £134 11s.[14]

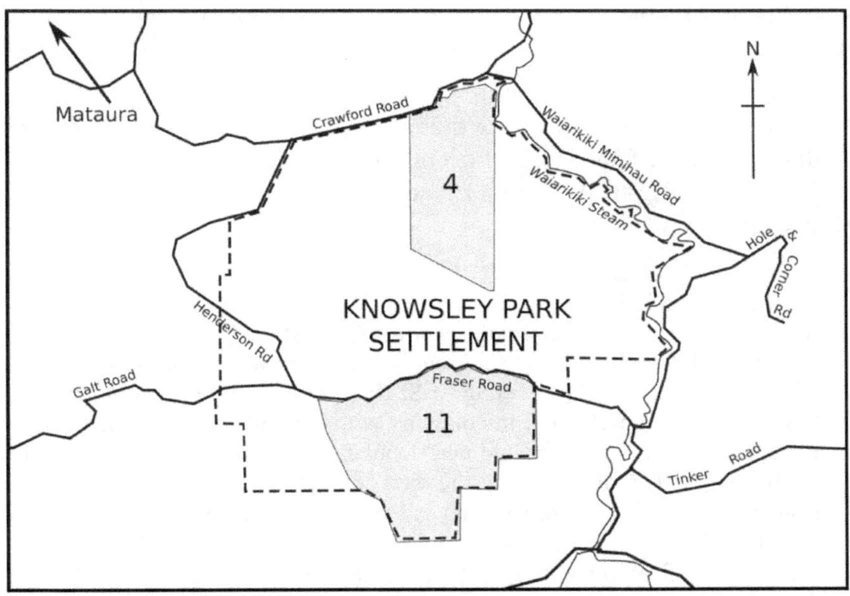

Figure 5.10. Map of the Knowsley Park Settlement near Mataura, Southland. Donald CHALMERS acquired Section 4, Block 6 (570 acres) and John Howe CHALMERS Section 11, Block 7 (912 acres). Modern roads shown. Source: after Tuturau Survey District Map, Wellington: NZ Department of Lands and Survey, 1955

It was about this time, when the youngest child Dora Grace, who had not long commenced school at Beaumont, made her first trip to Gibbston. She recalled some of her experiences: The family owned a big draught horse called Bluey that hated children. One day he made a rush at her, stamping his front feet. She was terrified and gave him a wide berth after that. Another unpleasant episode was when the working dogs were fighting over the offal from a sheep, killed for household use. 'Having no fear of dogs, which were my only playmates at times, I tried to stop them and received a nasty bite on my wrist that left a scar to remind me of the happening. My folk were very concerned because they thought I might become infected by the dreaded disease, rabies.'[15] Dora was enrolled at Gibbston School in 1916.[16]

Rabbits were a menace and had to be trapped or poisoned. On one occasion, two of her brothers were mixing pollard and phosphorous used to eradicate the pests when the mixture exploded, scattering small pieces. Some landed on Dora's clothes and woollen stockings where they smouldered, causing burns to her legs. Eleanor also had an unhappy experience with rabbits. She met with an unfortunate accident when she stepped into a rabbit burrow while walking along the road reading a book. Her left foot was badly strained and she suffered the effects for over four weeks.[17]

The most unfortunate member of the family to be affected by rabbits was William Howe. A fatal accident occurred on the CHALMERS' property on 21 August 1915 to William's friend Connor LESLIE that was to have even sadder consequences.

SAD FATAL ACCIDENT.
Young Man Killed.
It is with regret that we record the death of Connor LESLIE, youngest son of Mr James LESLIE, which occurred under very painful circumstances at Gibbston on Tuesday last. Young LESLIE was engaged in rabbiting on Mrs CHALMERS property, and in company with Mr Rupert CHALMERS was working on some rough ground near Doolans Creek, about five miles from Gibbston. On Tuesday morning the men commenced work on a rocky face near the creek. They were working independently, and shortly before noon CHALMERS saw LESLIE about two chains away. Shortly afterwards he heard noise of falling stones, and on looking round saw no sign of the lad. After a short search he found LESLIE lying near the bed of the creek, and the unfortunate lad had apparently fallen over a cliff about thirty feet in height. He appeared to be in great pain, and asked CHALMERS to go for a doctor.[18]

It was said by his brothers that Rupert provided warmth for Connie by tethering a sheep to his body. Rupert stayed for about an hour making Connie comfortable before running up over the Antimony Saddle to Gibbston to get help.[19] (See Figure 4.9.) A rescue party was assembled including William and Malcolm CHALMERS.

> Shortly after three o'clock a party consisting of Messrs Alex. SCOTT, W., J., and T. KINROSS, J. and S. COWAN, and M. [Malcolm] and W. [William] left for the scene of the accident. They arrived at Doolans Creek about five o'clock ... Fortunately the relief party had brought along a stretcher, and LESLIE was carried by relays over very rough country.[20]

William helped bring Connor out. As the stretcher party carried the injured young man out, they lit little fires on the way to show their progress for everyone watching from Gibbston.[21] Dr BROWN met the party at the foot of the hill but Connie had died on the way down

> Deceased, who was only nineteen years of age, was a bright, intelligent lad, popular with everyone, and the news of his untimely death cast quite a gloom over the community. He was a prominent member of the local Tennis Club, and also took a leading part in local concerts and dramatic entertainments. The sympathy of the whole district will be extended to the relatives in their sad bereavement. The funeral will take place tomorrow, leaving Gibbston at 10 a.m., and passing through Arrow about two o'clock.[22]

The inquest was held on 25 August 1915 at Gibbston before Mr Henry GRAHAM (Coroner).

> The inquest touching the circumstances surrounding the death of Connor LESLIE was held at Gibbston yesterday. Rupert CHALMERS said that on 21st August he was rabbiting with deceased on the property of witness's mother at Doolans Creek. He saw deceased about 11.45 a.m. He was then about two chains away. Witness heard a stone drop, and on looking round missed deceased. Shortly afterwards he saw deceased lying in the creek below. He considered that deceased must have fallen over a cliff about thirty feet in height. When witness reached the spot deceased was alive but appeared to be in great pain and was bleeding at the mouth. Witness remained with him for about an hour, and then left for Gibbston for assistance. Witness returned with several men and LESLIE appeared to be dead. The body was conveyed to Gibbston on a stretcher, the journey occupying seven hours. William Howe CHALMERS and Malcolm CHALMERS gave corroborative evidence in regard to the finding of the body at the foot of the cliff.[23]
>
> Dr Edmund Ewart BROWN said that he was called to Gibbston on Tuesday evening, and examined the body when it was brought in about 11.30 pm. Life had apparently been extinct for about ten hours. The principal injuries were about the head, and there were a few minor abrasions on the body. Witness said the cause of death was a fracture of the base of the skull. The Coroner

returned a verdict that deceased met his death by accidentally falling over a cliff at Doolans Creek.[24]

William Howe never recovered from the traumatic way in which he lost his friend Connie. No further electoral rolls contain his name. William Howe was in the army reserves in 1916.[25] After 1916 William was committed to Seacliff Mental Hospital and was later transferred to Cherry Farm where he remained for the rest of his life.

Figure 5.11. Seacliff Hospital, 1884, Samuel Calvert (1828-1913). Source: Public Domain, https://commons.wikimedia.org/wiki/File: Seacliff_asylum _1884.jpg

His niece, Thelma GEARY (née BOYLEN), recalls: 'He was not mentioned much. He was sitting on a chair on the verandah. She was told to be careful of him as "a mad person never forgets" and then he was taken away'. Although mental asylums still used what today would be considered barbaric and punishing practices, when William arrived he would have experienced the more liberal regime developed by Truby KING, the superintendent prior to 1920. Patients were housed in small dormatories and were given fresh air, exercise and good food. They were given productive tasks in the garden and on the Hospital's farm, both of which supplied much of the institution's food.[26] William's father and other family members visited him from time to time but he was unable to recognise any of them. William died on 15 May 1949 at Cherry Farm Mental Hospital, Waikouaiti. After having suffered from coronary atheroma for ten years the cause of his death was coronary thrombosis.

William was buried in the Andersons Bay Cemetery in Dunedin on 19 May 1949.[27]

Figure 5.12. Gibbston Valley, Little Mt Rosa (centre), Mt Mason (immediately behind to the left) and Mt Rosa (immediately behind to the right). (Refer to the map, Figure 4.9.) Source: painting by Barbara SMITH, great-grandaughter of John and Eleanor CHALMERS

There was much enjoyment to be had from the simple life at Gibbston. Dora enjoyed going to the neighbouring property of Mr and Mrs PERRIAM to collect water from their stream during the dry summer weather. A large barrel with a clean sack over the top was mounted on a sledge drawn by a quiet horse. It was filled with water from the stream.[28] Charles PERRIAM had applied for a water race regarding Mrs Eleanor Rebecca CHALMERS' run.[29] Eleanor missed the ferns and indoor plants that thrived in the humid climate at Beaumont but looked forward to creating a colourful garden in her new surroundings and imagined the scenery looked like Switzerland. Raymond CHALMERS, a grandson of John and Rebecca, described 'Mt Rosa' as a beautiful piece of land with a panoramic view, the best the family owned. Sheep grazed on its sunny slopes and they were easy to muster. (See Figure 5.11.)

World War I was underway in what seemed to be a very long distance from New Zealand. But as a member of the British Empire, the country had a duty to heed the call from Mother England to serve. Local Beaumont residents decided to hold a Patriotic Ball and provide entertainment in aid of New Zealanders at the war front. £15 was raised and Messrs CHALMERS and others were thanked for their donations.[30]

BUSINESS NOTICE.

I beg to notify to the residents of Beaumont and surrounding districts that I have disposed of my interest in the Beaumont Store to Messrs Douglas Chalmers and Philip Boylin, who will continue the same under the style of Chalmers and Boylin. In retiring from the business, I would solicit a continuance of the patronage so liberally conferred upon me during my eight years' residence in the Beaumont District.

J. H. CHALMERS.

In connection with the above we beg to state that it will be our earnest endeavour by careful attention to business to merit a continuance of the support bestowed upon our predecessor. Our stocks will be fresh and up-to-date, and customers may rely on their orders receiving prompt and careful attention.

D. CHALMERS.
P. BOYLIN.

Figure 5.13. Notice of business transfer of the Beaumont Store from John Howe CHALMERS to Douglas CHALMERS and Phillip BOYLEN. Source: Tuapeka Times. September 1, 1915.

In September 1915 a notice was put in the local paper informing the residents of John Howe's intention to relinquish his business ties and allow son Douglas Gollan to go into partnership with Philip BOYLIN (normally spelt BOYLEN). (See Figure 5.12.)

Perhaps John Howe felt that his time to retire from business had come and services were needed elsewhere as his sons fulfilled other duties, notably at Gibbston. No doubt Eleanor needed him. Donald had taken up residence at his Knowsley Park property and Norman joined him. Public transport was time-consuming, starting by coach to Queenstown where the lake steamer 'Earnslaw' or 'Mountaineer' would take passengers to Kingston. From there, a train went to Gore or Mataura and a vehicle would be required to get to Knowsley Park or Waiarikiki. Donald enrolled Norman at Waiarikiki School in 1915 and later he attended Gore High School.[31] (See Figure 5.14.)

War clouds were expanding on the horizon and volunteers to fight the distant enemy were sought. In New Zealand all the unmarried men were being called up in the ballot, also men who had married since May 1916. Violet wrote to the family in England: 'William, Douglas and John [Jack] were included. Willie had enlisted previously but had not seen the doctor, and would not yet know whether he would pass as fit in the meantime. Jack had been before the medical board but did not pass, the action of his heart not being right. Douglas made a good pass medically and was sent to Trentham.'[32]

Figure 5.14. Norman CHALMERS, c.1916. The Mora Studio, Gore. Source: author's collection

Patriotism was given as the main motivation for future soldiers to sign up for war service. Seeking adventure and the opportunity to go overseas also had appeal for many young men. Despite his family and other responsibilities Malcom offered his services to the Empire out of duty. The *Lake Wakatip Mail* reported that 'The example set by these young men and many others who have preceded them should surely be our incentive to many other eligibles who still remain in this district. A send off will be tendered 30 November at Arrowtown.'[33]

While living at the hotel by the Kawarau River, Malcolm was only a few miles from the Gibbston property where he was able to continue providing assistance when needed. The community there also recognised his contributions. However, the call to prepare to serve his country put everything on hold. 'Messrs Malcolm CHALMERS, J. COURTNEY and J. SMITH, who will shortly be leaving for Trentham, will be entertained at a social by the residents of Gibbston on Tuesday evening next.' Two days later Malcolm was on his way to Trentham Military Camp.[34]

This was an added loss and worry for Eleanor who felt the need to keep Malcolm's hotel running while he was away. The following April Malcolm visited his parents at Gibbston on final leave.[35] He would see his mother for the last time. His Majesty's New Zealand's troop ship 55, the SS *Tofua* sailed from Wellington on 27 May 1916 with Malcolm as part of D Company 13th Reinforcements aboard.[36]

Just prior to Malcolm's departure two happy events took place with the combined weddings of the twins, Gertrude Elizabeth and Constance Eleanor at Dunedin on 20 May 1916. Both grooms were Catholics of Irish descent. Gertrude married Philip BOYLEN who had taken over the family store in partnership with Douglas Gollan at Beaumont, while Constance married a policeman, James McKIBBIN from Dunedin.[37] (See Figure 5.15.)

Figure 5.15. The twins Gertrude and Constance CHALMERS and friends, Beaumont, 1915. Source: author's collection

A few months later Eleanor died at Dunedin after a long battle with exhaustion and depression. She had spent time at the Lawrence Hospital and later at St David's Private Hospital in Dunedin.[38]

> DEATHS
> CHALMERS. – On October 29, at Dunedin, Ellenor Rebecca, the beloved wife of John Howe CHALMERS, of Gibbston, Otago; aged 53 years. 'At rest.' Private interment – Hope and Kinaston, undertakers.[39]

Eleanor died of asthemia, exhaustion and mental depression after a period of seven months.[40]

The family members who had been living at Gibbston would have moved back to Beaumont after Eleanor's death. Dora Grace CHALMERS was re-enrolled at Beaumont School on 14 November 1916. She left there on 27 July 1917 when the family moved to Donald's property at Knowsley Park.[41]

It was now up to Violet Hoppner to let her mother's remaining sister Martha (See Figure 6.10), who had arrived for a visit to New Zealand with Eleanor in 1882, know what had happened to her mother and to share her grief with distant relatives. Writing from Gibbston she explained how the family always hoped that she would get through the illness, but Eleanor became increasingly thin and depressed.[42]

Figure 5.16. Malcolm CHALMERS (marked with a cross) in England. Source: author's collection

In December 1916 Malcolm wrote from 'Somewhere in France', which was the only address ever given for security reasons, to a relative in

England. 'What a soldier goes through seeing his comrades fall around him [he] gets terrible hardened to it, it will be a good thing for the world when the war is ended. Sometimes I think the dear ones at home feel it the worst. I feel for my dear mother. I wish she would not worry. I always pray for her. However I look on the bright side trusting she is in God's loving care and that she may get quite well. I am always thinking of you all.' Due to the slowness of mail delivery at that time Malcolm was not aware that his mother had died six weeks earlier.

Eleanor had suffered the loss of her sister Clara with whom she had been very close through letters to and from England. A tragic accident on her Gibbston property resulted in loss of life and was emotionally shattering to son William who never recovered. In losing William Eleanor also lost manpower that was vital to keeping the run going. On top of that Malcolm, who also worked on the run, was called to serve in the war. John employed someone to help with the Beaumont store when he left for Gibbston but by this time he was almost seventy years of age and no longer capable of hard physical work. Eleanor also wanted to keep Malcolm's hotel at Victoria bridge viable while he was away. All of this weighed heavily on her and she succumbed to depression.

Figure 5.17. Malcolm CHALMERS, 1915. Source: Author's collection

It was February of 1917 when Malcolm wrote: 'I shall be glad when the day comes when we will be able to meet again (God willing) I should have written sooner but, owing to hearing the sad news about my Dear

Mother's death, I was very much upset – did not feel much like writing the worst news for a soldier to hear about his best friend – however it is a great consolation to think I shall meet her again some day in heaven above – in God's loving care away from the trials and troubles of this world.'

Malcolm described a training march that was made in heavy drizzling rain: 'as rough as it was we enjoyed the march, it getting darned near the real thing. Notice we are in step.' (See Figure 5.16.) 'Some of the men were laying in water during the night under some trees. No tents when night comes on we have to find shelter whatever we can. CHALMERS happened to be one of the unlucky ones.'

Jack was the most senior family member in a position to manage the Run, along with Rupert Gordon and Violet Hoppner. Others were married, working on their own land or at war. He gave his signature to The Public Trust at its request, believing that, as his mother died intestate, the property no longer had a title holder and that the Public Trust Office had become the trustee.[43] In turn, approval to transfer the lease to another was granted and announced in the newspaper. A report by the Otago Land Board stated that the application of the Public Trustees, in the estate of Eleanor CHALMERS, to transfer small grazing Run 345E, Kawarau and Nevis, 5450 acres, to Alexander William SCOTT was approved.[44]

The deed for the Lease of Small Grazing Run No. 613 did not involve any lump sum payment and was merely a contract to lease the property. Not all members of the CHALMERS family realised that 'Mt Rosa' Run was leasehold and was not actually owned by the family. They resented what they believed was the sale of their property, for which they received no money so that they lost their inheritance. This misunderstanding resulted in an ongoing family conflict that lasted for many years. According to Jack, the last legacy of £1,000 that Eleanor received from England was needed to finance the Run. However, it had been spent, instead, on buying properties for the two oldest sons. The decision was controversial amongst the family and had been stressful for Eleanor.

> The Memorandum of Transfer of 'ALL THAT area of Crown Lands situated in the Kawarau and Nevis Survey Districts containing by estimation 5450 acres ... being Run Numbered 345E ... in a Deed of Lease ... the sum of TWO THOUSAND POUNDS (£2000) by Alexander William SCOTT.[45]

In June 1917 Malcolm wrote of recent war events: 'I suppose you will have heard all about the great push when the bombardment and mines went off. When this commenced it was just like as if the gates of hell had just opened. I had some very narrow escapes along with a few of my mates. We had a pretty hot time for a few days, expect to have another go shortly.'

Violet endeavoured to maintain family relationships in England by exchanging photos and sent one of Dora Grace, aged 8 years, as she was at the time.[46] (See Figure 5.18.)

In the same letter Violet reported that the 'Mt Rosa' Run had been 'sold' and that she expected to be leaving Gibbston before long. Violet wrote, 'I am glad to leave here in one way, it is rather lonely. I have not had anyone to help me for the last five months. Gertie used to be here, but complained of her nerves & seems to have left here for good. I got run down in health being left with all the work and the doctor ordered me to take a holiday, which has done me a lot of good. I miss our dear mother very much and at times it seems dreadful.'[47]

Figure 5.18. Dora Grace taken by Gibbston School teacher, 1917. Source: Family Collection

Eleanor had died intestate and her estate became the responsibility of The Public Trust Office. Claims by creditors and others were called for by advertisement. (See Figure 5.19.)

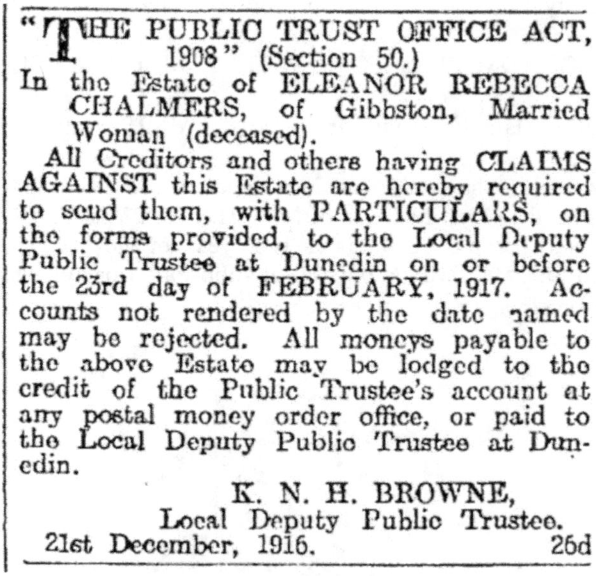

"THE PUBLIC TRUST OFFICE ACT, 1908" (Section 50.)
In the Estate of ELEANOR REBECCA CHALMERS, of Gibbston, Married Woman (deceased).
All Creditors and others having CLAIMS AGAINST this Estate are hereby required to send them, with PARTICULARS, on the forms provided, to the Local Deputy Public Trustee at Dunedin on or before the 23rd day of FEBRUARY, 1917. Accounts not rendered by the date named may be rejected. All moneys payable to the above Estate may be lodged to the credit of the Public Trustee's account at any postal money order office, or paid to the Local Deputy Public Trustee at Dunedin.

K. N. H. BROWNE,
Local Deputy Public Trustee.
21st December, 1916.　　　　26d

Figure 5.19. Notice to creditors having claims against Eleanor CHALMERS' estate. Source: Otago Daily Times. December 26, 1916.

Eleanor's estate was settled on 30 April 1918. The beneficiaries were all of the CHALMERS family. John Howe, as widower, received one third which totaled £625.11s.1d. The rest was divided equally between the twelve children, amounting to £104 5s.2d each.[48]

The war raged on and Malcolm was in the thick of it. 'It was terrible the last battle I was in. We got a bad cutting up owing to the very rough weather (making it) difficult to advance, very hard to get our guns up etc. I got gassed through a gas shell bursting close to me while there was a strong wind blowing towards me and did not give me a great deal of time to get my helmet on. My eyes were badly burnt also received some in my lungs.'[49] Malcolm was a stretcher-bearer, for which he was suited due to his big strong build. He continued to write home regularly. His brothers,

Douglas and Donald who followed him to war also wrote from England and France. Newspaper reports gave some details:

SECOND EDITION. THE ROLL OF HONOUR.
NEW ZEALAND CASUALTIES.
OTAGO AND SOUTHLAND NAMES
In the casualty list issued last night the following Otago and Southland names appear:
WOUNDED, ADMITTED TO HOSPITAL. MACHINE GUN CORPS.
(October 16.)
CHALMERS, Malcolm Shaw (Mr J. H. CHALMERS. Mataura, father).[50]

Private Malcolm Shaw CHALMERS, reported wounded and gassed on October 16 is the eldest twin son of Mr J. H. CHALMERS, of "Knowsley Park," Mataura. Born at Tauranga, he is 35 years of age. He was educated at Kurow and followed farming pursuits at Gibbston prior to leaving with the 13th Reinforcements as a stretcherbearer.[51]

Figure 5.20. Malcolm CHALMERS with cousin Agnes Greig CHALMERS, Dunoon, Scotland, 1917. D. and W. Prophet. Source: author's collection

Before returning home, Malcolm was given the opportunity to visit family in the United Kingdom. At Dunoon, Argyll in Scotland he met with the family of John Howe's brother George and wife Mary. He was photographed with their daughter Agnes. (See Figure 5.20), also Chapter 21.)

Douglas was called up for war service but appealed to the Military Service Board for an extension of time to get the family businesses in order before committing to training. He appeared before the Military Service Board early in March 1917.[52]

MILITARY SERVICE BOARDS
APPEALS AT LAWRENCE. The No. 2 Military Service Board met at Lawrence yesterday; present – Messrs V. G. DAY, S.M. (chairman), Robert BREEN, and A. S. ORBELL. Captain STEVENS was military representative. .

Douglas Gollan CHALMERS (baker, Beaumont) urged that his customers were widely distributed, and his calling up would be a cause of inconvenience. He further stated that his father was old, and appellant was in charge. In addition, he had a farm, which was about to be sold, as his brother was going to the war. He would like a little time to allow him to sell. The appellant was allowed until May 14, and his case is to be brought under the notice of the Efficiency Board.[53]

Figure 5.21. Douglas CHALMERS in uniform, 1917. Source: author's collection.

Douglas was posted to E Company, 29th Reinforcements on 6 June 1917. While at Trentham, the Beaumont Presbyterian Church met and 'A presentation was made on behalf of the Beaumont congregation to Private Douglas CHALMERS, for whom, in his unavoidable absence, his father replied. Beaumont congregation has given a send-off in this way, with a parting gift, to every young man who has gone to war.'[54] Douglas embarked at Wellington on HMS *Mokoia* and arrived at Sling Camp, Wiltshire, England on 2 October.

In June 1918, he wrote: 'I managed to win a prize of ten francs which was given to the best bomb thrower in my company.' Douglas was posted to the N.Z. Rifle Brigade and wounded in action on 26 October 1918. He was admitted to Number 10 General Hospital at Rouen, France on 29 October and transferred to Brockenhurst on 14 November.[55]

Figure 5.22. Old dray at Mt Rosa run. Source: author's collection

NOTES

---

[1] Gibbston School APW Register: Reg. No. 175, admitted 1912, last school Gibbston, last date 24 Oct 1913. Southern Branch NZ Society of Genealogists, HKN AG438/1/376.

[2] Dora GRUBB, pers. com.

[3] Letter from Eleanor (4 April 1912) to her sister Clara STOKES.

[4] Ibid

[5] Ibid.

[6] CHALMERS, John Howe, farmer, Gibbston, Otago, Wakatipu Electoral Roll, 1914; CHALMERS, Eleanor Rebecca, Gibbston, Otago, Wakatipu Electoral Roll, 1914; CHALMERS, Malcolm Shaw, farmer, Gibbston, Otago, Wakatipu Electoral Roll, 1914; CHALMERS, William Howe, Gibbston, Otago, Wakatipu Electoral Roll, 1914.

[7] Postcard to Clara STOKES (26 January 1913).

[8] Ibid.

[9] *Mataura Ensign.* "Closer Settlement." August 6, 1913.

[10] Copy of Deed for Knowsley Park, Settlement Register Application 3811, New Zealand Department of Lands and Survey Deed Register-book, Vol. 99, Fol. 113.

[11] Raymond CHALMERS, pers. com.

[12] Mortgage No. 61218, 6 November 1914, New Zealand Lands and Deeds Index Archive.

[13] Anne Cook, *The Gibbston Story* (Dunedin: Otago Heritage Books, 1985); Dora GRUBB, pers. com; Raymond CHALMERS, pers. com.

[14] Copy of Deed for Knowsley Park, Settlement Register Application 3811, New Zealand Department of Lands and Survey Deed Register-book, Vol. 99, Fol. 113.

[15] Dora GRUBB, pers. com.

[16] Education Department, Index Gibbston School, APW Register, Invercargill Public Library.

[17] Letter from Eleanor to her sister Clara STOKES, from Dora GRUBB.

[18] *Lake County Press.* August 26, 1915.

[19] Family tradition.

[20] *Lake County Press.* August 26, 1915.

[21] Family tradition.

[22] *Lake County Press.* August 26, 1915.

[23] *Ibid.*

[24] *Ibid.*

[25] CHALMERS, William Howe, 1st Division, Beaumont, Tuapeka, Clutha, New Zealand Army WWI Reserve Rolls, 1916-1917.

[26] "Seacliff Lunatic Asylum", last modified 24 February 2018, https://en.wikipedia.org/wiki/Seacliff_Lunatic_Asylum

[27] Certificate of Death, William Howe CHALMERS, February 26, 1937,Invercargill Southland. RGO Wellington. Copy in possession of the author.

[28] Dora GRUBB, pers. com.

[29] *Lake County Press*. July 27, 1911.

[30] *Tuapeka Times*. May 29, 1915.

[31] Education Department, Index of Waiarikiki School, APW Register Index, Invercargill Public Library.

[32] Letter from Violet CHALMERS to family in England.

[33] *Lake Wakatip Mail*. November 23, 1915.

[34] *Lake County Press*. November 25, 1915.

[35] *Lake County Press*. April 27, 1916.

[36] Malcolm Shaw CHALMERS, WW1 23516, Army R21893278, Archives New Zealand, Wellington.

[37] Marriage Certificate, Philip Boylen; NZRGO, Marriage Register, 1916/9020, Constance Eleanor CHALMERS, James MCKIBBIN; NZRGO, Marriage Register, 1916/9021, Gertrude Elizabeth CHALMERS, Philip BOYLEN.

[38] Dora GRUBB, pers. com.

[39] *Otago Daily Times*. November 1, 1916.

[40] Certified Copy of Entry of Death, Eleanor Rebecca CHALMERS, Dunedin, Otago, 29 October 1916, RGO, Dunedin; NZRGO, Death Register, 1916/8289, CHALMERS Eleanor Rebecca, 53 years.

[41] Otago Schools APW Registers Index, Hocken Library, Dunedin.

[42] Letter from Violet (19 November 1916) to Martha TIMS.

[43] Letter from J.C. CHALMERS (14 January 1946) to Arnold GRUBB.

[44] *Lake County Press*. July 19, 1917.

[45] Memorandum of Transfer, Dunedin, 16 August 1917.

[46] Letter from Violet (23 June 1917) to Martha TIMS.

[47] Ibid.

[48] The Estate of Eleanor Rebecca Chalmers – Deceased, Statement of Account of the Public Trustee's Administration, 29 October, 1916 to 30 April 1918, Public Trust Office.

[49] Letter from Malcolm CHALMERS (28 October 1917) to cousin Maggie STOKES.

[50] *Mataura Ensign*. November 6, 1917.

[51] *Mataura Ensign*. November 10, 1917.

[52] Douglas Gollan CHALMERS, baker, Beaumont. Military Callup, p158, *New Zealand Gazette* 1917; *Otago Daily Times*. March 21, 1917.

[53] *Otago Daily Times*. March 21, 1917.

[54] *Tuapeka Times*. August 4, 1917.

[55] Douglas Gollan CHALMERS, WW1 57293, Army 21893266, Archives New Zealand, Wellington.

PART 4: Southland

Mataura Map

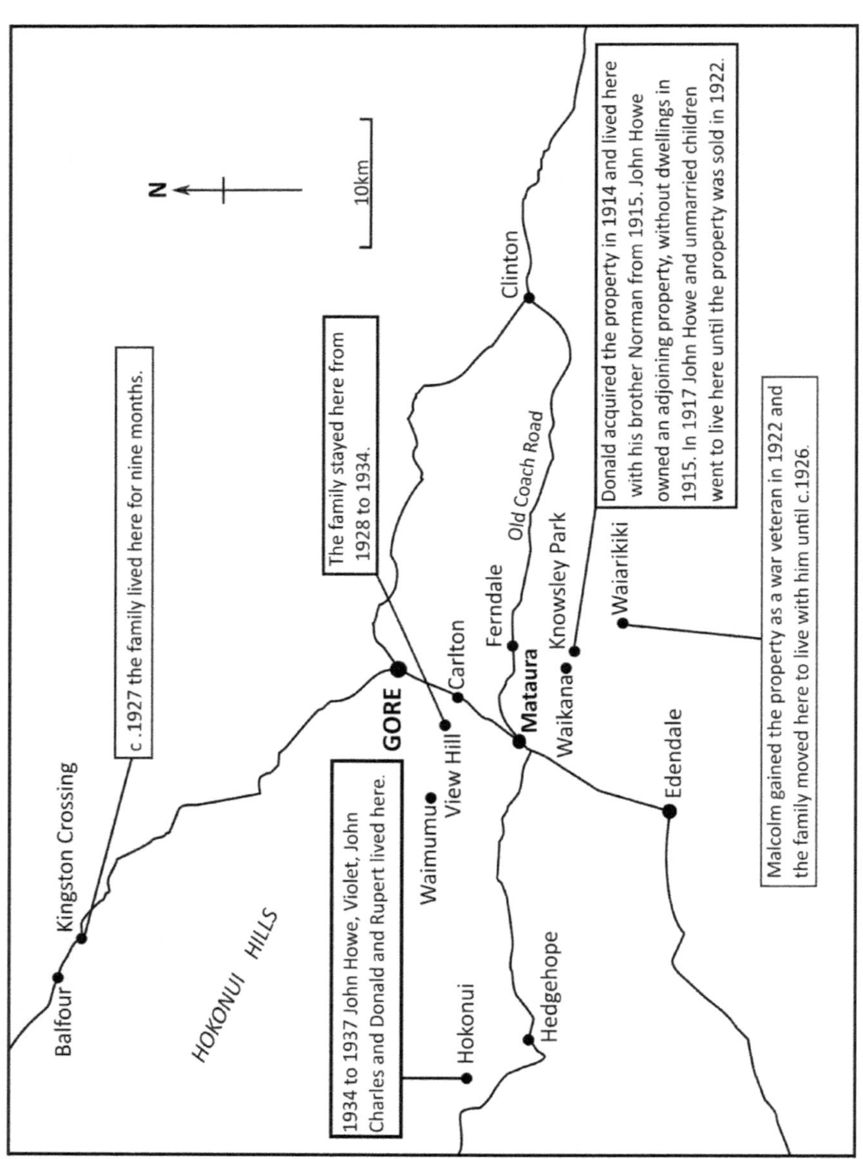
N
10km
c.1927 the family lived here for nine months.
The family stayed here from 1928 to 1934.
Donald acquired the property in 1914 and lived here with his brother Norman from 1915. John Howe owned an adjoining property, without dwellings in 1915. In 1917 John Howe and unmarried children went to live here until the property was sold in 1922.
Malcolm gained the property as a war veteran in 1922 and the family moved here to live with him until c.1926.
1934 to 1937 John Howe, Violet, John Charles and Donald and Rupert lived here.
Kingston Crossing
Balfour
HOKONUI HILLS
Hokonui
Waimumu
View Hill
GORE
Carlton
Ferndale
Old Coach Road
Mataura
Waikana
Knowsley Park
Waiarikiki
Edendale
Hedgehope
Clinton

6 Mataura

Following the sale of 'Mt Rosa' at Gibbston John Howe and many of the family moved to Knowsley Park. This property is south-east of Mataura and was owned by Donald Rolls. Dora had left Beaumont School on 27 July 1917 and this was most likely the time of the shift.[1] This was to be one of several moves within Southland, as shown on the Mataura Map (opposite). As family members married they moved away. However Donald and Rupert, in particular, with their families, rejoined their father and siblings in other places from time to time.

The property at Mataura where Donald had settled was expansive. (See Figure 5.10.) Existing buildings on Knowsley Park included an eight-roomed house and a men's hut with a brick chimney.[2] There would be plenty of room to accommodate the family. Living there at this time were John Howe, Donald Rolls and Violet Hoppner as well as the younger ones: Gordon Rupert, Norman Chamberlin and Dora Grace.

Figure 6.1. (See also Figure 6.2.) Original Knowsley Park homestead. Source: author's collection

Donald was also willing to share his property with the community. 'Access from the road to the homestead was difficult for many years as no track existed. Such inconvenience mattered little to party-goers of the time. The loft above the extensive stables was the venue for most district celebrations in the early days, and served as a hall.'[3] (See Figure 6.7.)

Another example of social activity at Knowsley Park included the annual school picnic: 'The annual Waikana School picnic was held on Wednesday on the grounds of Mr D. [R.] CHALMERS, "Knowsley Park".' Dora came second in the Committee race. 'At 9 p.m. the young people reassembled and held a dance in Mr CHALMERS' granary. ... Mr CHALMERS provided supper. ... The proceedings closed with a hearty vote of thanks to Mr CHALMERS for his kindness in lending his grounds and buildings year after year for public use on the occasion of the annual picnic. It may safely be said that this year's picnic easily eclipses any previous event of the sort held at Waikana.'[4]

Figure 6.2. The kitchen stove. Source: author's collection

Donald's name came up in the 8th and last Ballot: 'CHALMERS, Donald Rolls, farmer, "Knowsley Park" Homestead, Mataura.'[5] With his call to war service, Donald was faced with the prospect of his farm needs being neglected and he applied to the Military Service Board for time to get his farm in order before going to training. He was granted an extension of time.

A Sitting of the Otago No. 2 Military Service Board was held at Gore on the 10th September. The board consisted of Messrs V.G. DAY, S.M. (chairman), A.S. ORBELL, and R. BREEN. Captain BARRETT was the military representative. ... Donald Rolls CHALMERS (sheep farmer, Mataura), an adjourned case, applied for time. He stated that a portion of his ewe flock were now lambing, and the remainder would lamb in October. He would like to have the mustering done before he went into camp. The adjournment was allowed until December 11.[6]

Donald was the last of the three brothers to go to war. He left from Wellington with B Company, 39th Reinforcements on 28 April 1918 on

HMS troop ship SS *Athenic*. It was stranded at Jamaica en route for a time. He was also posted to Sling Camp and given special marksmanship training. Like Douglas, he was said to be a good shot with a rifle. However he did not reach France before the Armistice was signed.[7]

Figure 6.3. Private Donald CHALMERS in uniform, 1918. Source: Author's collection

In December 1918 Donald had seen his brother and wrote: 'I had been to Hornchurch and made enquiries to where Douglas was. Being told Hut 18. And I can tell you I was excited to see him straight away. I said is that you Douglas. Of course he said yes ... I was highly interested to listen to what Douglas had to say about his great adventure and having such narrow escapes. Douglas was laughing telling me about the stretcher bearers carrying him under shell fire puffing for all they were worth and all at once a shell dropped. If I remember right Douglas was dropped too. The shell bursting 10 or 11 yards from them and shrapnel flying over their heads ... No doubt we have to thank many a brave soldier for the lives that they have saved in great danger.'

Donald noted that he 'was glad to see Douglas look so well considering the hardships he has come through, though he is not as stout as he used to be.'[8]

*Figure 6.4. Douglas CHALMERS in uniform,
1917. Source: author's collection*

On 6 December 1918 Douglas wrote from Greytowers Convalescent Hospital at Hornchurch, to his cousin Maggie [Margaret STOKES, daughter of Eleanor's sister Clara] in England: 'I may say he [Donald] was lucky not having to go to France. I wish I had been so fortunate, he escaped untold misery and strenuous times. ... I can hardly believe I am here after what a fellow has gone through under terrible heavy shell fire and machine gun fire, amongst the groaning wounded & being waist deep in mud & stuck 3 days & 3 nights with little or no sleep. Very little to eat is not much of a joke. I feel quite happy at present. I have every reason to be as I am getting well looked after "

Figure 6.5. Postcard sent to cousin Margaret with the caption 'A Proposal in Flanders'. 'The point of Jean's pitchfork awakens a sense of duty in a mine that shirked'. Source: author's collection

By 30 December Douglas' elbow wound had healed and all voluntary movements above and below it were possible. The numbness caused by military duty had left.[9]

Meanwhile, at Knowsley Park and Waiarikiki, the local settlers were facing financial difficulties. Some wanted concessions in time for the payment of rents. Others, including Mr (J.H.) CHALMERS, preferred a straight out reduction in rent. Still others wanted a concession to procure lime. One settler's experience was that the ground was too sour to grow ryegrass or clover. He had tried 25cwt of carbonate of lime and he thought it was impossible to get on without it, having proved its efficiency, and was a great believer in its use. The lime cost 22/6d per ton at the Mataura railway station and it would cost ten or fifteen shillings to cart. Another settler favoured lime being supplied free to the settlers, who would do the carting.[10]

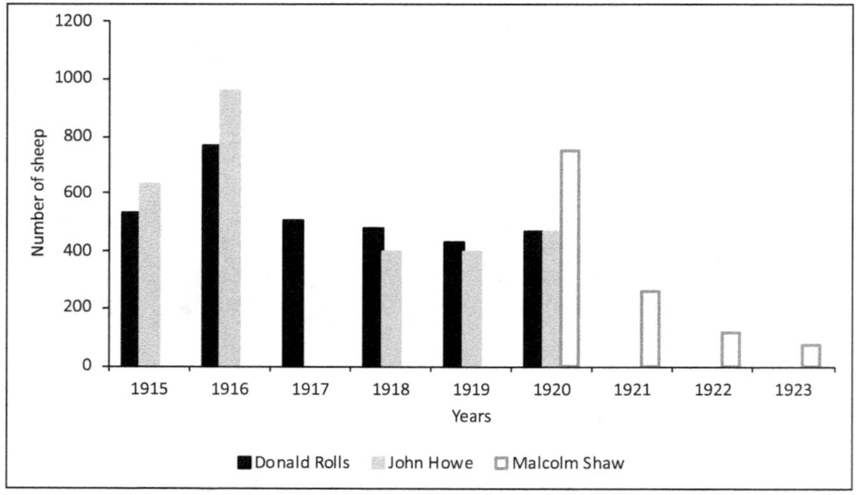

Figure 6.6. Sheep returns for Donald Rolls, John Howe and Malcolm Shaw CHALMERS at Knowsley Park, Mataura from 1915 to 1923. Source: Appendices to the House of Representatives: H-23 and H-23a, 1916-1923

On February 6 a party consisting of the Minister of Lands, Mr G. J. ANDERSON, M.P. and others left Gore at 1 a.m. to meet deputations 'at "Knowsley Park", Brydone, Stalker Settlement and Wyndham' where 'local requirements were brought [to] the notice of the Minister. At "Knowsley Park" Settlement, which was reached shortly after 8 o'clock, five settlers waited on the Minister.'[11]

> The Minister said it was apparent that the settlers were not satisfied. He advised them to submit a statement of their grievances to the Land Board, which would then be forwarded to him. and he would see what could be done.

He also urged them to send on samples of their soil to the Agricultural Department, where they would be analysed free of cost.[12]

Followup reports relating to the Minister of Lands suggestions have not been found.

After hospital treatment for gassing in France and England Malcolm was returned to New Zealand where he was 'but a shadow of his former self'. He was placed in The Cashmere Sanatorium, Port Hills, Christchurch, for the treatment of tuberculosis.[13] Malcolm was discharged on 21 March 1919.[14]

Figure 6.7. Good friends. The locals used the building in the background for social activities. Source: author's collection

On his release from military service and health care, Malcolm went to live on the property of his brother Donald at Knowsley Park, Mataura. While there Malcolm bought Dora a pony. (See Figure 6.8.) The family raised a goose and it became friendly with the pony. The pony would gallop home with the goose flying overhead. End of year came around and no-one had the heart to kill it for Christmas dinner.[15] (See Figure 6.7.)

A press cutting of 1919 reads: 'Mr Malcolm CHALMERS, who recently returned from the front, has been buckling to, and making some great improvements at the "Knowsley Park" homestead.' 'Originally a two-storied building, the "Knowsley Park" homestead was a landmark of the district. The top was removed and it was converted into what the [*Mataura*] *Ensign* described as a single-storey up-to-date residence.'[16] (See Figures 6.14 and 6.15.)

Figure 6.8. Dora with pony, c.1921. Source: author's collection

'Mr CHALMERS latest innovation is a tractor, the first in the district. Quite an amount of excitement was caused at Mataura when it was being unloaded from the railway truck, and there was a royal escort of interested admirers for the first mile out of Mataura. The tractor travels at a speed of 15 miles an hour. Mr CHALMERS gave a successful exhibition at the farm the other day.'[17] Malcolm had won the tractor, a Fordson with steel wheels.[18]

The CHALMERS family were the first in the district to own a car and were apparently a little careless with regard to registration:

> At the Magistrate's Court, Gore, yesterday before Mr E. O. MOSLEY, S.M. Malcolm CHALMERS was, on the information of Constable SNEDDON, fined 10s and costs 7s for failing to have a distinguishing number on the front of his motorcar on September 13 in addition to the one at the back of the car.[19]

There was no school at Knowsley Park. Dora had to ride double on an old horse with a Mrs RITCHIE. They would travel over the hill through private property to Ferndale School. Dora recalled the horse stumbling on a rabbit hole one day. She was thrown and became concussed. It was impossible to get in touch with the family so Dora rested in the playshed at school.[20] After being closed for a number of years Waikana School was reopened in 1918.[21] There Dora won the Special Prize for Sewing in Standard Three in 1919, the Class Prize and Most Popular Girl in 1920 and Second Prize for Standard Five in 1921.[22]

Figure 6.9. Malcolm on horseback, c.1921. Source: author's collection

At Waikana School Dora was taught by a Miss ANDERSON who boarded with the family at Knowsley Park. A report in the *Mataura Ensign* read: 'We cannot speak too highly of Miss ANDERSON's teaching ability.'[23] After leaving school Rupert, until his early twenties, had lived on the CHALMERS family farms and worked teams of horses.[24] Gordon Rupert married Janet Emily ANDERSON, teacher, on 28 December 1921 at Invercargill.[25]

Douglas was sent back to New Zealand on SS *Paparoa* via Glasgow, Scotland and discharged on 22 June 1919.[26] He returned to his former work as baker at Beaumont. At the same time Jack was storekeeper in the family business. He had returned to Beaumont after the loss of 'Mt Rosa' at Gibbston.[27] Douglas's business partner and Gertrude's husband, Philip BOYLEN, had also been called to military service and in 1919 he was working as a storeman at Heriot.[28]

The following year the Otago Land Board reported that John Howe CHALMERS, licensee of the Creek Reserve in Block 12, Dunkeld Town, containing two acres, 3 roods and 32 poles, applied for the issue of a new licence, as the original licence had been lost. This application referred to the family property, including the grocery and bakery business at Beaumont. A Declaration of loss had been lodged by John and a new licence was to be issued on payment of 10s 6d, being subjected to the usual conditions.[29] No further record pertaining to the property has been located to date.

Jack moved away from the family for a while and worked as a motor driver in Dunedin. He lived at 27 Mular Street, Dunedin North in 1919.[30] He had a lady friend named Nellie COLLINS whose address was 42 Mechanic Street, Dunedin North and who had been a schoolteacher at Beaumont where they probably met.[31] She was eight years older than Jack and was reputed to be a bright person.[32] The two were living in Dunedin North at about the same time. Jack wanted to marry her but the friendship was broken when Nellie left for Australia. The story goes that he pursued her there unsuccessfully.[33]

Figure 6.10. Donald in England with uncle William Robert STOKES and son and his aunt Martha TIMS, 1919. Source: author's collection

While in England Donald also visited relatives, members of the TIMS family on his mother's side. (See Figures 2.5 and 6.10) In September 1918 he wrote to his uncle, William Robert STOKES widower of his aunt Clara (his mother's sister) in England: 'Will be glad to send you word when I am likely to call on you all. I am quite sure I will enjoy myself as Malcolm and Douglas were delighted during the stay they were at your home. I am not a bit surprised at Malcolm driving a binder he is like myself very interested in that direction but I am afraid I will have to give up self interest in the meantime and fight for the glory of our great Empire.'

Despite the fact that the armistice had been signed in November 1918, New Zealand soldiers were still being held in camps in England well into 1919. Sling Camp was the temporary home of most of the men, being the chief New Zealand training camp in England. A bleak and lonely place, it was situated in the heart of the Salisbury Plains.[34] From Sling Camp Donald was transferred to Larkhill due to a measles epidemic in December. He felt that three weeks in isolation was just another term of imprisonment 'only we don't get it for a crime.' He was not alone in his feelings of frustration.

Figure 6.11. Sling Camp with kiwi carved into chalk hill in the background created by NZ soldiers. Source: author's collection

By March anger and resentment had built up to boiling point and hundreds of men rioted at Sling Camp. The men were enraged at repeated delays in scheduled sailings of troopships because of a British shipwright's strike. Cantabrians also complained of bias against South Islanders in decisions about sending men home. Other grievances included compulsory education, pointless guard duty and lack of leave. The total damage was said to amount to about £10,000. Troops from other Dominions misbehaved similarly after the war's end.[35]

Although not personally involved and nothing was achieved by the rioting, repeated requests for leave through to April 1919 were denied Donald. He wrote to family in England, saying that what he was experiencing was 'anything but a free life ... It doesn't matter where you go, you have somebody bringing you up to attention.' Perhaps by July he would be feeling a little happier, being part of a brass band.

After just thirteen months away Donald returned to New Zealand on HMS NZ troop ship SS *Cordoba*. He was discharged on 30 October 1919.[36]

The day before Donald's discharge the family had a notice put in the *Otago Daily Times*, in memory of their much-loved wife and mother who had passed away three years earlier.

IN MEMORIAM.

CHALMERS.—In loving memory of Eleanor Rebecca Chalmers, who departed this life on October 29, 1916.

Life is all the sweeter that she lived,
Death is all the easier that she died,
And Heaven is all the happier
That she is there.

—Inserted by her loving husband, sons, and daughters.

Figure 6.12. In Memorium Notice for Eleanor CHALMERS. Source: Otago Daily Times. October 29, 1919.

When Donald arrived home from the war he was upset to find the debts that had been accumulated by his family at his Knowsley Park property during his absence.[37] He decided that he would need to sell it to clear off the debts.

In the meantime he continued a friendship that had developed before leaving for overseas military service. Maribel PEART had corresponded with him throughout that time and would help Violet with the work at

Knowsley Park.[38] She was living on the property.[39] Donald and Maribel were married at Gore on 9 June 1920.[40]

Figure 6.13. Violet CHALMERS and 'Rough' the dog at Knowsley Park. Source: author's collection

In June 1921 Donald's property at 'Knowsley Park', Section 4, Block 6, changed hands. A family story goes that about 1919 a National Mortgage representative met Donald at the Gore or Mataura railway station and put pressure on him to sell. The buyer, by the name of SINCLAIR, promised to 'Do wonders'.[41] The lease was officially entered into the register and signed by Donald. The new lessee was Donald SINCLAIR of Mataura and the mortgage to the National Mortgage and Agency Company of New Zealand.[42] The remaining unmarried family members had lived off this property for two or three years.[43]

The following year, on 15 December 1922, John Howe's property at Knowsley Park, Section 2, Block 7 was forfeited for a new lease.[44]

Figure 6.14. The original Knowsley Park homestead. Source: author's collection

Figure 6.15. Renovated version of the Knowsley Park homestead. Source: undated Mataura Ensign cutting

NOTES

---

[1] Otago School APW Registers Index, Hocken Library, Dunedin.

[2] Copy of Deed for Knowsley Park Settlement Register Application 3811 Vol 99 fol 113.

[3] P.C.W. Muir, editor, *Mataura: City of the Falls* (Mataura: Mataura Historical Society, 1991).

[4] *Mataura Ensign*. January 20, 1917.

[5] *Southland Times*. June 7, 1917.

[6] *Otago Witness*. September 12, 1917.

[7] Donald Rolls CHALMERS, WW1 78478, Army R21893264, Archives New Zealand.

[8] Donald CHALMERS letter to English relatives.

[9] Douglas Gollan CHALMERS, WW1 57293, Army 21893266, Archives New Zealand, Wellington.

[10] *Southland Times*. "Minister Of Lands." February 7, 1919.

[11] *Ibid.*

[12] *Southland Times*. "Minister Of Lands." February 12, 1919.

[13] Dora GRUBB, pers. com.

[14] Malcolm Shaw CHALMERS, WW1 23516, Army R21893278, Archives New Zealand, Wellington.

[15] Dora, GRUBB, pers. com.

[16] P.C.W. Muir.

[17] Ibid.

[18] Kenneth CHALMERS, pers. com.

[19] *Mataura Ensign*. October 9, 1919,

[20] Dora GRUBB, pers. com.

[21] *Mataura Ensign*. June 3, 1918.

[22] *Mataura Ensign*. December 22, 1919; school book prizes, CHALMERS family archives.

[23] P.C.W. Muir. The original article in the *Mataura Ensign* has not been located.

[24] Dora GRUBB, pers. com.

[25] NZRGO, Marriage Register, 1921/10577, Janet Emily ANDERSON, Rupert Gordon CHALMERS

[26] Douglas Gollan CHALMERS, WW1 57293, Army 21893266, Archives New Zealand, Wellington.

[27] CHALMERS, Douglas Gollen, storekeeper, Beaumont, Bruce Electoral Roll, 1919; CHALMERS, John Charles, baker, Beaumont, Bruce Electoral Roll, 1919.

[28] BOYLEN, Philip, storeman, Heriot, Clutha Electoral Roll, 1919; Gertrude Elizabeth BOYLEN, married, Heriot, Clutha Electoral Roll, 1919.

[29] *Mt Benger Mail*. March 31, 1920.

[30] CHALMERS, John Charles, 27 Mular Street, Dunedin North Electoral Roll, 1919.

[31] Dorothy Mary Coburn, *Beaumont Primary School Centennial History 1872-1972* (Beaumont: Centennial Committee, 1972).

[32] NZRGO, Birth Register, 1884/1424 COLLINS, Nellie Sophia Smethe Jane Jordon, m. Ellen, f. Ralph.

[33] Thelma GEARY (née BOYLEN), pers. com.; CHALMERS, John Charles, motor driver, 27 Mular Street, Dunedin North Electoral Roll, 1919; COLLINS, Nellie, spinster, 42 Mechanic Street, Dunedin North Electoral Roll, 1914; COLLINS, Ellen, married, 42 Mechanic Street, Dunedin North Electoral Roll, 1914; COLLINS, Timothy, mechanic, 42 Mechanic Street, Dunedin North Electoral Roll, 1914.

[34] T.B.Drew, *The War Effort in New Zealand* (Auckland: Whitcombe and Tombs Ltd, 1923). Available from: http://nzetc.victoria.ac.nz/tm/scholarly/tei-WH1-Effo-t1-body-d15-d2.html

[35] Ministry for Culture and Heritage, "New Zealand troops riot in England", last modified 8 December 2016, URL: https://nzhistory.govt.nz/page/new-zealand-troops-riot-england,

[36] Donald Rolls CHALMERS, WW1 78478, Army R21893264, Archives New Zealand.

[37] CHALMERS, John Howe, farmer, Knowsley Park, Mataura, Mataura Electoral Roll, 1919; also present: Donald Rolls CHALMERS, farmer, Malcolm Shaw CHALMERS, farmer and Violet Hoppner CHALMERS.

[38] Dora GRUBB, pers. com.

[39] PEART, Amelia Maribel, spinster, Knowsley Park, Mataura, Mataura Electoral Roll, 1919.

[40] NZRGO, Marriage Register, 1921/4644 Amelia Maribell PEART, Donald Rolls CHALMERS.

[41] Dora GRUBB, pers. com.

[42] Department of Lands and Survey, Southland District Land Register, Vol. 99, Fol. 13.

[43] Dora GRUBB, pers. com.

[44] Department of Lands and Survey, Invercargill Register-book, Vol. 99, Fol. 183.

7 Waiarikiki, Balfour, Gore and Hokonui

Earlier in 1922 Malcolm had applied for a lease of Section 10 (643 acres 2 roods 17 perches) of the Waiarikiki Settlement in Southland. Soldiers in World War I were given an allowance for each day of service, over and above living costs provided for them. On their return from war, those interested in farming became eligible to enter a ballot for sections of land. The application was approved subject to evidence of military discharge.

> At yesterday's monthly meeting of the Southland Land Board the application of Malcolm Shaw Chalmers for Section 10, Waiarikiki Settlement, 643a 2r 17p, was approved subject to the production of military discharge. – Report adopted.[1]

Following the loss of Donald's farm at Knowsley Park, the family's next move was to Malcolm's newly acquired property at Waiarikiki. It was a big farm situated between 'Knowsley Park' and Ferndale. It had been divided up and the family lived on part of it. The house at Waiarikiki was very small. Violet and Dora shared a bedroom that had a kind of tallboy in it. Once she pulled out a drawer to find a rat looking at her. Rats were not uncommon and would be seen in the manure from the cowshed. Jack, who lived there for part of the time, slept in the other room. One end of the room was curtained off to form a bedroom, probably for John Howe, and Douglas and Norman probably slept on the verandah. Jack, Violet and Dora milked cows for a living. The cowshed was by a creek that was reached by path from the house. Dora couldn't start the oil-driven milking machine and milked the cows by hand. She recalled that Violet probably helped her.[2]

Because her labour was needed to help the family going through difficult times, Dora missed what should have been her first year at high school, having stayed home to milk cows. While at Waiarikiki she gained her proficiency certificate but was unable to commence secondary school as expected in 1923. Her brother Norman tried unsuccessfully to have her follow in his footsteps, requesting that she be admitted to Gore High School in the second term of that year.[3]

The family still owned the old Ford car that they had used at Beaumont and Gibbston. It was the first motorised passenger vehicle to be found at Waiarikiki at the time. The road was in extremely bad condition. It was impossible to drive a car on it and the vehicle had to be abandoned at Ferndale with the rest of the journey taking place by horse and sledge to carry supplies home. Violet and Dora would drive to Mataura in a buggy drawn by two horses.[4]

KINGSTON CROSSING

From Waiarikiki the remaining family members moved to Kingston Crossing, near Balfour, where they stayed for about nine months.

The move was no less challenging. They drove the stock by road the whole way. Jack rode on a horse or hack and Dora rode her pony. John Howe and Violet travelled by four-wheeled buggy. During the trip one of the animals, a bullock or steer with poor eyesight, went off the road and climbed through a fence into the CHALMERS' (no relation) property near the Ferndale School. Nightfall had descended by the time they reached the CHITTOCKS' house and these good people put everyone up for the night and housed the animals off the road.[5]

Dora vividly remembered the passage that ran for 36 feet through the Kingston Crossing house, from the front door to the back door. It was covered in line runner. Jack was appointed manager of the cow-milking business and Dora was relieved of the responsibility. At Kingston Crossing she was at last able to attend secondary school, by becoming a boarder at the Gore High School Hostel.

Desperate for financial relief, the family urged their father to do something to reclaim what they considered to be the illegal loss of the 'Mt Rosa' run. He travelled to Wellington where his petition to the Lands Committee of the House of Representatives was read: 'Praying for compensation for loss sustained owing to alleged precipitate sale of his deceased wife's interests in a Crown lease by Public Trustee.' The Committee's response was: 'I have the honour to report that in the opinion of the Committee this is not a matter for consideration by the Lands Committee, and the said Committee recommends that the petition be referred back to the Petitions Classification Committee. 18 September, 1924'[6]

The later petition was worded more strongly: 'Praying for compensation for monetary losses incurred by the beneficiaries in his deceased wife's estate, through the alleged forced sale of her interest in the Crown lease.' The response by the Public Petitions A to L Committee was no more encouraging and reads: 'I am directed to report that the Committee has no recommendation to make. 24 September 1924.'[7]

It cost John Howe £8 to travel to Wellington, a trip he could ill afford given his miserably low old age pension. To add to his woes, he was treated harshly by his complaining children on his return. Later, Dora said she felt ashamed of the way the family had treated their father.[8]

GORE

The family's next move was to the Gore district, south of the town near Waimumu. This property, known as 'View Hill', consisted of 402 acres 2 roods and 16 perches (162.9130 hectares). This had previously belonged to Jack EVANS and William (Billy) EVANS, and later to John DRISCOLL.[9]

In 1928 John Howe, Jack, Norman Chamberlin, all farmers, were living together with Violet Hoppner and Dora Grace at 'View Hill'.[10] At this time Malcolm was still on his property at Waiarikiki.[11] Douglas Gollan remained for some time as a farmer in the Mataura area, living and working with Malcolm at Waiarikiki, but does not appear at all in the 1928 electoral roll. Jack managed the 'View Hill' farm that was considered to be a good property. He owned a 'Hupmobile' car with beaded edge tyres that carried 18 hundredweight of lime at once.[12] Beaded edge tyres needed a high tyre pressure of 414kPa minimum and were used on most cars until around 1924.[13]

Figure 7.1. Dora on horseback at 'View Hill', c.1827. Source: author's collection

Dora was able to attend Gore High School from home and it was no longer necessary to be a boarder. Every day after school her father, who called her 'Dorry', would meet her at the end of the long driveway by the pond, at the gate. In all she spent six years of study from 1924 to 1929 at the school.[14] The rector, Joseph HUNTER wrote:

> While at school she passed the matriculation examination, and at the end of 1929 qualified for a Higher Leaving Certificate. During the present year she has been a probationer in the Gore Public School. Her work has always been of a high order, and conscientiously prepared. During her final year she was one of the school prefects, and exerted a strong influence for good among the girls. I am convinced that with training she should become an excellent teacher.[15]

A neighbour also wrote highly of Dora's keenness and determination in her scholastic enterprises, adding: 'I feel sure her strict morals and sound judgment will more than fit her to become an exemplary teacher in the near future.' He also commented: 'I cannot but stress the high standing of her Father who has travelled widely and whose high ideals and intellectual attainments are to be envied.'[16] Dora entered Dunedin Teachers' College in 1930 and graduated with a Trained Teacher's Certificate Class 6 on 1 February 1933.

There was a gap between leaving Teachers' College and securing an appointment with the Department of Education. Dora worked as a governess at Culverden in Canterbury, home teaching a boy who was sick while his brothers went to school by horse and buggy.[17]

Figure 7.2. Horse and buggy for going to school, 1933. Source: author's collection

Following that she was appointed to teach at Kapuka for three months only, as that was all teachers were allowed. This was Department of Education policy owing to the then current 'state of affairs' i.e. the Great Depression.

Later in the year Dora was teaching at Ohai, about 65 miles (105km) from Gore. Violet noticed that it was a much colder place than Gore, being fairly close to the mountains. 'Rupe and I could see them completely covered in snow, when we motored to a small place, not far from Invercargill, a fortnight ago.' She added: 'Dora is coming home next Saturday, for the term holidays. She and another girl are baching in a little cottage.'[18]

Violet seemed to finally get some time to herself: 'I entered in the weight-guessing competition, at the Dunedin Show, of a pen of sheep, and tied for the first prize. I got £1 6s. It is the first time I have tried in such a competition., but I have always been fairly good at guessing weights, or thought I would have a trial. Sheep can be rather deceiving at times, you have to take the age, etc into consideration.'[19]

In June 1933 Violet wrote to her cousin in England: 'Malcolm is on his farm at Victoria Bridge. Douglas is with him at present.' Malcolm Shaw had left the Mataura district and he traded his farm at Waiarikiki to return to Victoria Bridge by the Kawarau River. When he moved back to Central Otago he drove the tractor he had won while at Knowsley Park all the way to his property at Victoria Bridge by the Kawarau River in Central Otago.[20] He married Nellie HASTIE at Cromwell in 1935.

The Great Depression was well underway and, like all others, it had a huge impact on the CHALMERS family. The economic situation became so bad that Jack could not keep the farm running and was employed locally helping make the road at Carlton. Meanwhile, Billy EVANS, an unemployed Welshman, was taken on to milk cows for the family. This job lasted three weeks. He was paid thirty shillings for the first week but for the next two he received nothing.[21]

In October of 1933 Rupert and family came to live at 'View Hill'. Alterations in the way of furniture needed to be made and it took time to get things back in order. Violet liked the prospect of their planning to get another house built on the farm.[22]

On 18 January 1934 William EVANS conceded his share of the 'View Hill' mortgage, adding the names of Rupert Gordon CHALMERS, farmer, and Violet Hoppner CHALMERS, spinster, to that of Jack, thus giving the family total rights to the mortgage. They were tenants in common in equal shares. The tenancy was short-lived, however, as another transfer was sought by the end of the year and not finally settled until 29 March 1938.[23]

The hard times continued. Douglas returned to Waiarikiki in search of employment after spending time with Malcolm at Victoria Bridge. He and Norman were unable to find any work and took to cutting flax that ran alongside the small river that passed by the Waiarikiki School. From the river bank the flax was loaded onto a four-wheeled wagon drawn by two horses and taken to be sold.[24]

In 1935 Douglas returned once more to be with Malcolm at Cromwell where he tried his luck as a miner.[25] Douglas returned to his original work as a baker at some point and was employed at Gore, a few miles from Mataura.[26]

A keen walker, John Howe met with an accident. Gertrude wrote to her cousin Margaret STOKES in London: 'Father broke a small bone in his ankle. While confined to bed he contracted influenza and then congestion of the lungs. Greatly improved.'[27]

On 4 August 1937 Douglas Gollan married Violet Dina NATHAN at Caversham, Dunedin.[28] Violet was a qualified nurse.

Norman Chamberlin did not accompany the family to Hokonui. He left the area to find work further north and in 1935 he was a labourer at the state forest at Balmoral in the Hurinui District of Canterbury.[29] By 1938 he had moved south again to Taurina, near Allanton, in South Otago. He stayed in the Canterbury area seeking work where he could find it and laboured for a time at the Wigram aerodrome of the New Zealand Air Force.[30] By 1938 he had moved south again, to Taurina, at Allanton in South Otago where he continued to work as a labourer.[31] On 18 January 1940 Norman married Elizabeth Mary MARSHALL.

HOKONUI

At the end of 1934 the remaining family members moved west to a property known to the family as 'Hokonui', as it was situated near the Hokonui Hills between Hedgehope and Winton. A public road ran through the farm and around several other properties forming what was called the Hokonui Loop. A grass track made a shortcut to Hedgehope, while the shortest route to Gore was via Waimumu. The name of the farm was 'Pleasant Creek' and the postal address Hokonui/Otapori —

Winton/Southland. Consisting of 800 acres the farm contained three dwellings.[32]

Jack, Violet and Rupert again had shared ownership of the property near Forest Hill. The title referred to it under the name of Jack CHALMERS as Forest Hill Hundred 12/2834CV. A previous owner from 1895, the ANDERSON family had a road named after it. That may well be the public road that ran through the property. John Howe, Jack and Violet lived together in the top house, Rupert and family had the middle one and the dwelling at the far end was rented to a family by the name of FRISBY.[33]

Figure 7.3. The CHALMERS' property at Hokonui. Source: author's collection.

Dora had spent several years teaching in Southland, including a posting at Lochiel School.[34]

The last school she taught at before marriage was Gore Primary School where she was presented with a book as a token of best wishes on 1 March 1936.[35] On 11 May she married Arnold Henry McLeod GRUBB at Gore.[36]

Of her father, Constance Eleanor wrote to English relatives in 1933 stating: 'My father keeps in wonderful health considering his age (He was 86 at the time) and is very active both in mind and body. He has always been a great walker.' However, by the dend of his stay at 'View Hill' his health had deteriorated and he became an invalid. He was ill again at Hokonui. Violet was told by the doctors that his heart was very weak. Still, she was sure that a lot of young people could not have come through such a severe illness. John Howe was in need of a great deal of attention and it was decided to apply for home help. An organisation known as the Women's Division of Federated Farmers had been formed and Frances Louisa MITCHELL became a worker for the newly developed home help scheme. She lived at the family home and helped Violet with the care of her father. Jack married her on 22 December 1936.[37]

Figure 7.4. John Howe CHALMERS and grandson Kenneth CHALMERS c.1936. Source: author's collection

Early in 1937 John Howe was well enough to travel to Dunedin and he spent a holiday with Constance and her family. However, he did not survive for much longer and passed away on 22 February 1937 at Invercargill. His death was noted in the *Lake Wakatip Mail*:

PERSONAL.
The death occurred at Invercargill on Friday last of Mr John Howe CHALMERS a former resident of Gibbston. Deceased had reached the advanced age of 89 years.[38]

John Howe was buried with his wife Eleanor Rebecca at Andersons Bay Cemetery, Dunedin. The headstone reads simply 'CHALMERS'.

On reflection, Violet wrote to her distant relatives: 'I did not have any time to myself, what with all the others, work and father to look after. I seemed to stand it very well, but am now feeling very run down. To make matters worse I had a nasty kick on the chest, from one of my nice little jersey cows, caused by a cat coming near her, she hates the sight of cats. This happened three weeks ago, and I am hoping the chest will soon be rid of pain, and I will be feeling like myself again. Jack got married just before Christmas and I am glad to have his wife for company and help.'[39]

Violet kept house for the family. She was a very quiet, gentle person and often stayed with Gertie at Winton. Gertie's daughter Thelma remembers her lugging huge bags of flour, 25 to 50 lbs – and also the same sized bags of mash that she mixed with hot water for the hens. The smell was special.[40]

Violet was hoping there would be more leisure time for other things, commenting, "It is quite interesting on a farm so long as one is not tied too much to work. There is a lot of pretty native bush on the farm. ... We have a wireless set and get a lot of pleasure out of it. We listened to a relay of the ex-King's speech at the time of his abdication. Some of the people here think everything will most likely turn out for the best, as far as the throne is concerned." Violet was referring to King Edward VIII who left the throne in favour of marrying an American divorcée.

Figure 7.5. Violet with her sister Constance at Beaumont. Source: author's collection

When Rupert left the property, his share of the mortgage was taken over by Donald. The farm did not prove to be very profitable. A particular trace element, cobalt, was missing from the soil.[41] Added to that,

Southland has a very high rainfall and this had a leaching effect on the soil. Consequently trying to fatten lambs was a problem as they lost rather than gained weight. Discouragement set in and the property was sold for £4 an acre in 1937. On sale the stock was divided. Donald and Jack preferred sheep while Violet liked cows. However, she and Jack CHALMERS invested their share in a property at Roslyn Bush that accommodated their 600 sheep. Violet stayed for a while but soon sought independence and grazed cows at Kapuka where Donald and family had settled. She also liked dogs as pets and had a Pomeranian at one stage.[42]

Figure 7.6. Violet at Kapuka. Source: author's collection

Violet never married, though Dora thought she was more of a mother than a sister to her in her growing-up years, after their mother died.

NOTES

---

[1] *Mataura Ensign.* January 17, 1919.

[2] Dora GRUBB, pers. com.

[3] Ibid.

[4] Dora GRUBB, pers. com.; Kenneth CHALMERS, pers. com.

[5] Dora GRUBB, pers. com.

[6] Reports of the New Zealand Lands Committee, Appendices to the House of Representatives, 1924, Section I-05, p.4, No.33.

[7] Reports of the New Zealand Public Petitions A to L Committee, Appendices to the House of Representatives, 1924, Section I-01, p.5, No.33.

[8] Dora GRUBB, pers.com.

[9] Copy of Certificate of Title Under Land Transfer Act Register-book, Vol. 76, Folio 3.

[10] CHALMERS, John Howe, Farmer, View Hill, West Gore, Mataura Electoral Roll, 1928; also present: John Charles, farmer, Norman Chamberlin, farmer and Violet Hoppner, spinster and Dora.

[11] CHALMERS, Malcolm Shaw, farmer, Mataura, Mataura Electoral Roll, 1928.

[12] Ray CHALMERS, pers. com.

[13] Beaded Edge Tyres, Longstone Tyres, no date,
https://www.longstonetyres.co.uk/vintage-tyres/beaded-edge-veteran-
tyres.html?SID=icvom1gsfr22bjro99pnrulln0#page=1

[14] Dora GRUBB, pers.com.

[15] Personal reference by Joseph HUNTER, October 30, 1930.

[16] Testimonial signed by F. TREGARTHEN, Charlton Road, Gore, Tetipua R.D., October 30, 1930.

[17] Dora GRUBB, pers. com.

[18] Letter from Violet CHALMERS to Maggie (Margaret) STOKES.

[19] Ibid.

[20] Kenneth CHALMERS, pers. com

[21] Ibid.

[22] Violet's letter to Maggie (Margaret) STOKES.

[23] Copy of Certificate of Title Under Land Transfer Act Register-book, Vol. 76, folio 3.

[24] Dora GRUBB, pers. com.

[25] CHALMERS, Douglas Golleen [sic], Victoria Bridge, Central Otago, Central Otago Electoral Roll, 1935.

[26] Dora GRUBB, pers. com.

[27] Letter from Gertrude (February 1935 to cousin Margaret.

[28] NZRGO, Marriage Register, 1937/8153, Violet Dina NATHAN, Douglas Gollan CHALMERS.

[29] CHALMERS, Chamberlain Norman, labourer, State Forest, Balmoral, Hurunui Electoral Roll, 1935

[30] CHALMERS, Chamberlain Norman, labourer, Wigram Aerodrome, Riccarton Electoral Roll, 1938.

[31] CHALMERS, Chamberlain Norman, labourer, Taurina, Allanton, Central Otago Electoral Roll, 1938.

[32] Violet CHALMERS, pers. com.

[33] CHALMERS, John Howe, farmer, Hokonui, Awarua Electoral Roll, 1935; also present John Charles farmer, Rupert Gordon, farmer and Janet Emily, and Violet Hoppner, spinster.

[34] CHALMERS, Dora Grace, schoolteacher, Lochiel, Awarua Electoral Roll, 1935.

[35] Book in family archives.

[36] NZRGO, Marriage Register, 1936/6982, Dora Grace CHALMERS, Arnold Henry McLeod GRUBB.

[37] NZRGO, Marriage Register, 1936/13809, Frances Louisa Beaven MITCHELL, John Charles CHALMERS; Marriage certificate in CHALMERS family archives.

[38] *Lake Wakatip Mail*. March 2, 1937.

[39] CHALMERS, John Charles, farmer, Hokonui, Awarua Electoral Roll, 1938;
CHALMERS, Frances Louisa Beaver, married Roslyn Bush, Awarua Electoral Roll, 1938;
CHALMERS, Violet Hoppner, married, Hokonui, Awarua Electoral Roll, 1938.

[40] Thelma GEARY, pers. com.

[41] Martin CHALMERS, pers. com.; Southland soils were known to be deficient in iodine, copper, cobalt and possibly selenium. See E.D. Andrews, "Trace Elements in Relation to Animal Health in Southland," available: https://www.grassland.org.nz /publications/nzgrassland _publication _1821 .pdf

[42] Ken CHALMERS, pers. com.

PART 5: The Next Generation

8 Donald Rolls CHALMERS and Amelia Maribel PEART

Donald CHALMERS and Maribel PEART were married on 9 June 1920 at Gore.[1]

Figure 8.1. Donald CHALMERS.
Source: author's collection

Figure 8.2. Maribel PEART.
Source: author's collection

Maribel's paternal grandfather, Joseph Emerson PEART was born in Wolsingham, Durham, England in 1834. His father, John PEART, was a shoemaker.

Table 8.1 James and Elizabeth PEART's household, Margate Street, Weardale, Durham, 1841.[2]

John PEART	head	35	shoemaker	Durham, England
Elizabeth PEART	wife	35		Durham, England
George PEART	son	12		Durham, England
Jacob PEART	son	10		Durham, England
Joseph PEART	son	7		Durham, England
Jane PEART	dau	5		Durham, England
Thomas PEART	son	3		Durham, England
Elizabeth PEART	dau	6 mths		Durham, England

Aged 18 Joseph immigrated to Australia in 1855, arriving in Sydney from Adelaide on 6 October 1855 aboard the *Polly*.[3]

He moved to New Zealand where he met and married Margaret Hamilton MUIRHEAD on 27 February 1867 at Dunedin.[4]

Margaret was born on 20 March 1850 at St Cuthberts, Edinburgh, Midlothian, Scotland to James MUIRHEAD and Janet FRENCH.[5]

Margaret's father, James MUIRHEAD advertised that he had commenced business as blacksmith in Stuart Street, above the hospital, Dunedin 'and trusts, by strict attention and care in the execution of all orders with which he may be favoured, to merit a share of public patronage. Horse-shoeing and Smith-work in general'.[6]

Joseph took up his father's occupation as boot and shoemaker also in Stuart Street, Dunedin. The property in North East Valley was both a shop and dwelling.[7] By 1880 he had changed his business to fruiterer.[8] In the decade of 1883 to 1893 Joseph and his wife Margaret were millers at Vanguard Street, Nelson.[9] In between times, Joseph returned to Dunedin. From this point on he appears to have been living alone and working at different jobs, rabbiting at Mataura and as a labourer at Mandeville.[10] Before his death in 1907 Joseph was a farmer at Croydon Bush.[11]

Maribel's maternal grandparents were George McLEOD, born 12 December 1834 at Tongue, Sutherland, Scotland and Ann McDONALD, born 1 November 1842 at Kyle of Lochalsh, Scotland.[12] They were married on 12 March 1861 at Invercargill, Southland, New Zealand.[13]

In 1851 George's father was a farmer (crofter) of two acres. He was living with his wife Isabella SUTHERLAND and five children, George being the eldest.

Table 8.2. Donald and Issabella McLEOD's household, Braetongue, Tongue, Ship of Braetongue, Sutherland, Scotland, 1851.[14]

Donald McLEOD	head	42	farmer 2 acres	Tongue, Sutherland
Issabella McLEOD	wife	30		Tongue, Sutherland
George McLEOD	son	16		Tongue, Sutherland
Willimina McLEOD	dau	14		Tongue, Sutherland
Janet McLEOD	dau	11		Tongue, Sutherland
Neil McLEOD	son	3		Tongue, Sutherland
Barbra McLEOD	dau	2		Tongue, Sutherland
Christina McLEOD	dau	6		Tongue, Sutherland
William McLEOD	son	1		Tongue, Sutherland

Maribel was the daughter of James Muirhead PEART and Janet McLEOD, both of whom were born in New Zealand. (See Figure 7.3.)

Donald and Maribel's first child, Jessie Eleanor, was born at Gore while her parents were staying with Maribel's parents on their farm at Waimumu, twelve miles from Gore. In the early days of their marriage they moved to a dairy farm at Makarewa where Donald's main work was milking cows.[15]

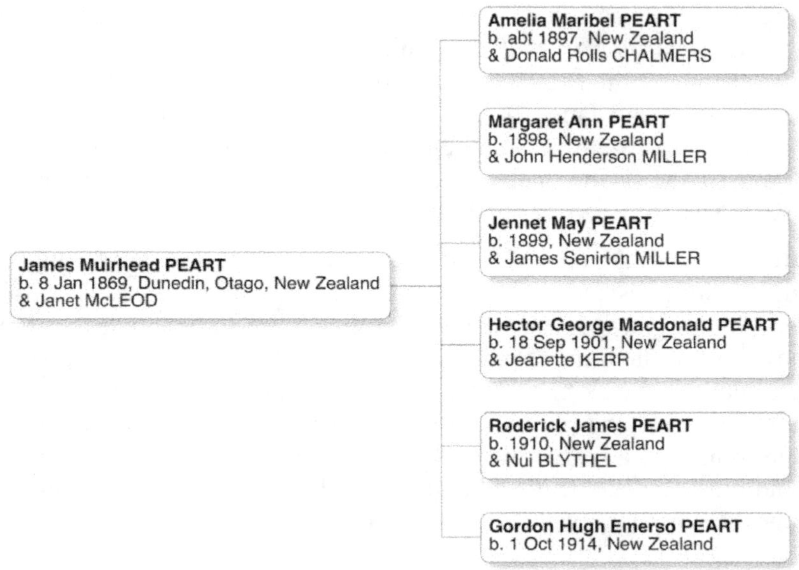

Figure 8.3. The children of James and Janet PEART

They moved to several places to earn a living. By 1926 they became settled for a while at Mimihau. The Wyndham Ridges property had been formerly owned by Andrew NOBLE, neighbour to the John and Rosa MITCHELL family.[16] (See Chapter 12.)

Raymond and George were born at Wyndham and that is where Jessie and Donald first attended school. Jessie remembered walking alone from school when she was bitten by a dog. The next day the teacher asked why she was wearing a bandage on her wrist. The boy from the farm concerned said that she had been throwing sticks and stones at the dog. This was a lie. From then on she dodged the gateway by going around a woolshed on the opposite side of the road.

On another occasion Jessie and her brother Don went through a paddock where carrots were scattered about. They ate some and wondered why their parents were alarmed when they told them. A Mr DODDS was poisoning rabbits and those carrots were the bait. Mercifully for the children they did not become seriously ill.[17]

Maribel had been a dressmaker and was a very successful gardener.[18] She would enter produce in the local show and won prizes for two years in succession. She was certain to win top prize for the third year, but by the time of the next show in 1929 the family had returned to Waimumu. They took up residence in a cottage near a coalpit on the property of Maribel's parents, James and Janet PEART, who did not ask for rent. It was two paddocks away from the main house and was the original pit house of a Mr WILLIAMS who had worked the mine.[19] The youngest child, Kenneth was born at Gore in 1930.

There was a burning coal-pit nearby that was always bright and could be seen for a long distance. Visitors were fascinated by it and used to walk around looking at it in wonder. When they were old enough the three young boys at the time, Donald, George and Raymond enjoyed playing in the coal dross making tracks for their toy vehicles to go along.[20] Ray remembered playing in the mine that was part open cast and part underground. As a little boy he would slide down the lignite and land in the bidibids. Ray also enjoyed holidays with the CHALMERS family at 'View Hill', not far away.[21]

Figure 8.4. The children of Donald and Maribel CHALMERS

Times were difficult during the Great Depression years. Donald had worked hard as a teamster, owned and operated his own farm and tended herds of dairy cows. When he became unemployed he relied on hard physical work to earn any sort of income. During the week he would stay with the CHALMERS family at View Hill, on the way to Waimumu.

Along with his brother Jack, he worked in gravel pits and at making roads. They earned a few shillings a day, but not enough to feed and clothe a family. Meanwhile, Maribel took in sewing to add to the family's income.[22]

In the early 1930s Donald, Maribel and their five children did a tour of Central Otago in the 1909 Model T Ford car. They camped in an open, empty section of road reserve in the Roxburgh area and got flooded out.

At Gibbston they were met by Donald's brother Norman who visited them while camping. He was amazed at the trouble Maribel had gone to: 'Oh, white sheets!' he exclaimed. No doubt they were a luxury for bachelor brothers. They went as far as Victoria Bridge where Malcolm, Norman and probably Douglas were living at the time. The family remembered the tasty apricots that had come from an orchard at Gibbston. At age eighty Jessie recalled the occasion: 'There were quite a lot of earwigs in the apricots and I was a little scared to go to sleep in case they got into my ears. They didn't make the apricots any less enjoyable to eat.' The shiny schist stone in the area also impressed the family.[23] In 1936 the Ford car was sold to a Bill WILSON for a bag of wheat.[24]

Figure 8.5. The young family. Jessie, Donald, Raymond, George, Kenneth, c.1935. Source: author's collection

Donald eventually found employment with the government forestry service at Dusky Forest, near Kelso. A tree planting project had been established there. In 1936 the family was living at Kelso on a property of fifteen acres with a four-roomed house and a cow. They paid 2s. 6d a week rent. The family moved to the town and lived on the main street. There was the added advantage of having Donald's sister Gertrude and husband Phil nearby. The BOYLEN family were neighbours and very supportive.[25] (See Chapter 13.)

Kelso was where George began to attend school for the first time. Jessie and Don had transferred from Mimihau School. Jessie went to secondary school by bus. The round trip to Tapanui District High School was twenty-seven miles and she spent the entire journey aboard as she was the first on and the last off. This was not a happy time for her. The family was unable to afford a school uniform and instead she would wear a cardigan previously owned by one of her cousins. She was teased by the other children and sat behind the bus driver for protection.[26]

When Donald's brother Rupert and wife Janet decided to move to Invercargill, Jack asked Donald to take his place. He was offered Rupert's share in the Hokonui property, along with existing interests held by Jack and Violet.[27] He stayed there on a trial basis and biked from Kelso to Hokonui several times. On one occasion he lost his way and must have decided that being so far apart was too stressful. He confirmed the offer and the family moved into the house that had previously been occupied by Rupert and family.[28]

Figure 8.6. Donald beside his children on horse-drawn jogger or dray. Source: author's collection

The family stayed at Hokonui for two years. Donald looked after the stock, including eight hundred ewes, and cultivation of the crops.[29] He worked for rent and food but did not receive any cash.[30] Maribel made clothes for everyone and grew vegetables.[31] She was kept very busy.[32] Before buses the children travelled to school by horse drawn covered jogger. It carried four CHALMERS and half a dozen other children.[33]

According to daughter Jessie, her father was of the 'old school' type and did not enter much into family activities.[34] He was a hard taskmaster and his severe ways caused conflict within the family. The boys hoped that he would stay away. Maribel was torn between the two.[35] He'd had to work hard early in life, but having come from an artistic background, he was interested in music and very fond of brass instruments and had played in bands. Each family member played a different instrument, having been taught by Donald. Donald played the cornet, Maribel the trombone, Jessie the flugelhorn, Don played bass or baritone, Ray the cornet and Donald transposed notes. The family played at a concert at Hokonui. Amongst a repertoire of simple songs, Jessie remembered playing 'Abide with Me'.[36]

Figure 8.7. The family with musical instruments. L to R: Donald (flugel horn), Maribel (valve trombone), Jessie (cornet), Donald Jnr (euphonium), Raymond (flugel horn), George (baritone) and Kenneth (cornet). Source: author's collection

Ken was aged seven in 1937 when his grandfather John Howe was still alive. He remembered being impressed with this beautiful farm that ran into bush. Ray had a yellow and white collie dog named Tim that he could play with.[37] While living at Kelso Ray took his dog Tim with him on a trip through Gore. The dog went missing and the family advertised for it. Someone found it and returned it to Kelso by bus. Tim was one very happy dog to be home again.[38]

Figure 8.8. L to R: Kenneth, Raymond with Tim the dog, George, Donald Jnr. Source: author's collection

Ken was very fond of his Uncle Jack who would take him for rides in his thirty hundred-weight truck. His Uncle Jack also built windmills and put them up in the trees.[39]

In her growing up years Jessie maintained close relationships with her extended family and was particularly close to her Uncle Jack and Auntie Frances. She loved babies and enjoyed watching and listening to their baby Rosalie learn to talk. Jessie spent a lot of time with her Auntie Dora and Uncle Arnold at Gore. The BOYLEN family also were not far away for visits, at Winton.[40]

Donald, in particular, hated the Southland climate and it was a frequent topic of his conversation. He made up some rhyming couplets to that effect:

Southland is famous for its clouds, rain and mud.
If you try and grow a crop of Lucerne you will come a thud.[41]
Leave it to the ducks and geese
When it starts to rain, you never know when it's going to cease.[42]
It makes the housewife curse with wrath
When the hens go off laying for want of sunshine and a dustbath.[43]

On one occasion Dora returned from another area where she was teaching and mentioned to Donald how cold and wet it was at Hokonui. This only added to Donald's misery and she kept her distance for a while.[44]

Figure 8. 9. Malcolm, Nellie, Donald and Maribel, Kapuka 1941. Source: author's collection

The Hokonui soils lacked the trace element cobalt and the abundant rain tended to leach what soil nutrients there were present. As a result lambs did not thrive on the impoverished pastures.[45] Hokonui consisting of unproductive land, coupled with family discontent, brought about the decision to sell the farm. The settlement between Donald and Jack was not an amicable one and some ill-feeling resulted. Donald felt disappointed but in the end said: "We're two families and all friends."[46] The land and buildings were sold for £4 an acre in 1937. The stock was said to have been divided unfairly and Maribel in particular was upset.[47] Donald took £100, 300 sheep and some cows. These, along with the old Mogul oil-driven milking machine were the basis of his farm at Kapuka where he and his family settled in 1938.[48]

Figure 8.10. L to R: Ken, Malcolm, Donald, Ray and Donald Jnr on the farm at Kapuka, c.1942. Source: author's collection

The road from Hokonui to Kapuka consisted of two big ruts. During the trip the vehicle got bogged down at one stage. They stayed at a Mr REED's place for tea. A meal of hot potatoes and mince was prepared over a black stove in a dark kitchen.[49]

In 1943 tragedy struck the family. During a polio (known at the time as infantile paralysis and later poliomyelitis) epidemic Donald Jnr, then aged eighteen and in his second or third year as an engineering apprentice at Melhop's Garage in Invercargill, became ill. He was losing movement in his limbs and could not stand, so his parents sent for the doctor who ordered an ambulance to take him to Kew Hospital in Invercargill. He was put in an iron lung to assist his breathing.

Figure 8.11. Donald Jnr with his bike, 1940. Source: author's collection

At the time, his sister Jessie was on her way to take up nurse aide work at Milton Cottage Hospital in South Otago. Instead, she went to Kew Hospital to visit Don. On arrival he told her to be careful and not let the sterilizers flow over. He had improved a little and was cheerful. Eventually he was taken off the ventilator for a few minutes each day. He was on a balcony where it was rather airy and apparently he contracted pneumonia which meant he had to be put back in the iron lung.

After seven weeks of nursing Jessie returned home for her first leave. She went straight to Kew Hospital from the train. A nurse met her at the bottom of the lift and told her that Don did not have much longer to live. All of the family came to see him. It was a sad night. Don passed away in the morning of 25 June, assured that he went to be with his Lord. He had quoted this Bible verse to Jessie: "Rejoicing in hope; patient in tribulation; continuing constant in prayer".[50]

Don had been writing to a penpal in Scotland by the name of Bessie MacASKILL. Ray wrote to tell her of the sad news of his passing. This was the beginning of a correspondence that lasted for about eight years.[51]

In 1943 George attended Southland Technical College for a year, focussing on rural industrial studies. In order to get there he needed to bike along a manuka-lined gravel road full of potholes and trenches to Kapuka where he caught the train to Invercargill.[52] On leaving school his first job was with his father, cutting flax at Lake Waituna. The flax mill at Gorge Road processed the flax. After some time he moved out on his own to work on a farm. While working at COPLAND's he fell from a horse, injuring his back. The pain and discomfort troubled him for the rest of his life.[53]

Figure 8.12. Ken following his father ploughing at Kapuka, 1945. Source: author's collection

Jessie began a three and a half years' training schedule at Gore Hospital in 1944. A nursing friend invited her to go to Sydney to advance her skills. On return to New Zealand she was required to do a further four months' training, the purpose given was to bring the nursing profession to New Zealand standards. Staying on in the Wellington area, she did maternity work in Lower Hutt and cared for the elderly at Upper Hutt.[54]

Donald and Maribel continued to live at Kapuka. The farm was worked by son Ray from the age of seventeen.[55]

However, Donald's longing for Central Otago persisted and in 1947 he bought 120 acres of land with an old cottage on the outskirts of Arrowtown for £500. The district gaol for those who ran foul of the law in the early days, was on the property. Meanwhile, Maribel was torn between the two places. Her husband wanted her to remain in Arrowtown, but she worried about the boys having to struggle by themselves at Kapuka. She lived in the two places, but as time went on she preferred Arrowtown.[56] Maribel was the practical one who did all of the gardening and orchard work. She kept the family, including nieces and nephews, who lived or stayed a while with her. Donald loved music and would spend hours at a time playing his cornet on the verandah and 'let the world go by'.[57] For many years Donald played 'The Last Post' at the Arrowtown ANZAC services.[58]

Figure 8.13. Jessie in nursing uniform, 1946
Source: author's collection

Jessie's chosen specialty was maternity nursing and she trained to become a maternity nurse at Tauranga.[59] She stayed at Tauranga for six months and then went on to nurse in Greenlane Hospital, Auckland where she was employed as a staff nurse and stayed for a year. From there she returned to Kapuka South for a time.[60] In February 1951 she visited her Uncle Malcolm and Auntie Nellie at Cromwell.[61]

Ray had full responsibility of the Kapuka farm from 1947.[62] He eventually came to own it. By this time Donald had ceased to work at Kapuka, choosing instead to stay in Central Otago and help Malcolm at Victoria Bridge as well as a Mr HELLER, owner of Mount Soho Station.[63]

In 1948 George and his brother Ken opened a lignite mine on the farm at Kapuka South. George remembered that they charged 11s ($1.10) per ton for the lignite. The coal was driven to Invercargill and sold for domestic fires. One of George's life-long dreams was that lignite would be developed for industrial uses.[64]

Figure 8.14. Ken and George mining lignite at Kapuka. Source: author's collection

A district nurse was required at the Queenstown area and, as there was no accommodation provided for a nurse, Jessie chose to live and spend time with her parents at Arrowtown.[65]

Donald and Maribel had a new home built for retirement on part of fifty acres of the property. It was financed by Jessie.[66] George and Ken took over the remaining seventy acres. They commenced running the Arrowtown farm in 1951.[67]

George and Ken would drive to Arrowtown to help look after the farm there and to spend time with family. Each autumn they harvested a type of grass known as browntop that grew in Southland and Central Otago. They went as far as Glenorchy in search of it.[68] It thrived in low-fertility soil. Improved by adding nitrogen fertiliser, it was one of the main grasses used on lawns and is still popular for golf greens.[69]

Figure 8.15. Work on the Arrowtown farm, c.1949. Source: author's collection

On 29 November 1951 Ray set sail from Auckland bound for Southampton aboard the *Rangitata*.[70]

Ray explained how his adventure to Scotland eventuated by saying that he 'wanted to see who was at the end of the pen!' In January 1952, after the boat docked in England, Ray made his way to the northern parts of Scotland. He was going to see Bessie MacASKILL who lived in the Outer Hebrides and with whom he had corresponded for many years after his brother Donald Jr's death.

There he met his penpal in person for the first time. It must have been a happy meeting as in February they became engaged. They were married in March 1952.[71]

In April Bessie said goodbye to her homeland and sailed with Ray to New Zealand. On 2 June 1952 he returned to New Zealand via Sydney aboard the *Wanganella* and disembarked at Wellington, with his bride Bessie as an immigrant.[72]

Ray had made bookings for the return trip before leaving home. He must have been very confident about his intentions as, prior to departing New Zealand and before he had even met Bessie, he booked a single cabin berth on the boat going to the UK but had booked a double cabin for the return trip home![73] Later Bessie's mother came from Scotland and lived at the CHALMERS house at Kapuka South with Ray and Bessie.

When Frances died suddenly on 27 June 1952 it was Maribel who went to the family's rescue. She stayed on the Greenhills property and saw to it that the children were fed and made comfortable for as long as was needed before they were removed to their new homes. Eight of the eleven children of John and Frances were eventually cared for by the extended CHALMERS family.

On 8 May 1953 George married Airlie HEAD from Woodlands. It was an affair of the heart that began when George was sixteen and Airlie was only thirteen.[74]

Figure 8.16. Josephine, c.1953. Source: author's collection

Figure 8.17. Martin and Charles with their Uncle Donald CHALMERS. Source: Charles CHALMERS

134

George and Airlie decided to become guardians of two of John and Frances CHALMERS' children. Immediately following his mother's death Martin Lovett was sent to live with neighbours at Greenhills. He stayed with John and Agnes McINTYRE, close friends of the family who had treated everyone with much kindness. The following year, Martin lived with his Uncle Donald and Auntie Maribel CHALMERS at Arrowtown. Meanwhile, Charles Hector had been living with his Uncle Roy and Auntie Isa MARTIN in Auckland and he joined the family in 1955.

George and Airlie had a caravan built on the property owned by Ray and Bessie and they accommodated and educated the boys at what must have been considerable sacrifice, being not long married and with limited resources. Martin went to Southland Technical College where he chose rural industrial studies. This led to a career as a public servant in the Ministry of Agriculture and Fisheries. Charles attended Southland Boys' High School and went on to Otago University to become a secondary school teacher.

Josephine Violet had been staying at Winton with cousins William and Eleanor EGERTON after the death of her mother, Frances. She then went to Arrowtown to live with her Uncle Donald and Auntie Maribel. She attended the local primary school and went on to Queenstown District High School where she qualified to become a student nurse at Wellington Public Hospital.

Ken married Ellen Georgina ADAM of Henley, Otago in June 1953.[75]

Like his older brothers, Ken took on independent farm work and in 1954 he was a farm labourer on a property at Otama. He became the manager.[76]

Jessie became married to Aike KIEL, an immigrant from Holland, in 1957 at Queenstown. The family of Jack and Frances CHALMERS came together again for the wedding. It was the first time many of the children had seen one another since the death of their mother.[77]

Donald died at Arrowtown in 1959.[78]

Maribel took up art in her later years and produced oil paintings of high quality. She was interested in painting scenic and still-life pictures, some of which are in the possession of the family.

While visiting her son Ray and his wife Bessie in Auckland in 1970, she suffered a stroke. She had used up the medication required for treating her high blood pressure. As she felt alright she failed to have the prescription renewed. She needed to be flown home to Arrowtown where she made a reasonable recovery. But she was not able to look after herself again and walked with a limp for the rest of her life.

Figure 8.18. Maribel with her painting of the Arrowtown cottage. Source: author's collection

Maribel's care was shared between her children and their spouses, mainly Ken and Ellen, George and Airlie and less often Jessie and Aike whose children were close together in age and rather noisy. Maribel continued to have little strokes and was finally looked after at the Riverton Hospital. Her niece, Jack's daughter Rosalie BLANCHARD (née CHALMERS) who was a nurse, supervised some of her care and attended to her personally. Family members visited her as often as possible. Maribel passed away on 18 September 1973.[79] Donald and Maribel are buried in the Eastern Cemetery, Invercargill, with their son Donald in Plot 27, Block 31.[80] The headstone reads:

In loving memory of
DONALD ROLLS CHALMERS
DIED 23RD MAY 1959 AGED 75 YEARS
ALSO HIS WIFE
AMELIA MARIBEL CHALMERS
DIED 18TH SEP 1973 AGED 76 YEARS
AND THEIR SON
DONALD RODERICK T CHALMERS
DIED 25TH JUNE 1943 AGED 18 YEARS[81]

NOTES

---

[1] Jessie KIEL, pers. com.

[2] 1841 England Census, Civil Parish: Wolsingham, Hundred: Darlington (North West Division), County/Island: Durham, Street Address: Margate Street, Registration district: Weardale, Sub-registration district: Wolsingham.

[3] New South Wales, Australia, Unassisted Immigrant Passenger Lists, 1826-1922.

[4] NZRGO, Marriage Register,1867/9046, Margaret MUIRHEAD, William PEART (Incorrect forename)

[5] MUIRHEAD Margaret, James MUIRHEAD/Janet FRENCH, FR164 (FR164)F 20/03/1850685/2390 212, St Cuthbert's Church Registers; Old Parish Registers (www.scotlandspeople.gov.uk)

[6] *Otago Witness*, December 18, 1858.

[7] PEART, Joseph E., boot and shoe maker and dealer, Stuart Street, Dunedin, 1872-1873, *Wise's New Zealand Post Office Directory* (Dunedin: H. Wise & Co., 1882-1995).; PEART, Joseph, Stuart Street, shop and dwelling house, Dunedin Electoral Rolls, 1875-1876; PEART, Joseph, bootmaker, Stuart Street, Dunedin, residence: Northeast Valley, Dunedin 1876, H. Wise & Co.

[8] PEART, Joseph E., fruiterer, Stuart Street, Dunedin Electoral Rolls, 1880-1881.

[9] PEART, Joseph, miller, residence: Vanguard Street, Nelson, 1883-1884, H. Wise & Co.; PEART, Joseph, Smith Street, Dunedin, 1886, *Stone's Otago and Southland Commercial Municipal and General Directory and New Zealand Annual* (Stone Son & Co.: Dunedin, 1884-1995); PEART, Joseph, rabbiter, Wantwood, Mataura Electoral Roll, 1890; PEART, Jos and Mrs PEART, millers, residence: Vanguard Street, Nelson, 1891, 1892-93, H. Wise & Co.

[10] PEART, Joseph, labourer, Mandeville, Wakatipu Electoral Roll, 1896.

[11] PEART, Joseph Emmerson, farmer, Croydon Bush, Mataura Electoral Roll, 1905-1906.

[12] NZRGO, Death Register, 1912/9025 McLEOD George, 78 years; NZRGO, Death Register, 1912/9022, McLEOD Ann, 82 years.

[13] CHALMERS family collection.

[14] 1851 Scotland Census, Civil Parish: Tongue, Town: Ship of Braetongue, County: Sutherland, Address: Braetongue.

[15] Jessie CHALMERS, pers. com.

[16] CHALMERS, Donald Rolls, farmer, The Ridges, Wyndham, Mataura Electoral Roll, 1928; CHALMERS, Maribel, The Ridges, Wyndham, Mataura Electoral Roll, 1928.

[17] Jessie CHALMERS, pers. com.

[18] Thelma GEARY (née BOYLEN), pers. com.

[19] Dora GRUBB (née CHALMERS), pers. com.; Jessie CHALMERS, pers. com.

[20] Jessie CHALMERS, pers. com.

[21] Raymond CHALMERS, pers. com.

[22] Dora GRUBB (née CHALMERS), pers. com.; Jessie CHALMERS, pers. com.

[23] Jessie CHALMERS, pers. com.

[24] Raymond CHALMERS, pers. com.

[25] Gertrude BOYLEN, pers. com.; Jessie CHALMERS, pers. com.

[26] Jessie CHALMERS, pers. com.

[27] Jessie CHALMERS, pers. com.; Raymond CHALMERS, pers. com.

[28] Kenneth CHALMERS, pers. com.

[29] Ibid.

[30] Raymond CHALMERS, pers. com.

[31] Ibid.

[32] Jessie CHALMERS, pers. com.

[33] Kenneth CHALMERS, pers. com.

[34] Jessie CHALMERS, pers. com.

[35] Kenneth CHALMERS, pers. com.

[36] Jessie CHALMERS, pers. com.

[37] Kenneth CHALMERS, pers. com.

[38] Raymond CHALMERS, pers. com.

[39] Kenneth CHALMERS, pers. com.

[40] Jessie CHALMERS, pers. com.

[41] Kenneth CHALMERS, pers. com.

[42] Jessie CHALMERS, pers. com.

[43] George CHALMERS, pers. com.

[44] Dora GRUBB, pers. com.

[45] Dora GRUBB and Martin CHALMERS, pers. com.

[46] Jessie CHALMERS, pers. com.

[47] Raymond CHALMERS, pers. com.

[48] CHALMERS, Donald Rolls, farmer, Kapuka, Mataura Electoral Roll, 1938; CHALMERS, Maribel, Kapuka, Mataura Electoral Roll, 1938;

[49] George CHALMERS, pers. com.

[50] Rom. 12: 12; Jessie CHALMERS; NZRGO, Death Register, 1943/30178 CHALMERS, Donald Roderick Tims, 18 years.

[51] Bessie MacASKELL, pers. com.

[52] Martin CHALMERS, pers. com.

[53] Eulogy notes for George CHALMERS.

[54] Jessie CHALMERS, pers. com.

[55] Raymond CHALMERS, pers. com.; CHALMERS, Donald Rolls, farmer, Kapuka, Awarua Electoral Roll, 1946.

[56] Jessie CHALMERS, pers. com.

[57] Thelma GEARY (née BOYLEN), pers. com.

[58] Dora GRUBB, pers. com.

[59] CHALMERS, Jessie Eleanor, nurse, spinster, Nurses' Home, Tauranga Electoral Roll, 1949.

[60] CHALMERS, Jessie Eleanor, spinster, Kapuka South, Awarua Electoral Roll, 1949.

[61] Visitors' Book M. CHALMERS, Victoria Bridge, CHALMERS family collection.

[62] Eulogy notes for George CHALMERS.

[63] Kenneth CHALMERS, pers. com.; CHALMERS, Raymond Hector, farmer, Kapuka, Awarua Electoral Rolls, 1949, 1954.

[64] Eulogy notes for George CHALMERS.

[65] Jessie CHALMERS, pers. com.; CHALMERS, Donald Rolls, farmer, Arrowtown, Wallace Electoral Roll, 1949.

[66] Lands and Deeds Index no 384/91.

[67] Eulogy for George CHALMERS.

[68] Obituary notes for George CHALMERS.

[69] Deric Charlton, "Pastures - Other grasses", Te Ara - the Encyclopedia of New Zealand, no date, http://www.TeAra.govt.nz/en/pastures/page-5; New Zealand Browntop, modified 2018, https://www.finelawn.co.nz/lawn-species/browntop/

[70] Raymond Hector CHALMERS New Zealand, Archives New Zealand, Passenger Lists, 1839-1973.

[71] Eulogy for Bessie CHALMERS; CHALMERS Raymond Hector, MacASKILL Bessie, 1952111/1 1 Harris North, Scotland Births, Marriages and Deaths Statutory Records, www.scotlandspeople.gov.uk.

[72] R. H. CHALMERS, New Zealand, Passenger Lists, 1839-1973, Archives New Zealand.

[73] Eulogy for Bessie CHALMERS.

[74] Obituary notes for George CHALMERS.

[75] Martin CHALMERS, pers. com.; Visitors' Book M. CHALMERS Victoria Bridge.

[76] Martin CHALMERS, pers. com.; CHALMERS, Kenneth James, farm labourer, Otama, Wallace Electoral Roll, 1954.

[77] Marriage of Jessie Eleanor CHALMERS to Aike KIEL, 16 Nov 1957, Queenstown, Central Otago, New Zealand, family record.

[78] NZRGO, Death Register, 1959/28933, CHALMERS, Donald Rolls, 75 years.

[79] NZRGO, Death Register, 1973/34704, CHALMERS, Amelia Maribel, 76 years.

[80] Invercargill City Council, Cemetery Database, https://icc.govt.nz/cemetery-result/?id=30850

[81] Ibid.

9 Malcolm Shaw CHALMERS and Nellie HASTIE

Figure 9.1. Two views of the Victoria Bridge property. Source: author's collection

Figure 9.2. Malcolm and his brother Donald. Source: author's collection

Like Donald, Malcolm had the desire to return to Central Otago. In 1933 he relinquished his unproductive property at Waiarikiki to take up his sixty acres of land at Victoria Bridge, Waitiri, in the Cromwell district. It was an area he knew well from hotel days. The hotel had been sited on a reserve and it was many years since it had been destroyed by fire. The land was described as rabbit-infested, dry and unproductive, of very poor quality. There were no buildings or amenities when he returned to live there. The stone walls were of the original stables and had no roof. Malcolm and two of his brothers, Douglas and Norman, lived in a tent within the walls.

Malcolm kept the Fordson tractor that he had driven from Waiarikiki and, being economy minded, he decided to switch from petrol driven to kerosene. He found that by lighting a fire under the tractor with a few pieces of matagouri, a thorny native bush, he could warm it sufficiently to start the engine using kerosene. This was just one example of his ingenuity. He became known in the district as 'a brainy sort of character' and one of Gibbston's most colourful and remarkable men.[1]

Known for his strength that was well used as a stretcher bearer in World War I, size twelve boots and his huge rough hands, he was also able to carry out intricate tasks with small objects. One of his prized World War I trophies was a German watch that he managed to keep going until 1950 at least. When it needed repairs, such as when two cogs became worn, he replaced them with others that had different teeth. This meant he had to make certain calculations in order to determine the correct time.

Malcolm created solutions to problems by putting together everyday items at no cost to him. He could be called the epitome of the Kiwi 'number eight wire' mindset of improvisation and adaptation. Malcolm made two mills to thresh his pea crops, using the wire base of a single bed as a sieve to clean the seed. He had an old Allis Chalmers header that he powered by a Model T car engine. Well known in the district, locals would give him machinery that was worn out or refused to go any more. One item was a large, two-cylinder Hart-Parr tractor that had beaten every mechanic in Cromwell. After half a day's tinkering, Malcolm had it going again and triumphantly drove it home to Gibbston.

He was also an inventor, though his inventions were not always patented. Malcolm devised a wire strainer, the main part of which was a spring from an old gramophone, that was light, powerful and worked well. There was a misunderstanding whereby the provisional protection application by Malcolm was not followed up and no publication of the invention took place through the Patent Office.[2] One patented invention was a rosehip picker. It was made from two oval fish tins, one smaller than the other. Attached was a light spring similar to that of a rabbit trap. Malcolm sold the patent to Reckitt and Coleman for £100 and the company tried to improve on the idea but only made it worse. [3]

Malcolm Shaw CHALMERS married Nellie HASTIE in 1935 when he was 53.[4] He obtained a three-roomed wooden building that he took up the hill and put within the stone stable walls of the old hotel. This became Malcolm and Nellie's home. It was simply 'a hut in a yard'. [5] (See Figures 9.3, 9.9 and 9.10.)

Figure 9.3. Nellie outside the stone walls of the Victoria Bridge property. Source: author's collection

Nellie HASTIE's grandparents, David Rankin HASTIE and Christina McADAM were born in Glasgow, Lanarkshire, Scotland. After their marriage they first lived at Hospital Street, Gorbals with their first child, William. David's occupation in 1841 was given as engineer.

Table 9.1 David HASTIE and Christina HASTIE's household, Hospital Street, Gorbals, Lanarkshire, Scotland Census, 1841.[6]

David HASTIE	head	20	engineer	Lanarkshire
Christina HASTIE	wife	20		Lanarkshire
William HASTIE	son	5 mths		Lanarkshire

By 1851 four more children had been added to the family and a servant was included as part of the household. David was a cabinetmaker, employing ten men.

Table 9.2 David and Christina HASTIE's household, 194 Main St, Gorbals, Lanarkshire, Scotland Census, 1851.[7]

David HASTIE	head	33	cabinet maker 10 Men	Lanarkshire
Christian [sic] HASTIE	wife	30		Lanarkshire
William HASTIE	son	10		Lanarkshire
James HASTIE	son	8		Lanarkshire
David HASTIE	son	5		Lanarkshire
John HASTIE	son	3		Lanarkshire
Robert HASTIE	son	1		Lanarkshire
Mary GRAHAM	servant	16		

In 1858 the family lived at 194 Main Street, Gorbals. David's business interests showed that he continued to prosper as a cabinet maker. His assets included houses, a workshop and byre.[8]

David is not found in the 1861 Scotland Census and Christina is recorded as head of the household and wife of a cabinet maker.

Table 9.3 Christina McADAM's household, 194 Main St, Glasgow Govan, Hutchesontown, Lanarkshire, Scotland Census, 1861.[9]

Christina McADAM Nattie	head	39	cabinet maker's wife	Renfrewshire
David HASTIE	son	14		Lanarkshire
John HASTIE	son	13		Lanarkshire
Hugh HASTIE	son	8		Lanarkshire
Isabella HASTIE	dau	7		Lanarkshire
Thomas HASTIE	son	2		Lanarkshire
Alexander HASTIE	son	1		Lanarkshire

It can be assumed that David had left for New Zealand by then as Christina's burial record indicates that she had arrived in their new country at about 1862.[10] (For some unknown reason and at some point in time, David and Christina changed their surname to THOMSON or THOMPSON.[11])

All nine of David and Christina HASTIE's children were born in Glasgow. Their second oldest son, James McAdam HASTIE (b.1843), did not accompany the family to New Zealand. On 26 September 1866 he married Maria JONES of Bristol, Gloucestershire. They lived at Bristol and four of their children were born there. They eventually decided to leave the United Kingdom and on 29 September 1879 the family arrived in Canterbury, New Zealand as assisted immigrants aboard the vessel *Invercargill*.[12]

> James HASTIE, 34, farm labourer, Lanark
> Maria HASTIE 30,
> James HASTIE 9
> Maria HASTIE 7
> Margaret HASTIE 5
> Isabella HASTIE [13]

Along with James' parents and siblings, the family settled in Dunedin where five more children were added to the family. Nellie was the eighth child.

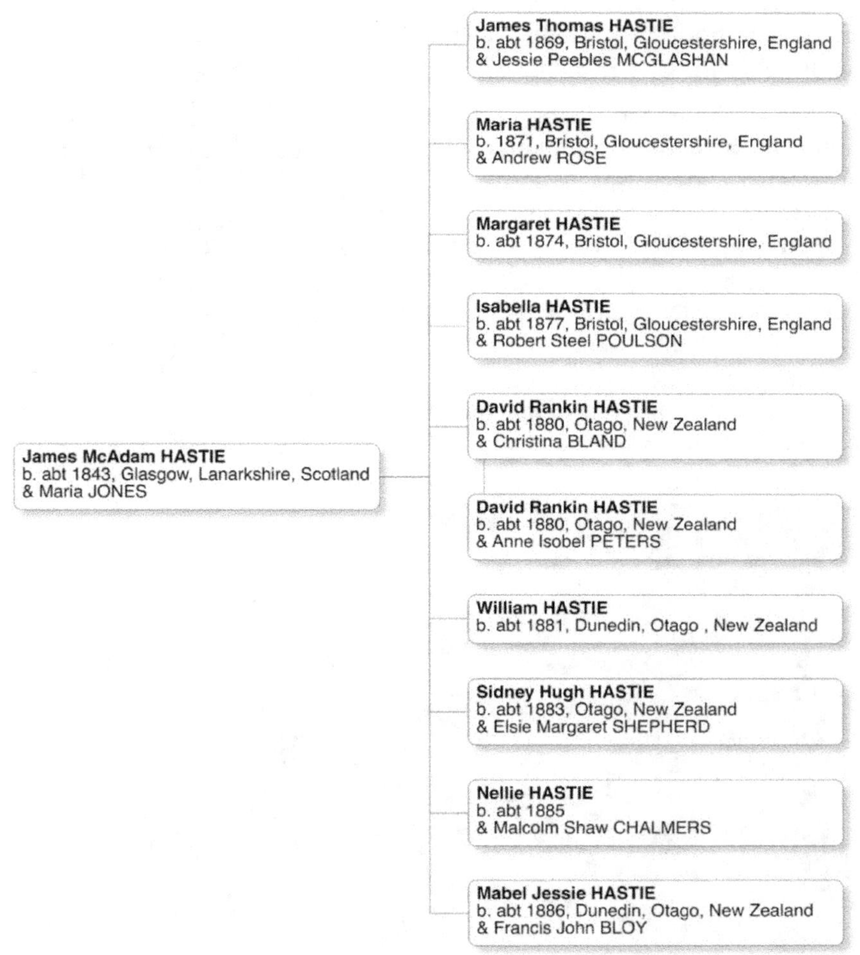

Figure 9.4. The children of James and Maria HASTIE

Nellie remained a spinster until aged fifty when she married Malcolm. She had lived in various places in Canterbury and Otago, including Christchurch and Dunedin, to which she returned in 1928.

In between these times she spent what was probably a considerable amount of time at Clyde in the Wakatipu District. She would have been familiar with Central Otago.[14]

Having been a bachelor for many years before marrying Nellie, Malcolm stayed with some of his unorthodox ways. For instance he boiled eggs in the water before adding it to the tea to be brewed.[15]

Nellie loved living at Victoria Bridge and, although the house was small, she kept it spotless. Laundry was done in a copper and tubs, outside. Water was collected from the roof or by lowering a bucket over the Kawarau River bridge. When Malcolm's sister Violet went to stay she would see that the water was boiled.[16] Soil was sluiced down the Kawarau River alongside the property and this made for a sizable patch of fertile land.[17]

Figure 9.5. Malcolm and Nellie walking on the bridge. Source: author's collection

Figure 9.6. Malcolm and Nellie at their Victoria Bridge property beside the Kawarau River. Source: author's collection

Malcolm and Nellie became known far and wide for their hospitality. The farm produced particularly high quality apricots that Nellie used for jam. She baked scones and the two together made a treat. Busloads of tourists used to stop by for her scones and cups of tea.[18] Added to that she gained popularity as a reader of teacups.[19] Family members were never long in turning up for a visit. Their visitors' book is also testimony of the many grateful friends they made from all over the world and whom they treated like family.[20]

In 1946 Malcolm and Nellie were still living at Victoria Bridge while the property was being farmed by Malcolm.[21]

Figure 9.7. Malcolm and Nellie panning for gold at the Kawarau River. Source: author's collection

Figure 9.8. Malcolm, Nellie and friends at Victoria Bridge. Source: author's collection

Figure 9.9. Malcolm, Nellie and friends at Victoria Bridge. Source: author's collection

Figure 9.10. Nellie, friend and Austin car at Victoria Bridge. Source: author's collection

Figure 9.11. Malcolm and friend. Source: author's collection

Figure 9.12. Malcolm and Nellie. Source: author's collection

Nellie did not keep good health. She had just one kidney and was said to have spent considerable time in hospital, having had fourteen operations for hydatids.[22]

In 1948 Malcolm did his best to save the life of a lorry driver who fell asleep at the wheel. This was not a new experience for him to help in life and death situations. As a young man with his brother William and rescue team Malcolm was first on the scene when his friend fell down a cliff while rabbiting at Gibbston. A stretcher bearer in World War I, he must have carried numerous wounded soldiers to safety.

TRUCK CAPSIZES
DRIVER RECEIVES FATAL BURNS
Richard Clifford STEVENSON, a married man, aged 33 years, a partner in the firm of Stevenson and Nolan, sawmillers of Gibbston, died at the Cromwell Hospital on Sunday morning as a result of severe burns received when his truck left the road and overturned, falling back on to the road and catching fire.
Stevenson was alone in the truck at the time, returning to Gibbston. his truck leaving the road at the approach to the Victoria Bridge about fifteen miles from Cromwell. Assistance was rendered by Mr Malcolm CHALMERS, who lives nearby, and when awakened by the smash, hastened to the scene where he found STEVENSON struggling in an attempt to extricate himself from the lorry, which was burning fiercely. After getting him clear, Mr CHALMERS then took him to his home, going then to Waitiri to obtain medical aid. The injured man was removed by ambulance to the Cromwell Hospital where he died a few hours later.
INQUEST. An inquest was held at Cromwell on Monday concerning the death of Richard Clifford STEVENSON who died at the Cromwell Hospital on Sunday morning, following an accident in which deceased sustained severe burns when his truck caught fire. Evidence of identification was given by John Grey HUNTER of Dunedin, who stated that deceased was 33 years of age, married, with no children. He last saw deceased, a motor driver by occupation on April 4th.
Malcolm Shaw CHALMERS, a farmer, residing at Victoria Bridge, Gibbston, stated that he was in bed about 1.30 a.m. on the 11th April, when he heard a motor smash at the other end of Victoria Bridge. He rushed across the bridge finding Messrs Stevenson and Nolan's lorry capsized and burning. The driver, Richard Clifford STEVENSON was struggling from the cab of the lorry. Gripping him round the body under the arm pits, he dragged him clear. The lower portion of his clothes was on fire. He removed clothing and returned to his home for an overcoat, leaving the victim on the side of the road, When he returned he found that STEVENSON had wandered down to the river bank. After taking him to his home, CHALMERS then went to Waitiri Station, where he rang for the Doctor and Ambulance. STEVENSON

was perfectly sober and there was no trace of liquor on him. He did not say what was the cause of the accident. The night was very dark but fine. John NOLAN, sawmiller of Gibbston, stated that deceased was his partner, and attended to the motor transport side of the business, being the only driver. Deceased left Gibbston about 2 p.m. on the 10th April to deliver a load of timber at Alexandra. He did not see him alive again. Under the supervision of Constable RUSBATCH he assisted in the removal of the lorry from the roadway where it was obstructing the traffic. The lorry was one year old and when driven by himself about ten days previously it was in good order, including the lights at that time. STEVENSON was a hard worker and frequently worked long hours, he had frequently told witness that he felt sleepy when driving, and viewing the scene of the accident, witness was of the opinion that it was caused by STEVENSON going to sleep while driving the lorry. It was a left hand drive with a current warrant of fitness and STEVENSON was the holder of a motor driver's license.

Richard Stephen RUSBATCH police constable, stationed at Cromwell, stated that he was advised by telephone by Dr. AUSTIN that an accident had taken place at the Victoria Bridge and that Richard Clifford STEVENSON, the driver of the lorry was a patient in the Hospital, his condition being serious. He went to the scene of the accident when he found the lorry lying on its left side on the road, blocking the approach to Victoria Bridge. From his observation he could see marks on the road where the lorry ran off and up a steep bank. It was thus apparent that the lorry had then capsized back on to the road below, a distance of about ten feet. The lorry was badly damaged by fire and was blocking the roadway. From the marks it did not appear that the lorry had been travelling at an excessive speed." Robert Erwin AUSTIN, medical practitioner gave evidence

Figure 9.13. Malcolm and Donald. Source: author's collection

that he was called to Victoria Bridge when he attended deceased at the residence of Mr Malcolm CHALMERS.[23]

Throughout their lives twin brothers Malcolm and Donald kept close contact, visiting one another frequently. Living at Arrowtown, Donald did not have far to travel to Victoria Bridge. The distance from Arrowtown to Waitiri was about sixteen kilometres. He helped Malcolm on his farm, as Malcolm had done for him at Kapuka. (See Figure 9.2.)

Many people found it difficult to tell who was who. Donald was a little taller and said to be the tidier of the two. Although they looked alike they had very different views on politics, Malcolm being a Labour supporter while Donald backed the National party. They were regarded as 'the friendliest pair of enemies anyone could know'.[24] A story goes that Donald and Malcolm travelled from Victoria Bridge to Arrowtown one time to vote. They went out for lunch and argued throughout the meal, then went to vote in the election. Afterwards they went home for a cup of tea and asked Nellie, "Who did you vote for?" She replied that she'd voted for the National man. She was so confused she voted for the wrong candidate, thus cancelling Malcolm's vote. [25]

Figure 9.14. Nellie and Malcolm. Source: author's collection

Malcolm and Nellie remained at Victoria Bridge for at least twenty years.[26] They retired to Cromwell and lived at Gay Street.[27] Nellie died in 1957 at Cromwell at the age of 72.[28] Nellie is buried in the Cromwell Cemetery.[29]

Malcolm maintained his membership of the Cromwell Returned Servicemen's Association throughout his life in the area. He also kept up his interest in music and was a member of the Cromwell Silver Band.[30] In his seventies he was still eligible to drive a car.[31]

Malcolm remained living in Cromwell as a widower.[32]

He died on 24 December 1964 and is buried with Nellie in the Cromwell Cemetery Section NC32, Plot 23.[33]

Following Malcolm's death, in 1967 his nephew and son of his brother Donald, Ray CHALMERS acquired the remaining two acres of the Victoria Bridge property and was still the owner in 1991.[34] Three years previously he had planted four apricot trees and a weeping willow. Rate payments of £200 per annum were difficult to maintain on a retirement income and no-one else in the family could afford to buy it at the time.

Figure 9.15. Malcolm with his grand-nieces Anita and Esther KIEL. Source: author's collection

NOTES

---

[1] Anne Cook, *The Gibbston Story* (Dunedin: Otago Heritage Books, 1985); Contributions by Chalmers family members.

[2] Letter to Malcolm from Henry Hughes Ltd International Patent and Trade Mark Agents, Wellington. Dated 9 September 1947.

[3] Anne Cook.

[4] CHALMERS, Malcolm, Victoria Bridge, Waitiri, Central Otago Electoral Rolls, 1935 and 1938.

[5] Ray CHALMERS, pers. com.

[6] Scotland Census 1841, Gorbals, Lanarkshire, Scotland

[7] Ibid.

[8] Glasgow, Lanarkshire, Scotland, Electoral Registers, 1857-1962

[9] Scotland Census 1861, Glasgow Govan, Hutchesontown, Lanarkshire, Scotland.

[10] Nothern Cemetery, Dunedin, New Zealand Cemetery Records, 1800-2007.

[11] New Zealand, Cemetery Records, 1800-2007: Christina THOMPSON, 3 November 1888, Northern Cemetery, Dunedin; David R. THOMSON, 1892, Northern Cemetery.

[12] Passenger Lists, 1839-1973, Archives New Zealand.

[13] Ibid.

[14] HASTIE, Nellie, spinster, 7 Atkinsons Road, Christchurch North Electoral Roll 1905-06; HASTIE, Nellie, spinster, Wain Street, Kensington, Dunedin South North Electoral Roll, 1911; HASTIE, Nellie, spinster, Clyde, Wakatipu Electoral Roll, 1919; HASTIE, Nellie, spinster, 31 Broughton Street, South Dunedin Electoral Roll, 1928; HASTIE, Nellie, spinster, Victoria Bridge, Wakatipu Electoral Roll, 1935.

[15] Anne Cook.

[16] Violet CHALMERS, pers. com.

[17] Ray CHALMERS, pers. com.

[18] Dora GRUBB, pers. com.

[19] Thelma GEARY (née BOYLEN), pers. com.

[20] *M. Chalmers Visitors' Book Victoria Bridge.* In family possession.

[21] CHALMERS, Malcolm Shaw, farmer, Cromwell, Otago Central Electoral Roll, 1946; CHALMERS, Nellie, Cromwell, Otago Central Electoral Roll, 1946.

[22] Ken CHALMERS, pers. com.

[23] *Cromwell Argus*, April 13, 1948.

[24] Ken CHALMERS, pers. com.

[25] Ray CHALMERS, pers. com.; Dora GRUBB, pers. com.

[26] CHALMERS, Malcolm Shaw, farmer, Cromwell, Otago Central Electoral Rolls, 1949 and 1954; CHALMERS, Nellie, Cromwell, Otago Central Electoral Rolls, 1949 and 1954.

[27] CHALMERS, Malcolm Shaw, retired, Gay Street, Cromwell, Otago Central Electoral Roll, 1957; CHALMERS, Nellie, Gay Street, Cromwell, Otago Central Electoral Roll, 1957.

[28] NZRGO, Death Register, 1957/39156, CHALMERS, Nellie, 72 years.

[29] Cromwell Cemetery, New Zealand Cemetery Records 1800-2007.

[30] Sympathy cards on Malcolm CHALMERS' death.

[31] Driving Testing Officer's Report, 11 June 1963.

[32] CHALMERS, Malcolm Shaw, retired, Cromwell, Otago Central Electoral Roll, 1963.

[33] NZRGO, Death Register, 1964/45513, CHALMERS, Malcolm Shaw, 82 years; New Zealand, Cemetery Records, 1800-2007.

[34] Raymond Hector CHALMERS, 23 June 1967 and 24 June 1970, Lands and Deeds Index.

10 David George CHALMERS and Betson Margaret CUNNINGHAM and Muriel Sophia Florence DANE

David George CHALMERS married Betson Margaret CUNNINGHAM at Oamaru in 1908.[1]

David's parents, John Howe CHALMERS and Eleanor Rebecca TIMS and Betson's grandparents, Robert CUNNINGHAM and Betson WILSON would have known one another. Both families farmed in the Kurow district as shown in this chart:

Table 10.1. Deferred Payment and Perpetual Lease Holdings, 14 August 1889[2]

Name of selector and district	Lease or license number	Acres Roods Perches	Original upset price per acre £ s d	Price agreed to be paid per acre £ s d
Robt. CUNNINGHAM, Kurow	6047	203. 1. 4	3. 0. 0.	3. 0. 0.
John H CHALMERS, Kurow	5057	302. 2. 15	1. 5. 0.	3. 0. 0.

Robert and Betson were married on 16 December 1848 at Forgan, Fifeshire, Scotland, their birthplace. Their first four children were baptised at St Andrews, Dysart, Fife, Scotland. In 1854 the family, along with Betson's sister Euphemia, set sail from Liverpool on the ship *Fulwood* and arrived in Australia in December of that year. The passenger list records:

Robert	CUNNINGHAM	30	farmer
Betson	CUNNINGHAM	28	wife
Jessie	CUNNINGHAM	4	daughter
John	CUNNINGHAM	3	son
Robert	CUNNINGHAM	1	son
Euphemia	WILSON	18	spinster Sister-in-law[3]

The most likely reason for leaving Scotland for Australia was the gold rush. The Victorian Gold Discovery Committee wrote in 1854:

> The discovery of the Victorian Goldfields has converted a remote dependency into a country of worldwide fame; it has attracted a population, extraordinary in number, with unprecedented rapidity; it has enhanced the value of property to an enormous extent; it has made this the richest country

in the world; and, in less than three years, it has done for this colony the work of an age, and made its impulses felt in the most distant regions of the earth. For a number of years the gold output from Victoria was greater than in any other country in the world with the exception of the more extensive fields of California. Victoria's greatest yield for one year was in 1856, when 3,053,744 troy ounces (94,982 kg) of gold were won from the diggings.[4]

Their next four children were born in Victoria, Australia. (See Figure 10.1.)

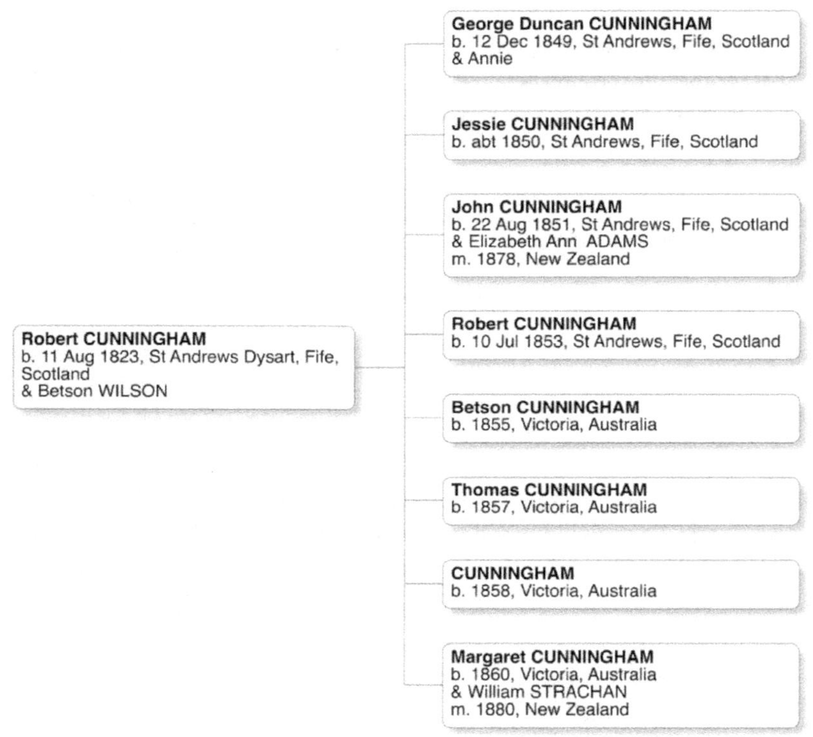

Figure 10.1. The children of Robert and Betson CUNNINGHAM

In January 1863 the family left Victoria, Australia in the *Lady Ann* bound for New Zealand, apparently attracted again by the lure of gold, this time in Otago.[5]

By 1864 they were living in New Zealand where they leased a property in Dunedin for seven years.[6] In 1870-71 Robert resided in the gold mining area of Mount Ida and Tuapeka where he lived in an iron building.[7]

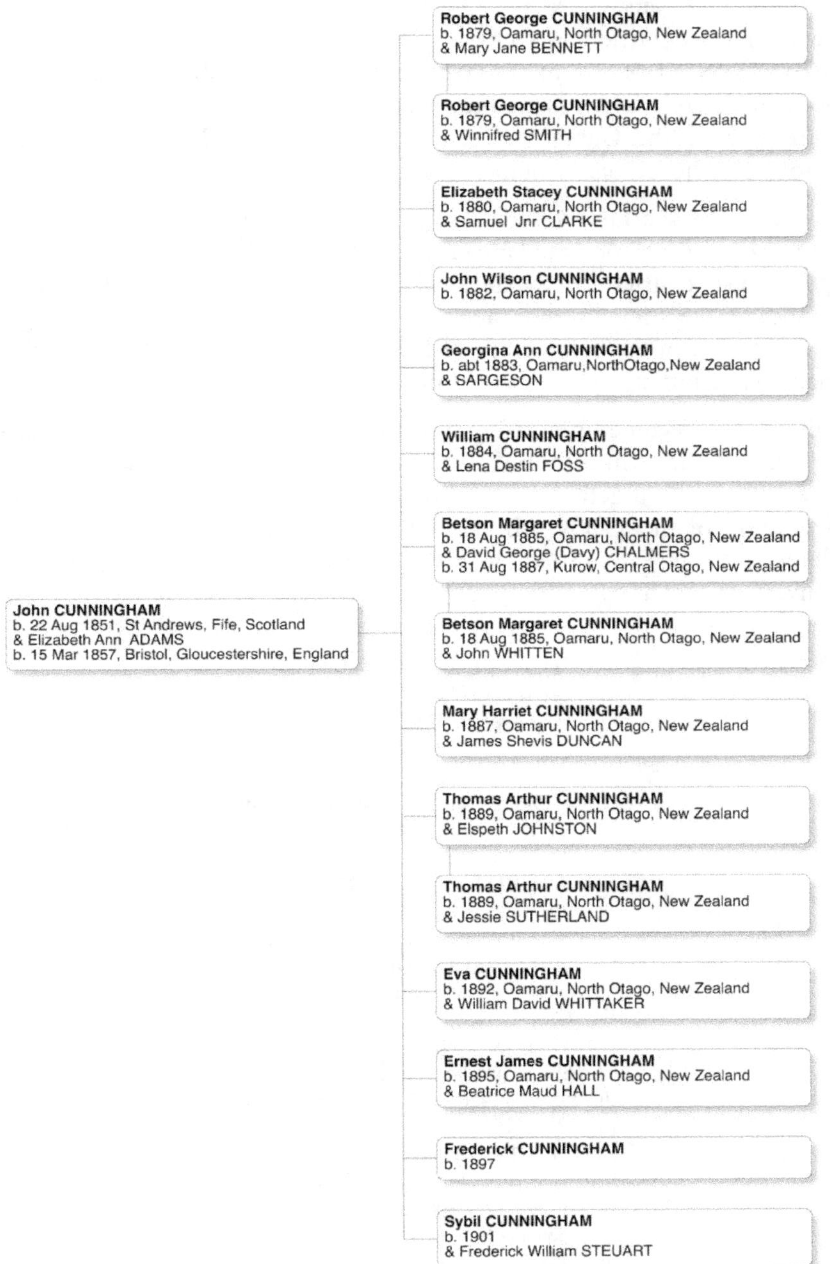

Figure 10.2. The children of John and Elizabeth Ann CUNNINGHAM

Between 1880 and 1896 the family was settled at Kurow where they owned land identified as Section 6, Block 2. (See Table 10.1.) Their son John CUNNINGHAM married Elizabeth Ann ADAMS in 1878. She was born in Bristol, Gloucestershire, England. All of their twelve children were born in the Oamaru area. (See Figure 10.2.) The children were enrolled at the Oamaru South School.[8]

In the 1890s the family was living in Wear Street, Oamaru.[9] Betson's family owned and operated a well-established coachbuilding business in the Oamaru district. The business also involved other forms of transport including the bicycle and their advertisement says: 'Now landing a consignment of the celebrated A1 and Vanguard bicycles (both English makes) at Cunningham's, Coachbuilder, Tyne street. [Advt.]'[10]

John's sons became involved in the family business, Robert George also as coachbuilder while John Wilson and William became coach painters. They all lived together at Ardgowan, not far from Oamaru, at the beginning of the 1900s.[11] In 1911 the business expanded and the site changed from Tyne Street to Coquet Street, Oamaru that was more convenient and allowed for greater expanse and modernisation.

IMPORTANT AUCTION SALE.
(Estate of Late J. S. DALZELL.)
Freehold Properties in the
Borough of Oamaru
Consisting of
Shops, Offices, Residences, and
Building Sites,
All Centrally Situated.
SATURDAY, JANUARY 28th, 1911,
At 2 p.m. sharp.
At the AUCTION ROOMS of
WILLIAM JARDINE, Wear street;
Oamaru.
IN CONJUNCTION with Messrs. J. HAMILTON AND SON & WILLIAM JARDINE has been instructed to Sell on the above-mentioned date the following PROPERTIES:
LOT 1 – Part Section 3, Block 3, Tyne Street, vacant; Section 4, Block 3, Tyne Street, together with large two-storey Wooden Factory and Stone Buildings (at present occupied by Mr John CUNNINGHAM, coachbuilder).[12]

John CUNNINGHAM was said to be the last coachbuilder and his transition to the motorcar can be seen in this business progress report.

BUSINESS PROGRESS.
MESSRS JOHN CUNNINGHAM'S NEW COACH FACTORY. After serving the public for over 50, years in Tyne street, Mr John Cunningham, proprietor; of 'The Original Coach and Carriage Works' has removed to a commodious and more centrally situated premises in Coquet street. The new factory on a section adjoining Mr O'BRIEN's stables, the buildings covering almost the whole of a quarter acre. The factory is complete in every detail for the purposes of an expanding business, the general layout being such that efficient work can be carried on with added regard to economy. Entrance is obtained from the front to the show room, 50 feet by 25 feet, and to the office, from which all parts of the factory are continuously under the eye. Leading from the showroom is a spacious workshop, 50 feet square, in which the different departments are conveniently situated. Back of the workshop is the paint shop, 50 feet by 25 feet, closely lined to prevent dust and well lighted. In the yard accommodation at the rear of the factory is a tire oven, which, besides saving fuel, does away with the old method of building a fire round the tires in the yard. The increasing popularity of the motor-car, instead of militating, against the coachbuilder's profession has enhanced it to the extent that the repairing and decoration of' the woodwork and trimmings have necessitated provision being made to meet them. Mr CUNNINGHAM has anticipated this growing class of trade and had his building so designed that a motor-car can be run through from front to rear and placed at any position handy to the workmen. Indeed, this applies to any kind of vehicle, which for no purpose whatever need be removed from the workman whose duty it is to deal with it.[13]

David <u>Lloyd</u> CHALMERS, son of David CHALMERS and Betson CUNNINGHAM, went to stay with his grandparents in Oamaru every year for a holiday. On one occasion he stayed for six months due to a polio epidemic when travel was restricted for fear of the disease spreading. He remembered the last hansom cab for hire in Oamaru and the end of an era. John CUNNINGHAM's huge coach building company was taken over by Woolworths. Lloyd's Uncle Ernie, Ernest James CUNNINGHAM (b.1895), worked for the Customs Department in Wellington.[14]

David George CHALMERS started his working life in the clothing business at Oamaru. It wasn't long before he was promoted to manager of the New Zealand Clothing Factory and transferred to Hokitika. The business was owned by Hallenstein Brothers whose businesses spread nationwide from Dunedin.[15] The couple's three children were born at Hokitika. (See Figure 10.4.)

Figure 10.3. The CUNNINGHAM sisters: Elizabeth Stacey (b.1880), Georgina Ann (b.1883), Betson Margaret (b. 1885), Mary Harriet (b.1887). Source: author's collection.

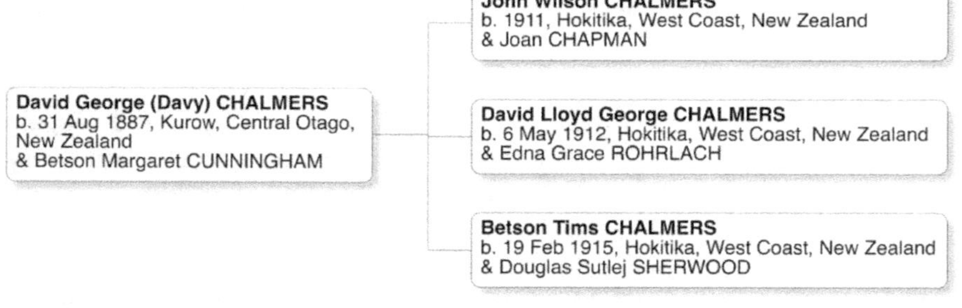

Figure 10.4. The children of David and Betson CHALMERS

By 1919 they had left the West Coast for Auckland where David worked as a travelling salesman for the menswear company of Sargood Son and Ewen. He stayed with the company for many years. They lived at two different addresses in Mount Eden during that year.[16]

During the 1920s the family moved from house to house, each bought for its potential to be done up and sold. Some of the addresses included:

Croydon Road, Fairfield Road, Prospect Terrace and Richmond Street, Grey Lynn. This lifestyle continued for possibly twenty-five houses in all and it meant frequent changes of school. Lloyd was able to recall twenty-one different primary schools that he attended while his brother John was enrolled at twenty-six. Lloyd began school at Richmond Road and finished at Cornwall Park, Mount Eden where he completed the first term of his standard six year. At that time the family moved to Reimers Avenue, Mount Eden. Rather than change schools again, Lloyd preferred to walk an hour each way and stay at Cornwall Park School. The house at Aratonga Avenue at the top of Farmers Hill, Great South Road was a lovely home that stayed in his memory.[17]

The marriage did not last. David and Margaret were divorced in 1928 and David was living alone at Aratonga Avenue, Parnell.[18]

Figure 10.5. David CHALMERS and Muriel NICHOLAS, 192 Karangahape Road, Auckland in January 1931. Source: author's collection

Figure 10.6. David CHALMERS and Muriel NICHOLAS, 1931, 192 Karangahape Road, Auckland in January 1931. Source: author's collection

Figure 10.7. Muriel. Source: author's collection

By 1935 David had become a fruiterer and he and Muriel were living at 422 Karangahape Road in Central Auckland.[19]

In 1935 David's former wife Betson was living at 218A Dominion Road, Eden with her son John Wilson who had followed in his father's footsteps and become an assistant draper.[20] The same year she married John WHITTEN, a blacksmith.[21] In 1938 Betson Margaret and John were living at 2 Cameron Street, Waitemata where John was working as a blacksmith.[22]

During 1935, her son David Lloyd CHALMERS married Edna Grace ROHRLACH.[23] The following year daughter Betson Tims CHALMERS married Douglas Sutlej SHERWOOD.[24]

David and Muriel moved to Australia, probably to be near Muriel's daughter Elsie. They lived at 27 Challis Avenue, Darlinghurst for a number of years. David was employed as a caretaker.[25]

Muriel's daughter Elsie was living at Sydney and married Llewellyn Edward John GREENLEES on 19 November 1938.[26]

Figure 10.8. Muriel at daughter Elsie's wedding. Source: author's collection

Figure 10.9. 189 Liverpool Road in Ashford, Sydney where the CHALMERS famly lived. Source: author's collection

Figure 10.10. David at the entrance to the house. Source: author's collection

Figure 10.11. David with stepdaughter Elsie, her husband Llewellen and daughter. Source: author's collection

Figure 10.12. David CHALMERS with CHALMERS grandchildren at Auckland, Source: author's collection

Figure 10.13. David and Muriel with David's brother Norman at Petone, Wellington. Source: author's collection

The last of the three children of David and Betson to wed was John Wilson CHALMERS who married Joan CHAPMAN in about 1940.

By 1945 David and Muriel had moved to 189 Liverpool Road in Ashford, New South Wales, where David was recorded as a residential proprietor.[27]

They returned to Auckland for retirement and were living at 278 St Andrews Road, Roskill, Auckland in 1954.[28]

David died at Auckland on 25 June 1955. He was cremated on the same day and was buried at the Waikumete Cemetery.[29]

Muriel continued to live at the same house and died on 28 April 1974. She was also buried at the Waikumete Cemetery.[30]

Betson Margaret CUNNINGHAM had died previously on 27 Jun 1957 at Auckland.

NOTES

---

[1] Folio No. 7824 Bride and Groom Collection (Oamaru Genealogical Society) New Zealand Society of Genealogists.

[2] *North Otago Times.* "Deferred Payment And Perpetual Lease Holdings." August 14, 1889.

[3] Victoria, Australia, Assisted and Unassisted Passenger Lists, 1839-1923.

[4] 'Victorian gold rush', Last modified, 2018. https://en.wikipedia.org/wiki/Victorian_gold_rush

[5] Robert CUNNINGHAM, Departure: Jan 1863, Place: Victoria, Australia, Destination: Otago, Ship: *Lady Ann*, Victoria, Australia, Outward Passenger Index, 1852-1915, p.1, available https://www.prov.vic.gov.au/ex...

[6] CUNNINGHAM, Robert, Clyde Street, Lease from 1864 for seven years, Dunedin, Electoral Roll, 1870-1871.

[7] CUNNINGHAM, Robert, Hamilton, iron building, Mount Ida and Tuapeka Electoral Roll, 1870-1871; CUNNINGHAM, George D Hamilton, iron building, Mount Ida and Tuapeka Electoral Roll, 1870-1871.

[8] AWP Register, Oamaru South School Reg. No. 5619, New Zealand Society of Genealogists.

[9] CUNNINGHAM, John, coach builder, Wear Street, Oamaru South, Oamaru Electoral Rolls, 1890 and 1896.

[10] *Oamaru Mail.* "Advertisements." September 7, 1897.

[11] CUNNINGHAM, John, coach builder, Ardgowan, Oamaru Electoral Roll, 1905-1906; CUNNINGHAM, Elizabeth Ann, wife, Ardgowan, Oamaru Electoral Roll, 1905-1906; CUNNINGHAM, Robert George ,coach builder, Ardgowan, Oamaru Electoral Roll, 1905-1906; CUNNINGHAM, John Wilson, coach painter, Ardgowan, Oamaru Electoral Roll, 1905-1906; CUNNINGHAM, William, coach painter, Ardgowan, Oamaru Electoral Roll, 1905-1906.

[12] *Oamaru Mail*. January 26, 1911.

[13] *Oamaru Mail*. August 22, 1911.

[14] Lloyd CHALMERS, October 27, 1991, pers. com.,; Ernest James CUNNINGHAM, Oamaru, 18 January 1912, Teacher and Civil Service Examinations and Licenses, 1880-1920, Wellington.

[15] CHALMERS, David George, Manager NZ Clothing Factory, Sewell Street, Hokitika, Westland Electoral Rolls, 1911 and 1914; CHALMERS, Betson Margaret, Sewell Street, Hokitika, Westland Electoral Rolls, 1911 and 1914.

[16] Lloyd CHALMERS, pers. com.; CHALMERS, David George, travelling salesman, 15 Richmond Road, Mount Eden, Auckland West Electoral Roll, 1919; CHALMERS, Betson, 15 Richmond Road, Mount Eden, Auckland West Electoral Roll, 1919; CHALMERS, David George, travelling salesman, 2 Croydon Road, Mount Eden, Auckland West Electoral Roll, 1919; CHALMERS, Betson, 2 Croydon Road, Mount Eden, Auckland West Electoral Roll, 1919.

[17] Lloyd and Betson CHALMERS (children of David and Betson), pers. com..

[18] Auckland Court Divorce File, 1928, no. 141 Ref.BBAE 4985, New Zealand Society of Genealogists; CHALMERS, David George, traveller, Aratonga Avenue, Auckland, Parnell Electoral Roll, 1928.

[19] CHALMERS, David George, fruiterer, 422 Karangahape Road, Auckland Central Electoral Rolls, 1935 and 1938; CHALMERS, Muriel Sophy Florence, 422 Karangahape Road, Auckland Central West Electoral Rolls, 1935 and 1938.

[20] CHALMERS, Betson, married, 218A Dominion Road, Eden Electoral Roll, 1935; CHALMERS, John Wilson, draper's assistant, 218A Dominion Road, Eden Electoral Roll, 1935.

[21] NZRGO, Marriage Register, 1935/10123, Betson Margaret CHALMERS, John WHITTEN.

[22] CHALMERS, Betson Margaret Whitten, married, 2 Cameron Street N 2, Waitemata Electoral Roll, 1938; CHALMERS, John Wilson, blacksmith, 2 Cameron Street N 2, Waitemata Electoral Roll, 1938.

[23] NZRGO, Marriage Register, 1935/7773, Edna Grace ROHRLACH, David Lloyd George CHALMERS.

[24] NZRGO, Marriage Register, 1936/420, Betson Tims CHALMERS, Douglas Sutlej SHERWOOD.

[25] CHALMERS, David George, caretaker, 27 Challis Avenue, Darlinghurst, East Sydney Electoral Rolls, 1937 and 1943; CHALMERS, Muriel, 27 Challis Avenue, Darlinghurst, East Sydney Electoral Rolls, 1937 and 1943.

[26] Sydney, Australia, Anglican Parish Registers, 1818-2011, Elsie Ina NICHOLAS, 19 November 1938, Sydney, New South Wales, Australia, Parish: Rose Bay St Paul, Father: David Washington NICHOLAS, Mother: Muriel, Sophia Florence NICHOLAS, Spouse: Llewellyn Edward John GREENLEES.

[27] CHALMERS, David George, residential proprietor, 189 Liverpool Road, Ashfield, New South Wales, Evans Electoral Roll, 1949; CHALMERS, Muriel, 189 Liverpool Road, Ashfield, New South Wales, Evans Electoral Roll, 1949.

[28] CHALMERS, David George, retired, 278 St Andrews Road SE3, Roskill Electoral Roll, 1954; CHALMERS, Muriel, 278 St Andrews Road SE3, Roskill Electoral Roll, 1954.

[29] Waikumete Cemetery, New Zealand Cemetery Records, 1800-2007.

[30] Ibid.

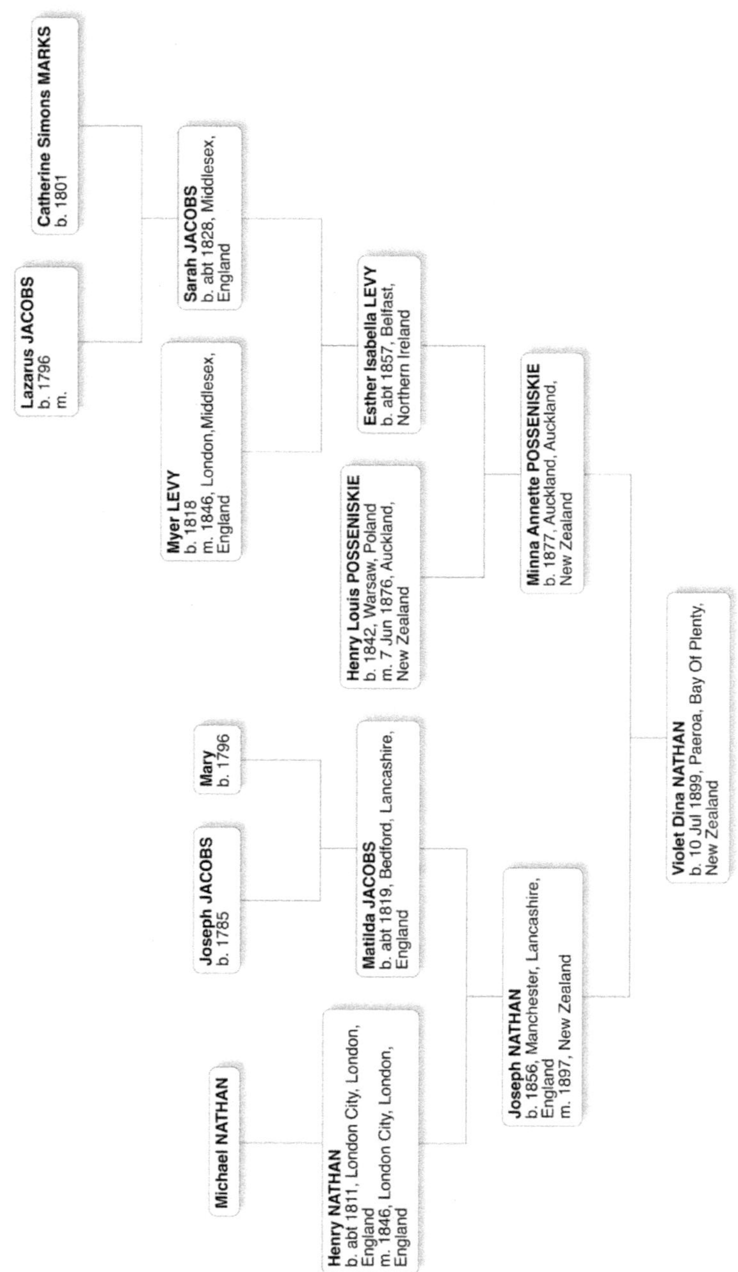

Figure 11.0. Pedigree chart for Violet Dina NATHAN

11 Douglas Gollan CHALMERS and Violet Dina NATHAN

Douglas Gollan CHALMERS and Violet Dina NATHAN were married on 4 August 1937 at Caversham, Dunedin.[1]

Violet's ancestors go back to Warsaw, Poland and Middlesex, England. (See Figure 11.0) Her paternal grandfather, Henry Louis POSSENISKIE was a Russian Jew who was born at Warsaw, Poland, in 1842. At age seventeen he went to London and spent five years learning his trade as a tailor. He came to New Zealand in the ship *Portland* in 1864, and was naturalised after residing here for 18 years. Shortly after arriving in Auckland Henry started business as a tailor and habit maker.[2] By 1875 his store on Shortland Street had become well known.[3]

On 7 June 1876 Henry POSSENISKIE married Esther Isabella LEVY, a daughter of Myer LEVY and Susan JACOBS of London, Middlesex, England.[4] Along with her siblings, Esther was born in Belfast, Ireland. The LEVY family had sailed for New Zealand aboard the 799 ton ship *Maori* and arrived in Auckland on 3 November 1859. The passenger list records:

> Mier LEVY
> Sarah LEVY
> Catherine LEVY
> Moss LEVY
> Lazarus LEVY
> Jane LEVY
> Julia LEVY
> Fanny LEVY
> Lewis LEVY
> Esther LEVY
> Albert LEVY
> Mary Ann LEVY[5]

Even in 1859 the *Maori* was regarded as 'an old New Zealand liner, and well known in the South, where, on her first arrival, her name, and her tattooed figure-head, gave great delight to the natives'. The ship sailed around ports in the South Island. As well as China she visited the Crimea where she 'was one of the vessels which rode out the gale in Balaklava harbour, when so many vessels were lost.'[6]

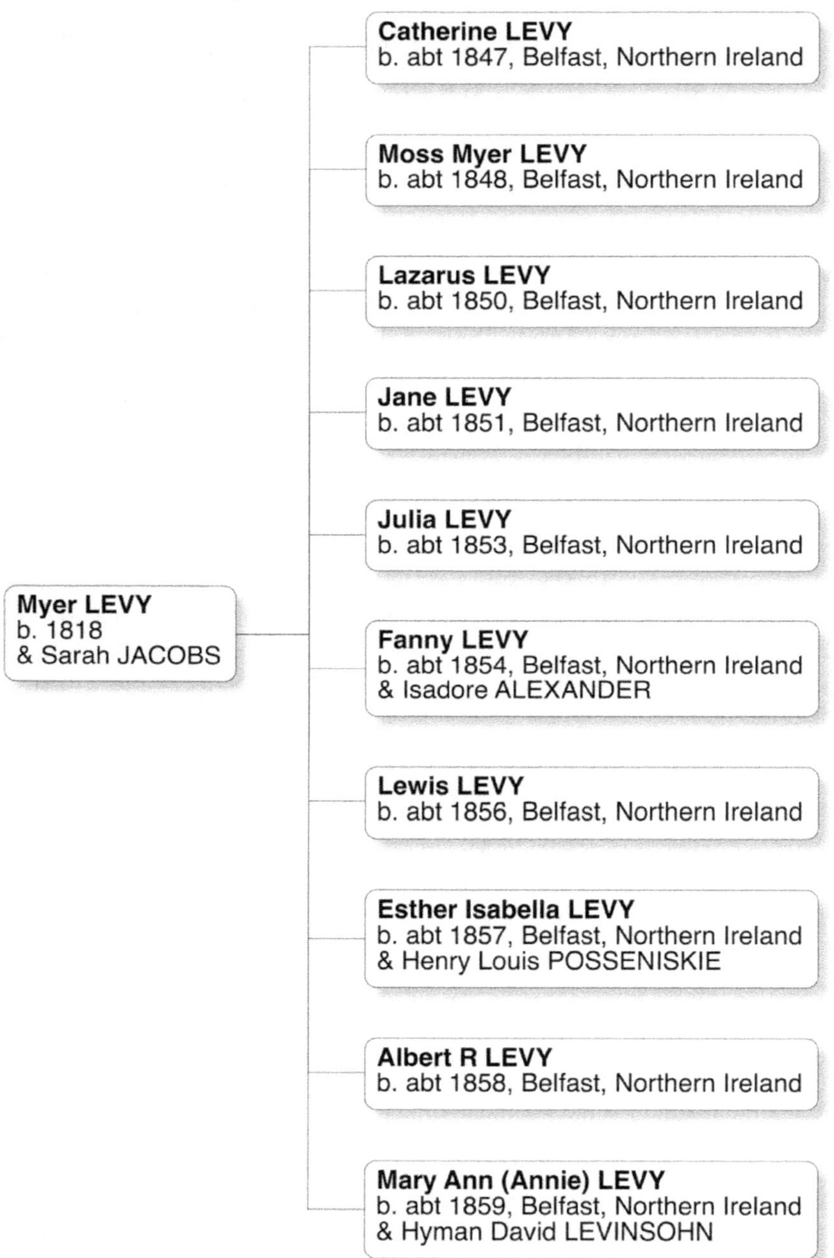

Figure 11.1. Children of Myer and Sarah LEVY

Ester's father Myer LEVY was a storekeeper. He tragically died after living in New Zealand for just over three years. It appears that the family was on an excursion in search of gold in the Coromandel area. Myer's son-in-law, George ISAACS was dissatisfied with the manner in which the inquest into Myer's death had been carried out. He was particularly concerned that no-one had examined the body.

INQUEST ON THE BODY OF MIER LEVY.
To the Editor of the *Daily Southern Cross.*
Sir, – Being a relation, and interested in the death of Mier LEVY, late of Victoria Street, Auckland, who was found dead in a hole (13 feet deep) at Coromandel, on the 31st January last, I think it my duty to ask you if it is the custom in New Zealand to hold an inquest without examining the body to see what were the probable causes of death, whether by accident or otherwise; as in this case of Mier LEVY there was no examination of the body, prior to, or during the inquest, although one person offered his services to bring the body out of the hole for examination during the inquest, but they were not accepted. This person is Mr JONES, digger, of Coromandel, who afterwards assisted in getting the body out of the hole. Now, sir, I think it my duty to bring this case before the public, that the like occurrence may not take place again, and to see who is to blame in the matter. I asked Mr TURTON, of Coromandel, to let me have a copy of the depositions taken at the inquest, he promised to do so, but has never fulfilled his promise. I have to apologise for taking up so much space in your valuable paper. G. ISAACS. Onehunga, February 13, 1863.[7]

Sarah, wife of Myer LEVY had a sister Esther who married George ISAACS and was, therefore, her brother-in-law.

CORONER'S INQUEST.
The following certified copy of the depositions taken at the inquest held on the 1st February, 1863, at the Victoria Hotel, Belleville, Coromandel, on view of the body of Mier LEVY, late storekeeper in Victoria Street, Auckland, has been forwarded to us for publication.
Before H. H. TURTON, Esq., Coroner, and a jury of twelve; of which Mr Joseph MASTERS was foreman. Hugh CHALMERS sworn, deposed: I am a bushman in the employment of Mr RING. Yesterday about half-past one o'clock, p.m., as I was about my work in the bush, and passing by an old shaft near the bottom of MURPHY's original claim, I looked in and I saw the body of the man which has now been seen by the jury. I then called my mates and told them there was a dead body in the hole, but I did not know it. We then sent down to tell the police.
George PARKER sworn, deposed: On Friday, the 16th of January, at about 7 or 8 o'clock in the evening, I was down at the Kapanga Beach at the time Mrs LEVY landed from the steamer. I believe she is the wife of the deceased. There were many others there at the same time; and we all returned together.

On the road I met Mr LEVY going towards the beach, and when I saw Mrs. LEVY he shook hands with her and kissed her and also his son – and then turned and came back with us. We called in at the Kapanga Hotel for light, and remained there about an hour. When we left to come away to the diggings, as I was carrying the baby I gave the lantern to Mr LEVY who carried it as far as the creek. As he lagged behind us about ten yards, being very slow, I took the light from him and told him to keep up with us. He made no answer, and we all came on.

By the Coroner: We were about twenty minutes in getting through the bush. We knew that Mr LEVY was not with us, but thought him close behind. Mrs B. LEVY told her husband that she wished to stop all night at the Kapanga, but he insisted on her coming up to sleep at the tent at Belleville. It was not very dark outside of the bush, and there we missed him, but came on saying that as the road was clear and well known to him there was no fear of his following after. It was about a quarter of a mile from that place to his I sensed. When we reached it Mrs LEVY declined to remain all night there, and so went on with Mrs PARKER and myself and her son to my house, where she slept, leaving her husband to occupy his tent when he should reach it.

By the Jury: I don't know exactly what clothes he had on. He had not a drop to drink during the time he was in the Kapanga. He was also asked to have tea but would not take any. I recognise the body now being in the hole as that of the deceased. When I saw him last he had trousers on and other clothes. He did talk rather strangely to his wife about the accommodation he had provided for her. Until we reached the house Mrs LEVY did not appear uneasy about him, but she said she was so afterwards and did not sleep during the night. This she said the next morning – but gave no intimation the night before of her wish that we should come and search for him. It was during the next day that I heard of his being missing.

George CHIPMAN, sworn, deposed: In the evening of February the 16th ult., I saw the deceased by the creek near RING's mill on the road to Belleville. I saw him rise the bank and come away. I called for him to come up and cross over. I spoke to him. He walked through the water, holding only the planks land stones, as if he thought it the safest way, for then the night, was dark, and it was bad and slippery over the rocks. He replied to my salutation, and I knew it to be the voice of the deceased. We then went our several ways.

Examined by the Coroner: It was not light enough for me to see how he was dressed. He seemed to speak in a hurry, but in good spirits. He was not in liquor that I could notice.

Corporal HASTIE, sworn: I well remember Mr LEVY's examination in the Court House on a late occasion. The whole style of his remarks was that of a sane and sensible person. He spoke with intelligence throughout, and in answer to all questions. That was on Saturday the 10th January. I have had frequent conversation with him, but he always appeared quite sensible, but he was of very careless and slovenly habits – in leaving the goods in his tent all in disorder and exposed to depredation and ruin.

Verdict of the jury, 'That the deceased was found lying dead in a shaft, but there is no evidence to show how or in what state of mind he came there.'[8]

Sarah JACOBS, wife of Myer LEVY, was the daughter of Lazarus JACOBS who was a stay maker at Plummers Row, Stepney, Middlesex in 1841. Her mother was Catherine Simons MARKS.

Table 11.1. Lazaris and Catherine JACOB's household, Plummer's Row, Stepney, London, Middlesex, England Census, 1841.[9]

Lazarus JACOBS	40	stay maker	Middlesex, England
Catherine JACOBS	40	stay maker	Middlesex, England
Isaac JACOBS	15	frame maker	Middlesex, England
Leah JACOBS	20	stay maker	Middlesex, England
Mary JACOBS	20	stay maker	Middlesex, England
Sarah JACOBS	15	stay maker	Middlesex, England
Julia JACOBS	15	stay maker	Middlesex, England
Morris JACOBS	10		Middlesex, England
Asher JACOBS	10		Middlesex, England
Esther JACOBS	5		Middlesex, England
John JACOBS			Middlesex, England

By 1861 Lazarus, a widower, had become manager of a looking glass factory. He was living alone in St Mark Chapel parish, Whitechapel, London.[10]

Following Myer's death in New Zealand his wife Sarah remained a widow for the rest of her life. She continued to live in Auckland for a time and moved to Sydney, Australia where she died in 1905.

LEVY – On September 18, at Sydney, Sara, relict of the late Myer LEVY, and beloved mother of Mrs. J. ALEXANDER and Mrs. H. L. POSSENISKIE, of this city.[11]

Henry POSSENISKIE and Esther Isabella LEVY spent their family lives in Auckland where their five children were born and raised.

The POSSENISKIE shop was a familiar part of Victoria Arcade. It had a top flat with a large workroom that employed about twenty hands. Several of Henry's employees remained with him for nearly a quarter of a century. He imported regular shipments from abroad and advertised the arrival of new stock that included English, Scotch, Bannockburn, Home, spun worsteds and other first class tweeds as well as special lines in blue and broadcloth, fancy coatings, and other vests.[12]

Henry appears to also have had a curiosity for gold, much like the LEVY family, as seen in this description in his shop window:

The old established tailoring business of Mr H. L. POSSENISKIE has been removed back to the site of his former establishment before the Victoria

Arcade was erected. Mr POSSENISKIE's new premises are in the commodious rooms at the Victoria Arcade lately occupied by Mr J. H. WITHEFORD, the mining and financial agent. Many habitants of the Arcade will be pleased to learn that the golden obelisk in the side window, representing the amount of gold obtained from Auckland goldfields, will be allowed to remain. No doubt both Mr POSSENISKIE and his patrons will find the new premises more central and convenient than the establishment further up Shortland-street.[13]

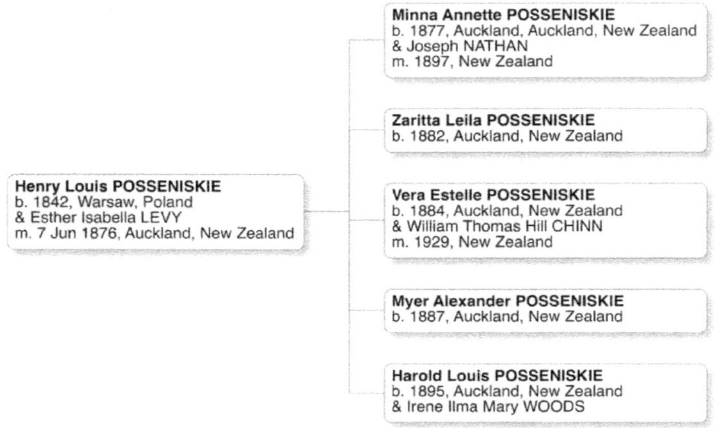

Figure 11.2. The children of Henry POSSENISKIE and Esther LEVY

It seems, even a person's weight came to be measured using gold as currency:

The Heaviest Man in Auckland.
A very weighty point in Auckland has at length been solved. Opinions differed greatly as to the heaviest man in town – Mr S. JAGGER and Mr ATKIN receiving the greatest support, while Mr EHRENFRIED was a good third. All doubts have now been set at rest by the declaration of Mr POSSENISKIE, who on his window, in large black letters on a gold background, says that his estimated weight is 2,132,742 ounces (12,694St 12lb 6oz), and his value £9,000,000, so that Auckland's heaviest man is also the richest.[14]

Henry's business flourished, but New Zealand's Long Depression seems to have affected his business and by 1892 he had filed for bankruptcy.

BANKRUPTCY.
Henry Louis POSSENISKIE, tailor, of Auckland, to-day filed a petition praying to be adjudged a bankrupt. Mr POSSENISKIE has not yet made out the schedule of his liabilities and assets, but the former are expected to

amount to about £1,200. His assets, represented by stock-in-trade, etc., have not yet been valued.[15]

Figure 11.3. Henry Louis POSSENISKIE. Source: The Cyclopedia of New Zealand: Auckland Provincial Districts (The Cyclopedia Company: Christchurch, 1902), 354.

Henry appears to have recovered from this setback. In 1911 and 1914 he and Esther, with unmarried daughters lived at 'Ardvair', Park Road, Parnell where Henry died in 1917.[16]

By the time of his death, Henry POSSENISKIE, husband of Esther Isabella LEVY, had become a wealthy man as shown in his 1917 property sales.

PROPERTY SALES. Mr. C. F. BENNETT will offer for sale by public auction, at the Chamber of Commerce, at noon to-day, several city properties in a deceased estate, comprising two cottages on corner allotments, Cook and West Streets; three cottages on two level sections in Adelaide Street, and three cottages in Kale Street; the residence of the late Mr. H. L. POSSENISKIE, in Park Road. Grafton; several sections of the Victoria Estate, Dominion Road, in Kensington Avenue and Marsden Avenue; four sections of the Panama Estate, Otahuhu, with frontage to Tamaki River; and residence of six rooms on large section directly opposite the tramway workshops at Epsom.[17]

Henry left the entire estate to his wife Esther Isabella LEVY.[18]

Figure 11.4. Headstone for Henry Louis POSSENISKIE. Source: author's collection

With the family property having been sold, by 1919 Esther had moved to Hobart West in Tasmania, most probably to live with one of her daughters.

A marriage has not been found for Zaritta who probably married a Mr. A. ALEXANDER.[19] The last record found for Zaritta is in 1914 when she was living with her parents at "Ardvair", Park Road, Parnell.[20]

Esther lived at 214 Warwick Street, Hobart West for several years.[21] She was visited by her son Harold in 1920.[22]

Harold had attended Auckland University College (now the University of Auckland) and became a licensed school teacher in 1912[23] He served in WW1 in the New Zealand Medical Corps.[24] (See Figure 11.5.)

Esther died in Hobart in November 1922.

Figure 11.5. Private Harold Louis POSSENISKIE, Reg. No. 3/3846, of the New Zealand Medical Corps. (Photo: Herman Schmidt, 1917). Source: Sir George Grey Special Collections, Auckland Libraries, 31-P4579B. No known copyright.

Henry belonged to the Hebrew Synagogue and Esther was among the pioneer women of the Auckland Jewish community.[25]

At the time, Esther was survived by one son, Mr Harold POSSENISKIE, three daughters, Mrs J. Nathan PAEROA, Mrs A. ALEXANDER of Hobart, and Miss POSSENISKIE, and a number of grandchildren.[26]

Mrs J. NATHAN of PAEROA, noted in Esther's obituary, referred to Minna Annette POSSENISKIE, her oldest daughter, who had married Joseph NATHAN in 1897, in New Zealand. Minna was a registered schoolteacher. She passed the Civil Service Junior Examination with merit in 1893.[27] Three years later she became a licensed teacher.[28]

Joseph NATHAN was the fourth child of Henry NATHAN, born in London, England and Matilda JACOBS. Joseph was born in 1856 in Manchester, Lancashire, England. His mother's birthplace was Bedfordshire. Matilda was the second daughter of Joseph JACOBS, jeweller, and his wife Mary. In 1841 Matilda, along with two sisters, worked as a laundress in Salford, Lancashire, England. The family had one servant.

Table 11.2. Joseph and Mary JACOB's household, Islington Street, Salford, Lancashire, England, Census, 1841.[29]

Joseph JACOBS	head	56	jeweller
Mary JACOBS	wife	45	
Caroline JACOBS	dau	24	laundry maid
Matilda JACOBS	dau	22	laundry maid
Dianna JACOBS	dau	20	laundry maid
Esther JACOBS	dau	18	
Isaac JACOBS	son	16	traveller
Murice JACOBS	son	14	
Zipporah JACOBS	dau	10	
Myer JACOBS	son	8	
Hart JACOBS	son	4	
Margaret JACOBS	dau	20	servant

In 1851 Henry and Matilda and family lived at Market Street, Manchester where Henry was a brush manufacturer.

Table 11.3. Joseph and Mary JACOB's household, 13 King Street, St Anns, Manchester, Lancashire, England, Census, 1851.[30]

Henry NATHAN	head	39	brush manufacturer	London
Matilda NATHAN	wife	32		Bedford
Sarah NATHAN	dau	2		London
Rosanna McDONALD			servant	

In 1861 they were living, and apparently Henry was working at, Artists' Repository and Envoy Depot. Joseph was a five year-old scholar at the time.

Table 11.4. Henry and Matilda NATHAN's household, 117 Artists' Repository, St Anne, Manchester, Lancashire, England, Census, 1861.[31]

Henry NATHAN	head	50	Artists' Repository & Envoy Depot	London
Matilda NATHAN	wife	43		Bedfordshire
Sarah NATHAN	dau	12	scholar	London
Michael NATHAN	son	9	scholar	Manchester
Maurice NATHAN	son	7	scholar	Manchester
Joseph NATHAN	son	5	scholar	Manchester
Annie NATHAN	dau	3		Manchester
Elias LEVY	nephew	11	shop boy	Woolwich, Kent
Ann MURPHY		22	house servant	Liverpool

In 1871 Joseph was an apprentice shopkeeper for his widowed mother. His two older brothers were shopkeepers and the family employed a servant.

Table 11.5. Henry and Matilda NATHAN's household, 44 Brunswick Street, St Paul, Chorlton, Lancashire, England, Census, 1871.[32]

Matilda NATHAN	widow	53	shopkeeper	Bedford, Bedfordshire
Sarah NATHAN	dau	22		London, Middlesex
Michael H. NATHAN	son	19	shopkeeper	Manchester
Maurice NATHAN	son	17	shopkeeper	Manchester
Joseph NATHAN	son	15	apprentice shopkeeper	Manchester
Annie NATHAN	dau	13	scholar	Manchester
Alice ROBERTS		18	domestic servant	Liverpool

His father, Henry NATHAN, had died in 1865 after spending two years in the Lunatic Asylum at Stockport Etchells, Cheshire where he suffered general paralysis. He died of a cerebral condition that lasted for 26 hours.[33]

In 1883 Joseph NATHAN immigrated to New Zealand.[34] In 1885-86 and 1890 he was working as a clerk at Nairn Street, Te Aro, Wellington.[35] He decided to go into business and moved to Inglewood, Taranaki as a stationer and tobacconist. While residing there, Mr NATHAN was, in 1893, placed on the Commission of the Peace.[36] In about the same year he moved to Ohinemuri in the Waikato where he is listed as tobacconist.[37]

In 1897 Joseph married Minna Annette POSSENISKIE.[38] (See Figure 11.2.)

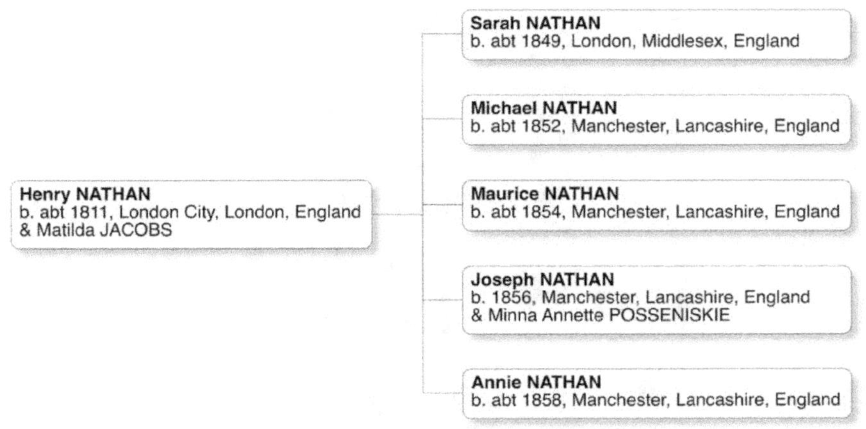

Figure 11.6. Children of Henry and Matilda NATHAN

They settled in Ohinemuri where they raised a family of four children, the oldest a son, followed by three daughters.

Figure 11.7. Minna NATHAN (née POSSENISKIE) on her wedding day. Source: author's collection

Figure 11.8. Joseph NATHAN. Source: author's collection

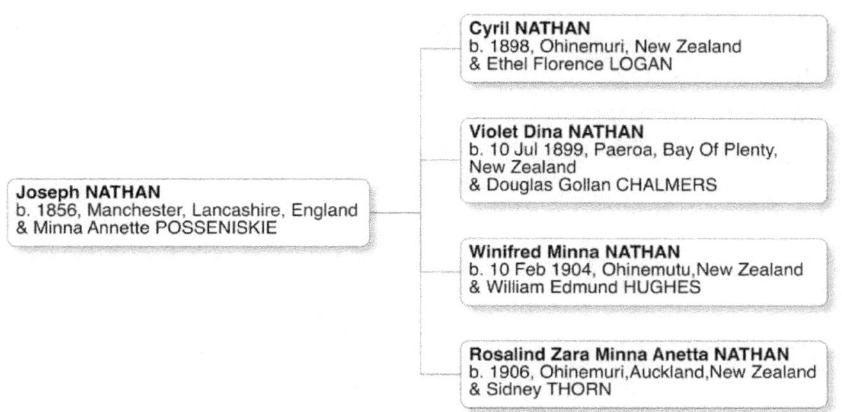

Figure 11.9. The children of Joseph and Minna NATHAN

Joseph served in the Ohinemuri Rifles and was elected a member of the local school committee in 1899.[39]

The family business was something of a general store. It sold and auctioned a wide range of goods. In 1900 Joseph's occupation was importer and he focussed on selling Christmas cards.[40]

Two years later he had a wide selection of sports equipment to sell.[41] Later in the year his stock had become diversified to include

> tobaccos, cigars, Havanna or Manilla, pipes, briar, clay or cherry, stationery plain or fancy, crockery china or earthenware, glassware British or American, fancy goods of every description, toys, dolls, basketware, etc., etc., etc. At Nathan's JOSEPH NATHAN BOOKSELLER, STATIONER, & IMPORTER, PAEROA.[42]

He remained in the business as bookseller at Puke Road, Paeroa from 1900 to 1914.[43] Joseph died in 1915.[44]

Minna was widowed for many years. At some stage she moved to Auckland where she died on 25 March 1951.[45]

Their daughter Violet Dina NATHAN had married Douglas Gollan CHALMERS in 1935. Douglas was a miner at the time and Violet was a nurse.[46] From nursing service in the Hospital Annex of the Domain Gardens at Auckland in 1928 she worked her way south to the Arawa (Maternity) Hospital at Ashburton.[47]

Violet's status as a registered nurse was shown in the New Zealand Register of Medical Practitioners and Nurses in September of 1929. At this time she was attached to St Helen's Hospital in Christchurch while living in Dunedin at 97 Elm Row.[48]

It was most likely in Dunedin where Violet and Douglas met. Violet was living at 52 High Street in 1935.[49] By 1938 they had moved to 27 Denton Street, Gore where Douglas recommenced his occupation as a baker.[50]

Figure 11.10. Douglas and Violet. Source: author's collection

Zelda Grace CHALMERS, born on 23 October 1940, was their only child.

Figure 11.11. Minna with daughter Violet and grandaughter Zelda.

Figure 11.12 Zelda. Source: author's collection

Figure 11.13 Douglas with daughter Zelda. Source: author's collection

By 1946 they had moved north to 26 Norwood Street, Dunedin North where Douglas was employed as a mill hand for several years.[51]

Changing his work to become a gardener, Douglas chose this as his last occupation before retirement. He and Violet moved to the North Otago region, known for its horticulture. They first went to Waianakarua, on a hill close to the main highway where they stayed for about five years.[52]

Continuing to garden for income Douglas and Violet spent some time at Kakanui, a productive horticulture area on the coast.[53]

They retired to Otepopo before their final move to 2 Aln Street, Oamaru.[54]

Zelda married George (Geordie) FRAME, brother of Janet FRAME the well-known New Zealand author.

Violet had suffered from diabetes for many years and eventually had to have both legs amputated.

Douglas died on 30 June 1976 and Violet on 17 December of the same year at Oamaru. They are buried at Block 516, Plot 71 in the Oamaru Lawn Cemetery.

NOTES

---

[1] NZRGO, Marriage register, 1937/8153, Violet Dina NATHAN, Douglas Gollan CHALMERS.

[2] *Auckland Star.* "Obituary." May 2, 1917.

[3] POSSENISKIE, Henry Lewis, Shortland Street, dwelling, Auckland East Electoral Roll, 1875-1876

[4] POSSENISKIE was also spelt POSSENNISKIE.

[5] LDS Film #0287464 (Excel file provided by Lindel), http://www.yesteryears.co.nz/shipping/ists/maori.html

[6] *Daily Southern Cross.* November 28, 1859.

[7] *Daily Southern Cross.* February 16, 1863.

[8] *New Zealander.* February 17, 1863; Myer LEVY, 1863, Registration Number1863/6544, New Zealand, Civil Records Indexes, 1800-1896, https://familysearch.org /ark:/61903/1:1:Q24J-L4VJ :); *New Zealand Herald.* September 21, 1905.

[9] 1841 England Census, Stepney, Ossulstone (Tower Division), Middlesex.

[10] 1861 England Census, Whitechapel, Middlesex.

[11] *New Zealand Herald.* September 21, 1905.

[12] *Auckland Star.* December 6, 1879; *The Cyclopedia of New Zealand: Auckland Provincial Districts* (The Cyclopedia Company: Christchurch,1902), 354.

[13] *Observer.* July 6, 1889.

[14] *Observer.* August 3, 1889.

[15] *Auckland Star.* October 22, 1891.

[16] POSSENISKIE, Esther Isabel, 'Ardvair', Park Road, Auckland, Parnell Electoral Rolls, 1911 and 1914; POSSENISKIE, Henry Louis, 'Ardvair', Park Road, Auckland, Parnell Electoral Rolls, 1911 and 1914; POSSENISKIE, Vera Estelle, 'Ardvair', Park Road, Auckland, Parnell Electoral Rolls, 1911 and 1914; POSSENISKIE, Zarella Leila, 'Ardvair', Park Road, Auckland, Parnell Electoral Rolls, 1911 and 1914; NZRGO, Death Register, 1917/1812, POSSENISKIE Henry Louis, 75 years.

---

[17] *New Zealand Herald.* July 26, 1917.

[18] Henry Louis POSSENISKIE, 1917, Probate Records 1843-1998, R21453024, Archives New Zealand, Auckland.

[19] NZRGO, Birth Register, 1882/9207, POSSENISKIE Zaritta Leila, Esther, Henry Louis.

[20] POSSENISKIE, Esther Isabel, 'Ardvair', Park Road, Auckland, Parnell Electoral Rolls, 1911 and 1914; POSSENISKIE, Henry Louis, 'Ardvair', Park Road, Auckland, Parnell Electoral Rolls, 1911 and 1914; POSSENISKIE, Vera Estelle, 'Ardvair', Park Road, Auckland, Parnell Electoral Rolls, 1911 and 1914; POSSENISKIE Zarella Leila, 'Ardvair', Park Road, Auckland, Parnell Electoral Rolls, 1911 and 1914.

[21] POSSENISKIE, Esther Isabel, 214 Warwick Street, Hobart West, Tasmania, Denison Electoral Rolls, 1919 and 1922.

[22] POSSENISKIE, H. L., Arrival Port: Hobart, 24 June 1920, Departure Port: Sydney, 22 June 1920, *Ulimaroa*, Tasmania, Australia, Passenger Arrivals, 1829-1957.

[23] Harold Louis POSSENISKIE, 17 January 1912, Wellington, New Zealand, Teacher and Civil Service Examinations and Licenses, 1880-1920 Civil Service Examinations.

[24] Harold Louis POSSENISKIE, Service Number 3/3846, http://www.aucklandmuseum. com/war-memorial/online-cenotaph/record

[25] The Cyclopedia Company, 354; *New Zealand Herald.* "Obituary." November 21, 1922.

[26] *New Zealand Herald.* "Obituary." November 21, 1922.

[27] Minna Annette POSSENISKIE, New Zealand Teacher and Civil Service Examinations and Licenses, 1880-1920, Civil Service Junior Examination, Merit, February 21, 1893, Wellington.

[28] New Zealand, Teacher and Civil Service Examinations and Licenses, 1880-1920, Minna Annette POSSENISKIE, Civil Service Junior Examination, February 25, 1896, Wellington.

[29] 1841 England Census, Salford, Lancashire.

[30] 1851 England Census, St Anns, Manchester, Lancashire.

[31] 1861 England Census, St Anne, Manchester, Lancashire.

[32] 1871 England Census, St Paul, Manchester, Lancashire.

[33] Certified Copy of an Entry of Death, GRO England Public Members Photos and Scanned Documents at Ancestry.com

[34] The Cyclopedia Company, 839.

[35] NZ Census 1885-86, Te Aro, Wellington.

[36] The Cyclopedia Company, 839.

[37] NATHAN, Joseph, stationer and tobacconist, Inglewood, Taranaki Electoral Roll, 1896; NATHAN, Joseph, tobacconist, Ohinemuri, Waikato Electoral Roll, 1896.

[38] NZRGO, Marriage Register, 1897/3740, Minna Annette POSSENISKIE, Joseph NATHAN.

[39] The Cyclopedia Company, 839.

[40] *Ohinemuri Gazette.* December 14, 1900.

[41] *Ohinemuri Gazette.* April 28, 1902.

[42] *Ohinemuri Gazette.* November 3, 1902.

[43] NATHAN, Joseph, bookseller, Puke Road, Paeroa, Ohinemuri Electoral Rolls, 1900, 1905-06, 1911 and 1914.

[44] NZRGO, Death Register, 1915/7931, NATHAN Joseph, 58 years.

[45] Minna Annette NATHAN, March 25, 1951, New South Wales, Australia, Index to Deceased Estate Files, 1859-1958.

[46] CHALMERS, Douglas Gollan, miner, Victoria Bridge, Central Otago Electoral Roll, 1935.

[47] NATHAN, Violet Dina, spinster, Hospital Annex, Domain Gardens, Auckland East Electoral Roll, 1928; NATHAN, Violet Dina, spinster, Arawa Hospital, Mid-Canterbury, Ashburton Electoral Roll, 1928.

[48] Violet Dina NATHAN, September 1929, Registers of Medical Practitioners and Nurses, 1873, 1882-1933, Nurses and Midwives Register of New Zealand, 1903-1933; Residence: Dunedin, New Zealand, St Helens Hospital, Christchurch, 1931.

[49] NATHAN, Violet Dina, spinster, 52 High Street, Dunedin C1, Dunedin Central Electoral Roll, 1935.

[50] CHALMERS, Douglas Gollan, baker, 27 Denton Street, Gore, Mataura Electoral Roll, 1938; CHALMERS, Violet Dina, 27 Denton Street, Gore, Mataura Electoral Roll, 1938.

[51] CHALMERS, Douglas Gollan, mill hand, 26 Norwood Street, Dunedin North Electoral Rolls, 1946 and 1949; CHALMERS, Violet Dina, 26 Norwood Street, Dunedin North Electoral Rolls, 1946 and 1949.

[52] CHALMERS, Douglas Gollan, gardener, Waianakarua, Oamaru Electoral Rolls, 1949 and 1954; CHALMERS, Violet, Waianakarua, Oamaru Electoral Rolls, 1949 and 1954.

[53] CHALMERS, Douglas Gollan, gardener, Kakanui, Oamaru Electoral Roll, 1957; CHALMERS, Violet, Kakanui, Oamaru Electoral Roll, 1957.

[54] CHALMERS, Douglas Gollan, retired, Otepopo, Waitaki Electoral Roll, 1963; CHALMERS, Violet, Otepopo, Waitaki Electoral Roll, 1963; CHALMERS, Douglas Gollan, retired, 2 Aln Street, Oamaru Electoral Rolls, 1969 and 1972; CHALMERS, Violet, married, 2 Aln Street, Oamaru Electoral Rolls, 1969 and 1972.

12 John (Jack) Charles CHALMERS and Frances Louisa Beaven MITCHELL[1]

Jack and Frances met at the Hokonui farm where Frances was employed by the Women's Division of Federated Farmers to provide home help for ailing John Howe CHALMERS who needed care.[2] They were married at Invercargill on 22 December 1936.[3]

Figure 12.1. Jack with his father John Howe at Hokonui. Source: author's collection

Frances' father, John MITCHELL was born on 26 December 1870 at Wyndham, Southland where his parents settled and farmed at nearby Mimihau. John MITCHELL Snr and Sarah MABEN arrived at Dunedin on the *Helenslee* in 1868. They came from Kirkcudbright in Scotland. John Snr died aged 46 leaving Sarah with 10 children and a farm to run. (See Figure 12.2) (See: Lindsay Watson, Lorraine Berry and Heather Bray, *Sunnyside: The Mitchell Family of Mimihau* (Ashburton, N.Z.: Lindsay R. Watson, 2018).

Her mother, Rosa PINK was born at Maidstone, Kent, England on 9 March 1873. Her parents, James Thomas PINK and Elizabeth PEARCE sailed for New Zealand on the *Wennington* when Rosa was nine months old. After a short period in the North Island the family settled at Waianiwa where James worked as a labourer and horticulturalist. They had 16 children, 11 of whom grew to adulthood. (See Figure 12.3) (See: Lindsay Watson and Lorraine Berry, *Of a Very Superior Class: The Pink Family of Waianawa* (Ashburton, N.Z.: Lindsay R. Watson, 2017)).

John and Rosa MITCHELL were married at Wyndham in 1894. They farmed in the area before moving near the PINKs at Waianiwa and after returning to Wyndham they ultimately lived at Invercargill.

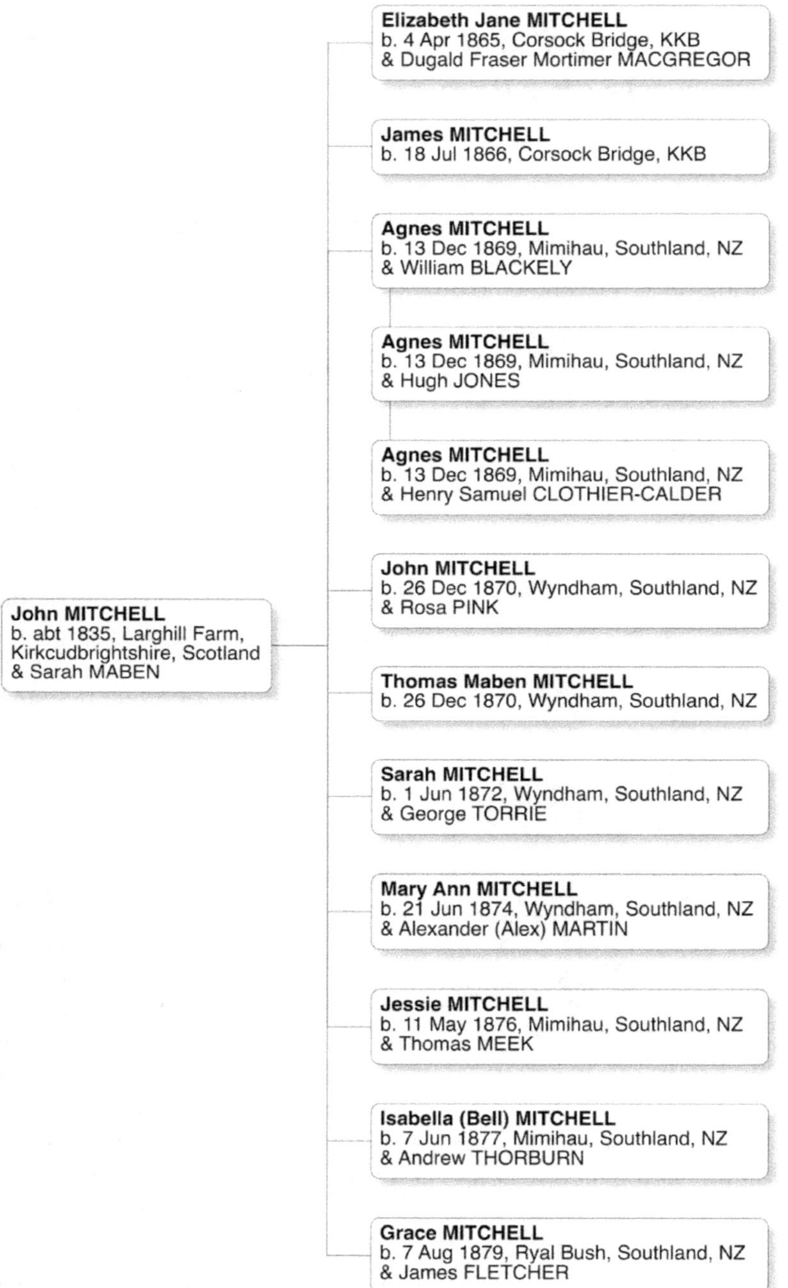

Figure 12.2. The children of John and Sarah MITCHELL

Figure 12.3. The children of James and Elizabeth PINK

Figure 12.4. Jack CHALMERS. Source: author's collection

Figure 12.5. Frances CHALMERS (née MITCHELL). Source: author's collection

After living for a while at Hokonui Frances had become tired of the bickering within the family. The farm was sold but the sharing of property was not amicable. Donald's wife Maribel thought it was unfairly divided.[4] The couple, with their baby, moved to Ryal Bush. Nephews Donald and Raymond CHALMERS, drove the horses and wagon for the move.[5] Their first child, Eleanor Rosalie had been born prematurely and needed extra care as she was not expected to survive. Violet enjoyed carrying her around and delighted in teaching her animal sounds.[6]

The family did not stay there for long and bought a property at Greenhills, seventeen miles south of Invercargill.[7] (See figure 12.8.) The Greenhills district extends in the south to Bluff, south-west to Barracouta Point and in the north from Omaui Island in the west to Moko-Moko Inlet.[8]

Jack's sister Violet remained close to Frances and chose to live with her and Jack for the rest of her life. (See Figure 12.7.)

Figure 12.6. Frances and baby Eleanor Rosalie CHALMERS. Source: author's collection

Figure 12.7. Violet, Rosalie and Allan at Greenhills, c.1938. Source: author's collection

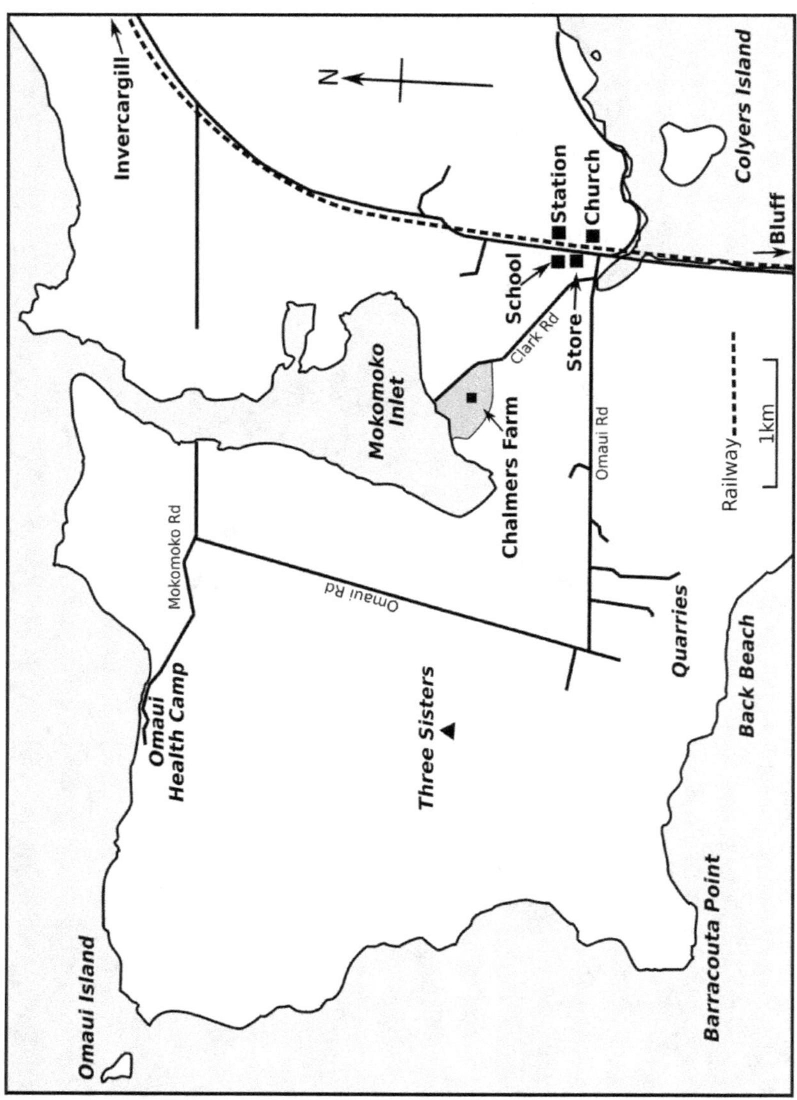

Figure 12.8. Map of the Greenhills District showing the position of Jack and Frances CHALMERS' farm. Source: based on a New Zealand topographical map.

The BOYLEN family at Winton also remained close, although Auntie Gertie did not travel. Cousins Eleanor and Thelma always enjoyed having the CHALMERS children come to stay.

Figure 12.9. Allan and Rosalie at Winton, c.1939. Source: author's collection

The Greenhills property consisted of twenty-eight acres and was typical of the small farms in the area. There was room to graze a couple of horses, a flock of sheep and cows for home supply. The land produced hay and grew crops such as swedes that also served as animal fodder. Otherwise tussock proliferated and there was an extensive hilly area covered in manuka trees. A large flower garden and strawberry patch, created and tended by Frances, overlooked the Moko Moko Inlet that was a tidal estuary. Strawberries were sold locally for several seasons. Down a hill on the other side from the house across a creek, was a henhouse that kept the family supplied with eggs.

During World War II as the enemy came closer to New Zealand's shores, steps were taken to defend it. Being on a hill, the CHALMERS property was chosen as a coastal defence site. The construction consisted of a circular concrete dugout with a lid and holes for guns to protrude. Jack was a member of the Home Guard and housed a gun, probably a .303 rifle if needed.[9] Later, the children knew it as 'The Pillbox' and a wonderful place to play. During blackouts grey blankets were hung from the windows. As with every other family, ration coupons for restricted food items were provided by the government and used at the local store. When the war ended the Invercargill to Bluff train sounded its whistle continuously, as did ships in the Bluff Harbour.[10]

Income was provided by a variety of work opportunities, often seasonal, and Jack spent varying amounts of time employed at the Ocean Beach Freezing Works, the Bluff wharf and the oyster grit mill. He worked at a foundry in Invercargill for a time. It would have suited his great understanding of machines.

There was a community spirit of helping one another, especially at ploughing and haymaking time. Harvesting was hard physical work that involved scything the hay and forming stooks that were added to build haystacks. Jack was often called upon when local farmers had trouble with mechanical things. Agnes FRASER, a neighbour, wrote: "There weren't many things Jack couldn't fix. I remember him having two or three people's brain[s in one]. Dan, Agnes' husband, and he were good friends. Jack sowed a paddock of grass for him. There was an art to that job. He had a bag tied on wire to put the seed in and a strap around the waist to support it. When I was cutting the hedges with the hand clippers he would stop as he was going by, sharpen the clippers and have a chat. Once when Dan was working in the paddock a stick got caught in the magneto and it flew apart. Jack picked up the pieces and put it back together straight away, even getting the timing right first time."[11]

Jack had an inventive mind that enabled him to design the woolpress, a valuable asset to sheep farmers. Unfortunately he did not have it patented and someone else took the rights. While at Hokonui he built windmills and placed them in the trees for more exposure to wind.[12] He developed a perpetual motion engine (his nephew Ray CHALMERS was in possession of the design plan) and worked out a smokeless underground heating system on the family property that could offset frosts that damaged fruit in Central Otago.[13] He paved and built stone walls around the family house. He also began, but did not complete, an extension to the house made of the same material.

Jack, and Frances had eleven children. They were known in the district as 'the smiling Chalmers'.

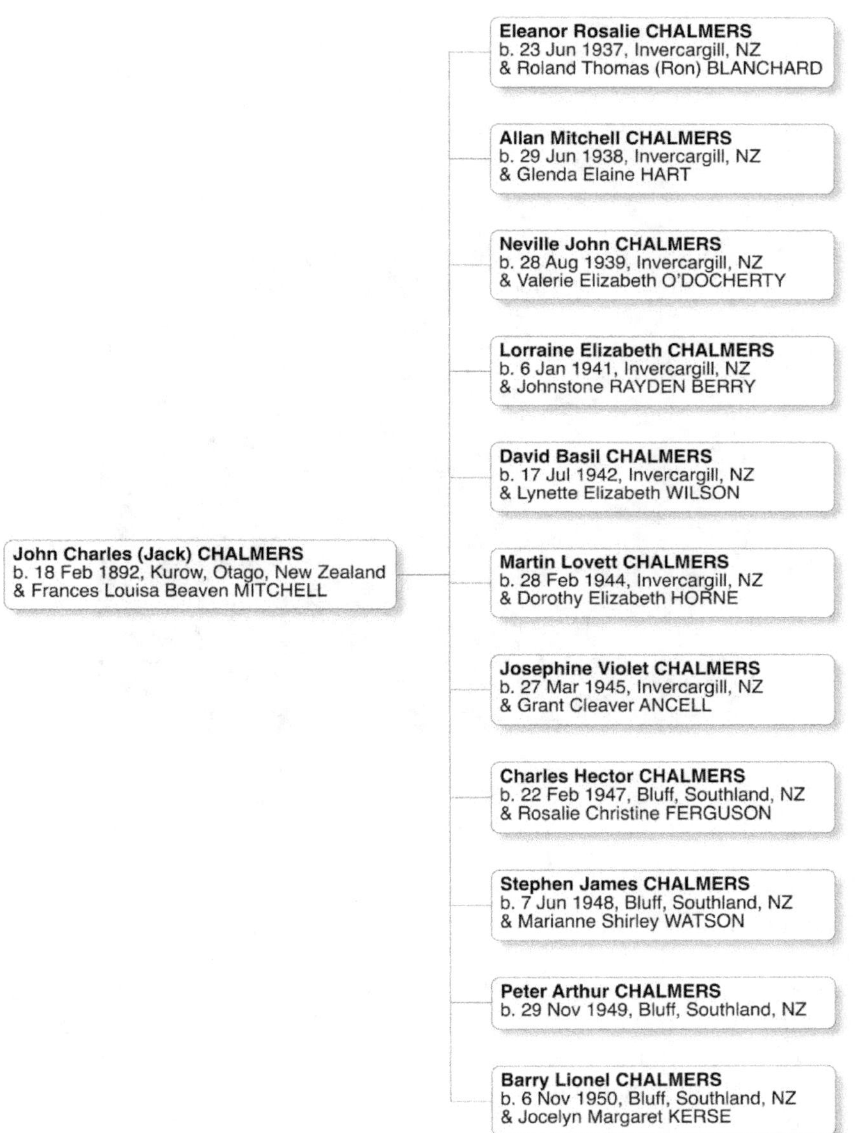

Figure 12.10. The children of Jack and Frances CHALMERS

Figure 12.11. The CHALMERS family at Greenhills, c. 1947, Front: Josephine; Second Row: David and Martin; Third row: Rosalie, Neville, Lorraine, Back Row: Frances holding Charles and Jack. Absent: Allan. Photo by Jessie KIEL (née CHALMERS).

The two-bedroom house was comparatively small with no modern facilities to speak of. A black coal range was used for cooking and heating water as there was no electricity. There was an open fire in the lounge. Candles and kerosene lamps were largely used for lighting. As the family grew in number more beds were called for and found in every room except the kitchen. Eventually the two older boys, Allan and Neville, moved into a hut across the lawn under the big macrocarpa trees. They took in the younger boys as needed. The older children were each assigned a younger sibling to care for.

The toilet was outdoors with a long drop, not enticing on cold winter nights. Open drains also needed regular cleaning with antiseptic. Bathing took place in a tin bath placed in the kitchen with one filling of tank water used by as many children as possible as water was scarce.

The nearest medical service was five miles away, at Bluff, and too expensive to attend. Fortunately everyone kept good health in the main, except for one case of scarlet fever suffered by Rosalie. Otherwise they survived the usual contagious diseases of the time such as measles, mumps, chickenpox and whooping cough. If any were experienced they are barely remembered. Cuts and bruises from minor accidents were treated at home so, without stitches, some scars remained. The worst accident happened when Martin's thumb became caught in the slats of Allan's homemade sled on its trial run. It required regular bathing for weeks.[14] Basic home remedies and supplements such as sulphur paste, tincture of iodine, epsom salts, cod liver oil, Lanes Emulsion, Throaties and Irish Moss were common.[15]

As each child turned five they were enrolled at Greenhills School, along a gravel road, a mile from home. In wintertime the potholes would be covered in ice that was fun to skate on but not so exciting when the cold of the morning turned to painful chilblains on the feet at night, attended to by Frances. On the main Invercargill to Bluff highway, it was a two-teacher school. Everyone feared the headmaster, Old Bill ANDERSON who was very liberal with corporal punishment and the older boys were frequent victims of his strap for out-of-school misbehaviour such as destroying the power pole insulators by shanghai on the way home.

Figure 12.12. Clark Road connecting home to school, with the Bluff Hill in the background. Source: Lorraine BERRY

Figure 12.13. Greenhills School, c.1944. Rosalie 2nd row 5th from right, Allan 1st row 2nd from right, Neville 1st row 4th from left. Source: author's collection

Figure 12.14. Greenhills School. Source: Josephine ANCELL (née CHALMERS)

There were lots of distractions and opportunities for mischief on the way home from school, mostly motivated by hunger. A loaf of bread from Percy SMITH's store seldom made it home intact, even swedes or turnips from a field tasted good and the neighbour's orchard was popular. There was always someone to serve as lookout for the elderly lady owner, Old Poonie [McDONALD] she was called because of the Scottish way she said "a poond of butter", who would be somewhere about. No doubt she would have allowed the children to have the fruit if they had had the courage to ask. Most ashamedly was the raiding of a tempting pantry of goodies that the lady owners kept well stocked. Forty years later one of the boys, David apologised for his behaviour and of course the old ladies had known about it all along.[16]

The end of year school picnics, with races and lolly scrambles, and concerts with prizes and items were highlights of the school year. Regular deliveries of fresh sets of library books from the National Library Service were looked forward to. A potbelly stove provided heat in wintertime. At morning playtime each child was provided with a bottle of milk, sometimes iced over by the cold and sometimes sour-tasting from warmth, and an apple. The cardboard bottle tops were used for making woollen pompoms. The use of looms for weaving with wool was part of the curriculum. Swimming took place at the beach area opposite Colyers Island (see Figure 12.7).

Figure 12.15. Percy SMITH's Greenhills store. Source: Lorraine BERRY

Violet was fanatical about diet but did not keep good health.[17] Gertrude wrote that Frances told her that she was recovering from a disordered liver at one stage and that she was concerned for her welfare. Gertrude thought it better for Violet to be moved to Winton where she lived, but husband Philip's car was not up to hauling the caravan that was Violet's home on the Greenhills property.[18]

Frances looked after her, but eventually she couldn't eat. She was particular with food and became anorexic and malnourished. After three days in Invercargill Hospital she died of pneumonia on 2 January 1947.[19] She was buried at Invercargill Eastern Cemetery Plot 58, Block 33.[20]

Loving Memory
VIOLET HOPPNER
CHALMERS
WHO PASSED AWAY 2ND JAN 1947
AT REST

The death in 1947 of Jack's sister Violet and the manner in which her possessions, particularly the caravan, were disposed of created more animosity. Family members were troubled because of missing items that supposedly had been held by Violet while living at Greenhills.[21] Again, this was upsetting to Frances.[22]

In 1948 the school reopening after the summer holidays was delayed due to a polio epidemic. The Correspondence School provided work through the mail. The activities were fun and each mailing was looked forward to with eager anticipation.

Frances would share Bible readings with her children in the evenings.

The CHALMERS children were regular attenders at the little church in the township. It had beautiful stained glass windows. The Sunday School teacher was Mrs NEEDHAM. The annual Harvest Festival transformed the little church with sheaves of wheat lining the ends of the pews and a colourful display of autumn vegetables and fruits up front that delighted the eye and tempted the taste. Restored in 2005, it now has a Category 2 rating in the New Zealand Historic Places Trust and is on the Bluff Heritage Trail.[23]

Figure 12.16. Greenhills Church. Source: Lorraine BERRY

Another annual event was Guy Fawkes day. Preparation started weeks before with the cutting down of manuka bush that was piled high waiting to dry out and become burnable. Ginger beer was the festive drink. Preparing it meant regular feeding of the ginger "bug" with sugar for several days. Close to the event a Guy would be made of old sacks stuffed with straw and with features added. He was placed on top of the wood pile awaiting his demise. When darkness fell, the big fire was lit and the celebration started with fireworks. Cutting bushes was also done to build huts to be used as hideaways.

Figure 12.17. Allan at Spar Bush, 1947. Source: author's collection

The MITCHELL family members visited from time to time. Frances' sister Elizabeth and husband Ted COLE would come in their much-admired Citroën car. As there were very few car owners at Greenhills a car of its type was a novelty. They would bring gifts and take older children for rides to Bluff.

School holidays were also spent with Grandma MITCHELL, Auntie Elinor and Mervan MACARTNEY at Invercargill, as well as Auntie Elizabeth and Ted COLE with their daughter Noeline and husband Bob WATSON at Spar Bush or later at Invercargill.

It was a family tradition to go by horse and dray across the Moko Moko for a picnic. Crossing the channel, where the water reached Bluey's waist and the current felt strong, was scary and it was a relief to reach the other side safely. It was quite spooky when the wind whistled through the gnarled old pine trees. An old steam engine from former days had been left to rust by a family of once skilled boatbuilders.[24] At the water's edge there were rock pools to explore. A hermit called Ginty lived there and would occasionally cross the estuary to visit his friend Jack. Jack, in turn, liked to take walks in the area and could be heard to mutter, "Ginty, how I envy him." Being father of a large family and struggling to provide for them must have felt overwhelming at times.

Bluey was a much more docile horse than the stormy Taupo. She would allow the children to ride bareback around the property. However, when she had had enough she would take them to a shrubbed area or one of overhanging branches to brush off the unsuspecting rider. Monty, the neighbours' Shetland pony was much more accommodating. The CHALMERS and McINTYRE children spent a lot of time together.

206

Figure 12.18. Photo of family on the dray going to a picnic, 1947. From the left: Lorraine, Frances with baby Charles, Rosalie, Josephine, David and Martin with Neville at the back. Absent: Allan. Source: Jessie KIEL (née CHALMERS)

The whole area from Omaui to Greenpoint and the back beach towards Stewart Island was a paradise for children, waiting to be explored. At the same time the back beach was rugged and treacherous. Rata trees on the Three Sisters hills made a blaze of colour at Christmastime. (See Figure 12.20.) The trees covering the area were said to be 'one of the finest stands of native bush in the country'.[25] Birdlife of many sorts flourished.

Bellbirds thrilled the ears and pigeons made a swishing sound as they flew from tree to tree. They were delicious to eat.[26] Crystal clear streams provided water for the thirsty young explorers. A favourite activity was rolling down the lupin-covered sandhills near the Omaui Health Camp across the Moko Moko. (See Figure 12.8)

Figure 12.19. The Moko Moko from the house. Source: Photo by Lorraine BERRY

Figure 12.20. The Three Sisters. Source: Photo by Lorraine BERRY

Tadpoles in the pond on the property were fun to catch in hopes of seeing them become frogs. Parents were probably unaware of how many birds' nests in the nearby bush were raided for no good reason, but to take the eggs. Tussocks provided a natural bed to lie in and watch the ever-changing clouds pass by and excite the imagination. Without artificial lighting to impede its magic, the night sky could be gazed at in awe and the aurora australis left an indelible memory of colourful, dancing lights.

Figure 12.21. Looking towards the pond and house site from the Moko Moko. Source: Photo by Lorraine BERRY

Frances was inventive with meals, making use of the natural environment when available. Water cress abounded in the clear streams, delicious with marmite as a sandwich. Fathen also served as greens.[27] Flounder netted in the channel of the tidal estuary, the occasional sack of oysters from Bluff or mussels, paua and lobster from the back beach all added to the diet. The annual migration of the southern muttonbird brought another delicacy. Although rather fatty, they were very satisfying. Seasonal gathering of blackberries and mushrooms were relished. Neighbours would share the meat of a pig or sheep from a kill. Frances thought that Jack made a very good baker. He was critical of commercially made bread and specialised in a type that expanded very quickly in the oven.[28]

Frances enjoyed reading books for relaxation. Frances Parkinson Keyes was a popular choice when Rosalie or Lorraine went to the London Book Shop in Invercargill to borrow books for her. Her other request was to come home with Pixie caramel bars, her favourite treat. The two oldest boys liked comics and wild west stories by Zane Grey. Neville was excited to be given a cowboy suit with two wooden pistols carved by his father.[29] The girls also liked authors such as Enid Blyton and the Pollyanna books. They had cloth dolls, usually made by grandma

MITCHELL, and celluloid kewpie dolls as well as paper cut-outs. Colouring in was popular. They also liked collecting pictures of film stars, though picture theatres were beyond reach, and pieces of coloured glass. Radio listening was limited to newscasts as it was battery run. Jack was a talented piano player and the family would have sing-songs to his music. He was also clever at drawing cartoons. He would quote Shakespeare easily and owned two large volumes of the writer's works.[30]

Jack was still troubled by the blame given him by one brother in particular for the 'loss' of the Gibbston run thirty years earlier. Much rancour had persisted through the years and, in response to an unexpected meeting between the two, he felt the need to explain to his brother-in-law Arnold GRUBB, who had witnessed the scene, by letter. He claimed that he had followed the law and whatever he did was for the love of his mother.[31]

Figure 12.22. Lorraine and Neville watching cousin Ken unload the Morris truck at Kapuka, c.1950. Source: author's collection

Raymond, George and Kenneth were fond of their Uncle Jack. Ray recalled a particular occasion when he was travelling with his brother Donald or George, a distance of 22.5 miles (36.3km) from Kapuka to Greenhills by horse-drawn vehicle. They went to do cultivation, to plough and work up the ground for winter feed. Their Uncle Jack also wanted contour drains around each paddock. The weather was wintery that day. They got wet and felt cold and miserable. The boys would take turns at driving the horses, Taupo and Bluey, and walking to keep their circulation going. Eventually it was so cold Ray couldn't walk any further. Allan CHALMERS never forgot the bitterly cold pervasive south-west winds that howled in the large macrocarpa trees that lined the property.[32] The predominant direction of the wind showed in the angle of all the trees and shrubs in the area. Visits by the Kapuka cousins also meant haircutting sessions for anyone who needed it and that was probably everyone.[33]

Cousins Ray, George and Ken would take the older children Rosalie, Allan, Neville and Lorraine to stay with them at Kapuka when Maribel was there to help. George and Ken would collect them and drive back to Kapuka in their truck. Lorraine remembered the bright lights of rabbits' eyes lit up by the car lights throughout the night-time journeys. It was fun on the farm. Ray allowed the children to 'drive' the tractor and George and Ken, from a distance, let them watch dynamite explosions to bring down the coal. (See Figures 8.4. and 12.22)

The girls' cousins would also go to Arrowtown, to spend summer school holidays. One summer at Arrowtown they used a bulldozer to make a swimming hole for the children to enjoy on hot days. Here is a letter from that time that Frances wrote to Maribel:

Dear Maribel
The girls are very pleased about going up to you tomorrow.
Lorraine's things are not as nice as I would have liked them to be. But I have had short notice & have been so busy with strawberry picking up to fifteen pounds every day for the last fortnight & still a lot to pick yet.
Rosalie will be pleased about going with the boys though. She was a bit worried about going on the bus on their own. It is good of the boys to take them.
I hope they will be good & Rosalie will be able to help you in the house. Lorraine is good at outside work.
I will send the money for their return fare up to you Marribel if you will tell me how much.
Lorraine's coat is very shabby & too short for her. I was going to get her one when I got the children's money on Tuesday but perhaps she won't need one much up there.
I must close as we have to be up early.
Love from Frances xx[34]

The trip to Arrowtown was scary, especially on the road around Lake Wakatipu. The Devil's Staircase winds its way at quite a height along the southern arm of the lake and from the truck it seemed there was nothing between it and the water below. (See Figures 12.23, 12.24 and 12.25.)

Figure 12.23. Cousins George and Ken with the CHALMERS Brothers' Morris truck and Rosalie and Lorraine on the way to Arrowtown. Source: author's collection

Figure 12.24. Rosalie and Lorraine in front of the CHALMERS' cottage at Arrowtown c.1948. Source: author's collection

Figure 12.25. Rosalie and Lorraine with a friend of Jessie at the Arrow River c.1948. Source: author's collection

Niece Jessie CHALMERS liked to go to Greenhills. She was fond of children and found her Auntie Frances to be kind and friendly, who did her best and was hospitable. She recognised that she did not have much to put together but Frances did what she could. In the summertime Jessie would join with the family for a picnic and remembered going into the bush by horse and dray.[35] Ray also recalled taking a horse and dray across the Moko Moko Estuary at the bottom of the farm and how the water came up to the horse's belly as it crossed the channel.[36]

As time went on, resources became more scarce. Jack was less able or inclined to take up work opportunities. He spoke of being in pain from time to time and was nearly sixty when the last child, Barry Lionel was born. Neighbour Agnes FRASER recalled a morning when he called at their place to see if they had seen his cow. They hadn't, but when he got home he found her in the bail where she had stayed from the previous night's milking. Agnes's husband 'Dan got him a job cutting grass in the orchard of another neighbour. It was a hot day and Jack decided to take a breather in the shade of an apple tree. He closed his eyes and nodded off. The neighbour was not too pleased!'[37] Allan enjoyed farm work and helped wherever he could, according to his age.

Eventually Social Welfare became the sole means of income and on benefit day Frances, or one of the older girls, would travel by train to Invercargill to buy the food supply. Usually they would be met at the station by someone to help carry the goods home by horse and dray or sled or the jogger that had pneumatic tyres and was driven by pedal power. It was designed and made by Jack with Allan's help.[38]

Rosalie was a big help until she reached secondary school age when her responsibilities were taken over by Lorraine. She attended Southland Girls' High School and would spend the week staying with Grandma MITCHELL and Mervan and Elinor MACARTNEY at their Elles Road South home in Invercargill. Her uniform and book requirements were paid for by them. Not many months after starting high school she began to stay over on Saturday nights and help with Saturday's housekeeping tasks and grocery buying. Grandad MITCHELL was able to get up and sit in a chair when the family lived at Fox Street, Cambden Road and Melbourne Street. But he had become bedridden with arthritis by the time they moved to Elles Road and Grandma spent her days looking after him. Adults found him difficult to help while Rosalie was able to distract him by having him cut out pictures from the Auckland Weekly for her scrapbook.[39]

Allan attended Southland Technical College when he finished primary school. Train travel was the means to get there from Greenhills.

Needs at Greenhills were met by Child Welfare supplemented by the Women's Division of Federated Farmers to which Frances still belonged. Percy SMITH, the local store owner, was generous in giving credit when the family ran out of money. After school he would always add broken biscuits to the grocery order, for hungry children. Kind neighbours, particularly the McINTYRE family, offered food and clothing from time to time. Grandma MITCHELL made dresses for the girls.

Frances was concerned with everyone's needs and perhaps no-one noticed hers. Despite her circumstances, she was not known to complain. She said to Lorraine several times that her

Figure 12.26. Rosalie in high school uniform, c.1950. Source: author's collection

heart hurt, but she would not have known what to do about it. And so it was that her death at the age of forty-three was unexpected. When Frances was on her way to catch the train or bus she collapsed on the road and died from a heart condition, angina pectoris. It was 27 June 1952.[40] The shock and grief experienced by the family, close and extended, was profound. According to his wife Vera, Frances' only brother Jack had never been so distraught or shown such sorrow.

214

Figure 12.27. Frances (right), her sister Elizabeth (Back) and their mother Rosa MITCHELL, 1951. Source: author's collection

At Greenhills when Jack answered the door to the police he was given the terrible news. Lorraine was at home looking after the younger children at the time. At least two of those who were at school that day were taken in by kind neighbours until new homes were found. Uncle Donald CHALMERS and Auntie Maribel came to the house and looked after those remaining. They stayed for about two weeks. Rosalie had turned fifteen just four days earlier and had taken up office work at Herbert Haynes store in Invercargill where she had been living. One by one those looked after by Aunty Maribel said goodbye to their father at the gate, never to return as a family.

Just over two weeks after Frances' passing her oldest sister Elizabeth COLE returned to the property and recorded her feelings:

Yesterday Ted and I went back to the house again, just our two selves. It was awful – so suddenly quiet – so absolutely desolate. … It was a lovely winter afternoon, across the beach it was like a mirror. But so quiet – so forsaken. Ted went back to the car and I went around Frances' garden alone. I looked at the flowers & shrubs. I leaned on the fence and sobbed. The cat came out from the bushes and rubbed against my legs. I went to the house to find the furniture was gone and the house cleaned. But the awful stillness – you know all the thoughts that crowded my mind and not a thing can be altered now. It seemed the only time I had given her alone. ... All the time my mind calls Frances. Frances. Frances. – the little girl she once was. I'm going to miss her terribly. Because in spite of all the worry she was to us there was a courage and a strength about her that I knew was always there that I could depend on. As a little girl she never complained. She would have toothache all night but never bother anybody. If she was sick she would just lie so quiet and now she is so quiet. She was always so worried if we were sick. She came straight up to see Ted when she knew he had to be x-rayed. But her death was so tragic.

Figure 12.28. CHALMERS' family home remains many years later. Source: author's collection

Jack was adamant that the family remain together, but who would be in charge and how would they be supported? Rosalie also wished for that to happen but she was too young. It remained for the two families to decide where and by whom the children would be cared for. Most of the aunts and uncles were older with grown-up families and no-one was well off financially. For those who took on the responsibility it must have been at great sacrifice. Family meetings, chaired by Mervan MACARTNEY, were ongoing until resolutions were found.[41] Visits and correspondence were maintained over many months, even years.[42]

Inevitably the practical solution was that the children should be cared for by separate branches of the family:

Eleanor Rosalie remained with Grandma MITCHELL and the MACARTNEY family in Invercargill. After their mother's death, brother

Peter came to stay. She cried and begged Cyril and Edith BUXTON not to take him away for adoption. They said they would never separate him from her. Later she became married to Ron BLANCHARD, neighbour of the BUXTON family. Having trained as a nurse Rosalie was called on to help with problems as time went on and take younger children to relieve caregivers, provide nursing care during sickness and for holidays.[43] Rosalie married Roland Thomas BLANCHARD at Invercargill on 30 January 1960.

- Allan Mitchell lived with cousins Robert and Noeline WATSON and family at Spar Bush. He attended Southland Technical College, took up fencing work in the Te Anau district and eventually settled on his own farm there. Allan married Glenda Elaine HART at Auckland on 14 October 1960.

- Neville John moved to Winton with Auntie Gertie and Uncle Phil BOYLEN. After completing secondary school at Winton District High School he entered banking as a career. Neville married Valerie Elizabeth O'DOCHERTY at Lumsden on 9 October 1965.

- Lorraine Elizabeth went with Uncle Arnold and Auntie Dora GRUBB (née CHALMERS) to Gore. She attended Gore Primary and Gore High Schools, spent a year as a nurse aide in the maternity wing of Gore Hospital and took up primary schoolteaching from Dunedin Teacher's College. Lorraine married Johnstone Rayden BERRY at Perth, Australia on 24 December 1964.

- David Basil was taken in by Uncle Rupert and Auntie Jen (Janet) CHALMERS who lived at Invercargill and shifted to Christchurch later on. At school leaving age he returned to Invercargill to become a telegraph delivery boy. From there he moved to Wellington for further training with the post office. David married Lynette Elizabeth WILSON at Wellington on 1 September 1962.

- Martin Lovett spent the remainder of the year with the John and Agnes McINTYRE family at Greenhills. From there he moved to Arrowtown and spent a year with Uncle Donald and Auntie Maribel CHALMERS. Then he moved to Kapuka to be with cousins George and Airlie CHALMERS. After time in the army, Martin took up employment with the Department of Agriculture and Fisheries. He married Dorothy Elizabeth HORNE at Mosgiel on 20 April 1968.

- Josephine Violet went to Winton initially and stayed with William and Eleanor EGERTON (née BOYLEN). Later she moved to Arrowtown to be with Uncle Donald and Auntie Maribel CHALMERS. After attending Queenstown District High School she moved to Wellington to train as a nurse. Josephine married Grant Cleaver ANCELL on 23 December 1974.

- Charles Hector went with Auntie Isa MARTIN (née MITCHELL) and husband Uncle Roy to Henderson, Auckland. He stayed for about eighteen months before returning south to join Martin living with George and Airlie CHALMERS at Kapuka. Charles attended Southland Boys' High School and studied at Otago University to become a secondary school teacher. Charles married Rosalie Christine FERGUSON at Dunedin on 22 December 1970.

- Stephen James stayed with George and Florence McRAE, friends of Frances' MITCHELL family at Mokoreta for a while, then joined Lorraine and Barry at Gore. Later he went to a children's home at Invercargill run by the Presbyterian Social Services Association. He attended Southland Boys' High School and trained to be a physiotherapist at Dunedin. Stephen married Marianne (Mandy) Shirley WATSON at Timaru on 11 September 1971.

- Peter Arthur was the only child who was adopted. He would become part of the family of Cyril and Edith BUXTON and their two daughters at Flint's Bush in Southland. Edith was a younger sister of Frances' close friend Mavis JEWITT of Spar Bush and later of Riverton. Peter attended Southland Boys' High School and became a hairdresser. Eventually he went to London and managed theatres there.

- Barry Lionel lived with Arnold and Dora GRUBB at Gore, along with Lorraine and eventually Stephen. He attended Gore Primary and High School and studied to become a landscape architect. Barry married Jocelyn Margaret KERSE at Tapanui on 6 March 1974.

Jack was admitted to Riverton Hospital and ultimately committed to Seacliff Mental Hospital. He had had the right to refuse the adoption of any of his children. Once he was committed, his wish of keeping the family together would be denied and children could be adopted outside of the family.[44]

As registered nurses, Rosalie and Josephine did not agree with the diagnosis that he suffered from senile psychosis (10 years).[45] It is more likely there was no-one to take care of him and a matter of convenience. All three daughters kept in touch with him through the years. There was no doubt that he was depressed. Letters and visits to see him at Cherry Farm Hospital at Waikouaiti showed a lonely man who grieved for a very long time, who loved his children and was still concerned for the welfare of each.[46]

Jack died on 16 September 1963. He and Frances are buried together at Eastern Cemetery, Invercargill. (See Figure 12.28) The headstone reads:

IN LOVING MEMORY OF
FRANCES LOUISA BEVAN CHALMERS
DIED 27TH JUNE 1952
AND HER BELOVED HUSBAND
JOHN CHARLES
DIED 16TH SEP 1963

Figure 12.29. Jack and Frances CHALMERS headstone. Source: author's collection

More about each of the children and their careers is told in the various chapters of this book as well as the MITCHELL and PINK books, mentioned earlier. Peter Arthur was never forgotten. As promised, the BUXTON family included Rosalie as one of their own. When Peter went to London to live she made trips to visit him there. He had trained to be a hairdresser in New Zealand and pursued his interest in the arts by becoming a theatre manager in London. Prior to his death in 1994 Peter made one last visit to New Zealand and met with each of his birth family members. Rosalie made a final trip to London to attend to his affairs. She brought back his ashes. They lie with those of the BUXTON family at Calcium Cemetery at Isla Bank in Southland. Although he had been out of touch with all his other siblings throughout his life, he had not forgotten them. Peter had chosen momentos of his life for each of his brothers and sisters and they were distributed by Rosalie on her return.

Figure 12.31. Rosalie with Peter BUXTON at a picnic, c.1953. Source: author's collection

Figure 12.32. Peter, c.1956. Source: author's collection

Figure 12.33. Peter BUXTON in London. Source: author's collection

Figure 12.34. The BUXTON headstone at the Calcium Cemetery, Isla Bank. Source: author's collection

Figure 12.35. John and Frances CHALMERS' children, 1957. L to R: David, Charles, Lorraine, Josephine, Rosalie, Barry, Alan (back), Stephen, Martin, Neville. Absent: Peter. Source: author's collection

Five and a half years later the family was reunited for the wedding of cousin Jessie CHALMERS to Aike KIEL at Queenstown. (See Figure 12.30.)

Beginning in 1977, Jack and Frances CHALMERS' children held a reunion every five years at which Peter was remembered. These have been well documented by photographs.[47] One special occasion was the 1992 reunion at Omaui, near Greenhills, in honour of their parents. The 2007 reunion at Queenstown, near Arrowtown and Gibbston, was in recognition of the CHALMERS grandparents, John Howe CHALMERS and Eleanor Rebecca TIMS. (See Chapter 1.) Extended family members also attended.

Jack's and Frances' family of eleven children produced thirty-two grandchildren.

NOTES

[1] Where not otherwise stated most of the text came from: *Early Childhood Memories* by Eleanor Rosalie BLANCHARD (née CHALMERS); *Memories of Greenhills Thru the Mind of Neville Chalmers* by Neville John CHALMERS; *Memoirs of Greenhills* by Lorraine Elizabeth BERRY (née CHALMERS) *Origins: Omaui Greenhills* by Martin Lovett CHALMERS.

[2] Ray CHALMERS, pers. com.

[3] Marriage Certificate, John Charles CHALMERS and Frances Louisa Beaven MITCHELL, 22 December 1936, Invercargill, RGO Wellington, in possession of the author.

[4] Jessie KIEL (née CHALMERS), pers. com.; Thelma GEARY (née BOYLEN), pers. com

[5] Ken CHALMERS, pers. com.

[6] Jessie KIEL (née CHALMERS), pers. com

[7] CHALMERS, John Charles, farmer, Greenhills, Awarua Electoral Rolls, 1946 and 1949; CHALMERS, Frances, Greenhills, Awarua Electoral Rolls, 1946 and 1949.

[8] J.E. Bremner, *The History of Greenhills* (details unkown).

[9] Neville CHALMERS, pers. com.

[10] Rosalie BLANCHARD (née CHALMERS), pers. com.

[11] Letter from Agnes FRASER to author, March 1992.

[12] Ken CHALMERS, pers. com.

[13] Dora GRUBB (née CHALMERS), pers. com.

[14] Martin CHALMERS, pers. com.

[15] Rosalie BLANCHARD (née CHALMERS), pers. com.

[16] Eulogy notes for David CHALMERS.

[17] Dora GRUBB, pers. com.

[18] Letter by Gertrude BOYLEN née CHALMERS) to relatives in England.

[19] Death Certificate, Violet Hoppner CHALMERS, 1947/19503, CHALMERS, Violet Hoppner, 61 years.

[20] Invercargill City Council, Cemetery Database, https://icc.govt.nz/cemetery-result/?id=30825

[21] Rosalie BLANCHARD (née CHALMERS), pers. com.

[22] Robert WATSON, pers. com.

[23] Jan Mitchell, *A history of Greenhills area & the oldest remaining wooden church in the Invercargill area.* (Details unknown.)

[24] Jan MITCHELL, pers. com.

[25] Ibid.

[26] Neville CHALMERS, pers. com.

[27] Ibid.

[28] Rosalie BLANCHARD (née CHALMERS), pers. com.

[29] Neville CHALMERS, pers. com.

[30] CHALMERS family collecfion.

[31] Letter from J.C. CHALMERS to Arnold GRUBB, 1946.

[32] Allan CHALMERS, pers. com.

[33] Martin CHALMERS, pers. com.

[34] Letter from Frances CHALMERS to Maribel CHALMERS, undated.

[35] Jessie KIEL (née CHALMERS), pers. com

[36] Ray CHALMERS, pers. com.

[37] Letter from Agnes FRASER to the author, March 1992.

[38] Martin CHALMERS, pers. com.

[39] Rosalie BLANCHARD (née CHALMERS), pers. com.

[40] Newspaper death notice.

[41] Mervan MACARTNEY, pers. com.

[42] Letters in CHALMERS family collecfion.

[43] Letters to Rosalie BLANCHARD (née CHALMERS) from Dora GRUBB.

[44] Letters by family members in CHALMERS family collecfion.

[45] Notice of Death Under the Mental Health Act 1911. Signed 17 September 1963 by the medical superintendent.

[46] Letters from J.C. CHALMERS to Lorraine CHALMERS; Letter from the hospital chaplain, Seacliff Hospital Presbyterian Church of New Zealand 11 July 1962 to Josephine CHALMERS.

[47] Author's collection.

13 Gertrude Elizabeth CHALMERS and Philip BOYLEN

Figure 13.1. Gertrude CHALMERS. Source: author's collection

Gertrude CHALMERS' future husband, Philip BOYLEN, was born at Tapanui, New Zealand on 9 February 1893.[1] His parents were of the Catholic faith and born in Ireland. They had married in November 1885 at Ballyscullion, Ireland. John BOYLEN was a labourer aged 27 and Susan SCULLION was aged 25 at the time.[2]

Their year of immigration to New Zealand and names of any accompanying children are not known. In 1890 John BOYLEN was a successful applicant for land by ballot in acquiring Section 40, Block IV at Greenvale, on the west side of the Blue Mountains between Heriot and Beaumont. It consisted of 3 acres 1 rood 6 perches with an annual rent of 10 shillings. Thirty-eight sections in the Greenvale, Crookston and Warepa districts had been thrown open under the village homestead system for the purpose of providing homes for villagers. Holders of other lands exceeding one acre in extent were not eligible as selectors. Married men were given preference.[3]

In 1900 the family was living at Heriot where John worked as a surfaceman (road worker) until about 1911.[4]

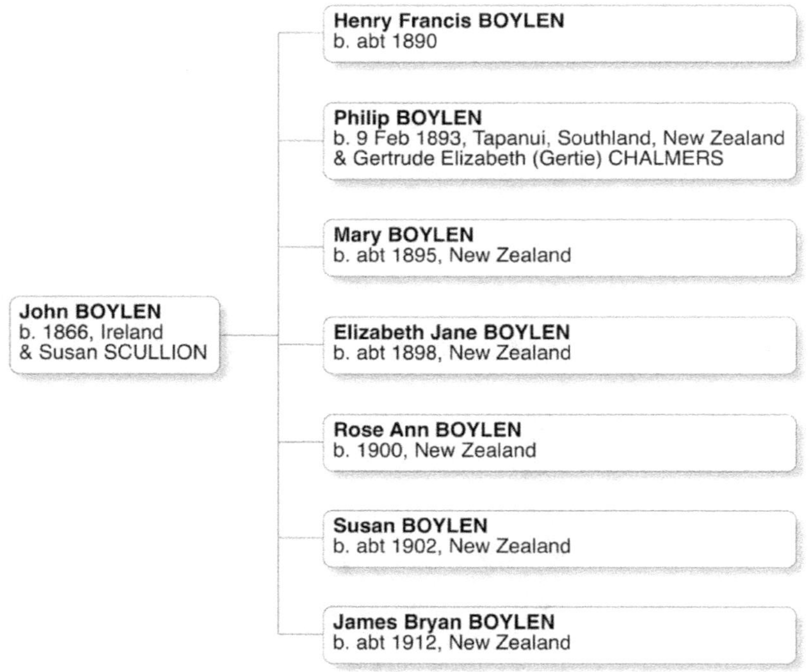

Figure 13.2. The children of John and Susan BOYLEN

By 1912 their family of seven known children was complete. The identities of any children born outside of New Zealand have not been found. The names of six children, including that of Philip, appear in the New Zealand register of births, deaths and marriages. (See Figure 13.2.) Henry's birth is shown in his N.Z. certificate of death.

In 1914 John and Susan BOYLEN bought property at Wangaloa on the coast southeast of Balclutha.

> WANGALOA.
> FROM OUR OWN CORRESPONDENT. A great many changes have taken place in this district since I wrote last. First, Mr CARSON sold his farm to Mr BOYLEN, of Heriot.[5]

They spent the rest of their lives working as farmers at Wangaloa in the Bruce district.[6] In 1914 Philip was a clerk at Heriot where he lived with his brother Henry.[7] By 1 September 1915 he had moved to Beaumont where he became joint owner of the Chalmers Store with Douglas CHALMERS.[8] He quickly became involved in social and sporting activities in the district and, along with John Howe CHALMERS, contributed items in a programme of songs and recitations in honour of a couple who had sold their run and were moving to Nightcaps.[9]

Philip and Gertrude Elizabeth CHALMERS were married on 20 May 1916 at St Joseph's Catholic Church vestry at Dunedin. Philip's occupation was a soldier at the time. Also married on the same day and in the same place were Constance Eleanor CHALMERS and James McKIBBIN, Constance being Gertrude's twin sister.[10]

The CHALMERS twins were not of the Catholic faith, therefore they were married in the vestry rather than before the altar in the main part of the church. Within a matter of days following his marriage, Philip was to leave for military service and a farewell social was held in his honour.

Figure 13.3 Philip BOYLEN.
Source: author's collection

SOCIALS AND PRESENTATIONS. To Private P. BOYLEN. On Friday evening, May 26th, a social and dance was held in the Public Hall, Beaumont, to bid farewell to Private BOYLEN who was on his final leave before leaving for the front with the 14th Reinforcements. The hall was packed with friends and wellwishers to say good-bye to the departing soldier who was a favourite in the district. Excellent music was supplied by Mrs T. DWYER in the early part of the night. After a few dances, Mr J. A. TEMPLETON sang a Patriotic song which was received with applause. Mr A. THOMSON then presented Private BOYLEN with a silver mounted fountain pen from his many friends in Beaumont. While making the presentation, Mr THOMSON referred to Private BOYLEN's connection with the local cricket, tennis, and football clubs in which he took a leading part during just three years' stay in Beaumont. He also referred to Private BOYLEN's latest step in taking unto himself a wife before he left for the scene of action. Mrs BOYLEN is a local lady, having been connected with our local store for the last eight years, and a great favourite with all who came in contact with her.

She was congratulated on the great sacrifice she was making in letting her husband go to the war. After refreshments had been handed round, dancing was commenced in real earnest by both old and young, the guest of the evening taking a leading part. Owing to there being a slight misunderstanding the musician did not turn up, but Mr W. BUCHANAN, a very old resident of Beaumont, came to light, and with the assistance of Mr Charles JOHNSON at the piano the music was worth going a long way to hear. Mr BUCHANAN's playing was something out of the ordinary and he fairly surprised the natives, and his services will be much sought after when the next batch of reinforcements leave Beaumont, and it is to be hoped he will come forward again. Dancing was kept up until early morning when all went home after thoroughly enjoying themselves. Thanks are due to the Beaumont Hall Committee for the free use of the hall, also to those who worked so hard to make the social such a success.[11]

Philip's war record gives his occupation on entering military service as baker at Beaumont. He became a lance corporal in the army on 7 October 1918 and was promoted to sergeant on 26 December 1918. Under the heading 'Special Instances of Gallant or Meritorious Conduct' Philip is mentioned in dispatches for distinguished and gallant service and devotion to duty during the period 16 September 1918 to 5 March 1919.[12] Philip had the added honour of being sergeant to the Prince of Wales' Guards when the soldiers marched to Germany after peace was proclaimed. He was given a certificate for special services in the field during the war. Gertrude had it framed to prevent it from being knocked about in any way.[13]

After the war he and Gertrude lived at Heriot where Philip worked as a storeman.[14] Philip was a keen rugby player and also played for the Heriot Cricket Team. They had two children, daughters Eleanor and Thelma. (See Figure 13.5.) Their first child was born on 3 February 1920.

BIRTH.
BOYLEN. – At Nurse McLean's, Tapanui, on February 3, 1920, to Mr and Mrs P. BOYLEN – a daughter.[15]

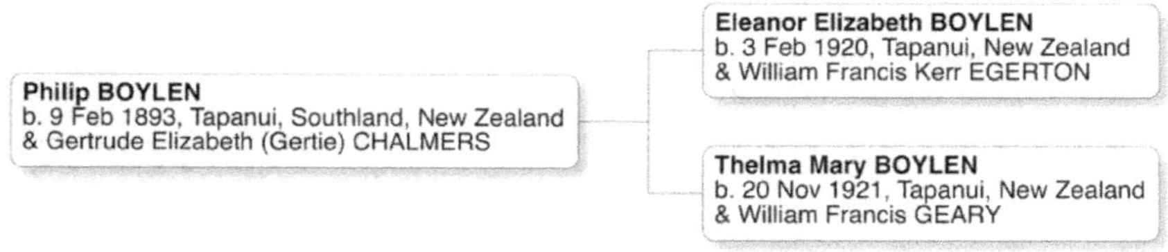

Figure 13.4. The children of Gertrude CHALMERS and Philip BOYLEN

Figure 13.5. Heriot Cricket Team, winners of the District Premiership. Back row (from left.): G. RICHARDS, H. MURPHY (scorer). D. DUN, W. TRIP, B. OTTREY (president), J. TRIP. Front row: S. OTTREY, M. O'DRISCOLL, P. BOYLEN, G. DUTHIE (captain), A. REID, A. OTTREY, W. HAUGH. Source: Otago Witness. April 20, 1920, Supplement

Figure 13.6. (L to R) Eleanor, Gertrude, Thelma and Philip. Source: GEARY family

In 1928 Philip became storekeeper in partnership with Sydney OTTREY at Kelso, just a few miles from Beaumont. (See Figure 13.6, Sydney is on the left in the front row.) Kelso is now an abandoned small settlement in Otago, located 10km north of Tapanui on the Crookston Burn, close to its junction with the larger Pomahaka River. A small dairy factory was a focal point in the village's early years. The township was first surveyed in 1875, and the first settlement began the following year. (See Figure 13.7.) It was named for the Scottish home town of one of the town's first settlers, James LOGAN. Originally intended as the main settlement in the West Otago area, this title eventually went to nearby Tapanui. The town was linked to Waipahi and the Main South Line railway on 1 December 1880 with the opening of the Tapanui Branch line. On 1 April 1884, this line was extended from Kelso to Heriot.[16] (See Figure 13.8.)

Figure 13.7. Kelso Dairy Factory. Source: author's collection

The township was frequently subject to flooding, notably in 1913 and 1917.[17] Philip and Gertrude remained there throughout the Depression years.[18]

Philip was popular keeping up the best traditions of a Kelso storekeeper in his stay of seven years. At that time it was the typical country store selling articles to meet the needs of the small farmer and township household. Billies hung from the roof, staples and nails came from a wooden box to be sold for 9d per pound, while all groceries were packed from a bulk supply as they were ordered over the counter. This meant loose biscuits from a tin, sugar and flour either by the bag (70 or 25 lb) or a brown paper bag. Eggs were sold by the dozen. These in turn came from the local farms as payment for store orders.[19]

At this time shop hours were changed. Friday closing at 9 p.m. replaced 10 o'clock on Saturday. The Wednesday half-day at that time was replaced by Saturday lunchtime closing. The *Otago Daily Times* was delivered by the railway bus at lunchtime. Papers were numbered for customers to collect on the step in the afternoon. During the week their place on the counter encouraged the additional daily purchase. Orders were delivered by van twice weekly by George BRANDIGAN who had been long in the employ of Phil BOYLEN. George, a bachelor, was deaf. Orders were shouted at him as the telephone was beyond his range of hearing.[20]

Philip was known for his generosity, as is shown by this donation:

THE CANCER CAMPAIGN
OTAGO AND SOUTHLAND LIST.
PUBLIC SUBSCRIPTIONS.[21]

Previously acknowledged	£13,406	3	0
BOYLEN and OTTREY, Kelso	£ 3	3	0
Total	£13,400	6	0

Eleanor and Thelma attended the Convent School at Gore. It was situated near the bridge in West Gore. In a letter written in 1933 to her cousin Margaret Gertrude STOKES in England Gertrude wrote: 'My two girls have learnt music. I have Mother's piano, which is over forty years old, and still quite good. Mother was a clever pianist and I remember her saying Aunt Clara (Margaret's mother) was more clever than she.' Gertrude also taught her niece Jessie, daughter of Donald and Maribel CHALMERS, to play the piano. Eleanor had left school by the age of fourteen while Thelma continued as a weekday boarder at the convent in Gore, thirty miles away. She travelled home for the weekends.

Philip was an enthusiastic and successful fisherman.[22] In 1931 he was president of the Tapanui Anglers' Society.[23]

> A party of local anglers, comprising Messrs J. D. EDGAR, K. RODGER, J. S. VARCOE, P. BOYLEN and W. ELLIOTT, the latter from Dunedin, visited Makarora last week and report good sport amongst the quinnat salmon, most of which were caught at the mouth of the river where it enters Lake Wanaka. As the result of their expedition a total of 94 fish was caught, ranging from two to 19.5 lbs, the latter being caught by Mr P. BOYLEN, who also secured a nineteen pounder.[24]

The preliminary moves to build a new public hall at Kelso were made in 1933. Mr LUSK of the Agricultural and Pastoral Society was of the opinion that the public should build its own hall and leave his Society out altogether. The building committee consisted of nine members, including Phil BOYLEN. The starting date was decided on 4 March 1935 when the site was to be made ready and the committee reformed. The official opening of the Kelso Hall was held on Friday, 30 August at 8 pm.

Phil BOYLEN, as man of the hour, confident, as he had been throughout the campaign, called Laurie KIRK to the stage, describing him as 'a Kelso old boy who had given him a real good spin throughout.' Laurie KIRK, in turn, presented him with the key of the hall. The ball then was proceeded with, surely a great night for Kelso. Many names, now forgotten, gave willing help in finishing off the hall. Mrs BOYLEN and Cora BLAMIRES sewed and hung the curtains of blue and gold, which gave the interior a touch of glamour.[25]

Figure 13.8. Kelso railway station, 1915. Source: author's collection

On Saturday evening of 16 April 1934 the West Otago Ex-servicemen's sub-branch met at Kitchin's Hall, Kelso. There was a good attendance of returned soldiers. 'Mr P. BOYLEN said the meeting was called for the purpose of forming a sub-association in the district, covering the area from Tapanui to Moa Flat. Mr BOYLEN introduced and welcomed Messrs J. A. ROY and W. TAYLOR, of the Clinton association.' Mr P. BOYLEN was elected President.[26]

The BOYLEN family was able to get through the Depression years with much less difficulty than many others. They assisted struggling family members where they could. These included Donald and Maribel CHALMERS and Rupert and Janet CHALMERS and all of their children who were enrolled at the Kelso School. (See Table 13.1.) The fathers of

232

these children had found employment in the district at roadmaking and forestry.

Table 13.1. CHALMERS children who attended Kelso School 1933-1936[27]

Years	Pupils	Parents
1933-34	Jessie CHALMERS	Donald and Maribel CHALMERS
	Donald CHALMERS	
	Raymond CHALMERS	
	May CHALMERS	Rupert and Janet CHALMERS
1935	George CHALMERS	Donald and Maribel CHALMERS
1936	Kenneth CHALMERS	Donald and Maribel CHALMERS
	Albert Gordon (Sonny) CHALMERS	Rupert and Janet CHALMERS

By February 1935 both Eleanor and Thelma BOYLEN had left school. Their mother was not keen for them to become teachers and did not think it necessary to give them any further schooling. They took week about working with their father to help lighten his duties. As well as their help he employed a shop assistant and a delivery man.[28]

Figure 13.9. Eleanor BOYLEN at Kelso.
Source: author's collection

Gertrude Elizabeth had experienced complications after the birth of Thelma and was never comfortable walking after that. She sat for most of the time and ran the household by instruction. Trained by their mother, the girls became very good cooks.[29]

The girls took a keen interest in basketball (latterly known as netball). They felt very pleased with themselves on their Kelso team gaining second place. Gertrude liked seeing them having fun together at home. She needed one of the girls to be with her to call on for help at all times. She was grateful for Phil's willingness to chop the firewood and keep the coal bucket full.[30]

In 1936 Gertrude's sister Dora and her fiancé Arnold GRUBB came to stay for a fortnight so that she could do all she could to help with wedding preparations in the absence of their mother. Arnold had provided the family with an all-wave Gulbransen radio that they found very impressive in keeping the family informed of important events in the world.

Other family members came to visit. They included Norman McKIBBIN, son of Gertie's twin sister Constance. Her brother Malcolm also came from time to time. Eleanor and Thelma spent holidays with their paternal grandparents, John and Susan BOYLEN at Wangaloa, on the coast sixty three miles from Kelso.

Figure 13.10. 'Roseneath,' the BOYLEN farm at Wangaloa. Source: GEARY family

Gertrude enjoyed her home and a garden that produced colourful displays of traditional flowers. There was also a productive vegetable garden. She was happy to spend most of her time indoors, apart from weekly outings to church and Bible class. At the same time she liked to see Philip taking time out from business concerns to take part in outdoor activities that duly changed from team field games to golf, fishing and seasonal duck shooting expeditions.[31]

Figure 13.11. The BOYLEN Family (L to R): Thelma, Eleanor, Philip (son), Mary (née SCULLION), James Bryan (son), John, Susan (daughter) and Gertrude (née CHALMERS). Source: GEARY family

Philip was frequently involved in local and district interests. He represented the Kelso Domain Board at a meeting held to discuss the pros and cons of amalgamation between the various local bodies, known as domain boards, that was proposed by the Government's Amalgamation Bill.

A conference of representatives of Tuapeka County and of all the local bodies within the area of Tuapeka County for the purpose of discussing the Government's proposed Amalgamation Bill which will be brought before the House of representatives at the next session of Parliament was held in the Tuapeka County Council Chamber, Lawrence, on Friday afternoon. Among the delegates for the various bodies were: – Kelso Domain Board. – Mr BOYLEN.

BOYLEN and J. SIM, representing the various Domain Boards, expressed the opinion that amalgamation would be of no benefit to these bodies; that their revenue was infinitesimal, and their administrative costs nil. After a lengthy discussion in which various views regarding the nature of the motion expressing the meeting's views, the following resolution was passed: – Moved: 'That this meeting consisting of representatives of local bodies in the Tuapeka County, is of the opinion that amalgamation of any of these bodies in undesirable, for the following reasons, (1) The services of members of these bodies are given free of cost. (2) That the present system takes full advantage of the local knowledge of members. (3) That amalgamation, if carried, would result in an increase of cost and corresponding loss of efficiency; the present system being more economical and efficient. (4) The valuable means of educating the youngest settlers to manage civic affairs would be lessened.'[32]

Philip BOYLEN was one of the returned servicemen from four districts who was given the opportunity to join with fellow Anzacs for Anzac Day celebrations in Australia. According to the *Otago Daily Times* "Country News" of 21 April 1938:

Returned Soldiers
Messrs J. S. ADAM and A. BATHGATE (Crookston). P. BOYLEN and D. GIBSON (Kelso), A. G. DUMBLETON, J. C. CAMERON, H. J. HAY, J. W. JOHNSTON, A. W. MUNYARD, and C. MURRAY (Tapanui) left on Sunday morning to join the special train at Waipahi en route for Wellington to join the New Zealand delegation of returned soldiers who will take part in the Anzac celebrations in Sydney with the returned soldiers and sailors of the Imperial League of Australia.[33]

At about the same time the family was given a farewell by the Kelso community.

Farewell Gathering
A large and enthusiastic gathering of district residents tendered a farewell social to Mr and Mrs P. BOYLEN and family at Kelso last Wednesday evening on the eve of their departure for Winton, where Mr BOYLEN has purchased a business.[34]

The person who bought the Kelso Store from Philip was the last owner until its demolition.[35] Today, little remains to indicate the location of Kelso, other than a stone memorial and faded wording referring to the township on several remaining buildings.[36]

In May of 1938 the BOYLEN family moved to Winton, sixty-seven miles from Kelso, where Philip took up business as a draper. They stayed there for the rest of their lives.[37]

Soon after the family arrived at Winton Philip applied to have his membership with the Returned Servicemen's Association transferred accordingly. 'The West Otago and Mataura Sub-Associations had respectively 38 and 19 financial members. Applications from the Winton Association for a transfer for P. BOYLEN, and the Dunedin Association for C. V. THOMPSON were granted.'[38]

With a population of 1,000 at the time, Gertrude recognised the business opportunity that Winton offered Phil. At the same time she missed the country lifestyle and all of her friends and felt that Kelso would always hold a treasured corner in her heart. The family lived in the flat above the shop where the rooms were bigger than Gertrude was used to. The upstairs offered lovely views from all windows. Window boxes were the only garden. The wash-house was downstairs.[39] She imagined how lovely it would have been for her if her dear mother had been able to sit back and relax in such comfortable surroundings, adding that her big family had been too much for her. [40]

The drapery business was a bigger concern, employing four girls compared with the Kelso shop that was served by only Cora, with the help of one of the girls, for nearly nine years. Cora also boarded with the family there. It was intended that she would take up duties again, at Winton, on the marriage of the head girl. The family had become fond of her. Winton would offer shorter hours and cash payments.

Figure 13.12. The BOYLEN family home in Durham Street, Winton. Source: GEARY family

Eleanor became employed at a boot and shoe shop not far down the street from the family shop, while Thelma was Gertrude's house assistant.[41]

With New Zealand's involvement in World War II looming, activities involving the services became more common. Royal Air Force trainees were invited by management to attend a weekly town hall dance event at Dunedin. It was also attended by Eleanor BOYLEN (Winton) who wore blue florals.

> Despite the heavy rain that had fallen all afternoon and evening there was a particularly large crowd of dancers and spectators, who seemed to enjoy themselves to the full. Members of the Royal Air Force came in all the way from Wingatui to attend the dance, and their attractive uniforms added a touch of colour to the scene. A new dance entitled 'The Patty Cake, Patty Cake' was demonstrated by two pupils of Miss Connie POTTS. Miss Joyce MEINUNG and Mr Corry DONOVAN. The demonstration was much enjoyed, and the dance attracted considerable interest. Five vocalists assisted Dick COLVIN's Band on Saturday night and all their numbers were greatly enjoyed.[42]

The BOYLEN interest in horse racing appeared in a 1903 publication and Philip seems to have maintained some involvement. His trotter, *Securus* was one of a field of thirteen horses set to take part in the Winton Juvenile Stakes.

> Winton Trotting Club Handicap, of £270.
> Winton Juvenile Stakes, of £250. One mile and a-quarter. – P. BOYLEN's *Securus*.[43]

World War II was moving closer. Phillip felt that the young men currently serving overseas were experiencing a more difficult time than he had had in World War 1. Despite not being obliged to serve, he was prepared to go to war again. Gertrude feared that her two youngest brothers, Rupert and Norman, would be eligible. Although married, Rupert was called up in the last ballot but did not serve. Being amongst those working in essential industries he was unlikely to be sent to camp for military training in the near future.[44]

By 1942 the Japanese were getting closer to New Zealand and tests for blackouts were taking place. Britain was experiencing food shortages and Gertrude wanted to help in some way, suggesting that she send a 2lb tin of cheese to her English relatives. A bulk supply was eventually sent to the U.K. by the N.Z. government. Food in New Zealand was readily available, especially fruit and vegetables. Current prices were: onions 5lb for 1/-, 4 oranges for 1/-, boiled sweets 1/- per lb, mutton birds 1/3 each, butter 1/6 per lb, eggs 2s 6d per dozen and a 40 lb case of dessert apples cost 5s 6d. Within a year or so food shortages were being felt locally, too.[45]

The government took man-power under its control to ensure that important services were provided for. Thelma was within the age bracket and was told to leave the family business and work at the linen flax factory two miles from home. The dust in the air there bothered her so she applied to be transferred to the army. Her Uncle Rupert was also working there at the time. Gertrude thought the idea was much like making women into men.[46]

On 18 April 1944 Thelma married William Francis GEARY at Winton and on 26 July of the same year Eleanor married William Francis EGERTON at Invercargill.

Nieces and nephews were always welcome at the BOYLEN home. With a live-in housekeeper Gertrude was able to cope with younger children who came on holiday, particularly those of Jack and Frances CHALMERS' family. They enjoyed the food and loved to play the pianola.

Figure 13.13. Thelma in army uniform. Source: GEARY family

Auntie Gertie shared Bible readings and tape recordings of prominent evangelists of the time, such as Oral ROBERTS. Uncle Phil was a kind and jolly man who would press a very generous ten shilling note into a hand when an older child left to go home.

Of her parents, Thelma said: "Mum was always a very correct person and we were conscious of being polite to others, being kind and considerate and careful in what we said. We always knew how important her religious beliefs were to her and her Bible was always on reach on the table by her chair. She was always concerned about how family members were making out, especially Violet and Frances, with her many children, at Greenhills. Dad was the one who encouraged hospitality and generosity and that was what he practised himself." Their parents willingly took children for holidays and Eleanor and Thelma loved to have them come to stay.[47]

Figure 13.14. Eleanor and Thelma BOYLEN. Source: GEARY family

When Frances CHALMERS died suddenly at Greenhills in 1952, Uncle Phil and Auntie Gertie took care of twelve year old Neville John until he became independent.[48] Neville attended Winton Primary School and Winton District High School and when he left he took up banking as a career. Bill and Eleanor EGERTON looked after Josephine Violet for a while until she went to live at Arrowtown with her Uncle Donald and

Auntie Maribel.

Gertrude had a stroke and died on 15 August 1958.

Figure 13.15. (From left) Neville with brothers David and Allan CHALMERS at Durham Street, Winton for Auntie Gertie's funeral, 1958. Source: GEARY family

Philip remained living at Durham Street and working at his drapery store until his retirement. During the 1960s the address of the family home changed from 53 Durham Street to 11 Queen Street.[49] A widower for eighteen years, he died on 6 March 1976 at Invercargill.

Philip and Gertrude are buried in Plot 19, Block 5 at the East Winton Cemetery.

Figure 13.16. Philip BOYLEN. Source: GEARY family

NOTES

---

[1] NZRGO, Birth Register, 1893/5421, BOYLEN Philip, Susan, John.

[2] Certified Copy of Entry in the Register-Book of Births in the District of Tapanui for Philip BOYLEN b. 9 February 1893.

[3] *Otago Witness.* "Disposal Of Crown Lands." September 24, 1891.

[4] BOYLEN, John, surfacemen, Heriot, Tuapeka Electoral Rolls, 1900, 1905-06 and 1911; BOYLEN, Susan, Heriot, Tuapeka Electoral Rolls, 1900, 1905-06 and 1911.

[5] *Clutha Leader.* July 17, 1914.

[6] BOYLEN, John, farmer, Wangaloa, Bruce Electoral Rolls, 1914, 1919, 1928 1935 (with John Jr) and 1938; BOYLEN, Susan, Wangaloa, Bruce Electoral Rolls, 1914, 1919, 1928 1935 and 1938.

[7] BOYLEN, John, clerk, Heriot, Otago Central Electoral Rolls, 1914 (with Henry).

[8] *Tuapeka Times.* September 1, 1915.

[9] *Mt Benger Mail.* "Social And Presentation." September 1, 1915.

[10] Copy of Register of Marriage by Officiating Minister, 1916, Marriage in the District of Dunedin, 20 May 1916 at St Joseph's Catholic Vestry, Dunedin.

[11] *Tuapeka Times.* May 31, 1916.

[12] Philip BOYLEN, WW1, 13866 Army Record, R22278168, Archives New Zealand, Wellington.

[13] Letter from Gertrude to cousin Margaret.

[14] BOYLEN, Philip, storeman, Heriot, Clutha Electoral Roll, 1919; BOYLEN, Gertrude Elizabeth, Heriot, Clutha Electoral Roll, 1919.

[15] *Otago Daily Times.* "Birth." February 6, 1920.

[16] May Brownlie, *Kismet for Kelso* (Tapanui, NZ: M. Bownlie, 1992).

[17] "Kelso, New Zealand", 2017, https://en.wikipedia.org/wiki/Kelso,_New_Zealand

[18] BOYLEN, Philip, storeman, merchant, Kelso, Mataura Electoral Rolls, 1928, 1935 and 1938; BOYLEN, Gertrude, Kelso, Mataura Electoral Rolls, 1928, 1935 and 1938.

[19] May Brownlie.

[20] May Brownlie.

[21] *Otago Daily Times.* January 9, 1930.

[22] Letter to cousin Margaret in London.

[23] *Otago Daily Times.* "Tapanui News." September 25, 1931.

[24] *Dunstan Times.* May 2, 1932.

[25] May Brownlie.

[26] *Otago Daily Times.* "Returned Soldiers." April 18, 1934.

[27] May Brownlie.

[28] Letter from Gertrude BOYLEN (née CHALMERS), to Margaret STOKES (cousin in England).

[29] Jessie KIEL (née CHALMERS), pers.com.

[30] Letter from Gertrude BOYLEN (née CHALMERS), to Margaret STOKES (cousin in England).

[31] Ibid.

[32] *Mt Benger Mail*. "'Local Bodies' Amalgamation Bill." February 3, 1937.

[33] *Otago Daily Times*. "Country News." April 21, 1938.

[34] Ibid.

[35] May Brownlie.

[36] "Kelso, New Zealand", 2017, https://en.wikipedia.org/wiki/Kelso,_New_Zealand.

[37] BOYLEN, Philip, draper, Winton, Awarua Electoral Rolls, 1938, 1946, 1949, 1954; BOYLEN, Gertrude, Winton, Awarua Electoral Rolls, 1938, 1946, 1949, 1954; BOYLEN, Philip, draper, Durham Street, Winton, Wallace Electoral Roll, 1957.

[38] *Otago Daily Times*. "Country News ." June 27, 1938.

[39] Letter from Gertrude BOYLEN (née CHALMERS),15 November 1938, to Margaret STOKES.

[40] Letter from Gertrude BOYLEN (née CHALMERS), to Margaret STOKES.

[41] Ibid.

[42] *Otago Daily Times*. "Town Hall Dance." October 31, 1939.

[43] *Otago Daily Times*. December 17, 1940.

[44] Gertrude BOYLEN (née CHALMERS), pers. com.

[45] Ibid.

[46] Ibid.

[47] Thelma GEARY (née BOYLEN), 12 December 2006.

[48] BOYLEN, Philip, draper, Durham Street, Winton, Wallace Electoral Roll, 1957; BOYLEN, Gertrude, Durham Street, Winton, Wallace Electoral Roll, 1957.

[49] BOYLEN, Philip, draper, 10 Durham Street, Winton, Wallace Electoral Roll, 1957; BOYLEN, Philip, retired, 11 Queen Street, Winton, Wallace Electoral Rolls, 1969 and 1972.

14 Constance Eleanor CHALMERS and James McKIBBIN

Figure 14.1. Constance Eleanor CHALMERS. Source: author's collection

Constance Eleanor CHALMERS married James McKIBBIN at Dunedin on 20 May 1916, on the same day and in the same place as her twin sister Gertrude Elizabeth. It is most likely that Constance and James met when he was working as a carpenter and staying at the Bridge Hotel at Beaumont.[1] (See Figure 14.3.)

Figure 14.2. James McKIBBIN. Source: author's collection

James was of Irish descent. He was said to have other relatives who lived in New Zealand, but none have been identified. An aunt was living at Brydone in 1933.[2] She may have been one of the McDOWELLs. The McDOWELL family were very close friends of the McKIBBINs. They 'adopted' James as a young man who had emigrated from Ireland. Nancy McDOWELL was like a sister to him.[3] She lived with Robert and Pamela

McKIBBIN in her later years and enjoyed spending time in the garden and with the family dog.[4]

Figure 14.3. The mail coach at Hunt's Bridge Hotel, Beaumont. The first change of horses took place here for Roxburgh. Source: Otago Witness, October 16, 1901.

At the end of 1916 James' name was drawn in the second ballot for recruitment to serve in World War I: 'McKIBBIN Jas., Beaumont, carpenter'.[5] A possible service record has not been found.

James and Constance had two children, Robert James and Norman Chamberlin.

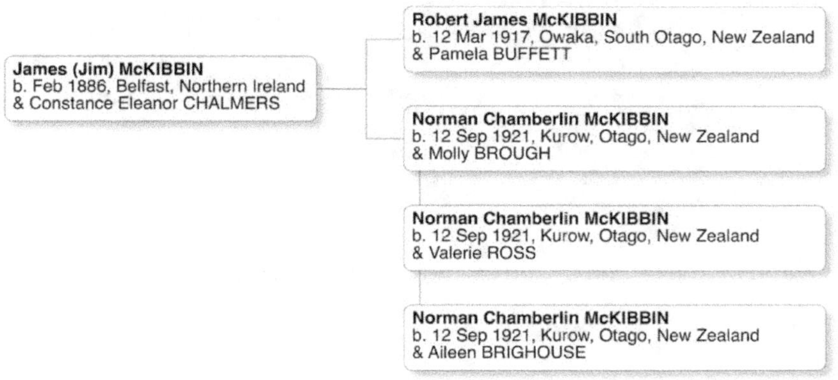

Figure 14.4. The children of James and Constance McKIBBIN

Figure 14.5. James and Constance McKIBBIN with their son Robert, c.1920. Armstrong Photo Dunedin. Source: author's collection

Early in their married life, after leaving Beaumont, James worked in Dunedin with the police as a constable for a time.[6]

Figure 14.6. (Left to right) Sons Robert and Norman (with unknown woman behind), James and Constance, c.1926, Dunedin Botanic Gardens. Source: author's collection

James soon returned to carpentry in Dunedin, living at different addresses for about thirty years. It is highly likely that James built houses, lived in them for a time and moved on. In 1928 they were at 8 Islington Street, North East Valley, Dunedin North.[7]

In the middle of the Depression building construction was almost out of the question. James travelled the one hundred miles to Cromwell where he worked as a carpenter in 'The Ounce Ltd' goldmine. He probably stayed with Constance's brother Malcolm and wife Nellie, of necessity leaving Constance at home. One consolation was living in Dunedin, just a short distance from the sea, as Constance enjoyed walking along the sandhills.[8]

Figures 14.7. and 14.8. James carpentering at the goldmine. Source: author's collection

Soon after he left school Robert James took a position in an auctioneer's office. While his wages were greatly reduced, even a small wage was to be appreciated under the circumstances.

In 1935 and 1938 their address was 104 Tainui Road, Andersons Bay, Dunedin E.[9]

Norman served as a gunner with the New Zealand Army in World War II.[10] Following the war he worked as a storekeeper in Dunedin but became bankrupt in 1948.[11]

The final family residence in Dunedin was at 18 Oakland Street. By this time son Norman was married to his first wife, Molly Hetty BROUGH and they were living there with his parents.[12]

While living in Dunedin Norman suffered severe injuries to his face as the result of a head-on collision while riding his motorbike. He lived most of his life as a pensioner as he was unable to sustain regular work.

> In 1972, a friend wrote, "I loved Connie very much and it was a sad loss to me when she went so far away. I helped [her] shift out of six houses in Dunedin. She always had something to give us a good laugh. She was a brave lovely lady and had some times to bear."[13]

Constance was used to visiting her twin sister Gertrude and husband Philip twice a year at Winton, usually at Christmas and Easter. By 1949 she and James were also living there, at New River Road.[14]

James built a house at Gap Road, not far from Phil and Gertie BOYLEN. They saw quite a lot of each other and the cousins got to know one another. 'Uncle Jim was quite a wit. Eleanor (BOYLEN) had a musquash fur coat, expensive at twenty pounds, and didn't want to wear it in the rain. Uncle Jim jokingly said: "Don't be stupid! Have you ever seen a rabbit with an umbrella?"'[15]

Robert James had married Pamela BUFFETT in 1948 and they were living in Auckland when James and Constance decided to move north also. Robert's parents bought a house at 4 Violet Street, Mt Albert. Norman's second wife, Valerie ROSS lived with them for a time.[16]

Figure 14.9. Constance and Vanguard car outside 4 Violet Street, Mt Albert, Auckland. Source: author's collection

Norman's third wife was Aileen BRIGHOUSE. He had a problem with alcohol and was desperate for money at one point. Norman had in his care the CHAMBERLIN family scroll that had been prepared by the College of Arms in London for Thomas Chamberlin TIMS. Norman sold it to a pawnbroker who displayed it in his shop window. Over ten years after Norman's death, family members Dora GRUBB, Raymond CHALMERS and Lorraine BERRY were able to reclaim the important piece of family history by negotiation and the payment of $300. Thomas Chamberlin TIMS (b. 17 November 1866, London) had his name legally changed to Thomas Chamberlin CHAMBERLIN in honour of his great-great-great-grandfather's brother who did not have a son to inherit the coat of arms.

Figure 14.10. Norman with his mother Constance.
Source: author's collection

James built a house for Robert and Pamela at the corner of Koromiko and Konini Roads, Titirangi.[17] It was at least two storeys high in a bush setting with panoramic views. James had become manager of a millinery factory and lived comfortably. James and Constance retired to live at 51 Rata Street, New Lynn.[18]

Figure 14.11. Robert with his mother Constance. Source: author's collection

Figure 14.12. Constance at 51 Rata Street New Lynn. Source: author's collection

Norman's second marriage ended in divorce in 1968.[19]

James died on 20 July 1968 and Constance passed away the following year on 22 November 1969. They are buried together at Plot 84, Row 9, Protestant Lawn C in the Waikumete Cemetery in Auckland.

In 1969 Norman was living with his third wife Aileen at 31 Gilbert Street, Orara. He died on 27 May 1970 at Auckland and an inquest into cause of death was held.[20] He was buried at the Otahuhu RSA Cemetery, Auckland.[21]

Figure 14.13. Memorial plaque on the grave of Norman Chamberlin McKibbin, Otahuhu RSA Cemetery. Source: author's collection

NOTES

[1] McKIBBIN, James, carpenter, Bridge Hotel, Beaumont, Otago Central Electoral Rolls, 1914 and 1919; McKIBBIN, Constance, Bridge Hotel, Beaumont, Otago Central Electoral Roll, 1919.

[2] Constance McKIBBIN (née CHALMERS), pers. com.

[3] NZRGO, Death Register, 1987/37034, McDOWELL, Nancy Millar, DOB 6 December 1899; McDOWELL, Nancy, spinster, Nurses' Home Leven Street, Invercargill Electoral

Roll, 1928; McDOWELL, Nancy, spinster, Hospital Balclutha, Clutha Electoral Rolls, 1935 and 1938; McDOWELL, Nancy, spinster, 4106 Great North Road, New Lynn, Auckland Electoral Rolls, 1935 and 1938.

[4] Pamela McKIBBIN, pers. com.

[5] *Tuapeka Times*. December 16, 1916.

[6] McKIBBIN, James, constable, 27 Millar Street, Dunedin North Electoral Roll, 1919; McKIBBIN, Constance, 27 Millar Street, Dunedin North Electoral Roll, 1919.

[7] McKIBBIN, James, carpenter, 8 Islington Street, North East Valley Dunedin North Electoral Roll, 1928; McKIBBIN, Constance, married, 8 Islington Street, North East Valley Dunedin North Electoral Roll, 1928.

[8] Letter from Constance McKIBBIN, 12 August 1933, to cousin Margaret STOKES.

[9] McKIBBIN, James, carpenter, 104 Tainui Road, Dunedin E.1, Dunedin Central Electoral Rolls, 1935 and 1938; McKIBBIN, Constance, 104 Tainui Road, Dunedin E.1, Dunedin Central Electoral Rolls, 1935 and 1938.

[10] McKIBBIN, Gunner Norman Chamberlin, Death: 23 May 1970, Burial: Otahuhu RSA, Auckland, New Zealand Cemetery Records, 1800-2007.

[11] McKIBBIN, Norman Chamerlain, Dunedin, storekeeper, 1948, Dunedin High Court.

[12] McKIBBIN, James, carpenter, 18 Oakland Street, St Kilda, St Kilda Electoral Roll, 1946; McKIBBIN, Constance, married, 18 Oakland Street, St Kilda, St Kilda Electoral Roll, 1946; McKIBBIN, Norman Chamberlin, pensioner, 18 Oakland Street, St Kilda, St Kilda Electoral Roll, 1946; McKIBBIN, Molly Hetty, married, 18 Oakland Street, St Kilda, St Kilda Electoral Roll, 1946

[13] Incomplete letter. Author unknown.

[14] McKIBBIN, James, carpenter, New River Road, Winton, Wallace Electoral Roll, 1949; McKIBBIN, Constance, married, New River Road, Winton, Wallace Electoral Roll, 1949.

[15] Thelma GEARY (née BOYLEN), pers. com.

[16] McKIBBIN, James, builder, 4 Violet Street, Auckland, Mt Albert Electoral Rolls, 1954 and 1957; McKIBBIN, Constance, married, 4 Violet Street, Auckland, Mt Albert Electoral Rolls, 1954 and 1957; McKIBBIN, Valerie, married, 4 Violet Street, Auckland, Mt Albert Electoral Rolls, 1954 and 1957.

[17] McKIBBIN, Robert James, Cnr Koromiko and Konini Roads, Titirangi, Waitakere Electoral Rolls, 1954 and 1957; McKIBBIN, Pamela, Cnr Koromiko and Konini Roads, Titirangi, Waitakere Electoral Rolls, 1954 and 1957.

[18] McKIBBIN, James, 51 Rata Street, Auckland SW4, New Lynn Electoral Rolls, 1963; McKIBBIN, Constance, married, 51 Rata Street, Auckland SW4, New Lynn Electoral Rolls, 1963.

[19] Auckland Divorce files, McKIBBIN, Norman Chamberlin v. McKIBBIN, Valerie , 1967, 1968, High Court Auckland, Department of Justice.

[20] Coroners Inquest, Auckland, McKIBBIN, Norman Chambelain, 1970, New Zealand Justice Department.

[21] McKIBBIN, Gunner Norman Chamberlin, Death: 23 May 1970, Burial: Otahuhu RSA, Auckland, New Zealand Cemetery Records, 1800-2007.

15 Gordon Rupert CHALMERS and Janet ANDERSON

Gordon Rupert CHALMERS and Janet Emily ANDERSON were married on 28 December 1921 at Invercargill.[1]

Figure 15.1. Wedding of Gordon Rupert CHALMERS and Janet Emily ANDERSON, 1921. Source: author's collection

Janet's family lived at Greenhills where she was born.[2] Her parents, John ANDERSON and Helena Christina LUCK were married on 30 April 1879 at Waimate.[3]

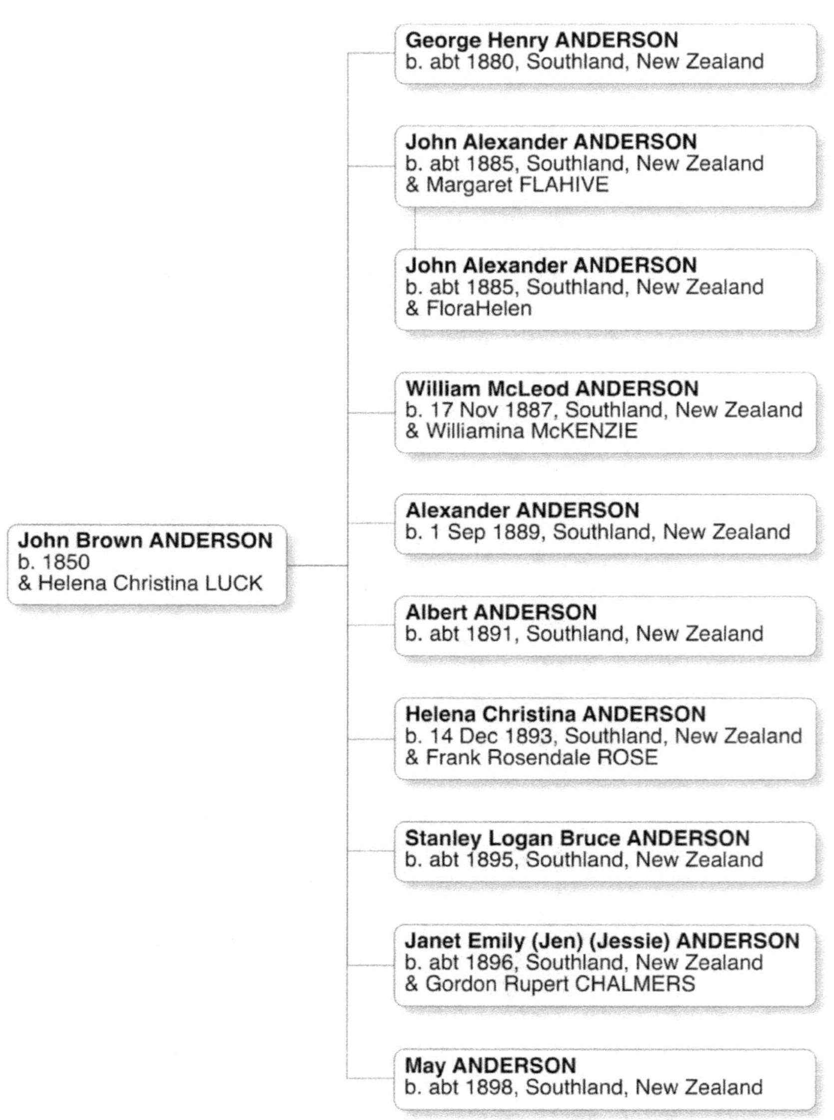

Figure 15.2. The children of John and Helena ANDERSON

John, her father, worked as a gardener at Strathearn (formerly Seaward Bush), Invercargill and became a labourer at Greenhills from 1890 to 1911.[4]

The ANDERSON family appears to be of Scottish descent but no records to prove this have been found. Janet's mother, Helena Christina LUCK was born in London, England in 1858. Family tradition is that she was of German descent, in explanation of her fiery temper.[5] By way of contrast, Rupert had a quiet and gentle nature and was a good artist.[6] He had won an art prize while attending Beaumont School.

Rupert and Janet met while the CHALMERS family was living at Knowsley Park in the Mataura district. Rupert had spent his teenage years working on the family farms. Janet was a schoolteacher at Waikana School and boarded with the CHALMERS family.[7] The couple returned to live with or near CHALMERS family members from time to time.

By 1928 Rupert was also teaching, at Mokoreta School.[8] They had two children, May Eleanor and Albert Gordon (Sonny). Janet had lost seven babies through miscarriage prior to May's birth.[9]

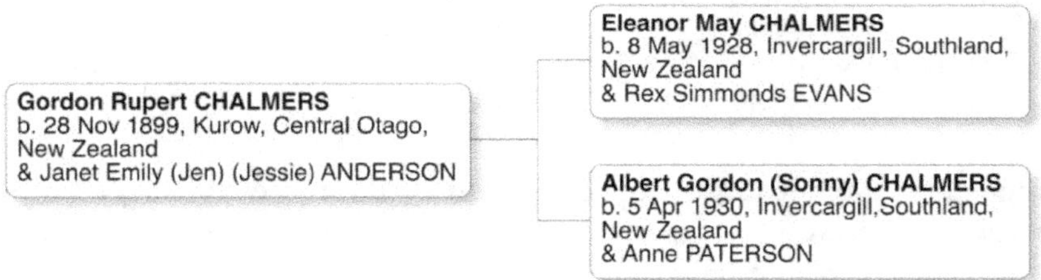

Figure 15.3. The children of Rupert and Jessie CHALMERS

When the children were young the family lived at Duntroon, in the Waitaki Basin, where Rupert's parents first settled before his birth. His parents returned to Duntroon from Kurow years later.

With the onset of the Depression, Rupert and Janet went to live at 'View Hill' near Gore where Rupert's father, John Howe CHALMERS and unmarried brother Jack and sisters Violet and Dora were living. He became a joint owner of the property with Jack and Violet. A long row of trees lined the driveway. The farm was up a hill. It had many cows and one angry bull. To avoid the cows and the bull May would stay close to the fence. On one occasion her leg became caught in the barbed wire. Her Uncle Jack was chased by the bull once and he shot over the fence without touching it.[10] Although the house was large, they sought to have a separate dwelling on the property.[11]

Figure 15.4. Eleanor May and Albert Gordon (Sonny) CHALMERS, c.1930, Duntroon. Source: author's collection

Figure 15.5. Rupert beside his Chevrolet car at Duntroon, c.1930. Source: author's collection

Apparently the house for Rupert and family did not eventuate, as from 'View Hill' May went to live with her Auntie Gertie and Uncle Phil BOYLEN at Kelso. She started her infant school education at the Kelso School. Phil's and Gertrude's daughters, Eleanor and Thelma were eight and six years older, respectively, and were like big sisters to her. For fun they would wheel her around in a pram. Once they lost control, the pram tipped over and May ended up in a ditch that ran into a stream with a bridge over it near the property gate.

When 'View Hill' was sold Rupert and Janet took up residence in one of the three houses on the new property at Hokonui. Rupert transferred his share of the Gore property to Hokonui, as did the other owners.[12]

By this time May's grandfather, John Howe CHALMERS, had become elderly and frail. She remembered him sitting at the kitchen table eating porridge. Her Auntie Violet had to thin it down to make it drinkable. His hands were shaky and he needed both to get the cup to his mouth.

Travel between home and school was by horse-drawn cart that could carry six or so children. On one occasion the horse dropped dead. Passing motorists helped get the horse off the road. Miss McKENZIE was told off for being late for school.[13]

Figure 15.6. Rupert and Janet.
Source: author's collection

Figure 15.7. Arnold and Dora with Janet, May and Sonny having a picnic, c.1937. Source: author's collection

Rupert and his brother John (known as Jack) did not see eye to eye. Rupert claimed that he was lazy and lounged around when there was work to be done. He needed to get outside help to keep up. This was the beginning of another family dispute. In May's opinion her Uncle Jack was plausible and had the knack of making people feel sorry for him.[14]

Things came to a head and this may have been the time that Rupert suffered his first nervous breakdown. Rupert and family decided to move out and go to Kelso. Rupert's escape was to travel selling Rawleigh products.[15]

They were near the families of Donald and Maribel CHALMERS and Philip and Gertrude BOYLEN. With Phil's knowledge, he and Gertie were involved with the sharing of property. The children attended Kelso school together.[16] (See Table 13.1.) May continued her education at standard one level at Kelso. Donald was also struggling to keep his family clothed and fed and worked in forestry. In 1938 Rupert was employed at Conical Hills making roads through the forest to transport logs. He worked as a lorry-driver.[17]

The family lived in a wooden house on 'The Terrace', but over the railway on a rise so that it escaped flooding that was typical of the area. A row of macrocarpa trees lined the street side. They kept three cows, one of which was called Jenny, that produced enough milk to supply neighbours as well.[18]

Although Rupert was enlisted in the army he was not called to serve.[19] However, his brother-in-law, Arnold GRUBB did go to war and was sent to the Pacific theatre, leaving his wife Dora at home alone. May was asked to take the bus to Gore to keep her company and happily returned to Kelso on the weekends as she found her Auntie Dora to be unnecessarily strict. She put on lipstick to be attractive to her mother and pleaded so that she would not make her return to Gore. She commenced her secondary school education at Gore High School in 1942. Arnold and Dora GRUBB were frequent visitors at Kelso. They wanted children of their own. Before she died, Dora apologised to May for treating her harshly.[20]

The onset of World War II meant that employment was prioritised by the government's demands for certain goods. The linen flax mill at Tapanui, not far from Kelso, produced flax fibre that was used to make parachute cords and camouflage nets, an essential wartime industry. Rupert spent time working there until he transferred to the Woodlands branch of the mill, near Invercargill. He took up a promotion as foreman. The manager lived next to the factory and the CHALMERS family next again to it.[21]

The mill closed at the end of the war and Rupert commuted to Invercargill, working in the grocery business. He worked at the Single Profit Stores for many years.[22] The dream of owning a home in Invercargill eventuated and the family moved into their newly-built house at 403 Elles Road Invercargill South.[23]

Directly opposite the house was the Kew Bowling Club where Rupert spent many leisure hours and became a very proficient bowler.[24]

Figure 15.8. Rupert and Janet CHALMERS' house at 403 Elles Road, Invercargill. Source: author's collection

Janet's parents had retired to a house at the corner of Elles Road and McQuarrie Street and her father had been living alone since the death of his wife in 1937.[25]

On 27 June 1952 Rupert's sister-in-law Frances CHALMERS died suddenly, leaving a large family of young children in need. Along with other relatives, Rupert and Janet took a share of responsibility by caring for David Basil CHALMERS. David first met them at Woodlands in 1947 when he was aged five.

May married Rex Simmonds EVANS at Invercargill on 8 December

1948. Janet's father passed away in 1949 and when May's twins were born she wanted to be near her daughter and family who were living in Christchurch. At first they took up residence at 10 Angela Street in Fendalton where Rupert continued in the foodstuffs business working as a grocer's assistant.[26]

A move to 10 English Street, Riccarton meant a change of job and Rupert became a factory hand at the Laminex division of the Crown Crystal Glass Factory. There were risks involved in being a machine operator and Rupert met with an unfortunate accident that resulted in the loss of a hand. The trauma resulted in another nervous breakdown from which he recovered. Eventually this disability did not hinder his ability to work in the garden, drive the car and return to his previous employment. He also did the work required to complete their new house at Riccarton.[27]

Figure 15.9. Wedding of May CHALMERS and Rex EVANS, Invercargill, 1948. Source: author's collection

David had accompanied the family when it moved to Christchurch. He remembered helping clean the section ready for planting a garden.[28] Following his Uncle Rupert's accident he spent time at Gore with his Auntie Dora and Uncle Arnold GRUBB. They had taken responsibility for the care of siblings Lorraine, Stephen and Barry after the death of their mother. Having met as teacher and pupil, Janet and Dora remained close throughout their lives. Janet probably influenced Dora in taking up the same profession.

Figure 15.10. Janet CHALMERS and sister-in-law Dora GRUBB, c.1950 Source: author's collection

Figure 15.11. David CHALMERS with his sister Lorraine, Gore, c.1953. Source: author's collection

When David reached independence at the age fifteen, Janet arranged for him to return to Invercargill to work as a telegram delivery boy. He stayed in a boarding house.

Son Albert, known as Sonny, lived in Balclutha. He trained there and became a practising engineer from about 1949.[29] Sonny married Anne PATERSON in 1953 and they had two sons.[30] But the marriage did not last.[31]

Rupert died on 14 April 1959 at Christchurch at the age of sixty.[32]

Figure 15.12. Albert (Sonny) with his two sons,
Clive and Niven. Source: author's collection

Albert Gordon did not remarry and he died at the age of 32 on 17 September 1962 at Ashburton.[33] Albert left his entire estate to his two sons and willed that they be under the care of his sister May until they reached maturity.[34]

Janet passed away on 2 June 1963 at Christchurch.[35]

Albert, Rupert and Janet are all buried at the Waimairi Cemetery at Christchurch.[36] Rupert's probate was filed on 22 May 1959 and Janet's on 13 August 1963.[37]

NOTES

---

[1] Copy of marriage certificate; Gordon Rupert CHALMERS, Janet Emily ANDERSON, 28 December 1921, Invercargill, Anderson Folio No.10573, NZ Society of Genealogists.

[2] Ibid.

[3] Personal account of May EVANS (née Eleanor May CHALMERS), daughter March 6 2003; New Zealand Marriage Index, 1840-1937, Christina LUCK, 1879, John ANDERSON, Folio 1411.

[4] ANDERSON, John, gardener, Strathearn, Awarua Electoral Rolls, 1880-1881; ANDERSON, John, labourer, Greenhills residential, Awarua Electoral Rolls, 1890, 1896 and 1900; ANDERSON, John, labourer Greenhills, Awarua Electoral Rolls, 1905-1906 and 1911; ANDERSON, Helena, Greenhills, Awarua Electoral Rolls, 1905-1906 and 1911; ANDERSON, James, woodcutter, Greenhills, Awarua Electoral Rolls, 1905-1906; ANDERSON, James, labourer, Greenhills, Awarua Electoral Roll, 1911.

[5] Thelma GEARY (née BOYLEN), pers. com.; England & Wales, Civil Registration Birth Index, 1837-1915, Helena Christina Luck, 1858 Apr-May-Jun, St George in the East London, Vol. 1c, p.413.

[6] Thelma GEARY (née BOYLEN), pers. com.

[7] May EVANS (née Eleanor May CHALMERS), March 6 , 2003, pers. com.

[8] CHALMERS, Rupert Gordon, schoolteacher, Mokoreta, Mataura Electoral Roll, 1928.

[9] May EVANS, pers. com.

[10] Ibid.

[11] Violet CHALMERS (sister of Rupert), pers. com.

[12] CHALMERS, Rupert Gordon, farmer, Hokonui, Awarua Electoral Roll, 1935; CHALMERS, Janet, Hokonui, Awarua Electoral Roll, 1935.

[13] May EVANS, pers. com.

[14] Ibid.

[15] Ibid.

[16] May Brownlie, *Kismet for Kelso* (Tapanui, NZ: M. Brownlie, 1992).

[17] CHALMERS, Rupert Gordon, lorry-driver, Kelso, Mataura Electoral Roll, 1938.

[18] May EVANS, pers. com.

[19] Ibid.

[20] Ibid.

[21] Letter from Gertrude BOYLEN to cousin Margaret STOKES; CHALMERS, Rupert Gordon, foreman, Woodlands, Awarua Electoral Roll, 1946; CHALMERS, Janet, Woodlands, Awarua Electoral Roll, 1946

[22] Thelma GEARY (née BOYLEN), pers. com.

[23] CHALMERS, Rupert Gordon, foreman, 403 Elles Road, Invercargill, Awarua Electoral Roll, 1949.

[24] May EVANS, pers. com.

[25] ANDERSON, John, retired, 1 McQuarrie Street, Invercargill, Awarua Electoral Roll, 1946; New Zealand, Cemetery Records, 1800-2007, Helena Christina ANDERSON, 19 March 1937, Eastern Cemetery Invercargill; John B. ANDERSON, 25 Jul 1949, Eastern Cemetery Invercargill.

[26] CHALMERS, Rupert Gordon, grocer's assistant, 10 Angela Street, Christchurch, Fendalton Electoral Roll, 1954; CHALMERS, Janet, Janet 10 Angela Street, Christchurch, Fendalton Electoral Roll, 1954.

[27] CHALMERS, Rupert Gordon, factory hand, 10 English Street, Christchurch, Riccarton Electoral Roll, 1954; CHALMERS, Janet, Janet, 10 English Street, Christchurch, Riccarton Electoral Roll, 1954.

[28] David CHALMERS, pers. com.

[29] CHALMERS, Albert Gordon, engineering cadet, James Street, Balclutha, Clutha Electoral Roll, 1949.

[30] CHALMERS, Albert Gordon, engineering cadet, Douglas Street, Balclutha, Clutha Electoral Roll, 1954; CHALMERS, Ann, Douglas Street, Balclutha, Clutha Electoral Roll, 1954.

[31] CHALMERS, Albert Gordon, engineer, 177 Charlotte Street, Balclutha, Clutha Electoral Roll, 1957.

[32] NZRGO, Death Register, 1959/24784, CHALMERS, Rupert Gordon, 60 years; New Zealand, Cemetery Records, 1800-2007, Rupert Gordon CHALMERS, 14 April 1959, Waimairi Cemetery Canterbury, Spouse: Janet Emily CHALMERS, 20 July 1963.

[33] NZRGO, Death Register, 1962/36932 CHALMERS, Albert Gordon, 32 years.

[34] Albert Gordon CHALMERS, Ashburton, Probate, 1962, Christchurch, R20530098, Archives New Zealand, Christchurch.

[35] NZRGO, Death Register, 1963/44264, CHALMERS Janet, 65 years.

[36] New Zealand, Cemetery Records, 1800-2007, Rupert Gordon CHALMERS, 14 April 1959, Waimairi Cemetery Canterbury, Spouse: Janet Emily CHALMERS, 20 July 1963; New Zealand, Cemetery Records, 1800-2007, Albert Gordon CHALMERS, 17 September 1962, Waimairi Cemetery, Canterbury.

[37] Rupert Gordon CHALMERS, factory hand, NZ Probates Christchurch, CAHX CH 171 500/59, 22 May 1959; Janet Emily CHALMERS, NZ Probates, CAHXCH 171 1067/63.,13 August 1963 Christchurch Court.

16 Norman Chamberlin CHALMERS and Elizabeth Mary MARSHALL

As a single man Norman lived and worked with different family members: Donald at Knowsley Park, Malcolm at Waiarikiki and Victoria Bridge and John Howe and other family members at 'View Hill', Gore.[1]

He trained to be a railway engine worker at some stage and took up employment in the Balmoral State Forest as a labourer.[2] He also laboured at Taurina, Allanton near Mosgiel and at Wigram Aerodrome, Riccarton, Christchurch.[3] At the end of the Depression he worked as a cook for threshing mill gangs.[4]

On 18 January 1940 he married Elizabeth (Betty) Mary MARSHALL in Christchurch.[5]

Figure 16.1. Norman and Betty on their wedding day, 1940. Source: author's collection

Betty was older than Norman, having been born about 1892 to Edwin MARSHALL and Elizabeth Mary O'ROURKE who had married in New Zealand in 1890.[6]

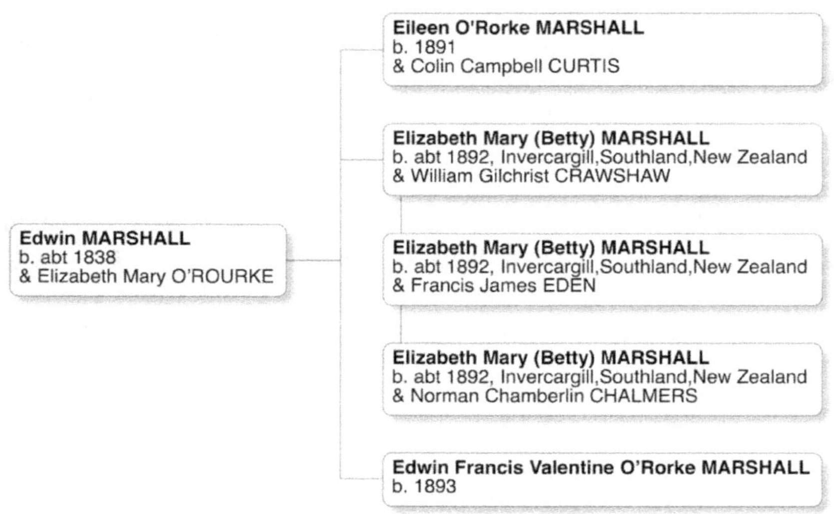

Figure 16.2. The children of Edwin and Elizabeth MARSHALL

Betty had been married twice before. Her first marriage was to William Gilchrist CRAWSHAW in 1915.[7] Four years later she was living alone at 87 Hanover Street, Dunedin West.[8]

At the same time, in 1919 Mary and William were recorded as living together at 32 Jackson Street, St Kilda, Dunedin. William worked as a railway guard.[9] By 1928 Elizabeth was living alone again at 12 Lambeth Road in Dunedin North.[10] In 1931 the couple were legally divorced.[11]

Shortly afterwards, in 1931, Elizabeth married Francis James EDEN.[12]

By 1935 they were living apart, Elizabeth at 393 Barbadoes Street, Christchurch North while Francis, a miner, resided at 161 Chester Street, Christchurch East.[13]

By 1938 Elizabeth had again filed for divorce.[14]

For several years Norman was caretaker for St Paul's Presbyterian Church in Christchurch where a testimonial recommended him as being sober, industrious and pleasant-mannered. In addition, he gave every satisfaction and was a thoroughly reliable and trustworthy man.[15]

The same was said of his service at an apartment house where he had worked for over two years. The letter was signed for Paul FRANKS per A.H. ALDERSON, 280 Oxford Terrace, Christchurch.

At one boarding establishment he provided breakfast on a tray as room service, for long-term residents who then went out to work for the day.

When Norman married Betty, as Elizabeth was known, he continued to work in the hospitality industry.[16]

Norman's name came up in a ballot during World War II, but he did not serve overseas.[17] He had had surgery for a shoulder injury at some stage which may have affected his eligibility for service.

Figure 16.3. Norman with Ginger the cat at the reserve near the river, Barbadoes Street, Christchurch c.1942. Source: author's collection

Figure 16.4. Norman and Betty outside 172 Chester Street with their Morris 8, Christchurch, 1942. Source: author's collection

After the Second World War Norman and Betty moved to Wellington where he took up work as an apartment proprietor at 303 Cuba Street.

Figures 16.5. Norman and Betty outside 303 Cuba Street. Source: author's collection

He kept close contact with his mother's cousin, Thomas Chamberlin (TIMS) CHAMBERLIN and his wife Edith Winifred TOVEY who lived at Khandallah, a Wellington suburb.[18]

Figure 16.6. Norman and Edith (TIMS) CHAMBERLIN at Paekakariki Beach, 1949. Source: author's collection

Figure 16.7. Norman fishing at Wellington wharf. Source: author's collection

In 1951 Norman took out a mortgage on a property at 18 Nairn Street, Wellington. Two years later the Hibernian-Australasian Catholic Benefit Society commended him for always being regular with payments and not having caused the trustees any concern.[19]

Figure 16.8. Norman with twin brothers Malcolm (left) and Donald (right) at Petone Beach, Wellington, 1951. Source: author's collection

Figure 16.9. With brother David and wife Muriel at Petone Beach, Wellington, 1950s. Source: author's collecton

Figure 16.10. Photo of Norman and Betty with cat, 1961. Source: author's collection

Norman and Betty moved to Auckland where they became owners of a large two-storeyed boarding house at 42 View Street, St Marys Bay in Auckland Central.[20]

Figure 16.11. 42 New Street, St Marys Bay, Auckland. Source: author's collection

Figure 16.12. Norman and Betty at the entrance to 42 New Street, Auckland, c.1963. Source: author's collection

Figure 16.13. Norman's brother Malcolm on the steps at 42 New Street, Auckland, c.1963. Source: author's collection

They retired and moved to 9 Herne Bay Road, Auckland.[21] (On 1 July 2017 the New Street property was valued at $5.7 million and the Herne Bay house was worth $2.675 million.)

Figure 16.14. 9 Herne Bay Road, Auckland. Source: author's collection

Betty died on 5 January 1970 at a private hospital and was buried in the Mangere Cemetery in Auckland.[22]

Following Betty's death, Norman moved to Flat 4 at 48 View Road, Mt Eden in Auckland.[23] In late 1971 or early 1972 he made a trip to the South Island to attend a Beaumont School jubilee. [24] (See Table 4.1.) Another friend thought that he had looked ill, while a third, Emily WATSON, had hoped 'that the trip wouldn't be too much for him'.[25]

Norman passed away suddenly at Auckland Hospital on 6 February 1972 and was buried with Betty at Mangere Cemetery.[26] An unidentified friend later wrote of Norman to Dora GRUBB:

> Norman died of heart trouble (I think) some years ago. His wife died first. They had no children. They were a very pleasant, very quiet couple and made me very welcome on a number of occasions – at Herne Bay, Auckland.
> Mr CHALMERS said that he was one of a large family from the South (perhaps Oamaru?) had been a baker – had a very pale skin – & slight build – suppose he'd have been 60-65 old – at a guess.
> He had not had a good education but was intelligent & 'a real gentleman' in manner – I remember thinking that 'blood will tell' – you'd have liked him,

I'm sure – he was greatly interested in his history – I think the CHALMERS came from Aberdeen & the CHAMBERLIN-TIMS side from Banbury, Oxfordshire.
I attended his funeral (though I can't remember where now) and sat beside a youngish man who was, I think, a nephew:
Mr R. J. McKIBBIN
Corner Koromiko and Konini Roads
Titirangi Auckland 7[27] (See Chapter 14.)

Norman left his personal and household effects to Eileen Rose PLUMRIDGE, including a picture of the English artist, John HOPPNER R.A. and the schedule setting out his family tree. This is a curious matter as there is no known CHALMERS family connection to Eileen PLUMRIDGE. She may be Betty's sister or relative. John HOPPNER is an ancestor in the TIMS line. Norman also bequeathed $200 each to five of his closest nieces with the balance of his estate to be bequeathed evenly to The Mother Aubert Home of Compassion Trust Board of Island Bay, Wellington, The Lepers' Trust Board (Inc.), Christchurch and Auckland School for Deaf Society (Kelston) Incorporated for the general purposes of the School for Deaf in Auckland.[28]

NOTES

---

[1] CHALMERS, Norman Chamberlin, View Hill, West Gore, Mataura Electoral Roll, 1928.

[2] Dora GRUBB, pers. com.; CHALMERS, Norman Chamberlin, labourer, State Forest, Balmoral, Hurunui, Canterbury Electoral Roll, 1935.

[3] CHALMERS, Norman Chamberlin, labourer, Taurina, Allanton, Central Otago Electoral Roll, 1938; CHALMERS, Norman Chamberlin, labourer, Wigram Aerodrome, Riccarton Electoral Roll, 1938.

[4] Ray CHALMERS, pers. com.

[5] Dora GRUBB, pers. com.

[6] NZRGO, Marriage Register, 1890/3814, Elizabeth Mary O'ROURKE, Edwin MARSHALL; NZRGO, Birth Register, 1892/15001, MARSHALL Elizabeth Mary Araike, Elizabeth Mary, Edwin.

[7] NZRGO, Marriage Register, 1915/6043, Elizabeth Mary MARSHALL, William Gilchrist CRAWSHAW.

[8] CRAWSHAW, Elizabeth Mary, married, 87 Hanover Street, Dunedin West Electoral Roll, 1919.

[9] CRAWSHAW, William G., railway guard, 32 Jackson Street, St Kilda, Dunedin South Electoral Roll, 1919; CRAWSHAW, Elizabeth Mary, 32 Jackson Street, St Kilda, Dunedin South Electoral Roll, 1919.

[10] CRAWSHAW, Elizabeth Mary, married, 12 Lambeth Road, Dunedin North Electoral Roll, 1928.

[11] CRAWSHAW, Elizabeth Mary v CRAWSHAW, William Gilchrist, Dunedin Divorce Files 1931, 1938, Dunedin High Court, Archives New Zealand, Dunedin.

[12] NZRGO, Marriage Register, 1931/7248, Elizabeth Mary CRAWSHAW, Francis James EDEN.

[13] EDEN, Elizabeth Mary, married, 393 Barbadoes Street, Christchurch North Electoral Roll, 1935; EDEN, Francis James, miner, 161 Chester Street, Christchurch East Electoral Roll, 1935.

[14] CRAWSHAW, Elizabeth Mary v CRAWSHAW, William Gilchrist, Dunedin Divorce Files 1931, 1938, Dunedin High Court, Archives New Zealand, Dunedin. (1938 must be the year of Elizabeth's divorce from Francis James EDEN.)

[15] Chairman Board of Management, St Paul's Church at St Albans, undated testimonial.

[16] Ray CHALMERS, pers.com.

[17] CHALMERS, Norman Chamberlin, labourer, 393 Barbadoes Street, Christchurch, New Zealand, World War II Ballot Lists, 1940-1945, 1942.

[18] Ray CHALMERS pers. com.; CHALMERS, Norman Chamberlin, apartment proprietor, 303 Cuba Street, Wellington, Brooklyn Electoral Rolls, 1946 and 1949; CHALMERS, Elizabeth Mary, 303 Cuba Street, Wellington, Brooklyn Electoral Rolls, 1946 and 1949.

[19] Commendation from the New Zealand District of the Hibernian-Australasian Catholic Benefit Society; CHALMERS, Norman Chamberlin, apartment proprietor, 18 Nairn Street, Wellington, Wellington Central Electoral Rolls, 1954 and 1957; CHALMERS, Elizabeth Mary, 18 Nairn Street, Wellington, Wellington Central Electoral Rolls, 1954 and 1957.

[20] CHALMERS, Norman Chamberlin, apartment proprietor, 42 New Street W1, Auckland Central Electoral Roll, 1963; CHALMERS, Elizabeth Mary, 42 New Street W1, Auckland Central Electoral Roll, 1963.

[21] CHALMERS, Norman C., retired, 9 Herne Bay Road, Grey Lynn Electoral Roll, 1969; CHALMERS, Elizabeth Mary, 9 Herne Bay Road, Grey Lynn Electoral Roll, 1969.

[22] Newspaper death notice; Elizabeth Mary CHALMERS, 5 June 1970, Mangere, Auckland, New Zealand Cemetery Records, 1800-2007.

[23] Christmas card to Dora and Arnold GRUBB.

[24] Letter from Doris SIMMONs to Norman's sister Dora, 8 February 1972.

[25] Extracts from letters of condolence to Dora GRUBB.

[26] Norman Chamberlin CHALMERS, 6 February 1972, Mangere, Auckland, New Zealand Cemetery Records, 1800-2007.

[27] Letter from unknown person at 18 Woodglen Road, Glen Eden, Auckland 7 to Dora GRUBB.

[28] Norman Chamberlin CHALMERS, retired, Auckland Court, NZ Probates Record, Archives Ref BBAE 1570 0524/72, filed 28 February 1972, hard copy in family possession.

17 Dora Grace CHALMERS and Arnold Henry McLeod GRUBB

Dora Grace CHALMERS married Arnold Henry McLeod GRUBB at Gore on 11 May 1936. At the time Arnold was a mechanic living at Thomas Street Gore in a house he had had built.[1]

Figure 17.1. Shooting party: Henry Joseph GRUBB, Arnold's father on the left. Source: author's collection

Arnold's early ancestors were from England and Scotland. His great grandparents, Henry GRUBB and Elizabeth Thompson HOBBS were a Colonial Tasmanian Family, having been among the first to settle there when Tasmania was no longer a pena l colony. (See Figure 17.2.) Henry GRUBB was a mariner of Hobart. He was master and part owner of the cutter *Victoria* in 1841 and became sole owner in 1847. He sold the *Victoria* in 1851.[2]

The fourth child of Henry and Elizabeth was Henry Hobbs GRUBB. He married Jane McLEOD on 11 November 1867. Jane's parents, Hugh McLEOD and Elizabeth COWPER were of Scottish origin and also became a Colonial Tasmanian Family. They were married in 1830 at Gorbals, Lanarkshire, Scotland. Henry Hobbs GRUBB and Jane McLEOD became the parents of thirteen children. (See Figure 17.3.)

Figure 17.2. The children of Henry and Elizabeth GRUBB

A mariner like his father, Henry was a boatbuilder. On 2 March 1894 Henry HOBBS and his son Hugh were drowned in a boating accident. The sea was rough at the time. A death notice appeared in the *Mercury* newspaper:

Deaths
GRUBB, – On March 2, 1894, accidently drowned off Blackman's Bay, Henry Hobbs Grubb, boatbuilder, in the 48th year of his age, leaving a wife and eight children to mourn their loss. Also, Hugh B. J. GRUBB, second son of the above, in the 14th year of his age. Respected by all who knew them.[3]

It appeared that their bodies were never found as their names were not included in the index of inquests held.

Henry Joseph GRUBB, also called 'Harry', the fourth surviving child, had taken up employment in Hobart. By 1901 he was seeking testimonials to help him gain employment further afield. Past employers in Tasmania such as Brownell Brothers, Warehousemen, 'London House', wrote in 1901 that Henry had good general knowledge of the trade and especially of the Manchester department where he held a senior position. He was regarded as a tasteful window dresser, a good salesman and stock-keeper. Edmund MULCALEY of 80 Murray Street, Hobart stated that as a draper's and clothier's assistant he was a conscientious worker, a smart hand, intelligent and pushing with ability as a window dresser with honesty. The Commercial Club, of which Joseph was a member, appreciated all that he had done from the Club's inception as one of its best valued members and would welcome him back at any time.[4]

Figure 17.3. The children of Henry and Jane GRUBB

From 13 May 1901 Henry Joseph was employed by J. Ballantyne and Co. at Christchurch, New Zealand, and on 6 February 1902 he was seeking leave of absence on account of poor health. He was offered one week's respite with the possibility of an extension of time. Henry resigned from a position in the fancy drapery department after having also worked in the mercery and manchester departments.[5]

The following year, on 26 March 1903 Henry married Agnes Clara BEESLEY who was six years older than himself. His occupation was given as draper. The marriage took place at the house of the Rev. Dr ERWIN of Papanui Road, St Albans, Christchurch and was witnessed by Agnes' sister, Emily Ann BEESLEY and E. McNAMARA, draper, 5 Clothier Street, Linwood.

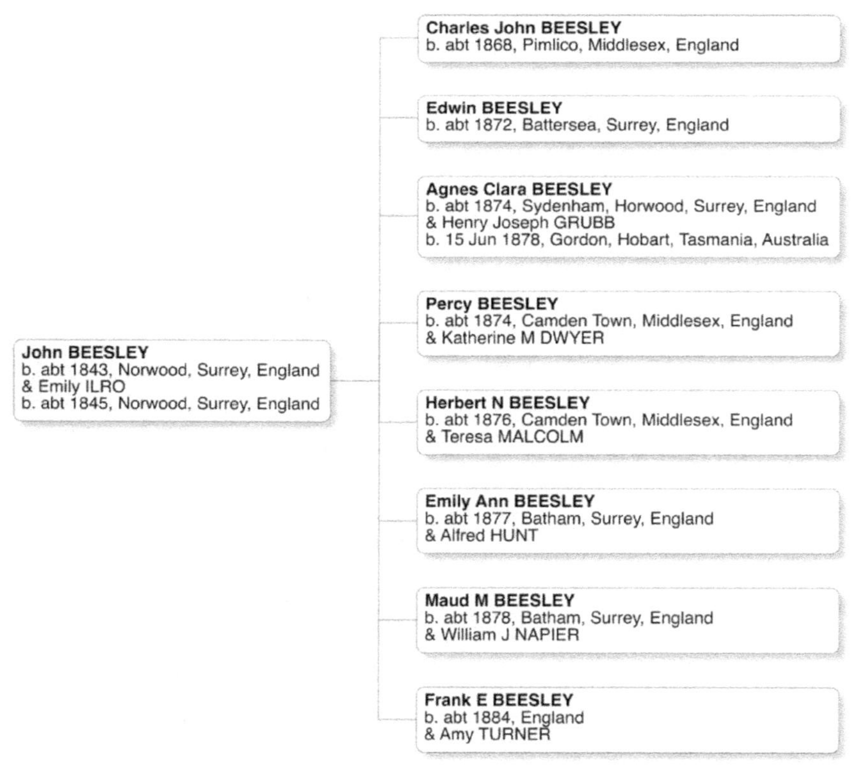

Figure 17.4. The children of John BEESLEY and Emily ILRO

Agnes' parents John BEESLEY and Emily ILRO were both born in Norwood, Surrey, England. John was a commercial traveller in ironmongery.[6] Throughout the births of their children they lived in at least five different towns or cities in England. The family eventually moved to New South Wales, Australia with two of John's brothers, Henry and George with their respective families on the same ship. The brothers lived and remained close to one another throughout their lives.[7]

Figure 17.5. BEESLEY brothers, from left: Henry, George and John. Source: author's collection

When mother died at Newtown, New South Wales in 1893 Agnes, the oldest daughter, took care of her younger siblings. A talented performer, Agnes took part in and produced stage and musical shows.

Figure 17.6. Agnes Clara BEESELY, Kerry & Co., George Street, Sydney. Source: author's collection

Figure 17.7. One of Agnes's plays. Agnes fourth from left. Source: author's collection

In 1904 R.H. Abbott, Importers and Warehousemen of Auckland engaged Henry as a traveller. He earned a salary of £4 per week, with travel expenses to be paid by the company for six months.[8]

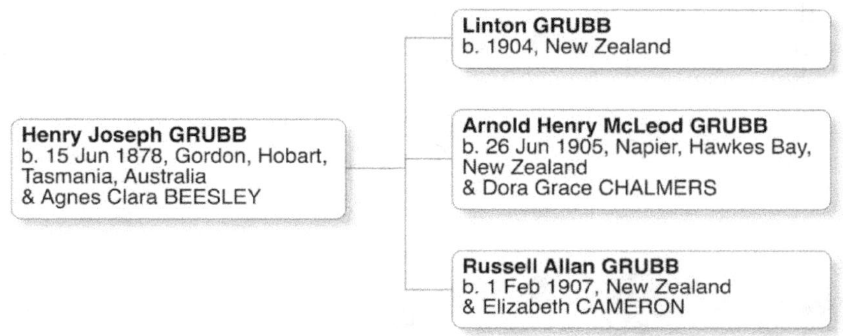

Figure 17.8. The children of Henry and Agnes GRUBB

Figure 17.9. GRUBB family from left, front: Arnold, Russell. Back: Agnes and Henry. Late 1920s. Source: author's collection

Linton (b. 1904), the first-born child of Henry and Agnes, did not survive. Arnold Henry McLeod GRUBB was born at home in Coote Road, Napier on 26 June 1905.[9]

He was baptised later at St John's Church, Roslyn, Diocese of Dunedin.[10] By this time the family had moved to 32 Sligo Terrace, Roslyn in Dunedin. It was originally known as 53 Town Belt. Henry worked as a warehouseman and Agnes became a teacher of music and voice production.[11]

Figure 17.10. House at 32 Sligo Terrace, Dunedin. Source: author's collection

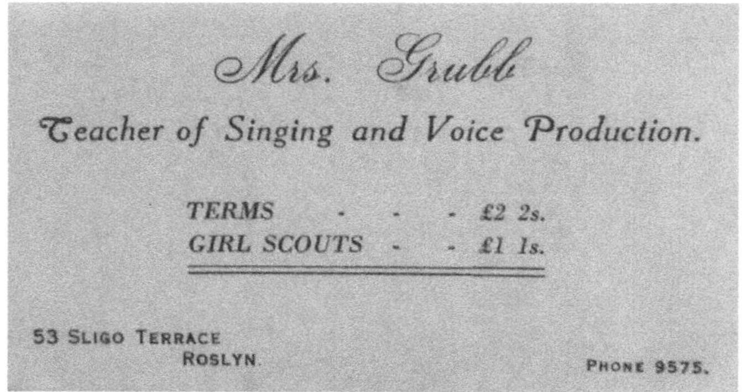

Figure 17.11. Agnes' Business Card. Source: author's collection

Arnold and his younger brother Russell attended Kaikorai Primary School, followed by Otago Boys' High School where Arnold won medals for swimming achievements. He was also a capable skier. Arnold developed a keen interest in radio and began experimenting as a teenager.[12] By 1923 he was licensed to establish and operate an amateur

288

radio transmitting and receiving station. His call sign was L4AL, later to become ZL4AL He was among the first half dozen New Zealand 'hams' to communicate with England by radio.[13]

Figure 17.12. Arnold as a young man. Source: author's collection

Figure 17.13. Arnold's radio shack, Sligo Terrace pre-1923. Source: author's collection

In 1925 the GRUBB family were still living at Roslyn, Dunedin.

SALE OF WORK. ST. JOHN'S, ROSLYN,
St. John's Hall, Roslyn, presented an animated scene yesterday afternoon and evening, when the annual sale of work in aid of the church funds was commenced. There was an attractive array of goods of all kinds. In the evening an entertainment arranged by Mrs GRUBB gave general satisfaction. The stallholders are as follow: – Guild – Mesdames BURNETT, HOLD, SHEPHERD, and FITCHETT; evening guild – Mrs CHAPMAN, and Misses CHAPMAN and HAIGH; produce, Mesdames BENZOIN and GRUBB.[14]

The family moved from Dunedin to Waikouaiti where they settled and established a family business.[15] They ran a general store on the main road. In 1933 Agnes directed a programme for the Waikouaiti Choral Club.[16]

She also produced plays for the Waikouaiti Dramatic Club.

The family lived at 17 Beach Street, Waikouaiti. The house was built around 1912. Even today the large ornamental trees at the front are a reminder of early days when the gardens ran alongside the cement path up to the front door. The original water tank at the back door remains, albeit covered in ivy. A well once stood behind the house near the tank stand. Locals hope that it will be restored.[17]

Figure 17.14. 17 Beach Street, Waikouaiti. Source: author's collection

Agnes died at Dunedin in 1937.[18] Joseph passed away at Waikouaiti in 1951.[19]

Russell married Elizabeth (Bessie) CAMERON and they remained at Waikouaiti as storekeepers throughout their lives. They had two sons, Alan and Lyall, both of whom married. Russell died in 1976 and Bessie lived until her hundredth year in 1912.

Arnold arrived in Gore in 1926. In 1928 he was living at Irwell Street and working as a mechanic.[20]

Two years later he was a radio expert employed by MacGibbon and Co. He took a leading part in detecting leaks from transformers and the like that interfered with radio reception. He was able to isolate the worst affected area of the town.[21]

Arnold had many community interests that reflected his particular talents. In 1930 he was a member of the forty-voice Gore Male Choir.[22] Soon after, he joined the newly formed Gore Tramping Club.[23] In 1932 Arnold was living at 10 Trafford Street when he was elected a Member of the New Zealand Radio Institute (Inc.). As speaker at a luncheon of the Gore Rotary Club, Arnold gave a comprehensive talk on the transmission of sound, from the announcer to the listener.[24] He was president of the Club for a term and became an honorary life member.

Dora's sister Gertrude had helped prepare for her wedding at St Andrews Hall, Gore on 11 May 1936.[25] Her niece, Gertrude's daughter Eleanor, was bridesmaid.

Figure 17.15. The wedding of Arnold GRUBB and Dora CHALMERS. Bridesmaid Eleanor BOYLEN. Source: author's collection

Dora and Arnold lived their entire married life at 19 Thomas Street in Gore. Arnold had bought the land, being Lot 58 Gore and part of Section 137, Block LXXI, Hokonui District, in January 1935.[26]

A member of the platoon of the Gore Battalion of the Home Guard, Arnold was involved in the establishment of signal points throughout the district.[27] He had been enrolled according to the National Service Emergency Regulations 1940.[28] On 20 January 1942 he was called up for service with the Territorial Force and began service on 9 May.[29]

Moved to Harewood base by January 1943 Arnold had achieved the rank of aircraftman.[30] He then trained at Wigram Air Force base and held the rank of driver.

Figure 17.16. Dora (right) and friends at 19 Thomas Street, c.1938. Source: author's collection

On 17 August 1944 Arnold was transferred to Ohakea Air Training Base where he became an aircraftman and took typing classes.[31] He was promoted to leading aircraftman from November 1944. On 27 April 1945 he sent a telegram to Dora telling her that he was leaving for overseas with Haigh Draft, New Zealand Air Force APO 361.[32] He reached Guadalcanal on 13 May 1945 and remained there serving as a radio technician until disembarkation. He arrived at Whenuapai on 22 November 1945. Arnold was discharged on 24 January 1946 and was awarded the Pacific Star medal, War Medal 1939-45 and NZ War Service Medal.[33]

Figure 17.17. Dora and Arnold at Wigram Air Force Camp, 1943. Source: author's collection

The War Service Gratuity was paid at the rate of 8d a day for service within New Zealand and 2s 6d for service outside of New Zealand. This was not enough to sustain a household and Dora continued to work as a teacher at Gore Primary School in Arnold's absence. At home she had the company of her niece May CHALMERS of Kelso who attended Gore High School. (See Chapter 15.)

Until this time Arnold had been working in partnership with another radio technician. On 20 November 1945 he decided to branch out on his own and rented a shop at 72 Main Street Gore, conducting business under the name of Arnold Grubb Ltd. The property was initially leased for a period of five years at the rate of two pounds ten shillings per week.[34] Arnold was registered as a radio serviceman.[35] The shop came to sell a range of electrical appliances as well as radios. Electrical repairs were an important part of the business. He employed a radio technician and an office assistant.

Figure 17.18. Arnold in air force uniform. Source: author's collection

Keen to have a family and still childless by 1949, the couple considered surgery as a last resort, keeping in mind the possibility of adoption. Dora spent time at Dunedin seeking all the data she could find to help in the decision.[36] They were not to know that Dora's sister-in-law Frances was to die suddenly in 1952 leaving husband Jack CHALMERS and his eleven children. Arnold worked out a formula for the sort of family that would suit them. They became guardian to twenty-month-old Barry and eleven-year-old Lorraine to begin with. Stephen, who was aged four at the time, had been staying with the McRAE family, friends of Frances, who lived at Mokoreta. This initial caregiving arrangement did not last and Arnold and Dora decided to add him to their family. Having three children almost simultaneously would have been a huge change for them as inexperienced parents. It was decided that they were to be known as mum and dad by the boys and aunt and uncle by Lorraine. (See Chapter 12 Jack CHALMERS and Frances Louisa Beaven MITCHELL.)

This was a difficult adjustment for Lorraine who had been very close to her mother who was warm and relaxed. In contrast she found her Auntie Dora to be a disciplinarian of the old school. She could be hard to please. Her niece Thelma BOYLEN described her as stern-looking while Arnold was quiet and stayed in the background.

Arnold and Dora were still able to maintain their joint interests and attend relevant meetings and conferences during weekends with Lorraine as babysitter. These included Men of the Trees, The Soil Association, NZ Amateur Radio Transmitters and wholesale electronic companies.

Dora kept up her friendships, mainly from Dunedin Teachers College days. Two of the ladies who lived at Gore, Rita MARRIOT and Lena DAVIS, would visit for afternoon tea and hair perming sessions. The whole family often spent Sunday after church meetings with Bert and Ella BYARS on their farm at Otama. After exploring the outdoors, a huge meal or 'high tea' with lots of fancy foods awaited.

Dora had won first prize at Gore High School for home science and housecraft.[37] She followed guidelines set by the Home Science branch of Otago University and she was a very good housekeeper and cook who provided tasty, nutritious meals. The garden, with a glasshouse, produced a variety of vegetables. Arnold would drive to the nearest beach to gather a trailer load of seaweed to supplement nutrients in the soil. Potatoes and root vegetables were stored in the cellar for winter use. In season the family would drive to Central Otago and take home a load of stone fruit. The next week would be taken up with bottling the fruit to be used a jar at a time on winter Sundays.

The children all attended Gore Primary School, known as Gore Main.

Lorraine and Barry completed their secondary school education at Gore High School, the former being amongst the first intake of the new building on Coutts Road that was opened in February 1954.

With the slowing of the business economy in 1957, at the end of term two Lorraine was forced to leave school and help in the shop. She spent the following year doing nurse aide work in the maternity wing of Gore Hospital and moved to Dunedin in 1959 to begin studies at Dunedin Teacher's College.

Both Dora and Arnold were avid readers. Arnold preferred books on electronics and self-improvement. He was a keen reader of philosophy and psychology, along with other sciences of life, the studies of which formed the basis of his life. Arnold was a seeker of truth and believed that many of the ideas of modern youth stemmed from Zen Buddhism in order to break from formal religion.[38] He also believed in the healing power of intelligent love as espoused by Christ while being a student of the Ancient Mystical Order Rosae Crucis.[39] Arnold believed that this catholic idea of diversity of thought would lead to a synthesis of wholism.[40] Dora frequented the public library for a variety of reading tastes, including gardening and travel.

Figure 17.19. Dora, Barry, Arnold, Stephen and Lorraine at 19 Thomas Street, c.1957. Source: author's collection

Arnold continued with his interest in amateur radio transmission and had set up a shack with long distance aerial reception at 19 Thomas Street. It was the custom for radio hams to mail their personalised card, known as a QSL card, as confirmation of their contact by radio. He liked to spend evenings making and receiving calls around the world.

Arnold was the holder of an Experimental (Research) Station licence for use in the testing and demonstration of radio transmitting equipment.[41] He was communications officer for the Civil Defence Corps. He organised an annual drill whereby a transmitter was set up on the highest point surrounding the town to ensure communication in times of emergency or disaster.

Figure 17.20. Dora in the garden at 19 Thomas Street. Source: author's collection

Figure 17.21. One of the last QSL cards received by Arnold ZL4AL. Source: author's collection

Figure 17.22. Arnold at work on the crib with Lake Wakatipu in the background, c.1958. Source: author's collection

Figure 17.23. The finished crib (bach) at Lake Wakatipu, c.1958. Source: author's collection

During the 1950s, as a family project, Arnold designed and built a crib (otherwise known as bach) at Frankton Arm by Lake Wakatipu. (See Figure 17.22 and 17.23.) It overlooked the lake. Long weekends and holidays were spent there.

In 1961 Lorraine was in her first year of teaching at Waikouaiti School and boarded for a time with Bessie GRUBB's mother who was living there. It was also an opportunity to visit her father (Jack) at the nearby Cherry Farm Hospital.

Figure 17.24. Arnold, Barry and Dora, c.1962. Source: author's collection

During the year Dora experienced an emotional crisis and took time away from home. Her sister-in-law in Christchurch, Janet CHALMERS, who had become widowed, stayed with Dora at the Frankton crib while Arnold and Stephen remained at Gore. Dora also spent time with her brother and his wife, Douglas CHALMERS and Violet who were living at Kakanui, out of Oamaru.[42] She felt unable to cope with a teenager, in Stephen, and arrangements were made for him to live at a children's home in Invercargill run by the Presbyterian Social Services Association. He attended Southland Boys' High School where he became reunited with two brothers closest in age, Charles and Peter who were fellow students at the time.

Dora and Arnold took a trip to Australia in 1965 and toured the Gold Coast. When Arnold returned to New Zealand Dora continued along the coast, stopping over in Sydney and Melbourne.[43] After attending the 1970 Expo at Osaka, Japan they sailed via Hong Kong, Manilla and Indonesia to Australia and in 1974 they took a world tour that started in and involved stopovers in the United States. On that trip they toured ancestral sites in England and in Scotland where they visited extended family. They also saw living relatives and friends in different places including the George CHALMERS family at Dunoon. (See Chapter 21.) A highlight for Arnold was his planned visit to Philips Electrical Industries headquarters in Eindhoven, Holland with a particular interest in the showroom of the sales organisation and service workshop. He had long dealt in the sale and maintenance of the company's products but was surprised to find himself receiving V.I.P. treatment. Other hosts in Europe as in Hanover, Germany treated the couple royally. Arnold and Dora returned home by ship via the Cape of Good Hope and Australia.[44]

Figure 17.25. Dora and Armold with cousin Elsie CHALMERS in Dunoon, Scotland, 1974. Source: author's collection

Arnold recognised a dream by building, in large part, an 18 foot cabin cruiser. Having joined the Gore Boat and Water Ski Club in 1967 and was commodore in 1969-70, 'he had been a keen, active member supporting many organised cruises and Club working bees and was also largely instrumental in the radio communications field during those early marathons and organised events.'[45] He was awarded a 'Gore Boat Club Service Award' in the form of a plaque, suitably worded and framed.[46] He and Dora would take the boat seventy to a hundred miles to Lakes Manapouri and Te Anau, sleeping in it over the weekend. Arnold was planning a trip to Tasmania, the home of his seafaring ancestors, but it was not to be.[47]

Figure 17.26. Group tramping in the Hokonui Ranges. Arnold and Dora together, upper right. Source: author's collection

In 1970 Arnold achieved another milestone by acquiring a private pilot licence and renewed it annually until 1978. He was a member of the Southern Districts Aero Club Inc. and had the distinction at the time of being the oldest student in NZ to gain a licence at the age of 63 years.[48] Following on, he revived his interest in tramping, with Dora, combining outings with Native Forest Action Group activities at the Hokonui Ranges, Piano Flat and Haast Pass.

Arnold Grubb Ltd was dissolved as a company in 1978.[49] (See Figure 17.27.) Arnold had retired long before, continuing part-time helping people where needed.[50] In October the following year he felt that his declining health necessitated his rendering an apology for non-attendance at the NZ Association of Radio Transmitters and he lodged his vote for the incoming controller to take his place. The following month he was elected a member of the American Radio Relay League Inc. with all the rights and privileges of an associate member for a period of one year.[51] Also relinquished was his position as Chairman of the Board of Trustees Advisory Committee for the Royal New Zealand Foundation for the Blind.[52]

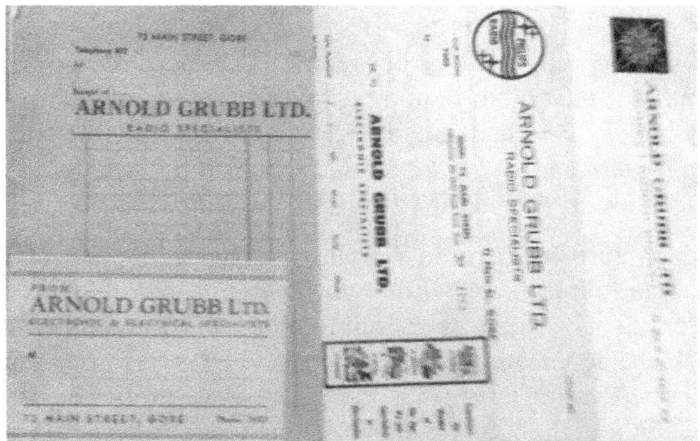

Figure 17.27. Arnold Grubb Ltd letterheads over the years. Source: author's collection

Arnold died at home on 18 June 1980. In all, he had served in fourteen different organisations and 'His standing in the community was reflected in the very large attendance at his funeral.'[53]

Figure 17.28. CHALMERS nieces and nephews at Arnold's funeral (Dora third from right), 1980. Source: author's collection

In her first year of widowhood Dora felt a great comfort in the children she had looked after, all of whom had taken up different careers.[54] Stephen trained to be a physiotherapist while Barry's interest in the environment led him to becoming a landscape architect then on to managing the development of regional parks and open spaces. All three had become married with children.

Dora maintained the interests and friendships that she had developed over the years, attended club and school reunions, visited family members in different parts of the country and renewed her enthusiasm for genealogy and family history. She had already accumulated a valuable collection of documents, letters and photos. Lorraine had also become more involved and together they furthered the research.

In 1986 Dora fulfilled Arnold's wish of visiting his ancestral ties in Tasmania. She found a companion with whom to travel. This was to be her last overseas trip. She was honoured by the Gore and Districts Travel Club that she had helped found and had been a member of the first executive. The citation noted that 'She has gone about her life humbly and quietly without thought of acknowledgement or reward – a rare breed these days – and who has helped found a workable and successful club.'[55]

The garden had always been a source of delight and peace for Dora, but by mid-1990 she felt the work involved, along with house maintenance, was more than she could manage. She decided to sell the property and the newspaper advertisement described it as being the 'Best Character Home Around. Mint condition, sunny, lovely plaster ceilings the nicest one we have seen and three car garaging.'[56]

Figure 17.29. 19 Thomas Street, Gore. Source: newspaper advertisement

Dora invested in a unit at Kitchener Street but realised later that it was a mistake, being a financial commitment that precluded maximum return in her estate. She bought, instead, a separate dwelling at 11 Ardwick Street in Gore.

Figure 17.30. Dora outside her home at 11 Ardwick Street, c.1991. Source: author's collection

In January, 1992, Dora attended the John and Frances CHALMERS family reunion at Greenhills, between Invercargill and Bluff. It was the birth home of her children: Lorraine, Stephen and Barry. (See Chapter 12).

Figure 17.31. Dora with Lorraine at the Greenhills Reunion, January 1992. Photo of Dora's mother in the background. Source: author's collection

Later in the year Dora took ill with a severe stroke and was taken to Gore Hospital accompanied by her niece Ellen CHALMERS. After a short stay she passed away on 27 June 1992. By coincidence or destiny, it was the 40th year to the day since the children's mother, Frances Louisa Beaven CHALMERS (née MITCHELL), passed away, ensuring that both would be remembered.

Dora and Arnold were cremated at Invercargill and buried in the CHALMERS family plot at Andersons Bay, Dunedin.

NOTES

[1] GRUBB, Arnold Henry McLeod, mechanic, Thomas Street, Gore, Mataura Electoral Roll, 1935.

[2] CUS 38/2-3; Letter from Principal Archivist to Arnold GRUBB 17 October 1978, Archives Office of Tasmania, 91 Murray Street, Hobart 7000.

[3] Ibid.

[4] Testimonials on record.

[5] Letter of approval by I. Ballantyne for I. Ballantyne & Co., Dunstable House, Christchurch, 7 April 1903.

[6] 1871 England Census; 1881 England Census.

[7] Letters from Constance HAKE and Max HUNT (BEESLEY descendants living in Australia) to Dora GRUBB.

[8] Memo of Engagement by R.H. Abbott, Importers and Warehousemen, Strand Arcade, Queen Street, Auckland. 25 January 1904.

[9] Certified Copy of Entry in the Register-book of Births in the District of Napier, Arnold McLeod GRUBB, 26 June 1905.

[10] Copy of Baptism Register, St Johns, Roslyn, Dunedin.

[11] GRUBB, Henry Joseph, warehouseman, 53 Town Belt (Later renamed 32 Sligo Terrace), Roslyn, Dunedin West Electoral Rolls, 1911, 1914, 1919; GRUBB, Clara, 53 Town Belt (Later renamed to 32 Sligo Terrace), Roslyn, Dunedin West Electoral Rolls, 1911, 1914, 1919.

[12] Arnold GRUBB, pers.com. Medals sighted.

[13] Original copy of license and schedule; Notes from Gordon BROWN, Nelson, on Arnold's early radio communications.

[14] *Otago Daily Times.* September 16, 1925.

[15] GRUBB, Henry Joseph, salesman, Beach Street, Waikouaiti, Oamaru Electoral Roll, 1935; GRUBB, Agnes Clara, Beach Street, Waikouaiti, Oamaru Electoral Roll, 1935; GRUBB, Russell Alan, salesman, Beach Street, Waikouaiti, Oamaru Electoral Roll,

1935; GRUBB, Henry Joseph, salesman, Beach Street, Waikouaiti, Oamaru Electoral Rolls, 1938-1949; GRUBB, Russell Alan, salesman, Beach Street, Waikouaiti, Oamaru Electoral Rolls, 1938-1949; GRUBB, Elizabeth (née CAMERON), Beach Street, Waikouaiti, Oamaru Electoral Rolls, 1938-1949;

[16] Programme of Concert, Waikouaiti Choral Club

[17] Waikouaiti Coast Heritage Centre, http://www.wchc.org.nz/Researchcentre/LocalStories.aspx 1912

[18] NZRGO, Death Register, 1938/21564, GRUBB Agnes Clara, 64 years.

[19] NZRGO, Death Register, 1951/20259, GRUBB Henry Joseph, 77 years.

[20] GRUBB, Arnold Henry McLeod, mechanic, Irwell Street, Gore, Mataura Electoral Roll, 1928.

[21] *Mataura Ensign*. "Looking Back Through the Files of the *Ensign* 50 years ago." November 11, 1980.

[22] *Mataura Ensign*. "Musical Recollections of Twenty Five Years Ago." Date unknown.

[23] *Mataura Ensign*. "Looking Back." August 21, 1981.

[24] *Mataura Ensign*. "Looking Back 50 Years." July 23, 1982.

[25] Letter from Gertrude BOYLEN to Margaret (cousin).

[26] Certificate of Title, Section 137 Block 71, Hokonui Survey District.

[27] *Mataura Ensign*. "1941 – 50 Years Ago." Date unknown.

[28] Certificate of Enrolment.

[29] GRUBB, Arnold Henry McLeod, Radio employee, 19 Thomas Street, Gore, 468793, New Zealand World War II Ballot List, January 20, 1942.

[30] GRUBB, Arnold Henry McLeod, Registration No. 468793, National Service.

[31] Palmerston North Technical School admission slip.

[32] Telegram from Arnold to Dora GRUBB.

[33] Leading Aircraftman 131170, Arnold Henry McLeod GRUBB, service record.

[34] Tenancy agreement, 72 Main Street, Gore.

[35] GRUBB, Arnold Henry McLeod, Registration No. 468793, National Service.

[36] Letter from Arnold GRUBB to Dora GRUBB, June 12, 1949.

[37] Gore High School book prize, in family possession.

[38] *Mataura Ensign*. "Personality Parade No 3." August 25, 1971.

[39] Letter to Dora, 11 September 1961; Student No. 312 274XB.

[40] *Mataura Ensign*. "Personality Parade No 3." August 25, 1971.

[41] Letter from the Resident Engineer at the Invercargill Office, May 1, 1952.

[42] Letters from Arnold to Dora GRUBB.

[43] Letter from Dora to Arnold GRUBB.

[44] Travel diaries by Dora and Arnold GRUBB.

[45] Tribute to Arnold by the Gore Boat and Water Ski Club.

[46] Letter from secretary of the Gore Boat & Water Ski Club, March 22, 1980.

[47] Note by Dora GRUBB.

[48] "Break-In" magazine, Jan/Feb 1981.

---

49 Letter from Assistant Registrar of Companies, Invercargill. April 4, 1978.

50 Dora GRUBB pers. com.

51 Certificate, American Relay League Inc.

52 Letter from the Secretary Royal New Zealand Foundation for the Blind, July 2, 1980.

53 Silent Key Arnold GRUBB ZL4AL; "Break-In" (magazine) January/February, 1981.

54 Dora GRUBB, June 1981, pers. com..

55 Citation for Gore and Districts Travel Club Life Membership Award, Mrs D. GRUBB.

56 *Mataura Ensign*, date unknown.

PART 6: Early Scotland

18 Early CHALMERS Families

The first part of this chapter covers some of the descendants of John CHALMERS and Isabel HILL as shown in this chart:

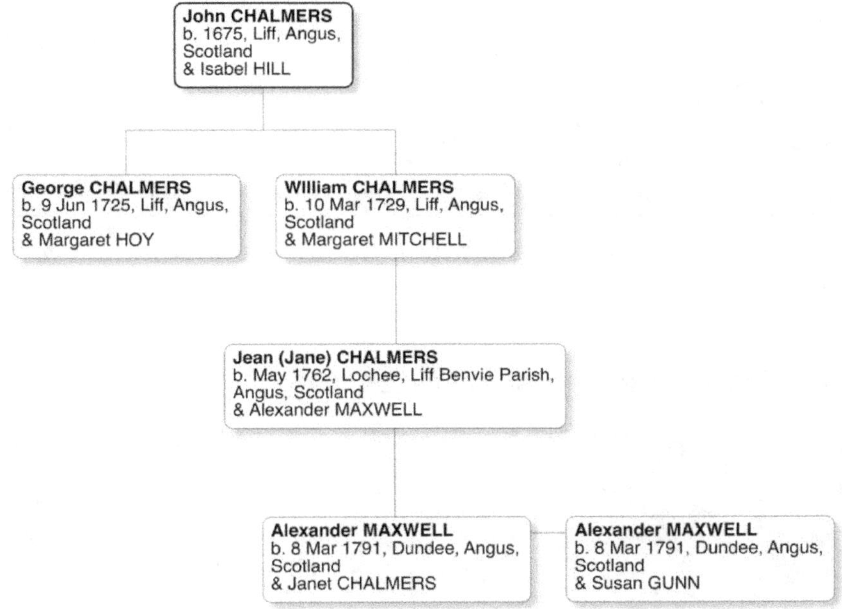

Figure 18.1. Descendants of John and Isabel CHALMERS

Alexander MAXWELL (b.1791) (See Figure 18.1) whose grandparents were William CHALMERS (b.1729) and Margaret MITCHELL (b.1733), wrote his family's history in a publication entitled *Genealogical Notabilia*. His son, David added to the manuscript. Where possible, direct quotes from these works are used so that either one or the other is telling the story. Modern research technology has been used to verify the content. All of the CHALMERS ancestors featured through to John Howe CHALMERS (b.1847) and beyond are direct descendants of William CHALMERS (b.1729) and either of his two wives, Margaret MITCHELL or Jane MONCUR (b.1742) (John Howe CHALMERS' great-grandmother).

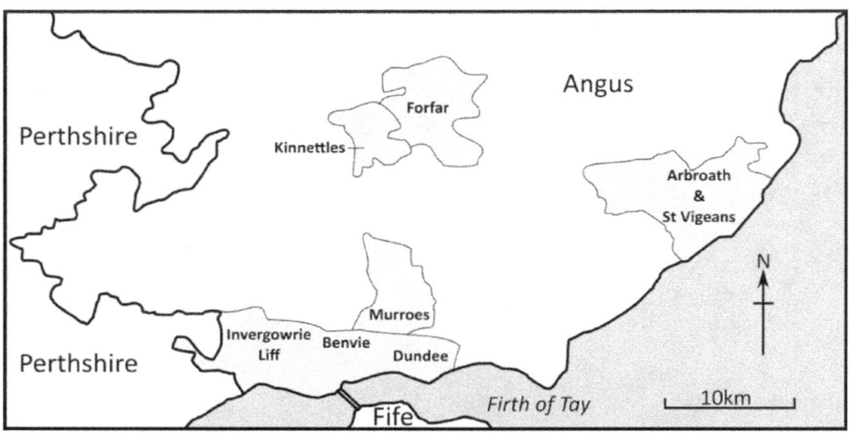

Figure 18.2. Parishes in Angus (formerly Forfarshire until 1928). Source: after http://www.kinnaird.net/images/angus.gif

John CHALMERS and Isabel HILL

The earliest known record of the CHALMERS family in Scotland is that of John CHALMERS born about 1675 and Isabel HILL born about 1685, both of Liff, Angus. They were married in 1714 and became the parents of nine surviving children.[1]

John and Isabel's children were all born in the Parish of Liff, near Dundee.

Figure 18.3. Kirkton of Liff Parish Church. Source: Lorraine BERRY

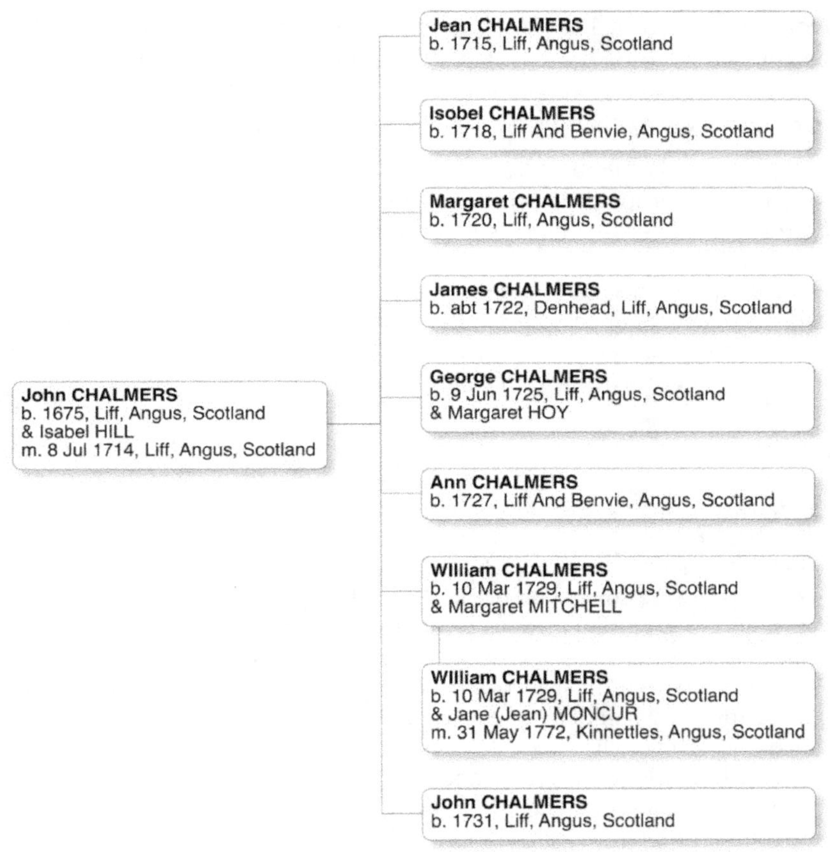

Figure 18.4. The children of John CHALMERS and Elizabeth HILL[2]

Something of the family's struggles were told to and recorded by Alexander MAXWELL, a grandson of William. (See Figure: 18.1.) Alexander's wife Janet CHALMERS was a granddaughter of George. (See Figure 18.5.)

Alexander writes: 'The family appears to have been settled there [in Liff, Angus] for some time. The headstone which they claimed in the churchyard seems of a considerable age, but I could not find a date upon it.'

A Tale of Two Boys

George was born in 1725, William in 1729. (See Figure 18.1.) The first account we have of the two boys is in the year 1739, they being then fourteen and ten years old respectively. Their father had been dead seven years, and their mother was in very poor circumstances:

> but she managed to furnish a pack with small wares, with which she sent her 'laddies' as chapmen (i.e. hawkers) over the countryside. It was a time of great distress; – two bad harvests in succession, and there were not then as now foreign imports of corn to mitigate scarcity at home. Fearful later of these bad old times were current in my childhood; of famine in Dundee, with its attendant privations, sufferings and death; of people leaving the town for the country, in search of food, and of dead bodies being found in dens and on moors, with wild herbs in their mouths.[3]

> In the spring of 1740, – 'in the time of the harrows', as I have heard my grandfather tell the story, – the two young merchants were plying their vocation in the neighbourhood of Forfar. As night came on, with aching hearts and hungry bellies – they begged for quarters at a farm-house but were rudely denied. It happened that a young man and young woman – farm servants – were doing a bit of outside courtship, and love may have opened their hearts to pity for the poor boys: they secreted them in the barn, and left them to repose amongst the straw. In the morning the lass rose before any of the family were astir: she woke the lads, gave them all she had in her power to bestow – the half of a pease-meal bannock [a flat, round, unleavened loaf] and sent them on their way. They had to trudge ten miles before they could get anything else to eat. At Pourie they went in on a ploughman making his brose, and solicited a share. He was willing to give each of them a large spoonful for a pair of scissors to clip his beard with. The times were hard, but like starving Esau they were obliged to comply. They had no other food until they reached their mother's house at Denhead.[4]

The famine of 1740-41 was due to extremely cold and then rainy weather in successive years, resulting in a series of poor harvests. 'Hunger compounded a range of fatal diseases. The cold and its effects extended across Europe, and it is now seen to be the last serious cold period at the end of the Little Ice Age of about 1400-1800.'[5] During the time of the boys' childhood the kirkton (i.e. church town) of Liff was a clachan, or small hamlet associated with a church where joint farming activities gave the crofters social and economic unity. Besides farming, however, the weaving of coarse linen cloth had by then 'become the principal employment'.[6]

George CHALMERS (b.1725) and Margaret HOY and Janet BARRIE

Little further is known of George, the older of the two brothers. He appears to have led a quiet life away from city activities.

I cannot tell much about his early life. His wife's name was Margaret HOY, they settled at Denside in the Parish of Monikie and I think at that time they belonged to John GLAS's people, but he left them afterwards and became a Baptist, being a man of some abilities he was leader in that sect but subsequently left them, and continued until the time of his death unconnected in any way.[7]

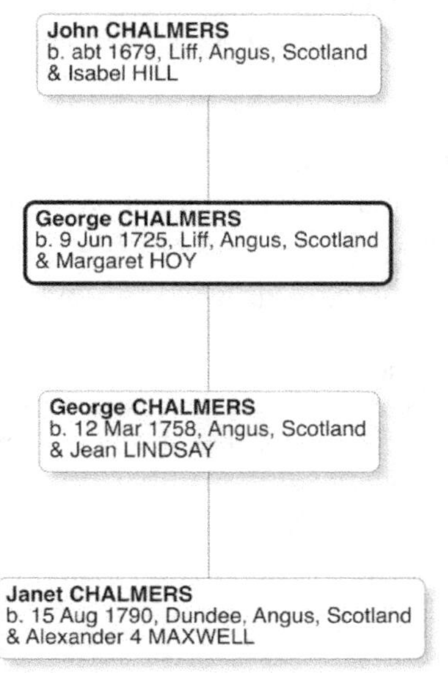

Figure 18.5. George CHALMERS parents and descendants

Figure 18.6. Kirkton of Monikie. Source: Lorraine BERRY

I recollect that amongst my father's books was an old coarsely-printed pamphlet on 'Melchizidek' – which had been written and published by my mother's grandfather, and was doubtless the first literary production in the family. I think that this was to prove that the ancient priestly king was an

313

earlier incarnation of Christ.; and I understood that his peculiar views got him into trouble with his church, even to expulsion from the brotherhood. The Glasites allowed no difference of opinion amongst their members on matters theological.[8]

The Glasites were a small Scottish sect founded by John GLAS in 1730. Glasite churches taught strict conformity and the sect spread to parts of Scotland, England and America.

He had a small farm or pendicle [a rented part of a large estate in Scotland] as it is called. His son George ... and two daughters I think were all his first family. After the death of his wife he married again Janet BARRIE who bore him one daughter, but their tempers seemed to be much unsuited to one another, and they finally separated soon after. About this time he seemed to have left his place and I think again travelled about the country as a chapman, he also wrote his treatise on Melchizidek about this time, and sold it through the country.[9]

Figure 18.7. High Street and Luckenbootes from the east, Dundee, 1836. Source: http://www.electricscotland .com/history/dundee

About the end of the century I think he had a shop about the High Street, and here he met with a considerable loss, a rogue named MALLOCH kept a small public house, and a billiard table in his neighbourhood; pretending to want change for a pound, discovered where the old man kept his money and plundered the hoard, the fellow was hanged in Perth two years afterwards for some other depridation, but was never charged with that offence.[10]

A later crime brought John MALLOCH before the courts and he was tried for housebreaking and theft on 23 October 1801. He was hanged in Perth on 18 December 1801.[11] The two month gap between John's sentencing and hanging was because 'the King and the Privy Council had to approve Scottish death sentences so there tended to be a greater time between sentence and execution or reprieve than in England due to the communications difficulty'. While hanging may seem an extreme punishment for theft, 'between 1800 and 1868, 273 people were publicly hanged in Scotland for various crimes including different forms of theft: housebreaking 55; robbery 30; highway robbery 13; theft 8; horse theft 7; sheep stealing 2; Stouthrief (robbing a dwelling house) 9 and Hamesucken ("the seeking and invasion of a person in his dwelling house") 3.'[12]

> My mother spoke of him [George] as having in his latter years lived with her and her sister at Pack Wynd, Hawkhill, Dundee. George's granddaughter, Janet CHALMERS spoke of his fine, fresh complexion, when his years exceeded fourscore.[13]

Although they may have lived very different lives and in different parts of the country, the bond between the two brothers was never broken. George's younger brother William, who outlived him by three years, 'insisted upon carrying his head to the grave'.[14]

The Linen Weavers

Throughout the generations the CHALMERS families were involved predominantly in the linen and jute industries and business interests. Linen had been a major industry in Scotland for hundreds of years. The industry was stimulated by an act of Parliament of 1686 stipulating that everyone had to be buried in linen winding sheets made from materials which had been grown. As time went on considerable business was being done in the manufacture of sail-cloth, fine linen, lawns, and cambric. Made from the blue-flowered linen flax plant, the manufacture of linen was based mainly in Fifeshire and Forfarshire, Dundee becoming its centre.[15] Handloom weaving tended to be a cottage industry and therefore would be carried out in the home and the cloth sold for local use. Therefore it was usual for weavers to own their own looms and to learn weaving skills from family members. In 1792 the linen weaving trade was in a flourishing state in Forfarshire. The principal kind of cloth made was a coarse plain fabric called 'osnaburg'. A weaver could earn from 15 to 20 shillings for weaving a piece of 120 yards in length, which occupied him eight or ten days.[16]

The Three Williams

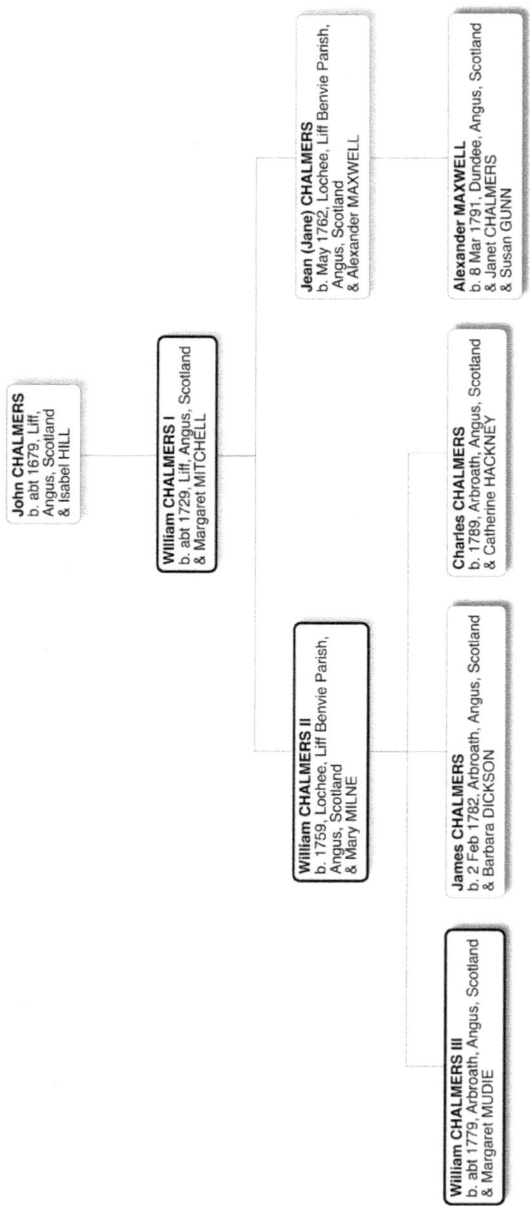

Figure 18.8. Three William CHALMERS

William I CHALMERS' first marriage to Margaret MITCHELL

George's younger brother William CHALMERS also married twice, his first wife being Margaret MITCHELL of Aberdeenshire, with whom he had six children.

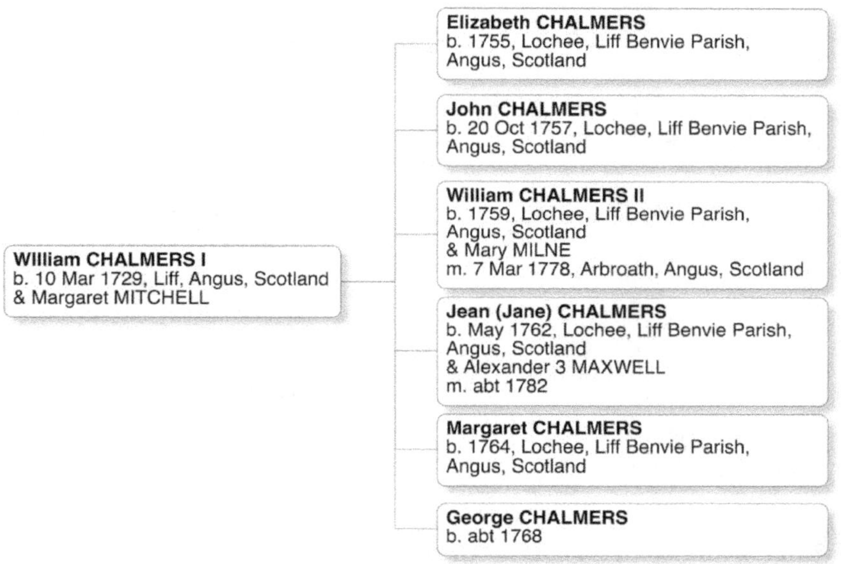

Figure 18.9. The children of William CHALMERS and Margaret MITCHELL[17]

'He built a house at Lochee, and took his mother to live with them.'[18] Margaret is said to have died giving birth to the youngest, George. A death record has not been found.

William I's second son to Margaret MITCHELL was also named William (II) and whose first son was also called William (III). Three generations of William can be more easily referred to as William I, William II and William III. Both William II and his son James became prominent citizens of Dundee. (See Figure A18.8.)

William II married Mary MILNE on 7 March 1778.[19] They were both aged nineteen. They settled in Arbroath and moved to Dundee later. William II became a jute manufacturer, as did his two sons, James and Charles, while William III was a bookbinder who opened the stationers shop near the top of Castle Street. The two youngest did not reach adulthood. Andrew died as a child and John passed away in 1807 at the age of eighteen. Their only daughter, Margaret married George BATCHELOR, a linen cloth merchant. They were childless.[20]

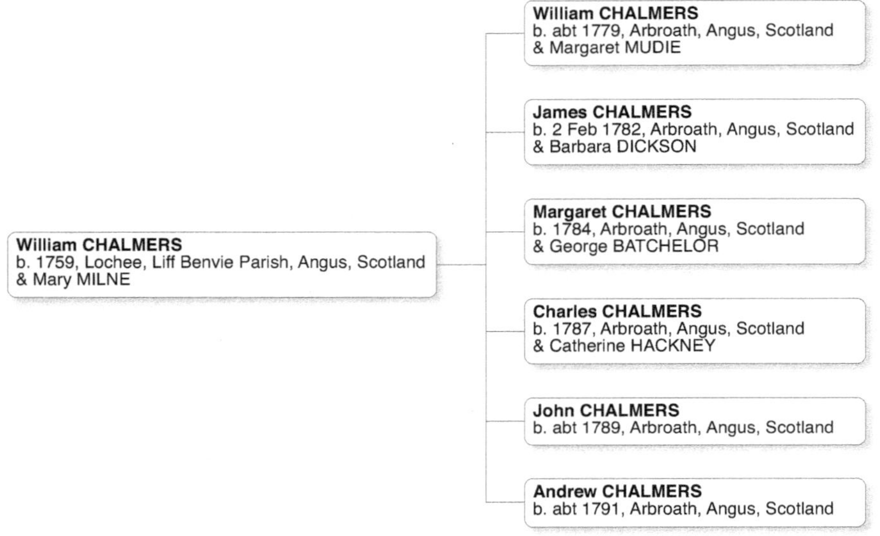

Figure 18.10. The children of William CHALMERS and Mary MILNE

The Booksellers, Printers and Publishers

Their son William III, born 1779 at Arbroath in Angus, trained to be a handloom weaver. But while still intelligent, scholarly and ambitious, he started a business with the help of his father in Castle Street, Dundee as a bookseller, bookbinder and seller of writing materials. The shop had been a baker's.[21]

Castle Street had opened in 1785, 'the second street formed from High Street/Nethergate to the Harbour'.[22]

It was a good business, involving interests close to William's heart, but his love of books could not compete with his other loves, drink and women. The first he was able to indulge at the Blue Bell Inn, near his shop in Castle Street – too near. The second apparently involved him with a collection of women, his health began to suffer, and so did his business. His cousin Alexander MAXWELL wrote: 'Poor William went from bad to worse, was repeatedly separated from his wife and at last died in a house in St Andrew's Street, where my mother had been prevailed upon to go and wait upon him'. His death in 1809 at the age of thirty-two, broke the hearts of his wife and his father, who, according to his cousin, had done all he could to reclaim the prodigal son.[23]

William II was concerned about the fate of the business and this was where his second son James (b.1782) comes at last on the scene. His father made him give up his occupation as weaver at the age of twenty-seven and sent him to Castle Street in an effort to rebuild the business. He seems to have made a success of his opportunity and to have extended the scope of the firm in a manner now known as diversification.[24]

Figure 18.11. Portrait of James CHALMERS. Source: author's collection

James CHALMERS, bookseller, in Dundee, was admitted burgess by the privilege of William CHALMERS, manufacturer, his father.[25] Being a burgess meant that James was permitted to trade in the burg free of charge.

On the 1st January, 1846, Mr CHALMERS was presented in the Town Hall of Dundee with a public testimonial in recognition of his services in improving the postal system, and as the originator of the adhesive postage stamp. On the 3rd March, 1883, the Town Council of Dundee formally passed the following resolution:

That, having had under consideration the pamphlet lately published on the subject of the adhesive stamp, the Council are of the opinion that it has been conclusively shown that the late James CHALMERS, bookseller, Dundee, was the originator of this indispensable feature in the success of the reformed penny postage scheme, and that such be entered upon the Minutes.

In the course of his career, Mr CHALMERS served in many positions of importance in the Town Council of Dundee, and in the public institutions of the town. Early in life he married Barbara DICKSON, eldest daughter of Bailie DICKSON, Montrose. He died in August, 1853, aged 71 years, and lies buried, in the Howff. His son, Charles Dickson CHALMERS, merchant, Dundee, was admitted Burgess on 17th December, 1840.'[26]

Figure 18.12. Dundee Town Hall, 1836. Source: http://www.electricscotland.com/ history/dundee

Testifying as to the truthfulness of James CHALMERS' claim, cousin Alexander MAXWELL (1791-1859) wrote: 'James, bred a manufacturer, but went into his brother William's shop, which he kept (being also Printer, Bookbinder, Pianoforte dealer and Ink Manufacturer), until his death in 1853. I was with him in 1833-34, as shop-boy, and P.D., and have a very pleasant memory of him as a kind master, and a courteous gentleman. ... The youngest son Patrick still survives: he was a tea-merchant in China – now resides in Wimbledon, London.'[27]

For several years he has persistently fought for his father's claim to be recognised as the original inventor of the adhesive postage-stamp. (See Figures 18.13 and 18.14) No doubt he was so. I have certain and precise knowledge on the matter, having seen and handled model stamps, gummed on the backs which the master had printed in the office before I left it. – and I left it at the end of October, 1834.[28]

The building next to the CHALMERS shop at 10 Castle Street was originally an hotel. In 1965 it was reborn as the Chalmers Hall of Residence of the University of Dundee in honour of James' invention of the adhesive postage stamp in the shop next door.[29] (See Figure 18.14)

Figure 18.13. Illustration of Original Stamps. Source: author's collection

Figure 18.14. Shop Sign. Source: author's collection

In addition to being credited with the invention of the penny postage stamp, James became a Burgh Councillor and served as Convener of the Nine Incorporated Trades. He became a strong supporter of the reform of local politics and, unsurprisingly given his business, campaigned for the repeal of taxes on newspapers and newspaper adverts.[30] As well, being a book publisher in his shop, James helped push Dundee's writing culture further.[31] His achievements are recognised by a plaque, one of ten, honouring residents of Dundee who contributed to the betterment of the world through social and scientific discovery and advancement. It can be seen on the Discovery Walk at Slessor Gardens, part of the new Water

Front, Dundee.[32]

Figure 18.15. Headstone of James CHALMERS, Houff Cemetery. Source: Lorraine BERRY

The Jute Manufacturers

While the Napoleonic War inhibited commerce, a huge demand for sailcloth, hammocks and cheap shirtings almost trebled Dundee's flax imports by its end, and though her total was less than half that of Hull, she had 36% of the Scottish trade and 16% of the British. The rate of shipping that had been increased by steamboats meant that jute could be imported from as far away as Russia and India. The production of hemp that was used for inferior linens and sacking, as well as rope, increased twelve-fold between 1789 and 1849. Steam powered factories with mechanised spinning eventually grew in number to sixty.

Table 18.7. Average Imports of Fibres at Dundee, 1789 and 1815-50 (tons)[33]

Year	Flax	Hemp	Jute	Total
1789	908	88	0	996
1815- 19	2,577	1,058	0	3 635
1820-24	5,609	2,016	0	7,525
1825-29	12,327	1,293	0	13,620
1830-34	18,628	2,535	0	21,163
1835-39	24,909	2,550	0	27,459
1740-44	25,464	648	3,704	29,816
1845-49	28,400	1,132	9,111	38,643

Alexander MAXWELL and Janet CHALMERS

Alexander MAXWELL spent just a few months of formal education at a dame school, an early form of a private elementary school in English-speaking countries. They were usually taught by women and were often located in the home of the teacher.[34] At a very early age he was sent out into the country to herd cows. However, his thirst for knowledge was not deterred though limited to the Scriptures, Scottish ballads and detached poems by Burns and Allan Ramsay. At the age of eighteen he was appointed to the joiner trade and worked for a few years in Dundee as a journeyman. An economic depression brought about his move to Edinburgh and later to Glasgow.[35]

Figure 18.16. Alexander MAXWELL. Source: unknown

Returning to Dundee in 1818, he settled there and married Janet CHALMERS on 4 December of that year.[36] Janet's parents were George CHALMERS born 1758 and Jean LINDSAY. Alexander and Janet had a family of five surviving children, the eldest being David born 1819 and for whom he wrote *Genealogical Notabilia*.[37] (See Figure 18.1)

To help ease his pain, Alexander wrote in detail to a friend recalling the events and physical and emotional suffering that went with the onset of scarlet fever followed by typhus that took the lives of two of his children throughout eighteen days. He wrote: 'Mary and William were remarkably fine children, and never did I see them in better health and spirits than they were that day. Full of life and gaiety Mary trip'd before me, making her childish but acute remarks upon passing objects, often turning and holding up her little round face to catch my smile or William's ready laugh.' Their sudden decline was painful for him to watch and a huge drain on the wellbeing of their mother. The situation and feelings fluctuated between hope and despair until 'Our wearied feelings now found rest, to concentrate to one point; the storm is over and like shipwrecked mariners we enjoy a melancholy respite to contemplate our loss.' Although his faith sustained him, Alexander lamented, 'Again will Spring visit desert Nature with a smile, but they shall no longer be the companions of my rural walks – while I pleased myself with showing the beauties of the town or assisted them in the fields to cull the fairest wild flowers.'

> In 1821 he obtained employment at the building of a spinning mill, on the starting of which the proprietor, who had taken notice of his intelligence and painstaking industry, employed him permanently.[38]

David MAXWELL described his father's working conditions under Charles CHALMERS who was the fourth child of William CHALMERS and Mary MILNE. (See Figure A18.10). William CHALMERS born 1879 and his brother James born 1782 written of earlier, were first cousins of Alexander: 'My father was employed about Tay Street Mills, – first as a millwright, – then as foreman of mechanics, and then as manager of the works, about thirty years', as shown in the 1841 and 1851 Census returns.[39]

Table: 18. 8. Hendersons Wynd, Dundee, Angus, 1841 Scotland Census[40]

Alexander MAXWELL	50	flax mill manager	Angus, Scotland
Janet CHALMERS	50		
David MAXWELL	22		
Elisabeth MAXWELL	13		
Charles MAXWELL	11		
George MAXWELL	19		

Janet died in 1847 and two years later Alexander became married to Susan GUNN.[41]

Table: 18.9. East Side 7 Hendersons Wynd, Dundee, Angus, 1851 Scotland Census[42]

Alexander MAXWELL	60	head	flax mill manager	Dundee, Forfarshire
Susan MAXWELL	52			
Charles C. MAXWELL	21			
John LINDSAY	19	visitor		

Alexander served 'the mester' faithfully, and – especially when his own health was failing – had to endure much from a captious temper, and an overbearing spirit.[43]

Figure 18.17. Tay Dundee Jute Mills, 1836. Source: http://www.electricscotland.com/ history/dundee

Charles CHALMERS (1789 - 1859) was a Millspinner – reckoned the head of the family – he ever seemed to surround himself with an atmosphere of austere dignity and hauteur. He married Catherine HACKNEY – sister to his business partner. They had only one child – a son, also Charles. (On one occasion) "Young Charlie", then nearly forty years old, was maudlin with drink, – insulting his father, and swearing at the two female servants who had been in the family since before he was born. Mr. C. was in evident dread of his son, and in Charles' absence from the room, he cried to us like a child. All his wealth and pride had come to this. When the young master came into possession, he took my brother Alexander into partnership, and until Charles' death in 1868, Alex had to manage both him and the business. After some legacies and annuities, my brother was residuary legatee. The annuitants were his cousin - the old servants, the gardener, and a boyfriend of Charlie's. Mr CHALMERS died 7 August 1859, just one month after my father, aged 71.[44]

'This situation he [Alexander] retained until failing health obliged him to resign in 1850.'[45] 'Shortly after retirement Alexander became utterly helpless through creeping paralysis, speech and motion being almost annihilated, but his mental power remained undimmed until his death in July 1859.'[46] His son thought his physical decline was most likely the consequence of a mill accident. 'Mr MAXWELL's favourite study was history, both ancient and modern - Josephus, Rollin, Gibbon, Goldsmith, Hume and Buchanan being authors with whom he was familiar. So retentive was his memory that any anachronisms or mis-statement, either written or spoken, was speedily detected by him.'[47]

Alexander's obituary reads:

At Isles' Lane, Hawkhill, Dundee, on the 7th inst. 1859. Mr. Alexander MAXWELL, late mill manager, in his 69th year. His intellect was vigorous, his information copious and minute, and his general attainments remarkable, considering that he was a self-taught man. His literary ability is not unknown to the readers of the 'Telegraph', several of his writings having appeared in its columns. We may specially instance the admirable series of papers concluded last week entitled 'Town and Country in the Olden Time' which were the product of his instructive pen. Of his spotless integrity, genial disposition and kindly heart it is unnecessary to speak at any length here. These are cherished in grateful remembrance by his family and friends.[48]

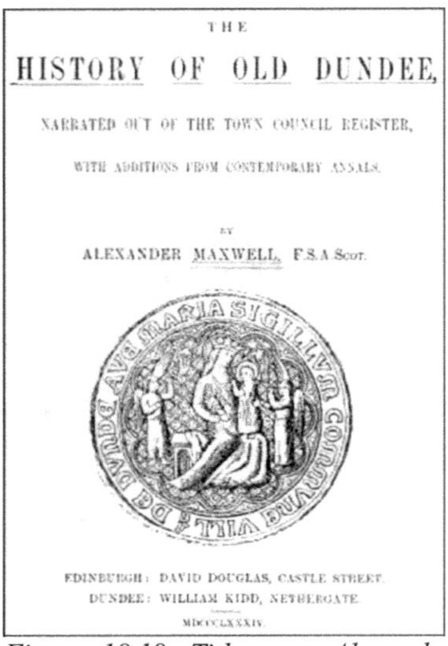

Figure 18.18. Title page Alexander MAXWELL's The History of Old Dundee. Source: electricscotland.com

Alexander was a recognised poet and historian. His published writings include:

- David Herschell Edwards, *Modern Scottish poets, with biographical and critical notes* (Scotland: Brechin, 1897)
- Alexander Maxwell, *Genealogical Notabilia*
- Alexander Maxwell, *The History of Old Dundee, Narrated Out of the Town Council Register, with Additions from Contemporary Annals* (Edinburgh: D. Douglas, 1884)[49]

In his introduction to the *Genealogical Notabilia* MAXWELL noted: 'And this must be the most extended genealogy which has ever be[en] compiled for prince or potentate, be as one single spray in the wide-spreading tree of descent appertaining to every human being. But it is ever interesting to know a few of the nearer links in the all-binding chain of humanity.'[50]

At least two of Alexander's sons became mill managers. Alexander Jnr took over his father's role as mill manager for his cousin Charles CHALMERS. They remained at Tay Street. In 1851 Alexander was married and was living at 2 St David's Lane, Dundee.

Table 18.10. Household of Alexander and Helen MAXWELL, 2 St Davids Lane, Dundee, Angus, Scotland, 1851

Alexander	30	Manager Of Flax Mill	Dundee, Forfarshire
Helen MAXWELL	32		

David returned to Dundee from working as an engine fitter in Portsea, England to take up mill management. In 1871 he was a widower living at 30 Tay Street Dundee with four of his children.

Table 18.11. David MAXWELL household, 30 Tay Street, St Peter, Dundee, Angus, Scotland, 1871[51]

David MAXWELL	51	head, manager	Dundee, Forfarshire
James MAXWELL	23		
Harriet MAXWELL	14		Portsea Island, Hampshire
David MAXWELL	12		Portsea Town, Portsmouth
Charles MAXWELL	10		Portsmouth, Hampshire
Kath CAMPBELL	30		
James SCOTT	28		

Alexander's son, of the same name, became a master flaxshire. His responsibility was to do away with waste and increase production by controlling the sorption capacity of cellulose. This was done by applying chemicals and heat treatment to salt-containing natural fibre materials. In this way they regulated the crystal and pore structure to produce strong 'oxide fibres'.[52]

During the peak of Alexander Jnr's business success he employed twenty-three men, one hundred and eight women and girls and fourteen boys. There were more women in employ because they were paid less which kept the costs down. It was not unusual for the man of the household to look after the home affairs while his wife worked at the mill. As a result, Dundee had very high male unemployment – the men who stayed home were known as 'kettle bilers' (kettle boilers).[53]

Table 18.12. Alexander MAXWELL household, 59 Magdalen Yard Road, St Peter, Dundee, Angus, Scotland, 1871[54]

Alexander MAXWELL	50	flaxshire, master employing 23 men, 108 woman & girls & 14 boys	Dundee, Forfarshire
Helen MAXWELL	52	wife	Dundee, Forfarshire
George F MAXWELL	16	son	Dundee, Forfarshire
Alexander MAXWELL	13	son	Dundee, Forfarshire
Mary WHITE	19		
Jessie G McLAREN	21		

Ultimately all the jute for the Dundee mills came from the Bengal region in eastern India, centered on the city of Calcutta (now known as Kolkata). From around 1870 Indian businessmen started to open their own jute mills knowing that they could undercut the Dundee industry by employing cheaper labour and also because the raw material was right 'on their doorstep'. Dundee had the experienced workers though, so for the next 90 years a steady stream of Dundee mill workers would travel out to India to work in and manage the Calcutta mills.[55] Following the move of the jute industry to India, Dundee's economy turned to jam and journalism, products for which the city became famous.[56]

Figure 18.19. Jute mill workers. Source:author's collection

Alexander rejected any ideas of moving to India and, by the age of seventy, he had retired from the jute industry and chose instead to become a bookseller, an occupation familiar to his family.[57]

By this time he had returned to the original CHALMERS home area of his great-great grandparents, John and Isabel CHALMERS, at Liff and Benvie.

Table 18.13. Alexander MAXWELL household, 9 Viewforth St, St Peter, Liff and Benvie, Angus, Scotland, 1891[58]

Alexander MAXWELL	70	head, bookseller	Dundee, Forfarshire
Helen MAXWELL	72	wife	Dundee, Forfarshire
George F MAXWELL	36	son	Dundee, Forfarshire

William CHALMERS I second marriage to Jane MONCUR

William and Jane MONCUR, William's second wife, were married at Kinnettles Parish Church on 31 May 1772.[59] (Refer to Figure 18.20.)

Jane was from the parish of Rattray and, like William's first wife Margaret MITCHELL, was a member of the Glasite Church. Her parents were David MONCUR and Jannet MARSHAL, also of Rattray, Perthshire.[60] Jane's father David MONCUR was a crofter of Muirhouses (Murroes). (See Figure 18.21.)

Added to his family of six with Margaret MITCHELL, William had eight more children with Jane MONCUR. (See Figures 18.21 and 18.22.)

Figure 18.20. Kinnettles Parish Kirk. Source: author's collection

The youngest child of William and Jane MONCUR, Thomas, died in childhood.[61] The ninth child has not been identified.

With such a numerous family it may easily be imagined my Grandfather had many difficulties to encounter – he had however a small bit of land and kept a Cow – this would greatly enable him to bring them decently up and at the same time maintain his own respectability. At the foot of his small garden a cristal Burn – at that time unspoiled by the Spinning mill and many other things that now defile it was his boundary he had a fine Bleaching green and a great trade in washing for wealthy people in Dundee – this they practised for a long series of years and I think kept a servant for the purpose even after some of the daughters were grown up … I was accustomed to see Grandfather working in his four loom shop – generally accompanied by one or more of his sons.[62]

Figure 18.21. Muirhouses, Murroes, Angus. Source: author

New Year's Day (old style), was quite a great affair with us youngsters. On that festive occasion the old man expected all his numerous progeny, who could attend, to dine with him. At the time of my earliest recollections he had nearly reached his seventieth year. He was rather grave in countenance and of sober deportment, – but withal cheerful and conversable, – much respected and esteemed by neighbours and acquaintances. He had been a comely man in his youth, and maintained a fresh complexion to the last; his ruddy locks never turning to gray, or leaving him bald.[63]

According to Alexander MAXWELL: 'The CHALMERS face had delicately cut features, and a pure red and white complexion. Portraits of Lord Nelson, always suggest to me the CHALMERS face.' [64]

In 1813, his second wife, Jane MONCUR died.[65] She had been his helpmate for nearly forty-five years; The old man had then become very frail. I often went out on Sabbath forenoon, to lead him into the meeting-house for which he was very thankful. His daughter Janet then kept house for him.[66]

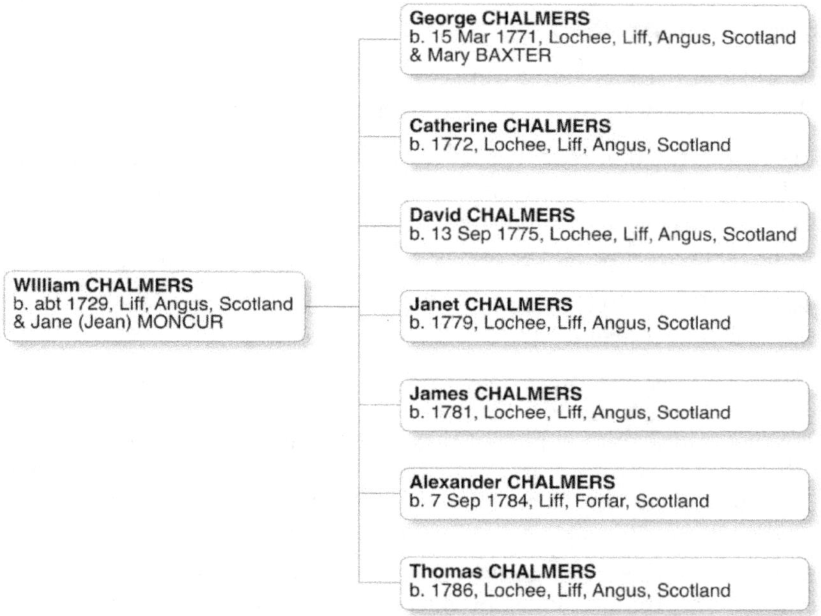

Figure 18.22. The children of William I CHALMERS and Jane MONCUR.

William remained a faithful member of the Glasite Church throughout his life. 'As a young man he said he had often heard of that man and would willingly go to hear him (Mr GLAS) preach. He did so and from that day he never went to any other Church.'[67]

All of the surviving children of William I CHALMERS and Jane MONCUR married, except for Janet who looked after her father in his later years. Following in their father's footsteps all of their sons began their occupations as weavers: While James and Alexander went abroad to seek their fortunes in North America, many of William I's sons had become jute manufacturers in Dundee. The sons who remained in Dundee were able to benefit from the flax and hemp industry that flourished there during their working years.

The Fortune Seekers

The brothers James and Alexander were perhaps the first known CHALMERS emigrants from Dundee. (See Figures 18.22 and 18.23.)

James CHALMERS

James CHALMERS, fourth son of William and Jean MONCUR was born in 1781. He went to New York City where he trained as a silk-dyer.

James had arrived in New York City as a seventeen-year-old on 18 June 1798. He became an American citizen on 25 April 1807.[68] In 1850 he was retired and living with a married daughter, Mary CLAYTON.[69] James died intestate in New York City in 1859.[70]

By 1867 James' offspring had little or no knowledge of their Scottish roots in Dundee. David MAXWELL, son of Alexander, wrote:

> 'James, a dyer by business. He went to New York and became rich. One of his grandsons, James M. CHALMERS, some twenty years ago, wrote to his second cousin James [b.1806], the eldest son of James CHALMERS [b.1782] asking particulars of family history, and extracts from my father's narratives were sent to him. There have been some wild notions of great wealth waiting for "next of kin" on the other side of the Atlantic.'[71]

James M. CHALMERS, grandson of James, dyer, was a lawyer in New York and was the one who sought information about his CHALMERS family history. He died at the age of 32 and did not marry.[72] However, others of his grandfathers'offspring did survive and became involved in a number of occupations including: merchant, carpenter, teacher, boarding house proprietor, clerk and clergyman. Many lived in New Jersey, United States.

Alexander CHALMERS

Alexander, the other fortune seeker, second son of William I CHALMERS and Jane MONCUR was born in 1784. He was a manufacturer and was said to have married a girl from Edinburgh and with her and their two children, settled in Canada in 1820.[73] Alexander married Ann DON on the fourth of August 1815 at St Cuthbert's, Edinburgh, Scotland.[74]

Shortly before his death William I gave his blessing on the marriage.

> 'August, 1815, his … son, Alexander married in Edinburgh, and brought his wife home to Dundee. I accompanied them out to Lochee on the presentation of the bride to the old man. He rose with some difficulty from his chair, took his blooming daughter-in-law by the hand and said, – "Ye are very welcome

to this kintra side, – and may the Lord be wi' you a' your days, to bless you and to you gude." The words, and the manner in which they were spoken were so impressive that I never forgot them. I never saw my grandfather afterwards: I went to Edinburgh shortly, and he died the January following, and was buried in the Liff churchyard – 87 years old – and his older brother George attained to the same age.'[75]

William I CHALMERS died on 18 January 1816 at Dundee and was buried in the Liff Churchyard.[76]

Four years later on 13 October 1820 Alexander, with his wife Ann and two children, did in fact sail from Scotland to Quebec, Canada. From there they boarded the vessel *New Swiftsure* that took them along the St Lawrence Seaway to Montreal.[77] They settled in a farming area centred on Granby, eighty kilometres east of Montreal. Their nine children were all christened at St Stephen Anglican Church in Granby.[78]

Son Alexander and wife Ann remained as part of the farming community in the village of Granby throughout their lives. As a widower Alexander lived with his son James and daughter-in-law Elizabeth.

Alexander died on 12 December 1878 at Granby where he was buried. His wife Ann had preceded him in death on 21 November 1864 and was buried in the same plot.[79]

Their eldest son Alexander continued to farm the land. He and wife Anna are also buried in the Cowie Cemetery at Granby. Most offspring remained in Quebec. However, later generations moved away, to western Canada and the United States, particularly Washington state where they became US citizens. Their daughter Elizabeth married Damon FULLER, farmer, who was an American citizen born in New Hampshire. Their eldest son George Damon FULLER was born in Quebec but immigrated to the United States and became a naturalised citizen. In 1910 George was living in Chicago Ward 7, Cook County, Illinois. He was professor of ecology, botany and zoology at Chicago University.[80]

George CHALMERS and Mary BAXTER

George, the oldest son of William and Jane MONCUR was born 15 March 1771 at Lochee, Liff, Angus. He married Mary BAXTER on 28 December 1798 at Dundee, Forfarshire.[81] Mary was the youngest child of John BAXTER, crofter and Mary DARLING of Muirhouses, Murroes. (Refer to Figure 18.21.) She was baptised there on 27 September 1778.[82] At the time of Mary's marriage her father was a labourer at Duntroon,

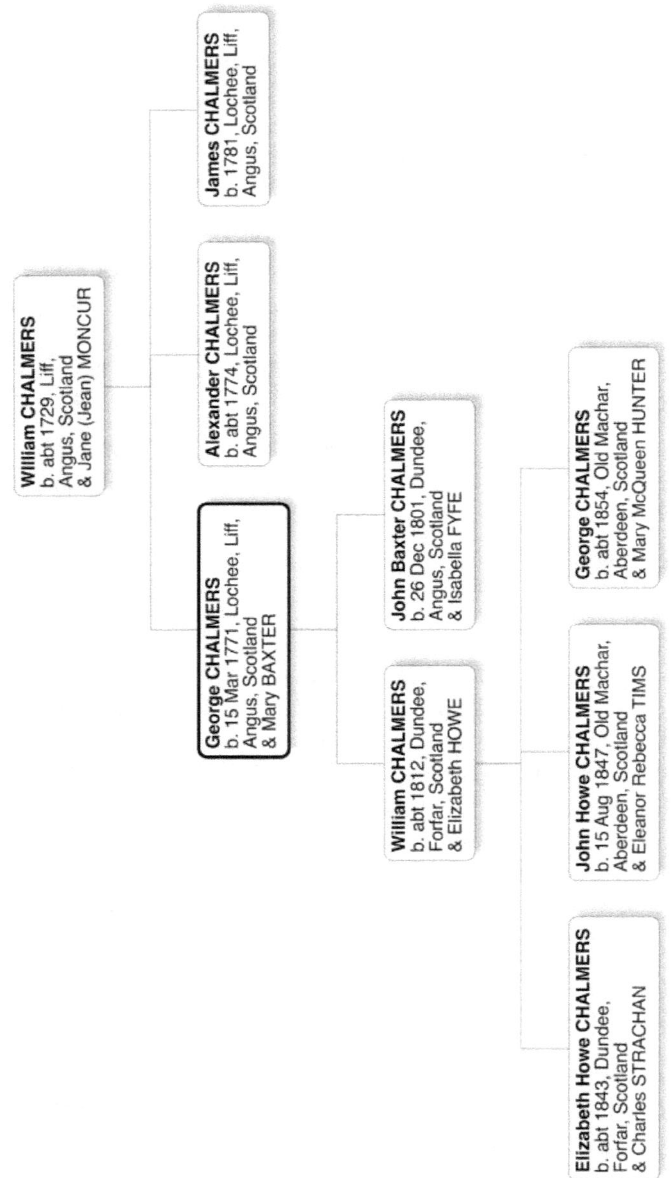

Figure 18.23. Descendants and parents of George CHALMERS

Argyllshire, Scotland.[83] In 1824 George and Mary were living at Westside Hilton, Dundee where he had become a jute factory owner and manufacturer in the thriving industry.[84]

Within five years George had moved to Maxwelltown, Dundee. This address was known as Chalmers Land. The property ran from Number 36 to Number 40 Jamaica Street.[85] When visited in 2006 by the author, any buildings were in the process of being demolished and the land laid bare for future development.

George CHALMERS died on 30 December 1836 at 36 Jamaica Street, Maxwelltown, Dundee, the Chalmers family home.[86] The cause of death was asthma.[87] His widow Mary of thirty years was still living there in 1861 and died at 40 Jamaica Street, Dundee on 31 December 1869. There was no medic in attendance and cause of death was given as old age.[88]

George had been buried in the Howff Cemetery at Dundee. His widow, Mary BAXTER was interred at the Eastern Cemetery in Dundee. Her name was added to the headstone erected by her eldest son John Baxter CHALMERS and his wife Isabella FYFE in remembrance of their children who had died young.

The new Howff Cemetery that was opened in 1836 was closed in 1870. The Dundee Council opened the Eastern Cemetery in 1863. As Isabella FYFE wanted the family to be together she sought permission for the names of those buried at Howff to be incuded on the CHALMERS' headstone at the Eastern Cemetery. The CHALMERS-FYFE headstone records:

'I AM THE RESURRECTION AND THE LIFE'

JOHN CHALMERS
IN AFFECTIONATE REMEMBERANCE OF
ISABEL FYFE HIS BELOVED WIFE
WHO DIED 18 FEB 1869 AGED 61 YEARS
AND OF THEIR CHILDREN
HELEN WHO DIED 3 DEC 1851 AGED 12 YEARS
GEORGINA WHO DIED 29 MAY 1854 AGED 4 YEARS
MARY WIFE OF JAMES LOGIE WHO DIED 3 DEC 1859
AGED 24 YEARS.
THESE THREE ARE INTERRED IN THE HOWFF[89]
JEANNIE WHO DIED 3 NOV. 1868 AGED 31 YEARS
AND DAVID C. DUFF HER HUSBAND
WHO DIED 14 NOV 1868 AGED 30 YEARS

ALSO OF HIS MOTHER MARY BAXTER
WHO DIED 31 DEC. 1869 AGED 92 YEARS
AND OF EMMA RICHARDSON.
WIFE OF HIS SON, WILLIAM CHALMERS,
WHO DIED 23 APRIL 1873 AGED 31 YEARS.
THE ABOVE JOHN CHALMERS,
DIED 18TH OCTOBER 1882, AGED 81 YEARS.
THE ABOVE NAMED WILLIAM F. CHALMERS
DIED 21ST AUGUST 1915 AGED 74 YEARS.
NANCY DAUGHTER OF THE ABOVE
JOHN CHALMERS
DIED 22ND FEBRUARY 1933.
IN MEMORY OF ISABELLA DUFF,
DAUGHTER OF THE ABOVE NAMED DAVID C. DUFF
WHO DIED 4TH APRIL 1943[90]

NOTES

---

[1] John CHALMERS christened 17 April 1675 at Liff Benvie and Invergowrie, Angus f. David; Scottish Church Records (1500s-1854) Batch no. C113012 1650-1773 Film nos. 0993484 – 0993485; 'Scotland Births and Baptisms, 1564-1950,' database, *FamilySearch* (https://familysearch.org/ark:/61903/1:1:XYJJ-3B7: 8 December 2014), Issobell Hill, 16 May 1685; Liff Benvie and Invergowrie, Angus, Scotland, reference, index based upon data collected by the Genealogical Society of Utah, Salt Lake City; FHL microfilm 0993484-0993485; Source Information John Chamers, 'Scotland Marriages, 1561-1910.' Ancestry.com. *Scotland, Select Marriages, 1561-1910* [database on-line]. Provo, UT, USA: Ancestry.com Operations, Inc., 2014.

[2] Scotland Births and Baptisms, 1564-1950, database, *FamilySearch,* https://family search.org citing Liff Benvie and Invergowrie, Angus, Scotland, reference, index based upon data collected by the Genealogical Society of Utah, Salt Lake City.

[3] Alexander Maxwell, *Genealogical Notabilia.* By 1791-1859 for his son David Maxwell, 1819-1899 and copied chiefly from his father's narrative by David MAXWELL The original, handwritten. Copy held by the author.

[4] Ibid.

[5] "Irish Famine (1740–1741)", updated 2017, http://enacademic.com/dic.nsf/enwiki /113615

[6] Liff, Angus, updated 4 April 2018, https://en.wikipedia.org/wiki/Liff,_Angus

[7] CHALMERS George, Margt. HOG, /11/06/1747282/120 100, Dundee. Scotland's People, www.scotlandspeople.gov.uk

[8] Alexander Maxwell.

[9] Alexander Maxwell; CHALMERS George Jannet BARRY/28/08/1773310/50 152 Monifieth, Church Register, Old Parish Registers Scotland.

[10] Alexander Maxwell.

[11] Scotland 1800-1868 and 1869-1899, no date, http://www.capitalpunishmentuk.org/scot1800.html

[12] Ibid.

[13] Alexander Maxwell.

[14] Ibid

[15] "Weaving and the Textile Industry", updated March 4, 2015, https://blog.findmypast.com/weaving-and-the-textile-industry-1406188754.html

[16] "The Industries of Scotland: Linen and Jute Manufacturers", no date, http://www.electricscotland.com/history/industrial/industry10.htm

[17] "Scotland Births and Baptisms, 1564-1950," database, *FamilySearch*, https://familysearch.org citing Liff Benvie and Invergowrie, Angus, Scotland, reference, index based upon data collected by the Genealogical Society of Utah, Salt Lake City.

[18] Alexander Maxwell.

[19] CHALMERS William, Mary Milne/07/03/1778272/50 65 Arbroath. Scotland's People, www.scotlandspeople.gov.uk

[20] Alexander Maxwell.

[21] W.J.Smith and J.E.Metcalfe, editors, *James Chalmers Inventor of the Adhesive Postage Stamp* (Dundee: David Winter & Son Ltd, 1970). Copy held by the author.

[22] Historical Environment Scotland, "Buildings at risk; Register for Scotland", Chalmers Hall, 1a-2 High Srret/ 2-6 Castle Street, Dundee, last modified 17 May 2016, https://www.buildingsatrisk.org.uk/details/914848

[23] W.J.Smith and J.E.Metcalfe.

[24] Ibid

[25] Ibid.

[26] From the Book of Eminent Burgesses of Dundee 1513 to 1885. © 2011 Friends of Dundee City Archives. All rights reserved. (Scottish Registered Charity SCO 006813.)

[27] 1861-1891 England Censuses.

[28] Alexander Maxwell.

[29] Historical Environment Scotland, "Buildings at risk; Register for Scotland", Chalmers Hall, 1a-2 High Srret/ 2-6 Castle Street, Dundee, last modified 17 May 2016, https://www.buildingsatrisk.org.uk/details/914848

[30] Undiscovered Scotland, "James Chalmers', last modified 2018, www.undiscoveredscotland.co.uk/usbiography/c/jameschalmers.html

[31] "Reasons why Dundee should be the city of culture: James Chalmers", last modified 2013, waracle.com/dundees-hidden-gems-that-youve-never-heard-of-james-chalmers/

[32] Plaque for James Chalmers Discovery Walk Phase 2 Slessor Gardens Dundee Scotland, last modified 2018, https://www.alamy.com/plaque-for-james-chalmers-discovery-walk-phase-2-slessor-gardens-dundee-scotland-april-2018-image183045621.html

[33] Gordon Jackson and Kate Kinnear, "The Trade and Shipping of Dundee 1780 to 1850," *The Abertay Historical Society Publication*, No. 31, Dundee, 1991, available from www.fdca.org.uk/pdf%20files/TradeShippingDundee.pdf

[34] "Dame School", last modified 20 September 2018, https://en.wikipedia.org/wiki/Dame school

[35] Obituary Alexander MAXWELL (b.1791), document by an unknown author, p.404, published Rob McIntosh per Ancestry.com

[36] Alexr. MAXWELL, 4 Dec 1818, Dundee, Angus, Scotland, Janet CHALMERS, Scotland, Select Marriages, 1561-1910, FHL Film Number: 993401.

[37] David MAXWELL, 10 September 1819, Dundee, Angus, Scotland, Alexr. MAXWELL, Janet CHALMERS, Scotland, Select Births and Baptisms, 1564-1950, FHL Film Number: 993402.

[38] Obituary Alexander MAXWELL (b.1791), document by an unknown author, p.404, published Rob McIntosh per Ancestry.com

[39] 1841 Scotland Census, Hendersons Wynd, Dundee, Angus.

[40] Ibid.

[41] Susan GUNN, 16 July 1849, Dundee, Angus, Scotland, Alexander MAXWELL, Scotland, Select Marriages, 1561-1910, FHL Film Number: 993404.

[42] 1851 Scotland Census, Hendersons Wynd, Dundee, Angus.

[43] Alexander Maxwell.

[44] Alexander Maxwell. Especially p.9 in original handwriting for the continuing account and details of their lives, CHALMERS family collection.

[45] Obituary Alexander MAXWELL (b.1791), document by an unknown author, p.404, published Rob McIntosh per Ancestry.com

[46] Ibid.

[47] Ibid.

[48] Alexander Maxwell.

[49] Copy in the author's collection.

[50] Alexander Maxwell. Especially p.9 in original handwriting for the continuing account and details of their lives, CHALMERS family collection.

[51] 1871 Census Scotland, 30 Tay Street, St Peter, Dundee, Angus.

[52] T.M. Ul'yanova and L.T. Sivakova, 'Spinning of oxide fibres made of natural cellulose materials', *Fibre Chemistry*, 29, 5, 1997. Available from: https://www.scribd.com/document/119635931/1997-0xide-of-Natural-Fibres-Using-Insulatng

[53] Natural Bag Co., 'Dundee and the Jute Industry', last modified 2015, http://naturalbagcompany.co.uk/jute-news/dundee-and-the-jute-industry/

[54] 1871Scotland Census, 59 Magdalen Yard Road, St Peter, Dundee, Angus.

[55] Natural Bag Co., 'Dundee and the Jute Industry', last modified 2015, http://naturalbagcompany.co.uk/jute-news/dundee-and-the-jute-industry/

---

[56] BBC, The Victorian achievement, "Victorian Dundee: Jute, Jam & Journalism", last modified 2014, bbc.co.uk/history/scottishhistory/victorian/trails_victorian_dundee.shtml

[57] BBC - History - Scottish History www.bbc.co.uk The interactive Scottish History Site of BBC Online

[58] 1891Scotland Census, 9 Viewforth St, St Peter, Liff and Benvie, Angus.

[59] "Scotland Marriages, 1561-1910," database, *FamilySearch*, 8 December 2014, https://familysearch.org/pal:/MM9.1.1/XTV5-R4G; William Chalmers and Jean Moncur, 31 May 1772; Kinnettles, Angus, Scotland, index based upon data collected by the Genealogical Society of Utah, Salt Lake City; FHL microfilm 993,441.

[60] Scotland Births and Baptisms, 1564-1950.

[61] CHALMERS Thomas, M, 25/03/1794282/240, 273, Dundee; CHALMERS Helen, F, 01/04/1800282/240, 327, Dundee, Old Parish Registers from National Records of Scotland, www.scotlandspeople.gov.uk

[62] Alexander Maxwell.

[63] Ibid

[64] Ibid.

[65] CHALMERS, Jean, MONCUR / Wm CHALMERS, F11/11/1813301/30, 336, Liff, Benvie and Invergowrie, Old Parish Registers from National Records of Scotland, www.scotlandspeople.gov.uk

[66] Alexander Maxwell.

[67] Ibid

[68] James CHALMERS, dyer, New York City, 1815, 1820, 1829-30 and 1835, New York, State and Federal Naturalization Records, 1794-1940, Genealogical Records, 1675-1920.

[69] 1850 United States Federal Census.

[70] James CHALMERS, Death: 6 May 1859, age 78, native Dundee, next of kin: son William, sons-in-law: William H. CURTIS and A. T. CLAYTON (Alexander T. CLAYTON, husband of Mary I CLAYTON, daughter), U.S., Newspaper Extractions from the Northeast, 1704-1930, Newspaper: New York Evening Post; New York, Wills and Probate Records, 1659-1999.

[71] Alexander Maxwell; A copy of a letter written 8 February 1867, received by James Chalmers, Castle Street, Dundee, from James M CHALMERS, New York, lawyer and grandson of James, son of William CHALMERS and Jane MONCUR is included in Alexander Maxwell's notes.

[72] James CHALMERS, Death, 23 Jul 1877, Bloomfield, Essex, New Jersey, 32 years, lawyer, single, Father: Wm CHALMERS, Mother: Abby CHALMERS, FHL Film Number: 494143 New Jersey, Deaths and Burials Index, 1798-1971.

[73] Alexander Maxwell.

[74] CHALMERS, Alexander, Ann DON, FR5575 (FR5575), 04/08/1815 685/2190, 171, St Cuthbert's, Old Parish Registers from National Records of Scotland, www.scotlandspeople.gov.uk

[75] Alexander Maxwell.

[76] CHALMERS, William, M, 18/01/1816282/250, 115, Dundee,www.scotlandspeople.gov.uk

[77] Alexr CHALMERS, wife and two children, Departure: 13 Oct 1820, Quebec, Canada, Arrival: Montreal, Canada, Vessel: *New Swiftsure.* Canada, St. Lawrence Steamboat Company Passenger Lists, 1819-1838.

[78] Quebec, Canada, Vital and Church Records (Drouin Collection), 1621-1968; 1861 and 1871 Canada Censuses for Quebec.

[79] Canada, Find A Grave Index, 1600s-Current for Alexander CHALMERS, died 12 December 1878 at Granby, Monteregie Region, Quebec, Canada.

[80] 1910 United States Federal Census; 'George Damon FULLER was born in Adamsville, Quebec on January 18, 1869. He began his pedagogical career teaching in small public schools in Quebec, before moving on to study at McGill University (B.A. 1901). Following several years of work as an educator and research fellow, Fuller entered University of Chicago as a graduate student in botany in 1907. Mentored by Henry C. COWLES, FULLER conducted research on the ecology of the Indiana Dunes and the Starved Rock area. After earning an S.M. in 1912 and Ph.D. in 1913, he went on to teach courses in ecology, botany and zoology at the university, serving on the faculty of the Department of Botany until 1934.

Like COWLES, FULLER emphasized the study of ecology in the field, leading trips to Colorado, Washington, British Columbia, Wisconsin and Michigan. Fuller's research on forest and prairie ecology in the Midwest resulted in several journal articles, and culminated in the exhaustive Vascular Plants of Illinois, co-authored with G. NEVILLE JONES and published in 1955. His professional activities included editorial positions with the journals Ecology and Botanical Gazette, and leadership in the Ecological Society of America and the Illinois State Academy of Science. Public education was important to FULLER throughout his career, and he was active as a science writer and educator for children and lay audiences. Magazines and newspapers published his writings about plant life, and he had a long association with the Illinois State Museum. Fuller married Louise Miller in 1908, and had a son (Damon) and daughter (Janet). He died on November 22, 1961 at age 92.' Guide to the George D. Fuller Papers 1887-1929', 2008, https://www.lib.uchicago.edu/e/scrc /findingaids/view.php?eadid=ICU.SPCL.GDFULLER

[81] George CHALMERS m. Mary BAXTER 28 Dec 1798 at Dundee, Forfarshire, Scotland Scottish Church Records (1500s-1854). LDS Family Search film no.993401 batch no. M112824.

[82] BAXTER Mary, John BAXTER/F, 27/09/1778,313/10,104, Murroes, Scotland, Select Marriages, 1561-1910; George CHALMERS, 28 December 1798, Dundee, Angus, Scotland, Mary BAXTER, FHL Film Number: 993401, www.familysearch.org, Church of Scotland (old parish registers) www.scotlandspeople.gov.uk

[83] Scotland Select Marriages, 1561-1910.

[84] *The Dundee Register and Directory* (Colville, A. & Co.: Dundee,1824-5), 1824.

[85] *The Dundee Directory and Register,* for 1829-30 (James Chalmers: Dundee, 1829).

[86] CHALMERS George, 66, M, 30/12/1836282/270, 79, Dundee, Church of Scotland (old parish registers), www.scotlandspeople.gov.uk

[87] National Records of Scotland. Old Parish Registers Deaths, Dundee.

[88] 1861 Scotland Census; CHALMERS Mary 92 DARLING 1869 282/4X 172 St Andrew (Dundee), Widow of George CHALMERS Linen Weaver, Daur of John BAXTER Crofter and Mary Baxter ms Darling; Informant: John CHALMERS, Son, 40 Jamaica, Street Dundee.

[89] This refers to the Howff Cemetery in Dundee.

'1815 by Jas and Helen Fyfe In Memory of their daughter Janet 17.11.1814, aged 3y 9m her mother 20.5.1815, aged 27, daughter Helen 4.8.1815 "Weep not for me, my husband dear, I am not dead but sleeping here … (7.9.1859. Permission to Mrs Isabella Fyfe or Chalmers to revise the headstone)

(East side) 1859, by John Chalmers and Isabella Fyfe In Memory of daughters Helen, d. 31.12.1851, aged 12; Georgina 29.5.1854, aged 4-1/2 y and Mary 3.5.1859, aged 24 (husband Jas Logie)'

(Pre-1855 Gravestone Inscriptions in Angus, Scotland Call no. 941.31 V3a V.4, Houff Cemetery, Entry no. 1428.)

[90] Headstone, Dundee Eastern Cemetery.

PART 7: Leaving Dundee

19 John BAXTER CHALMERS & Isabella FYFE

Neither of George's known surviving sons pursued careers in the jute industry. (Refer to Figure 18.23.) William was a mariner and later a flesher. (See Chapter 1.) By 1841 John Baxter CHALMERS had become a mason and lived with his wife Isabella, née FYFE, and four children at Union Street East Side. In a rapidly expanding city like Dundee, building construction would be in demand. However, their son William FYFE and their son-in-law David DUFF became jute merchants and David's father was a flax mill overseer.[1]

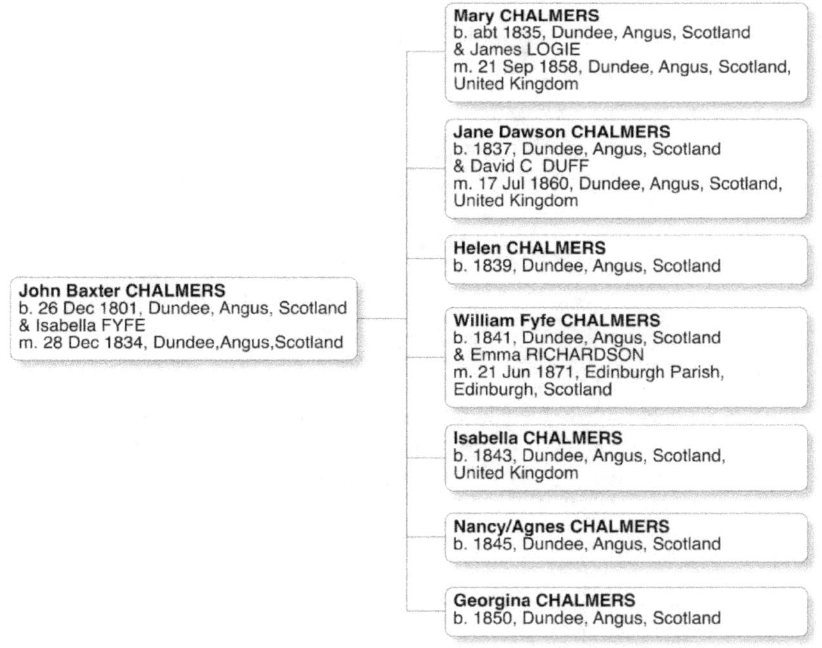

Figure 19.1. The family of John Baxter CHALMERS and Isabella FYFE

By 1851 John had changed his occupation from mason to grocer and spirits dealer, changing to grocer in 1861 and back to grocer and spirits dealer in 1871. By 1881 he had retired and died in 1882, also at the family home, 36 Jamaica Street, Dundee. The headstone that he had erected at the Eastern Cemetery at Dundee includes the names of John and his wife and those of their family.

Figure 19.2. Chalmers-Fyfe Headstone. See p.333-4 for a transcription. Source: author's collection

John and Isabella lost four of their six daughters: Isabella at birth, Georgina at the age of 4, Helen aged 12 and Mary aged 24. An even greater tragedy befell them when their second daughter Jane Dawson CHALMERS and her husband David DUFF both succumbed to tuberculosis within days of each other, although at different addresses, in 1868. Both were aged thirty. They left two young children who were cared for by their grandparents, John and Isabella CHALMERS. At the time, Isabella DUFF was aged six and David was only two. Isabella CHALMERS lived for less than a year after the death of the children's parents. In 1871 and 1881 the responsibility for their care was being undertaken by their grandfather, John Baxter CHALMERS along with his unmarried son, William Fyfe, unmarried daughter, Nancy/Agnes CHALMERS and a servant. They all continued to live at Jamaica Street until 1891 and possibly beyond.

William Fyfe had married Emma in 1871 and she died two years later, probably in childbirth. William did not remarry.

By 1901 the remaining family members had moved to Fifeshire, thus ending close CHALMERS family ties in Dundee.

Beyond Dundee

Figure 19.3. Isabella DUFF with her cousin William and his mother, Mary McQueen CHALMERS, c.1930 (See

Chapter 18). D. & W. Prophet, Dunoon. Source: author's collection

Isabella DUFF, became a schoolteacher and did not marry. In 1901 she was living with her uncle, William Fyfe CHALMERS, who continued to manage his business as a jute merchant, her aunt Nancy CHALMERS and a servant at Kilburn Terrace, Forgan in Fifeshire. They lived at this address for the remainder of their lives.[2]

Table 19.1. William Fife CHALMERS' Family, Kilburn Terrace, Forgan, Fifeshire, 1901[3]

W F CHALMERS	59	head
Nancy CHALMERS	55	sister
Isabel DUFF	39	niece
Jane GRANT	25	servant

Isabella died in 1943 at Forgan, Fifeshire.[4]

There are no known surviving descendants beyond the grandchildren of John Baxter CHALMERS and Isabella FYFE. It appears that David DUFF left for Australia in 1890. No further records have been found.[5] By 1901 the remaining family members had moved to Fifeshire, thus ending close CHALMERS family ties in Dundee.

NOTES

---

[1] 1841 and 1851 Scotland Censuses; Scotland Births, Marriages and Deaths Statutory Records for David DUFF, www.scotlandspeople.gov.uk

[2] 1901 Scotland Census.

[3] Ibid.

[4] DUFF Isabella, 81years, 1943, Ref 431/15, Forgan.

[5] Victoria, Australia, Assisted and Unassisted Passenger Lists, 1839-1923; Isabella DUFF became a schoolteacher and did not marry (1901 Scotland Census).

20 Elizabeth CHALMERS and Charles STRACHAN

Elizabeth Howe CHALMERS, the only surviving daughter of William CHALMERS (b.c.1812) and Elizabeth HOWE, married Charles STRACHAN on 24 December 1863 at Old Machar. Charles was born at Kincardine O'Neil, Aberdeenshire, where the family was living in 1851.[1] Charles was a son of Charles STRACHAN, farmer and Henrietta COOPER (b.1805). He was born on 20 April 1841 at Kincardine O'Neil, Aberdeenshire. The STRACHAN and COOPER (formerly COWPER) families were living in the area in the early 1700s and probably earlier.[2]

Charles and Henrietta had a family of six children.

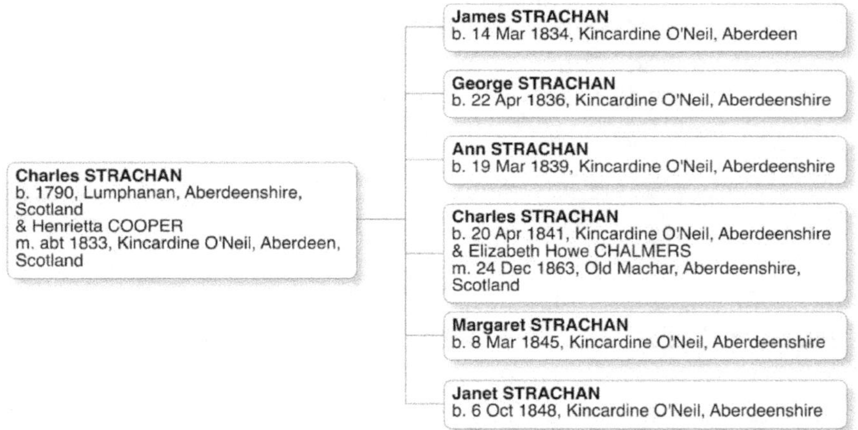

Figure 20.1. The children of Charles and Henrietta STRACHAN

Table 20.1. Household of Charles and Henrietta STRACHAN, Drumlasie, Kincardine O'Neil, Aberdeenshire, 1851 Scotland Census[3]

Charles STRACHAN	60	farmer 40 acres, 3 servants	Lumphanan, Aberdeenshire
Henrietta STRACHAN	46		Kin O'Neil, Aberdeenshire
George STRACHAN	15		Kin O'Neil, Aberdeenshire
Ann STRACHAN	12		Kin O'Neil, Aberdeenshire
Charles STRACHAN	9	scholar	Kin O'Neil, Aberdeenshire
Margt STRACHAN	6		Kin O'Neil, Aberdeenshire
Janet STRACHAN	2		Kin O'Neil, Aberdeenshire
James THOMSON	24	servant	
Elspet NIEL	17	servant	

In 1851 they were living at Kincardine O'Neil where Charles Snr was a farmer. (See Table 20.1.) Young Charles trained for four years as a merchant navy seaman between 1853 and 1857.[4] By 1861 he had taken up employment as a grocer's shopman, living as a boarder at 2 Washington Street at Anderston in Glasgow.

Table 20.2. Household of John and Isabella FORREST, 2 Washington St, Anderston, Glasgow, Lanarkshire, 1861 Scotland Census[5]

Isabella FORREST	22	sister	Glasgow, Lanarkshire
John FORREST	25	head green	Glasgow, Lanarkshire
Mary FORREST	15	sister	Glasgow, Lanarkshire
Robert CRIGHTON	23	stepman	
Ann CARMICK	18		
Charles STRACHAN	20	grocer's shopman	Aberdeen, Aberdeenshire

Having returned to the sea within a year or two, Charles obtained his Masters and Mates certificate, issued in 1863 and 1866.[6] At the time of his marriage he had left life at sea and reverted to the selling business as a commercial traveller and was living with his family near Glasgow.

Table 20.3. Household of Charles and Elizabeth STRACHAN, Mitchells Land, Cadder, Bishopbriggs, Lanarkshire, 1871 Scotland Census[7]

Charles STRACHAN	30	head	Kincardine O'Neil, Aberdeenshire
Elizabeth STRACHAN	37	wife	Dundee, Forfarshire
Elizabeth STRACHAN	6	daughter	Glasgow, Lanarkshire
Henrietta C STRACHAN	5	daughter	Glasgow, Lanarkshire
Charles STRACHAN	1	son	Glasgow, Lanarkshire
George STRACHAN	4 Mo	son	Glasgow, Lanarkshire

Figure 20.2. Elizabeth before leaving Glasgow. Source: author's collection

Cadder (Scottish Gaelic: Coile Dobhair) is a district of the town of Bishopbriggs, East Dunbartonshire, Scotland. It is located 7km north of Glasgow city centre, 0.5km south of the River Kelvin, and approximately 1.5km north-east of Bishopbriggs town centre, sited on the route of the Forth and Clyde Canal.[8]

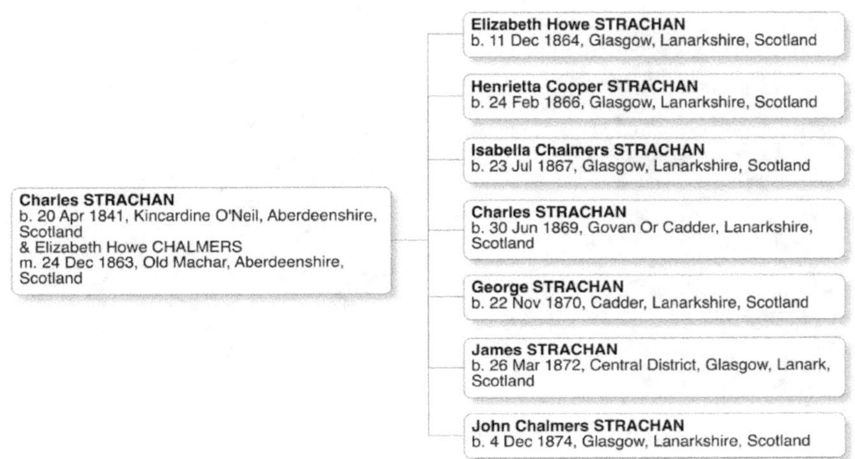

Figure 20.3. The children of Charles and Elizabeth STRACHAN

Of the seven children born to Charles and Elizabeth, three did not survive childhood. Isabella, born in 1867 did not live beyond a year, Charles born in 1869 and John born in 1874 each lived for about five years

In 1881 the STRACHAN family were residing at 49 Tillie Street, Glasgow. By this time Charles had migrated to New Zealand and Elizabeth remained with the support of her mother and brother George. She worked as a grocer.

Table 20.4. Household of Elizabeth STRACHAN, 49 Tillie Street, Glasgow Barony, Kelvin, Lanarkshire, 1881 Scotland Census[9]

Elizabeth STRACHAN	37	head grocer	Dundee, Forfarshire
Elizabeth STRACHAN	16	daughter	Glasgow, Lanarkshire
Henrietta STRACHAN	15	daughter	Glasgow, Lanarkshire
George STRACHAN	10	son	Glasgow, Lanarkshire
James STRACHAN	9	son	Glasgow, Lanarkshire
Elizabeth CHALMERS	69	mother	Dundee, Forfarshire
George CHALMERS	28	brother	Old Machar, Aberdeen

Figure 20.4. Elizabeth (Lizzie) 16.
Source: author's collection

Figure 20.5. Henrietta aged 15.
Source: author's collection

Figure 20.6. George aged 10.
Source: author's collection

Later that year Elizabeth STRACHAN and children sailed for New Zealand to join Charles who had already left Scotland to prepare the way for his family. The 1961 obituary for a daughter, Miss H.C. STRACHAN states that 'she came to New Zealand in 1881 at the age of 14 with her mother, sister and two brothers to join her father who had migrated here two years earlier.'[10]

On 15 July 1881 Elizabeth STRACHAN with her children: Elizabeth aged 16, Henrietta aged 15, George aged 10 and James aged 8 sailed on the *Jessie Readman* (962 tons) from Greenock, Scotland bound for Dunedin, Otago. The *Jessie Readman*, one of the last sailing ships to visit that port, arrived at Port Chalmers in November 1881.[11] The *Otago Witness* recorded their arrival:

> Arrived on Monday – *Jessie Readman*, Patrick Henderson's and Co.'s ship, 962 tons, Gibson, from Glasgow (July 15). Cargills, Gibbs, and Co., agents. Passengers listed in 2nd cabin:
>
> A.B. DOWNES
> Mr(s) E. STRACHAN
> Miss Elizabeth STRACHAN
> Henrietta STRACHAN
> George STRACHAN
> James STRACHAN
> David C. HELM
> Mrs BURNS[12]

The Passenger's Contract Ticket states that the cost was £102 and 8 shillings, a considerable amount at the time.

Figure 20.7. Passenger's ticket for the STRACHAN family. Source: author's collection

Figure 20.8. Charles and Elizabeth STRACHAN in New Zealand, c.1915. Source: author's collection

After living in Dunedin for a few months the family moved to Milton where they made their home for thirteen or fourteen years.[13] While living there one of the children met with an accident when a chemical explosion caused serious eye injuries.

The Milton Explosion.
All but the three principal sufferers by the late explosion of chemicals at Milton are out of the doctor's hands. No further hope is entertained of Mr James REID ultimately gaining the use of his eye. In the other two cases, Mr STRACHAN's son and Mr LANE's daughter, there is an improved perception of light in each, and it is believed they will be fully restored to sight.[14]

Shortly afterwards, at about 1895, the family settled in Timaru where Henrietta established a business as a millinery specialist, working on her own account.[15] Situated at 112 Stafford Street, it was known as 'Glasgow House'. By 1916 Henrietta's business had expanded to include a range of ladies' and children's clothing.

Miss H. C. Strachan
MILLINER,
LADIES' AND CHILDREN'S OUT-
FITTER.

NEW GOODS JUST ARRIVED IN
TIME FOR THE HOLIDAYS
:: AND SHOW ::
Per S.S. Arawa and Ionic.

SEE THE CHILDREN'S WINDOW
for Sweet Little Washing Dresses,
Coatees, Hats and Bonnets, in Voile,
Muslin and Embroidery—just what you
have been looking for—and the Goods
are MARKED VERY CHEAP.
IN SHOWROOMS UPSTAIRS you
will get suited with a Stylish Hat, Cos-
tume or Sports Coat. at a VERY
REASONABLE PRICE.

LARGE STOCK OF BLOUSES AND
CORSETS TO CHOOSE FROM.
NEW UNDERSKIRTS.
EVERY SHAPE IN PANAMAS.
At Prices from 6s 11d to 30s.
GREAT VARIETY
In
UNDERCLOTHING AND HOSIERY.

Call and See MISS STRACHAN'S
Show of the above Goods when in town
on Wednesday or Thursday.

Figure 20.9. Henrietta STRACHAN's advertisement. Source: Timaru Herald. October 23, 1916.

Figure 20.10. Ettie at the beach, c.1900. Source: author's collection

Charles had become a music teacher in Timaru and worked until 1919 and probably for longer.[16] He died in 1924 at the age of 83 and Elizabeth passed away in 1926, aged 82. They are both buried in Plot 318, Row 39 at the Timaru Cemetery.[17] Their headstones read:

IN
LOVING MEMORY
OF
CHARLES STRACHAN
DIED AUG. 3RD 1924,
AGED 82 YEARS.
LATE OF ABERDEEN.

IN
LOVING MEMORY
OF
ELIZABETH STRACHAN
DIED JUNE 2ND 1926,
AGED 82 YEARS.
LATE OF ABERDEEN.[18]

Nothing further is known of George and James, the two sons of Charles and Elizabeth. Their daughter Elizabeth Howe, a spinster, lived with her parents until their deaths and by 1928 she had moved to 1 Craighead Street, Timaru where her sister Henrietta also stayed.[19] No means of employment is given. Henrietta retired from her millinery business in 1927.[20]

Figure 20.11. Ettie 1928.
Source: author's collection

The names of all three children are included on the STRACHAN cemetery records but no further details are given.[21]

Henrietta Cooper STRACHAN outlived other family members by about thirty years. Following retirement she rented a portion of 12 Albert Street, the house that became her home for the rest of her life.[22]

Henrietta, known as 'Ettie', and her sister Elizabeth (Lizzie) took a prominent part in amateur theatricals.

Ettie made two trips to her homeland, the first in 1928. She sailed on the *Ormonde* via Melbourne, Sydney, Adelaide, Colombo, Naples, Gibraltar, Port Said, Fremantle and Southampton. She stayed with her maternal relatives, notably her uncle, George CHALMERS and family who lived in Dunoon, Scotland.[23] (See Chapter 21.) Her second overseas trip was for the coronation of King George VI in 1937.

Figure 20.12. Ettie's home at 12 Albert Street, Timaru. Source: author's collection

Figure 20.13. Lizzie in fancy dress. Source: author's collection

Figure 20.14. Ettie on board the Ormonde in a life buoy. Source: author's collection

Figure 20.15. Ettie on board in fancy dress. Source: author's collection

Figure 20.16. Henrietta in Highland dress, Scotland. Source: author's collection

Figure 20.17. Elderly Ettie. Source: author's collection

Ettie kept the best of health and was a regular swimmer in Caroline Bay until her eighties. She had a clear mind and memory and managed her rental property independently. At the age of ninety-four she was still keeping a written account of her income and expenditure.[24]

Henrietta died at Timaru on 1 June 1961 at the age of ninety-five. She is buried in the family plot at the Timaru Cemetery.[25] Henrietta willed her real estate to Chalmers Presbyterian Church in Timaru. She had been a regular attender and member of the choir.

Household effects to the value of £51 12s 8d were auctioned. To her closest living relative, Dora Grace GRUBB (née CHALMERS) she left her grandfather's clock, glassware, linen, ornaments etc and jewellery.

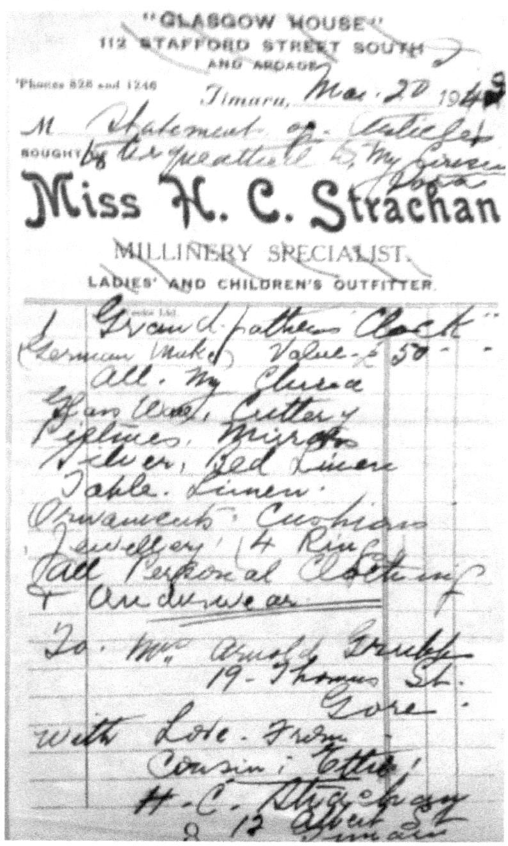

Figure 20.18. Henrietta's letter of bequest to Dora. Source: author's collection

There were no known marriages or further descendants of Elizabeth CHALMERS and Charles STRACHAN.

NOTES

---

[1] Charles STRACHAN, b. 20 Apr 1841, bapt: 6 Jun 1841, bapt. place: Kincardine O'Neil, Aberdeen, Scotland, Father: Charles STRACHAN, Mother: Henrietta COOPER Scotland, Select Births and Baptisms, 1564-1950, FHL Film Number: 993334.

[2] Ibid.

[3] 1851 Scotland Census.

[4] Charles STRACHAN, Military Service, 1853-1857, United Kingdom, Aberdeenshire, Birth: 1841, United Kingdom, Merchant Navy Seamen Records, 1835-1941, GS Film number: 1483722.

[5] 1861 Scotland Census.

[6] Certificate Number: 27.624, Charles STRACHAN, b. 1841, Birth: Aberdeen, Aberdeenshire, Issued: 13 Feb 1863 and 1866 at Aberdeen port, UK and Ireland, Masters and Mates Certificates, 1850-1927,

[7] 1871 Scotland Census.

[8] 'Cadder', 2018, https://en.wikipedia.org/wiki/Cadder

[9] 1881 Scotland Census.

[10] Obituary for Miss H.C. STRACHAN, newspaper cutting, 1961.

[11] Ibid.

[12] *Otago Witness*. "English Shipping." September 17, 1881.

[13] Obituary for Miss H.C. STRACHAN, newspaper cutting, 1961.

[14] *Star*. August 13, 1884.

[15] Obituary for Miss H.C. STRACHAN, newspaper cutting, 1961.

[16] Charles STRACHAN, music teacher, Le Cren's Terrace, Timaru, Timaru Electoral Rolls, 1905-1906, 1911 and 1919; Elizabeth Howe STRACHAN, Le Cren's Terrace, Timaru, Timaru Electoral Rolls, 1905-1906, 1911 and 1919; Elizabeth STRACHAN, Le Cren's Terrace, Timaru, Timaru Electoral Rolls, 1905-1906, 1911 and 1919; Henrietta Cooper STRACHAN, Le Cren's Terrace, Timaru, Timaru Electoral Rolls, 1905-1906, 1911 and 1919.

[17] Timaru District Council, Cemetery Database, https://www.timaru.govt.nz/services/community-and-culture/cemeteries/cemetery-search?BurialId=4181

[18] Ibid.

[19] Elizabeth Howe STRACHAN, spinster, 1 Craighead Street, Timaru, Timaru Electoral Roll, 1928.

[20] Obituary for Miss H.C. STRACHAN, newspaper cutting, 1961.

[21] Henrietta Cooper STRACHAN (daughter) Death Date: 1 June 1961, George; Elizabeth and James (children), Timaru Cemetery: 8th Row 393, New Zealand Cemetery Records, 1800-2007.

[22] Henrietta Cooper STRACHAN, spinster, 12 Albert Street, Timaru, New Zealand, Electoral Rolls 1935, 1938, 1949, 1954 and 1957.

[23] UK Incoming Passenger Lists, 1878-1960.

[24] Miss H.C. STRACHAN, accounts notebook.

[25] Henrietta Cooper STRACHAN, Timaru, 1961, Folio 2632, New Zealand, Death Index, 1848-1966.

21 George CHALMERS and Mary McQueen HUNTER

George CHALMERS was the youngest child of William CHALMERS and Elizabeth HOWE. (See Figures 1.2 nd 1.3.)

In 1881 George was living with his widowed mother Elizabeth and his sister Elizabeth STRACHAN and her children at 49 Tillie Street in the Kelvin district of Glasgow. At that time he was working as an assistant in the parochial office.[1]

Table 21.1. The household the STRACHAN family, 49 Tillie Street, Glasgow Barony, Kelvin, Lanarkshire, Scotland, 1881[2]

Elizabeth STRACHAN	37	head	
Elizabeth STRACHAN	16	daughter	
Henrietta STRACHAN	15	daughter	
George STRACHAN	10	son	
James STRACHAN	9	son	
Elizabeth CHALMERS	69	mother	
George CHALMERS	28	brother	Aberdeen, Aberdeenshire

Figure 21.1. George CHALMERS, c1890. Fergus photographer, Greenock, Dunoon. Source: Author's collection

In 1889 George married Mary McQueen HUNTER at Dunoon, Argyll.[3] Mary was the daughter of James HUNTER and Mary GREIG, both of whom were born at Clackmannanshire, Scotland. They were married at James' place of birth, Alloa, Clackmannanshire. In 1851 James' father Andrew and his mother Margaret PATERSON were living at Cambridge, Clackmannanshire where Andrew was working as a labourer.[4]

Table 21.2. HUNTER Family at Cambridge, Alloa, Clackmannanshire, Scotland, 1851[5]

Andrew HUNTER	52		
Margaret HUNTER	50		
James HUNTER	21	labourer	Alloa, Clackmannanshire

Andrew HUNTER
b. abt 1799, Alloa, Clackmannanshire, Scotland
m. 12 Jan 1824, Alloa, Clackmannanshire, Scotland

Margaret PATERSON
b. abt 1801, Alloa, Clackmannanshire, Scotland

James HUNTER
b. 26 Nov 1829, Alloa, Clackmannanshire, Scotland

Figure 21.2. The parents of James HUNTER

James was twenty-one at the time and within ten years he had accrued enough money to go into business as a fresh provision manufacturer employing four men and six women. The shop assistant living in his household was step daughter-in-law Sarah CONNEL.[6]

Table 21.3. The household of James HUNTER, 59 Clyde Place, Glasgow Govan, Tradeston, Lanarkshire, Scotland, 1861[7]

James HUNTER	31	fresh provision manufacturing employing 4 men 6 women	Alloa, Clackmannanshire
Sarah CONNEL	27	step daughter-in-law, shop server	

James married Jane GREIG on 3 December 1858 at Alloa, Clackmannan. The family remained living at Tradeston, Glasgow where James kept his business and where the first four of their seven children were born. From there they moved to Hunters Corner in Dunoon where James became employed as a gardener. By then his mother had passed away, in 1861 at Clackmannanshire, and his widowed father Andrew had come to live with the family.[8]

Table 21.4. The household of James and Jane HUNTER, Hunters House, Dunoon and Kilmun, Argyll, Scotland, 1871[9]

James HUNTER	41	head	gardener	Alloa, Clackmannanshire.
Jane HUNTER	35			
Andrew HUNTER	11			
Mary Mc Q HUNTER	8			
David G HUNTER	5			
Margaret P HUNTER	3			
Agnes G HUNTER	10 mo			
Andrew HUNTER	73			

Figure 21.3. The children of James and Jane HUNTER

Once settled in Dunoon James became a borough collector and remained so for at least ten years.[10]

Table 21.5. The household of James and Jane HUNTER, Grocer's Shop, Dunoon and Kilmun, Dunoon, Argyll, Scotland, 1881[11]

James HUNTER	51	head	borough collector	Alloa, Clackmannan
Jane HUNTER	45			
Mary Mc Q HUNTER	18			
David G HUNTER	16			
Margaret P HUNTER	10			
Agnes G HUNTER	10			
James Mc Q HUNTER	5			
John W HUNTER	3			

Their eldest daughter, Mary McQueen HUNTER married George CHALMERS at Dunoon on 6 June 1899. At the time George was working as a collector of poor rates. Within each parish a property tax was levied to provide relief for the poor.[12] Their first child, Janet Greig CHALMERS was born on 26 March 1891.[13]

Table 21.6. The household of George and Mary CHALMERS, Alexander St, Firth View, Dunoon and Kilmun, Argyll, Scotland, 1891[14]

George CHALMERS	37	head	collector poor rates	Aberdeen, Aberdeenshire
Mary CHALMERS	29			
Janet G CHALMERS	11 days			
Mary FLEMING				

Their family of four children was complete by 1901.[15]

Table 21.7. The household of George and Mary CHALMERS, Langpark, Auchamore Road, Dunoon and Kilmun, Dunoon, Argyll, Scotland, 1901[16]

George CHALMERS	47	head	collector of poor rates & factor	Aberdeen, Aberdeen
Mary CHALMERS	38	wife		
Jeanie CHALMERS	10	daughter		
William CHALMERS	6	son		
John CHALMERS	4	son		
Agnes CHALMERS	2	daughter		
315	22	servant		

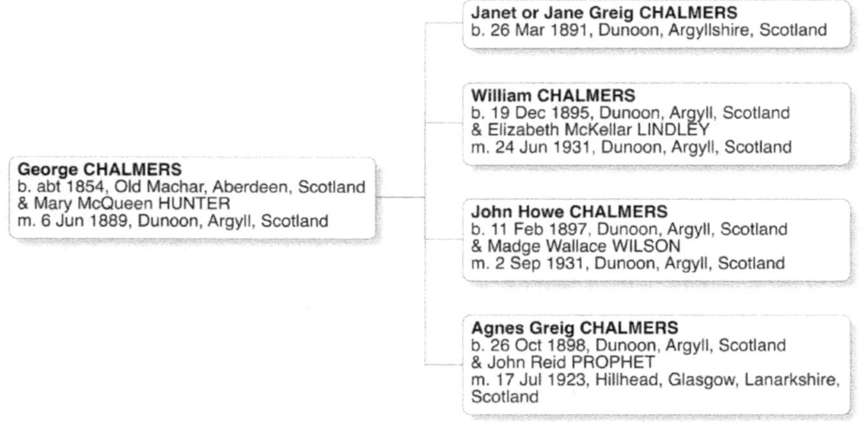

Figure 21.4. The children of George and Mary CHALMERS

The family was living at Langpark, Auchamore Road in Dunoon in 1901, by which time George had extended the scope of his work, adding factor as an occupation. (Factor is a Scottish term for real estate agent.) This became his fulltime work until his retirement. He was also said by the family to be the town clerk of Dunoon.[17]

Figure 21.5. George CHALMERS and Mary McQueen HUNTER, attr. D. and W. Prophet. Source: author's collection

George died at Dunoon on 26 May 1934 and Mary passed away in 1939 at Dunoon.[18]

Jane Greig CHALMERS, the eldest of their children, did not marry and died at the age of twenty in Dunoon.

William CHALMERS

William CHALMERS, George and Mary's eldest son

joined the 8th (County) Battalion, The Argyll and Sutherland Highlanders as a ranker in 1913 and was commissioned shortly after the First World War broke out. He took part in the bitter fighting at Arras, where many local lives were lost, and for his part in that action he was awarded the Military Cross, and a few months later received a bar to his decoration, and was promoted to the rank of Lieutenant-Colonel.[19]

Figure 21.6. William CHALMERS in military uniform, attr. Lafayette. Insignia reads 'Honi soit qui mal y pense'. Source: author's collection

On leaving the army at the close of hostilities William CHALMERS went out to New Zealand with a Mr Benjamin PRATT, a war-time comrade, to learn farm management. Later they set up their own business as grain dealers and millers in Hawera. However, the death of his partner Mr PRATT some four years later caused him to sell the business and return to his native Scotland and where he rejoined the army.[20] (See Figure 19.3.)

William married Elizabeth (Elsie) McKellar LINDLEY in 1931 at Dunoon.[21] Elizabeth's parents were Thomas ('Tom') LINDLEY and Elizabeth McArthur GOUDIE.

Figure 21.7. William CHALMERS and Elizabeth (Elsie) LINDLEY's wedding, attr. M. Greachen, Dunoon, 1931. On his right is William's brother George (best man). William's parents, George and Mary are seated at the end of the row to his left. Source: author's collection

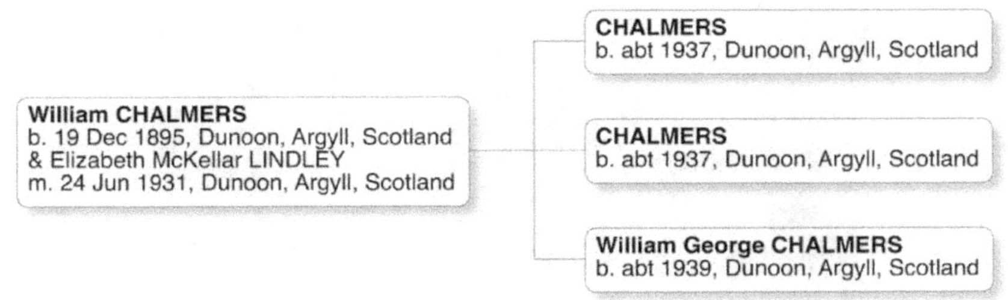

Figure 21.8. The children of William and Elizabeth CHALMERS

William and Elizabeth lost twin infants who died at birth in 1937.[22] They had one surviving child, named William George CHALMERS. He was born in 1939.

Figure 21.9. William, William George and Elsie CHALMERS, c.1937. Source: author's collection

Figure 21.10. The original CHALMERs family home at Dunoon. Source: author's collection

William and Elsie lived at Avon Bank, Auchamore Road, Dunoon, Argyll. The house was added to later.

During his lifetime William served as Honorary Sheriff-Substitute of Argyll for over twenty years. He carried out his duties on the Bench from time to time. William was Past President of the Dunoon Bridge Club and a member of the Coval Golf Club. He was a noted rifle shot and an angler, having been a member of the Duntroon and District Angling Club.[23]

Figure 21.11. William and Elsie's silver wedding anniversary, 1956. Front left: Elsie, William and Madge (John's Wife). Back: William (Billy, the son) and John Howe. Source: author's collection

William ('Will') died in 1960. He was buried at Dunoon Cemetery. Elizabeth was a widow for forty years. During that time she was visited by at least two cousins from New Zealand, Dora GRUBB (and husband

Arnold) in 1974 and Raymond CHALMERS (son of Donald who had visited during WWI) and his Scottish wife Bessie in 1990. (See Figure 17.25.)

William George CHALMERS

William George, known as Billy, studied at the Royal College of Science and Technology at Glasgow in the Food Science Department and became a food scientist in what was then a new discipline. He worked with the Nestlé Company and moved in Sao Paulo, Brazil, South America. He married Danielle at Old Church in Montreux, Switzerland on 19 September, 1981. Their only known child is Nathalie CHALMERS b. 19 December 1983.

With no brothers or sisters and son Billy and family living far away, Elsie CHALMERS became increasingly lonely as she aged, although she did keep regular contact with her sister-in-law Agnes.[24] Elsie died in 2000 at the age of ninety-two.

John Howe CHALMERS

John Howe CHALMERS served in World War I. He worked with his father George in a real estate agency dealing in property and house sales.

Figure 21.12. John CHALMERS in military uniform attr. M. Greachen, Dunoon, 1914. Source: author's collection

John married Madge Wallace WILSON in 1931 at Dunoon.[25]

Figure 21.13. The wedding of John Howe CHALMERS and Madge Wallace WILSON, 1931, attr. M. Brown & Co. Helensburgh. Source: author's collection

When his father died in 1934 John looked to his brother William to leave the army and join him in their real estate business. The two brothers were said to be quite different from one another, but they were able to work together successfully.[26] The business prospered until 1960 when William passed away. At this stage John felt unable to carry on alone and he sold out.

There were no children from this marriage.[27]

John died in 1991 at the age of ninety-four.[28]

The family business of William and John Chalmers was noted in 2013 as:

W & J Chalmers Ltd – Argyll St
Classification: Estate Agents W & J Chalmers Ltd is located in the city of Dunoon.
Address: 47 Argyll St Dunoon PA23 7HG Strathclyde GB
Phone: 01369 704097

The business W & J Chalmers Ltd – Argyll St in Scotland is listed in the category Residential Property Agents in the Yalwa Business Directory. W & J Chalmers Ltd was still in existence in 2018.

Madge died in 1995 at Dunoon.

Agnes Greig CHALMERS

Agnes Greig CHALMERS was said to be like her father by way of a keen sense of humour and a great capacity for living.[29] She married John Reid PROPHET at Hillhead, Glasgow, Lanarkshire on 17 July 1923.

Figure 21.14. Agnes Greig and John Reid PROPHET, attr. D. and W. Prophet. Source: author's collection

John was the eldest child of William PROPHET (b.1863, Perth, Perthshire) and Euphemia Lamb DUNCAN (b.1864, Dundee, Angus). William was a photographer. In 1901 the PROPHET family of parents and six children lived at Forgan in Fifeshire and by 1911 their address was Hillpath Road, Viewbank at Forgan. Two more children had been added to the family by then.[30]

Table 21.8. The household of William & Euphemia PROPHET, Forgan, Fife shire, Scotland, 1901[31]

William PROPHET	38	head	photographer	Perth, Perthshire
Euphemia PROPHET	36	wife		
John R PROPHET	9			
Freida PROPHET	7			
Ella W PROPHET	6			
William K PROPHET	5			
George L PROPHET	2			
James D PROPHET	1			
Julia WILSON	16	general servant		

Agnes was visited by her cousin Malcolm Shaw CHALMERS before returning to New Zealand from World War 1. (See Figure 5.19.)

John and Agnes were living at Newton Mearns near Glasgow in 1961.[32] They remained there until John's death in 1983. There are no known children from the marriage of John and Agnes.

NOTES

---

[1] 1881 Scotland Census.

[2] 1881 Scotland Census, 49 Tillie Street, Glasgow Barony, Kelvin, Lanarkshire.

[3] CHALMERS George, HUNTER Mary, married 1889, 510/1 16, Dunoon.

[4] 1851 Scotland Census.

[5] Ibid.

[6] 1861 Scotland Census.

[7] Ibid.

[8] 1871 Scotland Census.

[9] Ibid.

[10] 1881 Scotland Census.

[11] 1881 Scotland Census, James and Jane HUNTER, Grocers Shop, Dunoon and Kilmun, Dunoon, Argyll.

[12] 1891 Scotland Census; 'Poor Rate', last modified 2017, https://en.wikipedia.org /wiki/Poor_rate

[13] 1891 Scotland Census; www.scotlandspeople.gov.uk.

[14] 1891 Scotland Census.

[15] 1901 Scotland Census.

[16] Ibid.

[17] Marriage Certificate of William CHALMERS and Elizabeth LINDLEY, 24 June 1931, Dunoon, Scotland's People.

[18] CHALMERS George, 80, 1934510/1 71, Dunoon; CHALMERS Mary McQueen 76, 1939510/1 192, Dunoon.

[19] William CHALMERS Obituary, Dunoon newspaper.

[20] Ibid.

[21] Marriage Certificate of William CHALMERS and Elizabeth LINDLEY, 24 June 1931, Dunoon, Scotland's People.

[22] Letter from Elizabeth (Elsie) CHALMERS, 1961, to cousin Dora GRUBB.

[23] William CHALMERS Obituary, Dunoon newspaper.

[24] Letter from Elizabeth (Elsie) CHALMERS, 1982, to cousin Dora GRUBB.

[25] CHALMERS John Howe, WILSON Madge Wallace, 1931510/1 40, Dunoon.

[26] Letter from Elizabeth (Elsie) CHALMERS, 1961, to cousin Dora GRUBB.

[27] Ibid.

[28] CHALMERS John, 94, HUNTER, 1991532/ 73, Dunoon.

[29] Letter from Elizabeth (Elsie) CHALMERS, 1961, to cousin Dora GRUBB.

[30] 1901 Scotland Census.

[31] Ibid.

[32] Letter from Elizabeth (Elsie) CHALMERS, 1961, to cousin Dora GRUBB.

Index

NOTE: Family names and categories are in UPPERCASE. Categories are very broad e.g. DISTRICT includes place, suburb, geographical feature or simply a location; TOWN includes cities, towns and small villages.

ADAM
   Ellen Georgina, 136
   J. S., 236
ADAMS
   Elizabeth Ann, 160
ALDERSON
   A.H., 271
ALEXANDER
   Mr A., 180
   Mrs A., 181
   Mrs J., 177
ALLAN
   Rev., 60
ANDERSON, 259
   Bill, 201
   G. J., 94
   Janet, 259
   Janet Emily, 97, 257
   John, 259
ATKIN
   Mr, 178
ATKINSON
   Ranger, 35
AUSTIN
   Dr., 151
   Robert Erwin, 151
BARCLAY
   W. de R., 20
BARRETT
   Captain, 83, 90
BARRIE
   Janet, 314
BATCHELOR
   George, 318
BATES
   Mr, 61
BATHGATE

A., 236
BAXTER
   John, b.c.1738, 333
   Mary, b.1778, 333
BEESLEY
   Agnes Clara, 284, 285
   Emily Ann, 284
   George, 285
   Henry, 285
   John, 285
BENNET
   Mr, 61
BENNETT
   Mr C. F., 179
BENZOIN, 289
BERRY
   Lorraine, 252
BLANCHARD
   Roland Thomas (Ron), 217
   Rosalie, 136
BOYLEN, 124, 126, 197, 236, 239
   Eleanor Elizabeth, 197, 228,
      231, 233, 234, 237, 238, 239,
      240, 260, 291
   Gertrude Elizabeth, 124, 197,
      217, 227, 228, 230, 231, 234,
      237, 238, 239, 240, 241, 251,
      260, 262, 291
   Henry, 226
   John, 225, 226, 234
   Philip, 74, 76, 97, 124, 204,
      217, 225, 226, 227, 228, 230,
      231, 232, 234, 235, 236, 237,
      240, 241, 251, 260, 262
   Philip., 236
   Susan, 226, 234

Thelma Mary, 197, 228, 231, 233, 234, 237, 239, 240, 260, 294
BOYLIN. *See* BOYLEN
BRANDIGAN
George, 231
BREEN
R., 83, 90
BRIGHOUSE
Aileen, 252
BROUGH
Molly Hetty, 250
BROWN
Dr Edmund Ewart, 71
BUCHANAN
Mr W., 228
BUFFETT, 251
BURNETT, 289
BUXTON, 217, 219
Cyril, 217, 218
Edith, 217, 218
BYARS
Bert, 294
Ella, 294
CAMERON
Elizabeth 'Bessie', 290
J. C., 236
CAMPBELL
Kath, 327
CARMICK
Ann, 350
CARSON
Mr, 226
CEMETERY
Andersons Bay, 73, 112, 304
Calcium, Isla Bank, 219
Cowie, Granby, Quebec, Canada, 333
Cromwell, 152, 153
Dunoon, Argyll, Scotland, 371
East Winton, 241
Eastern, Dundee, Angus, Scotland, 335, 345
Eastern, Invercargill, 136, 204, 219
John Knox Churchyard, Aberdeen, 8
Liff Churchyard, Dundee, Angus, Scotland, 333
Mangere, Auckland, 277
Oamaru Lawn, 188
Otahuhu RSA, Auckland, 254
The Howff, Dundee, Scotland, 320, 335
Timaru, 356, 360
Waikumete, 168
Waimairi, Christchurch, 266
CHALMERS, 3, 20, 35, 50, 51, 52, 55, 74, 81, 96, 97, 112, 122, 125, 134, 197, 206, 259, 263, 315, 330, 348
Agnes Greig, b.1898, 366, 372, 374, 375
Airlie Christina Jean, 136, 217, 218
Albert Gordon (Sonny), 233, 259, 265, 266
Albert Rupert, 266
Alexander, 333
Alexander, 1784, 332
Alexander, b.1821, 325
Alexander, b.c.1774, 331
Allan Mitchell, 200, 201, 211, 213, 217
Amelia Maribel, 120, 122, 123, 125, 128, 130, 132, 134, 135, 136, 194, 211, 215, 217, 232, 233, 241, 262
Andrew, b.c.1791, 318
Ann, 333
Anna, 333
Barry Lionel, 218, 265, 294, 302, 303
Bessie, 135, 372
Betson Margaret, 163, 165
Betson Tims, 165
Charles Dickson, 320
Charles Hector, 135, 218, 298
Charles, b.1786, 326
Charles, b.1787, 324

Charles, b.1789, 325
Constance Eleanor, 34, 49, 50, 60, 69, 76, 111, 112, 227, 245
David, 5, 161
David Basil, 203, 217, 263, 265
David George, 40, 41, 157, 161, 162, 163, 165, 168
David Lloyd George, 163, 165
Don. *See* Donald Roderick Tims
Donald Roderick Tims, 121, 122, 124, 125, 128, 129, 136, 194, 210, 233
Donald Rolls, 35, 40, 41, 43, 52, 55, 58, 60, 66, 67, 69, 74, 76, 77, 82, 89, 90, 91, 92, 99, 100, 101, 113, 119, 120, 122, 123, 124, 125, 126, 127, 128, 130, 132, 135, 136, 142, 152, 153, 215, 217, 232, 233, 240, 262, 269
Dora Grace, 33, 42, 52, 63, 70, 73, 80, 89, 90, 95, 96, 97, 105, 106, 107, 108, 109, 111, 114, 126, 127, 234, 259, 281, 291
Douglas Gollan, 28, 35, 50, 74, 76, 82, 83, 84, 91, 92, 93, 97, 99, 107, 109, 110, 123, 142, 173, 185, 186, 187, 188, 227, 298
Eleanor May, 233, 262, 266, 293
Eleanor Rebecca, 25, 29, 30, 31, 32, 33, 37, 40, 41, 42, 50, 51, 52, 53, 54, 55, 56, 58, 60, 63, 64, 65, 66, 69, 70, 73, 76, 77, 79, 81
Eleanor Rosalie, 194, 209, 211, 213, 215, 216, 218, 219
Elizabeth, 8, 9, 13, 333
Elizabeth Howe, 349
Elizabeth Howe, b.c.1843, 9, 361

Elizabeth McKellar, b.c.1908, 371, 372
Elizabeth, b.1813, 351, 363
Elizabeth, b.1829, 333
Elizabeth, b.1843, 8, 9, 349
Ellen, 304
Frances Louisa Beaven, 126, 134, 135, 197, 201, 204, 205, 206, 209, 211, 213, 214, 215, 219, 223, 239, 240, 263, 294, 304
George, 8
George Howe, 121, 122, 124, 129, 132, 133, 134, 135, 136, 210, 211, 217, 218, 233
George, b.1725, 312, 313, 315, 317
George, b.1758, 314, 323
George, b.1771, 333, 335
George, b.c.1768, 317
George, b.c.1854, 8, 9, 299, 351, 357, 363, 364, 366, 367
Georgina, b.1850, 346
Gertrude Elizabeth, 34, 49, 50, 60, 76, 80, 110, 113, 204, 225, 227, 245
Gordon Rupert, 34, 49, 51, 52, 53, 54, 61, 70, 71, 79, 89, 97, 109, 111, 113, 124, 217, 232, 233, 238, 239, 257, 259, 260, 262, 263, 264, 265, 266
Helen, b.1839, 346
Hugh, 175
Isabella, b. & d.1843, 346
Jack. *See* John Charles
James, 333
James M. (New York), 332
James M., b.c.1845, 332
James, b.1781, 331, 332
James, b.1782, 317, 319, 320, 324
James, b.1806, 325, 332
Jane Dawson, b.1837, 346
Jane Greig, b.1891, 367
Jane, b.1742, 329

Janet, 124, 260, 263, 265, 266, 298, 315
Janet Emily, 232
Janet Emily (Jen) (Jessie), 217
Janet Greig, b.1891, 366
Janet, b.1779, 331
Janet, b.1790, 311, 323, 324
Jessie Eleanor, 120, 121, 123, 124, 125, 126, 129, 130, 131, 132, 213, 223, 231, 233
John b.c.1679, 309, 310
John Baxter, b.1801, 335, 345, 347, 348
John Charles, 33, 50, 60, 74, 79, 98, 105, 106, 107, 109, 111, 113, 123, 126, 134, 135, 191, 198, 209, 210, 213, 219, 223, 262, 294, 298
John Howe, 3, 5, 8, 9, 15, 16, 17, 18, 19, 20, 25, 26, 28, 29, 30, 31, 32, 33, 35, 37, 38, 39, 40, 42, 44, 51, 52, 58, 59, 60, 63, 64, 69, 74, 77, 82, 89, 94, 101, 106, 107, 110, 111, 112, 125, 157, 191, 194, 223, 227, 259, 260, 269, 309
John Howe, b.1897, 366, 372, 373
John Wilson, 163, 165, 168
John, b.c.1789, 318
Josephine Violet, 135, 217, 218, 240
Kenneth James, 122, 125, 126, 132, 133, 135, 136, 210, 211, 233
Lloyd, 161
Lorraine Elizabeth, 209, 211, 213, 214, 215, 217, 218, 265, 294, 298, 302, 303
Malcolm Shaw, 35, 40, 41, 42, 43, 56, 58, 60, 66, 67, 71, 75, 76, 77, 78, 79, 81, 82, 83, 95, 96, 99, 105, 107, 109, 110, 123, 132, 142, 143, 146, 147,

150, 151, 152, 153, 234, 250, 269
Margaret, b.1846, 318
Martin Lovett, 135, 201, 217, 218
Mary b.c.1838, 9
Mary, b.1778, 335
Mary, b.1862, 367
Mary, b.c.1835, 346
Mary, b.c.1862, 366
May Eleanor, 259, 260, 263
Miss, 59
Misses, 52
Muriel Sophia Florence, 165, 168
Nancy, b.1845, 348
Nancy/Agnes, b.1845, 347
Nathalie, b.1983, 372
Nellie, 132, 146, 147, 150, 152, 153
Neville John, 200, 209, 211, 217, 240
Norman Chamberlin, 34, 41, 49, 53, 54, 63, 74, 89, 105, 107, 110, 123, 142, 238, 269, 270, 271, 272, 274, 275, 277, 278
Patrick, b.1819, 320
Peter Arthur, 217, 218, 219, 298
Ray. *See* Raymond Hector
Raymond Hector, 73, 121, 122, 125, 129, 130, 132, 133, 134, 135, 153, 194, 198, 210, 211, 233, 252, 372
Stephen James, 218, 265, 294, 298, 302, 303
Thomas, b.1786, 329
Violet Dina, 187, 188
Violet Hoppner, 20, 40, 50, 55, 60, 74, 77, 79, 80, 89, 105, 106, 107, 109, 111, 112, 113, 114, 124, 146, 194, 204, 259, 260, 298
William, 5, 8, 9
William b.c.1812, 349
William Fyfe, b.1841, 347, 348

William George, b.c.1939, 370,
372
William Howe, 35, 50, 55, 58,
60, 70, 71, 72, 74, 150
William I, b.1729, 309, 311,
312, 315, 317, 329, 331, 332,
333
William II, b.1759, 317, 319,
324
William III, b.1779, 317, 318,
320
William, b.1784, 317
William, b.1879, 324
William, b.1895, 366, 368, 373
William, b.1960, 371
Zelda Grace, 186, 188
CHAMBERLIN, 252
Thomas Chamberlin, 252, 273
CHAPMAN, 289
A.H., 32, 37, 38, 39
Joan, 168
Mr A., 37
CHIPMAN
George, 176
CHITTOCKS, 106
CHURCH
Chalmers Presbyterian, Timaru,
360
Kinnettles Parish, 329
Old Church in Montreux,
Switzerland, 372
St Andrews, Gore, 291
St John's, Roslyn, Dunedin, 288
St Joseph's Catholic, Dunedin,
227
St Paul's Presbyterian, 270
St Stephen Anglican, Granby,
Quebec, Canada, 333
CLAYTON
Mary, 332
COLE
Elizabeth, 206, 215
Ted, 206, 215
COLLINS, 35
Nellie, 98

COLVIN
Dick, 238
CONNEL
Sarah, 364
COOPER, 349
Henrietta, b.1805, 8, 349
COUNTRY
Australia, 98, 119, 157, 165,
236, 299, 348
Britain, 238
Canada, 332
China, 173, 320
England, 82, 92, 95, 99, 100,
109, 133, 281, 285, 299
France, 77, 82, 91, 92, 95
Germany, 228
Holland, 135
Hong Kong, 299
India, 322
Indonesia, 299
Ireland, 225, 246
Russia, 322
Scotland, 3, 5, 9, 97, 129, 133,
134, 157, 191, 281, 299, 353
Sri Lanka, 13
Switzerland, 73
Sydney, 133
United Kingdom, 83, 144
United States, 299, 333
COURTNEY
J., 76
COWAN
J., 71
Mrs A., 42
S., 71
COWPER, 349
Elizabeth, 281
CRAWSHAW
Elizabeth Mary, 270
William Gilchrist, 270
CRIGHTON
Robert, 350
CROCKETT
Mr, 52, 60
CUMMINGS

Miss, 59
CUNNINGHAM
  Betson Margaret, 41, 157, 161,
    168
  Jessie, 157
  John, 157, 160, 161
  John Wilson, 160
  Robert, 157, 158
  Robert George, 160
  William, 160
DALZELL
  J. S., 160
DARLING
  Mary, b.c.1735, 333
DAVIS
  Lena, 294
DAY
  V.G., 83, 90
DEMPSEY
  J., 54
  Mr, 60
  Mr N., 52
  Mrs, 60
DICKSON
  Bailie, 320
  Barbara, b.1785, 320
DISEASE
  aneurism, 8
  angina pectoris, 214
  asthemia, 77
  coronary atheroma, 72
  coronary thrombosis, 72
  creeping paralysis, 325
  diabetes, 188
  general paralysis, 183
  liver cancer, 9
  mental depression, 77
  pneumonia, 129, 204
  polio, 128
  senile psychosis, 218
  stroke, 304
  tuberculosis, 95, 346
DISTRICT, 20
  Aberdeenshire, Scotland, 3, 6
  Allanton, 110

Alloa, Clackmannanshire,
    Scotland, 364, 365
Angus, Scotland, 324
Antimony Saddle, 56
Ardgowan, 160
Balmoral, 110
Balmoral State Forest, 269
Barracouta Point, 194
Bay of Plenty, 17, 20
Beaumont, 49, 50, 51, 52, 55,
    56, 58, 59, 60, 63, 64, 70, 73,
    76, 77, 83, 97, 98, 105, 225,
    226, 228, 230, 247, 248
Beaumont Burn, 49
Beaumont Ferry, 49
Beaumont River, 49
Bedfordshire, England, 182
Bengal, India, 328
Benvie, Dundee, Scotland, 328
Blackman's Bay, Tasmania, 282
Blue Mountains, 225
Bluff Harbour, 198
Bruce, 226
Brydone, 246
Cadder, Bishopbriggs,
    Lanarkshire, Scotland, 350,
    351
California, United States, 158
Canterbury, 108, 110, 144, 146
Cape of Good Hope, 299
Carlton, 109
Caroline Bay, Timaru, 360
Caversham, Dunedin, 110, 173
Central Lowlands, Scotland, 15
Central Otago, 109, 110, 123,
    130, 132, 133, 142, 146, 198
Chinaman Flat, 50
Clackmannanshire, Scotland,
    15, 364
Clutha River, 49
Conical Hills, 262
Coromandel, 175
Crimea, 173
Crookston, 225, 236
Crookston Burn, 230

Croydon Bush, 120
Diggers Gully, Kurow, 37
Doolan's Creek, 56, 70, 71, 72
Drumlasie, Kincardine Oneill,
    Aberdeenshire, Scotland, 349
Dundee, Angus, Scotland, 327
Dundee, Forfarshire, Scotland,
    327
Dunedin North, 98
Dunkeld, 44, 49, 97
Duntroon, 26
Durham, England, 119
Epsom, Auckland, 179
Fife, Scotland, 315
Fifeshire, Scotland, 157, 347,
    348
Flint's Bush, 218
Forfarshire, Scotland, 315
Forgan, Fifeshire, Scotland,
    157, 348
Frankton Arm, Lake Wakatipu,
    298
Gibbston, 54, 55, 56, 63, 64, 66,
    70, 71, 73, 74, 75, 76, 77, 80,
    82, 89, 97, 105, 112, 123,
    142, 150, 151, 223
Gibraltar, 357
Gloucestershire, England, 160
Gold Coast, Queensland,
    Australia, 299
Gorbals, Lanarkshire, Scotland,
    281
Greenhills, 194, 197, 206, 210,
    213, 214, 217, 223, 240, 257,
    259, 303
Greenpoint, 207
Greenvale, 225
Guadalcanal, 292
Haast Pass, 300
Hakataramea Valley, 40, 42, 43
Hedgehope, 110
Henderson, 218
Henley, 135
Hillhead, Glasgow, Lanarkshire,
    Scotland, 374

Hokonui, 110, 111, 124, 125,
    127, 128, 191, 194, 198, 260
Hokonui Hills, 110
Hokonui Ranges, 300
Hot Lakes District, 18, 19
Hurinui, 110
Kakanui, 187, 298
Kapanga Beach, 175
Kapuka, 109, 128, 130, 132,
    152, 210, 211, 217, 218
Kapuka South, 132, 134
Kawarau, 56, 58, 79
Kawarau Gorge, 63
Kawarau River, 54, 67, 75, 109,
    146
Kelso, 124, 125, 230, 231, 232,
    234, 236, 237, 260, 262, 293
Khandallah, Wellington, 273
King Country, 60
Kingston Crossing, 106
Kirkcudbrightshire, Scotland,
    191
Kurow, 28, 29, 30, 31, 32, 33,
    35, 36, 37, 39, 40, 41, 42, 45,
    82, 157, 160
Lake Manapouri, 300
Lake Waituna, 130
Lake Wakatipu, 55
Lake Wanaka, 231
Lanarkshire, Scotland, 143, 144
Makarewa, 120
Makarora, 231
Mataura, 109, 259
Maxwelltown, Dundee, Angus,
    Scotland, 335
Mayor Island, Tauranga, 16
Middlesex, England, 173, 177
Mimihau, 121, 191
Mitchells Land, Bishopbriggs,
    Lanarkshire, Scotland, 8
Moa Flat, 232
Moko-Moko Inlet, 194, 197,
    206, 208, 213
Mokoreta, 218, 294
Molyneux River, 64

Mount Eden, 162
Mount Tarawera, 19
Mt Ida, 158
Muirhouses (Murroes), Angus, Scotland, 333
Nevis, 79
Nevis River, 56
New Hampshire, USA, 333
New South Wales, Australia, 285
North America, 331
North East Valley, Dunedin, 120
North Otago, 187
Norwood, Surrey, England, 285
Norze Land, Dundee, Scotland, 5
Ochil Hills, Clackmannanshire, Scotland, 15
Ohinemuri, 183, 184
Old Machar, Aberdeenshire, Scotland, 5, 8, 9, 349, 351
Omanawha, 20
Omanua, Tauranga, 20
Omaui, 207, 223
Onehunga, Auckland, 175
Otago, 33, 135, 146, 158
Otahuhu, Auckland, 179
Otama, 135, 294
Otapori, 110
Otekaike, 27, 35, 42, 43
Otepopo, 187
Outer Hebrides, 133
Papakaio, 40
Perthshire, Scotland, 49
Piano Flat, 300
Pink and White Terraces, 18
Pomahaka River, 230
Port Hills, 95
Portsea, Hampshire, England, 327
Quebec, Canada, 333
Renfrewshire, Scotland, 144
Riccarton, Christchurch, 269
River Forth, Scotland, 15

River Kelvin, Lanarkshire, Scotland, 351
Roslyn Bush, 114
Roslyn, Dunedin, 289
Ryal Bush, 194
Salisbury Plains, England, 99
Seaward Bush, 259
South Otago, 129
Southland, 111, 133, 219
Spar Bush, 217, 218
St Cuthbert's, Edinburgh, Scotland, 332
St Lawrence Seaway, 333
St Mark Chapel, Whitechapel, London, 177
Strathearn, Invercargill, 259
Tamaki River, 179
Taranaki, 183
Tasmania, Australia, 282, 300, 302
Tauranga Harbour, 16
Taurina, 269
Te Anau, 300
The Terrace, 262
Three Sisters, 207
Tuturau, 66
Victoria Bridge, 109, 110, 123, 132, 142, 146, 147, 150, 151, 152, 153, 269
Victoria, Australia, 158
Victorian Goldfields, 157
Viewbank, Forgan, Fifeshire, 375
Waianakarua, 187
Waiarikiki, 74, 94, 105, 106, 107, 109, 110, 142, 269
Waikana, 90
Waikato, 183
Waimumu, 107, 110, 120, 122
Waipahi, 230, 236
Waitaki, 32, 45
Waitaki River, 33, 42
Waitaki River Basin, 29, 30, 259
Waitiri, 142, 150, 152

Wakatipu, 146
Wangaloa, 226, 234
Warepa, 225
West Coast, 162
Westside Hilton, Dundee,
    Angus, Scotland, 335
Wigram Aerodrome, Riccarton,
    269
Wigram, Christchurch, 110
Wimbledon, London, 320
Woodlands, 134, 262, 263
Wyndham, 121, 191
Wyndham Ridges, 121
DODDS
Mr, 121
DON
Ann, 332
DONOVAN
Corry, 238
DORSEY
Mrs, 52
DOWNES
A.B., 353
DRISCOLL
John, 107
DUFF
David, b.1840, 345, 346, 348
David, b.c.1864, 347
Isabella, b.c. 1862, 347
Isabella, b.c.1862, 348
DUMBLETON
A. G., 236
DUNCAN
Euphemia Lamb, b.1864, 374
DWYER
Mrs T., 227
EDEN
Elizabeth Mary, 270
Francis James, 270
EDGAR
J. D., 231
EGERTON
Eleanor, 135
Eleanor Elizabeth, 217, 240
William, 135

William Francis, 239, 240
EHRENFRIED
Mr, 178
ELLIOTT
W., 231
ERWIN
Rev. Dr, 284
EVANS
Jack, 107
Rex Simmonds, 263
William, 109
William (Billy), 107
FARM
Ardlussa, 66
Benmore Station., 35
Fortification, 66
Gibbston Run, 210
Kawarau, 54
Knowsley Park, 66, 67, 69, 74,
    77, 82, 89, 90, 94, 95, 96, 97,
    100, 101, 105, 259, 269
Kurow Run, 27
Mount Soho Station, 132
Mt Rosa, 54, 55, 60, 73, 80, 89,
    97, 106
Otekaike Estate, 44
Pleasant Creek, 110
Sauchie, 15, 19, 20, 25
View Hill, 107, 109, 111, 122,
    259, 260, 269
Waitiri Station, 150
Wentworth, 56
FARRER, 20
FITCHETT, 289
FLEMING
Mary, 366
FORREST
Isabella, 350
John, 350
Mary, 350
FRAME
George (Geordie), 188
Janet, 188
FRANKS
Paul, 271

FRASER
  Agnes, 198, 213
  Dan, 198, 213
FRENCH
  Janet, 120
FRISBY, 111
FULLER
  Damon, 333
  George Damon, b.1868, 333
FYFE
  Isabella, b.1810, 335, 345, 348
GARD, 35
GEARY
  Thelma, 72
  William Francis, 239
GIBSON
  D., 236
GILBERT
  Percy, 203, 214
GLAS
  John, 313, 314
  Mr, 331
GOUDIE
  Elizabeth McArthur, b.c.1875,
    369
GRAHAM
  Henry, 71
  Mary, 144
GRANT
  Jane, servant, 348
GREEN
  Joseph, 30
GREENLEES
  Llewellyn Edward John, 165
GREIG
  Jane, b.c.1836, 364
  Mary, b.c.1836, 364
GRUBB, 289
  Agnes Clara, 288, 289, 290
  Alan, 290
  Arnold, 210, 217, 218, 262, 265
  Arnold Henry McLeod, 111,
    126, 234, 281, 288, 290, 291,
    292, 293, 294, 295, 296, 298,
    299, 300, 301, 302, 304

  Dora Grace, 217, 218, 252, 262,
    265, 291, 292, 294, 295, 298,
    299, 300, 302, 303, 304, 360,
    371
  Elizabeth (Bessie), 298
  Henry, 281
  Henry Hobbs, 281
  Henry Joseph, 282, 284, 287,
    288, 290
  Hugh B. J., 282
  Linton, 288
  Lyall, 290
  Russell Allan, 288, 290
GUNN
  Susan, b.1799, 324
HACKNEY
  Catherine, 325
HAIGH, 289
HARWOOD
  John, 30
HASTIE
  Alexander, 144
  Christina, 143, 144
  Corporal, 176
  David, 143, 144
  David Jnr, 144
  David Rankin, 143
  Hugh, 144
  Isabella, 144
  James, 144, 145
  James McAdam, 144
  John, 144
  Nellie, 109, 143, 145, 146, 250
  Robert, 144
  Thomas, 144
  William, 143, 144
HAY
  H. J., 236
HEAD
  Airlie Christina Jean, 134, 135
HELLER
  Mr, 132
HILL
  Isabel, 309, 310
HISLOP

Mr, 31
HOBBS
Elizabeth Thompson, 281
HOLD, 289
HOPPNER
John, 278
HOWE
David, 5, 9
Elizabeth, 5
Ellen, 9
HOY
Margaret, b.1729, 313
HUGHES
Ranger, 30
HUNTER
Agnes Greig, b.1870, 365
Andrew, b.1859, 365
Andrew, b.c.1799, 364, 365
David Grieg, b.1864, 365
James McQueen, b.1872, 365
James, b.1829, 364, 365
Jane, b.c.1836, 365
John Grey, 150
John W., b.c.1878, 365
Joseph, 108
Margaret Paterson, b.1867, 365
Mary McQueen, b.1862, 364,
365, 366
ILRO
Emily, 285
ISAACS
Esther, 175
G., 175
George, 175
JACOBS
Asher, 177
Caroline, 182
Catherine, 177
Dianna, 182
Esther, 177, 182
Hart, 182
Isaac, 177, 182
John, 177
Joseph, 182
Julia, 177

Lazarus, 177
Leah, 177
Mary, 177, 182
Matilda, 182
Morris, 177
Murice, 182
Myer, 182
Sarah, 177
Susan, 173
Zipporah, 182
JAGGER
Mr S., 178
JARDINE
William, 160
JEWITT
Mavis, 218
JOHNSON
Charles, 228
JOHNSTON
J. W., 236
JOHNSTONE
Mrs Mammy, 67
JONES
Maria, 144
Mr, 175
KELLY
John, 42
Mr, 35
KIEL
Aike, 135, 136, 223
Jessie Eleanor, 136
KING
Truby, 72
KINROSS
J., 71
T., 71
W., 71
KIRK
Laurie, 232
LANE
Mr, 355
LEONARD, 43
Ranger, 56
LESLIE
Connor, 70, 71

James, 70
LEVY
  Albert, 173
  Catherine, 173
  Elias, 182
  Esther, 173
  Esther Isabella, 173, 177, 179, 180
  Fanny, 173
  Jane, 173
  Julia, 173
  Lazarus, 173
  Lewis, 173
  Mary Ann, 173
  Mier, 173, 175
  Moss, 173
  Mr, 176
  Mrs, 175, 176
  Myer, 173, 175, 177
  Sarah, 173, 175, 177
LINDLEY
  Elizabeth (Elsie) McKellar, b.c.1908, 369
  Thomas, b.c.1875, 369
LINDSAY
  Jean, 323
  John, 324
LOUCH
  Mr, 20
LUCK
  Helena Christina, 259
LUSK
  Mr, 231
MABEN
  Sarah, 191
MACARTNEY, 216
  Elinor Anne Pearce, 206, 213
  Mervan, 206, 213, 216
MacASKILL
  Bessie, 129, 133, 134
MALLOCH
  John, 314, 315
MARKS
  Catherine Simons, 177
MARRIOT

Rita, 294
MARSHAL
  Jannet, b.c.1709, 329
MARSHALL
  Edwin, 270
  Elizabeth Mary, 110, 269, 270, 271, 272, 275, 277
MARTIN
  Francis Roy, 135, 218
  Sarah Isabella (Isa), 135, 218
MASTERS
  Joseph, 175
MAXWELL
  Alexander b.1791, 309
  Alexander, b.1791, 311, 318, 320, 323, 324, 325, 326, 330
  Alexander, b.1821, 326, 327, 328
  Alexander, b.1924, 327
  Charles Chalmers, b.1829, 324
  Charles, b.1860, 327
  David, 332
  David, b.1819, 309, 323, 324, 327
  David, b.1858, 327
  Elizabeth Anderson, b.1827, 324
  George Flemming, b.1854, 327
  George Flemming, b.1917, 328
  George, b.1832, 324
  Harriet, b.1856, 327
  Helen, b.1818, 327, 328
  James, b.1848, 327
McADAM
  Christina, 143, 144
McDONALD
  Ann, 120
  Rosanna, 182
McDOWELL, 246
  Nancy, 246
McINTYRE, 206, 214, 217
  Agnes, 135
  John, 135
McKENZIE
  Miss, 261

McKIBBIN, 246
   Constance Eleanor, 234, 247,
      250, 251, 253
   James, 76, 227, 245, 247, 248,
      249
   Norman Chamberlin, 234, 247,
      250, 251, 252
   Pamela, 247, 253
   R. J., 278
   Robert James, 246, 247, 250,
      251, 253
McLAREN
   Jessie G., 327
McLEOD
   Barbra, 120
   Christina, 120
   Donald, 120
   George, 120
   Hugh, 281
   Issabella, 120
   Jane, 281
   Janet, 120
   Neil, 120
   William, 120
   Willimina, 120
McNAMARA
   E., 284
McRAE, 294
   Florence, 218
   George, 218
MEINUNG
   Joyce, 238
MEYER
   Caroline Elizabeth, 17
MILLER, 25
MILNE
   Mary, 317, 324
   Mr A., 60
MITCHELL
   Frances Louisa Beaven, 112,
      191, 194
   John, 121, 191, 213
   Margaret, 366
   Margaret, b.1733, 309

   Margaret, b.c.1733, 309, 317,
      329
   Rosa, 121, 191, 206, 213, 214,
      216
MONCUR
   David, b.c.1706, 329
   Jane, b.1742, 309
   Jane, b.c.1742, 329, 330, 331,
      332, 333
MOSLEY
   E. O., 96
MUIRHEAD
   James, 120
   Margaret Hamilton, 119, 120
MULCALEY
   Edmund, 283
MULVENIA
   Mary, 30, 31
MUNRO
   Tertius, 37
MUNYARD
   A. W., 236
MURPHY, 175
   Ann, 182
MURRAY
   C., 236
NATHAN
   Annie, 182, 183
   Henry, 182, 183
   Joseph, 181, 182, 183, 185
   Matilda, 182, 183
   Maurice, 182, 183
   Michael, 182
   Michael H., 183
   Minna Annette, 185
   Sarah, 182, 183
   Violet Dina, 110, 173, 185, 186
NEEDHAM
   Mrs, 205
NICHOLAS
   Elsie, 165
   Elsie Ina, 165
NIEL
   Elspet, servant, 349
NOBLE

Andrew, 121
NOLAN
John, 151
O'BRIEN
Mr, 161
O'ROURKE
Elizabeth Mary, 270
OCCUPATION
aircraftman, 292
baker, 6, 55, 83, 97, 228, 277
blacksmith, 120, 165
boatbuilder, 282
bookbinder, 317, 318, 320
bookseller, 185, 318, 319, 320,
328
borough collector, 365
brush manufacturer, 182
burgess, 319
bushman, 175
cabinet maker, 144
caretaker, 165
carpenter, 247, 250
cattle dealer, 8
coach builder, 160, 161
commercial traveller, 285, 350
contractor, 40
cook, 66
cooper, 6
coroner, 175
crofter, 120, 329
crown land commissioner, 30
dairy farmer, 120
digger, 175
district nurse, 132
domestic servant, 183
draper, 13, 27, 165, 241, 284
driver, 291
dyer, 332
engineer, 143
factor (real estate agent), 366
fancy draper, 284
farm labourer, 135
farmer, 9, 30, 55, 120, 150, 349
flax mill manager, 324, 327
flax mill overseer, 345

flaxshire, 327
flesher, 6, 8
food scientist, 372
fruiterer, 165
gardener, 187, 259, 364, 365
general servant, 375
general store keeper, 289
glass factory hand, 264
good salesman, 283
grain dealer, 368
grocer, 345
grocer's assistant, 264
grocer's shopman, 350
habit maker, 173
hairdresser, 219
hammerman, 6
handloom weaver, 318
head green, 350
head grocer, 351
Honorary Sheriff-Substitute,
371
house servant, 182
importer, 185
ink manufacturer, 320
ironmonger, 285
jeweller, 182
joiner, 323
jute factory owner, 335
jute manufacturer, 317, 335
jute merchant, 345, 348
labourer, 110, 225, 259, 269,
364
lance corporal, 228
laundress, 182
laundry maid, 182
lawyer, 332
leather merchant, 5, 9
linen cloth merchant, 318
linen flax factory foreman, 263
lorry driver, 262
magistrate, 83
manager, 135
manufacturer, 319, 320, 332,
364
mariner, 5, 281

mason, 345
maternity nurse, 130, 131
mechanic, 281
mechanics foreman, 324
medical practitioner, 151
merchant, 320
merchant navy seaman, 350
mill hand, 187
mill manager, 324, 326
miller, 120, 368
milliner, 357
millinery factory manager, 253
millspinner, 325
millwright, 324
miner, 110, 270
motor driver, 98
music and voice production
     teacher, 288
music teacher, 356
nurse, 185
parochial office assistant, 363
pawnbroker, 252
photographer, 374, 375
pianoforte dealer, 320
police constable, 151, 248
policeman, 76
poor rates collector, 366
printer, 320
professor of ecology, 333
provision merchant, 8
rabbiter, 120
radio serviceman, 293
radio technician, 292
railway engine worker, 269
railway guard, 270
ranger, 35
Rawleigh seller, 262
sawmiller, 150, 151
sergeant, 228
servant, 66, 182, 183, 348, 349,
     366
sheep farmer, 90
shoemaker, 6, 119
shop boy, 182, 320
shop server, 364

shopkeeper, 183
silk dyer, 332
soldier, 227
spirits dealer, 345
stationer, 185, 317
stay maker, 177
stock-keeper, 283
store owner, 214
storekeeper, 97, 175, 230, 250
storeman, 97, 228
surfaceman, 226
tailor, 6, 173
tea merchant, 320
teacher, 98, 180, 181, 259, 293,
     348
teamster, 43, 67
telegram delivery boy, 265
theatre manager, 219
threshing mill cook, 269
town clerk, 367
travelling salesman, 162
warehouseman, 288
weaver, 6, 319, 331
window dresser, 283
wright, 6
ORBELL
  A.S., 83, 90
ORGANISATION
  Agricultural and Pastoral
     Society, 231
  Agricultural Department, 95
  American Radio Relay League
     Inc., 301
  Arawa [Maternity] Hospital,
     185
  Argyll and Sutherland
     Highlanders, 367
  Arnold Grubb Ltd, 293, 300
  Artists' Repository and Envoy
     Depot, 182
  Auckland Hebrew Synagogue,
     181
  Auckland Hospital, 277
  Auckland University College,
     180

Bank of New Zealand, 17
Beaumont Horticultural and Industrial, 60
Beaumont Presbyterian Church, 84
Beaumont Presbyterian Home Mission, 59
Beaumont Public Library, 52
Beaumont School Committee, 60
Beaumont Sports Club, 52
Beaumont Sports Committee, 52
Blue Bell Inn, Dundee, 318
Bridge Hotel, Beaumont, 245
Brownell Brothers, 282
Cashmere Sanatorium, 95
Chalmers Brothers, 40, 43
Chalmers Store, 227
Chamber of Commerce, 179
Cherry Farm, 72
Cherry Farm Hospital, 72, 218, 298
Chicago University, 333
Child Welfare, 214
Christchurch School for Deaf, 278
Church of England, 43
Civil Defence Corps, 296
Commercial Club (Tasmania), 283
Commission of the Peace, 183
Coval Golf Club, 371
Cromwell Hospital, 77, 150
Cromwell Returned Servicemen's Association, 152
Cromwell Silver Band, 153
Cunningham's, Coachbuilder, 160
Customs Department, Wellington, 161
Department of Education, 108
Dick Colvin's Band, 238
Dundee Council, 335

Dunedin Teachers' College, 108
Dunoon Bridge Club, 371
Dunoon Sheriff Court, 9
Duntroon and District Angling Club, 371
General Hospital, Rouen, 84
Gibbston Tennis Club, 71
Glasite Church, 329, 331
Gore and Districts Travel Club, 302
Gore Boat and Water Ski Club, 299
Gore Hospital, 130, 304
Gore Magistrate's Court, 96
Gore Male Choir, 290
Gore Rotary Club, 291
Gore Tramping Club, 290
Greenlane Hospital, 131
Greytowers Convalescent Hospital, Hornchurch, 92
Hallenstein Brothers, 161
Henry Hobbs Grubb, 282
Herbert Haynes Ltd, 215
Heriot Cricket Team, 228
Hibernian-Australasian Catholic Benefit Society, 274
Home Guard, 198
Home Guard, Gore Battalion, 291
Hospital Annex, Auckland Domain Gardens, 185
Imperial League of Australia, 236
Invervargill Hospital, 204
J. Ballantyne and Co., 284
J. Hamilton & Son, 160
Kapanga Hotel, 176
Kelso Domain Board, 235
Kew Bowling Club, 263
Kew Hospital, 128, 129
Kurow Presbyterian Church, 41
Land Board, 94
Land Commission, 27
Land Purchase Board, 44

Lands Committee of the House of Representatives, 106
Lepers' Trust Board (Inc.),, 278
London Book Shop, 209
MacGibbon and Co., 290
Melhop's Garage, 128
Men of the Trees, 294
Milton Cottage Hospital, 129
Ministry of Agriculture and Fisheries, 135
Mother Aubert Home of Compassion, 278
National Library Service, 203
National Mortgage and Agency Company of New Zealand, 101
Native Forest Action Group, 300
Nestlé Company, 372
New Zealand Air Force, 110
New Zealand Amateur Radio Transmitters, 294
New Zealand Army, 250
New Zealand Association of Radio Transmitters, 300
New Zealand Clothing Factory, 161
New Zealand Historic Places Trust, 205
New Zealand Medical Corps, 180
New Zealand Radio Institute (Inc.), 291
New Zealand Rifle Brigade, 84
Nurse McLean's Maternity Unit, 228
Ocean Beach Freezing Works, 198
Ohinemuri Rifles, 185
Omaui Health Camp, 208
Otago Daily Times, 231, 236
Otago Land Board, 27, 28, 29, 30, 42, 56, 79, 97
Otago No. 2 Military Service Board, 83, 90

Otago University, 135
Philips Electrical Industries, 299
Presbyterian Social Services Association, 218, 298
Prince of Wales' Guards, 228
Public Trust Office, 79, 81
Public Works Department, 19
Returned Servicemen's Association, 236
Riverton Hospital, 136, 218
Rotorua Railway Company, 19
Royal Air Force, 238
Royal College of Science and Technology, Glasgow, 372
Royal New Zealand Foundation for the Blind, 301
Sargood, Son and Ewen, 162
School for Deaf in Auckland, 278
Seacliff Mental Hospital, 72, 218
Single Profit Stores, 263
Soil Association, 294
Southern Districts Aero Club (Inc.), 300
St David's Private Hospital, 77
St Helen's Hospital, 186
Stevenson and Nolan, 150
Stockport Lunatic Asylum, 183
Tapanui Anglers' Society, 231
Tauranga County Council, 19
Tauranga, Butter, Cheese and Bacon Factory Company, 20
Tay Street Jute Mills, Dundee, 324
Town Council of Dundee, 319, 320
Tuapeka County Council Chamber, 235
University of Dundee, 321
Victoria Hotel, 175
W & J Chalmers Ltd, 373
Waikouaiti Choral Club, 289
Waikouaiti Dramatic Club, 290

Waitaki County Council, 37, 42
Wellington Public Hospital, 135
West Otago Ex-servicemen, 232
Women's Division of Federated
    Farmers, 112, 191, 214
Woolworths, 161
OTTREY
Sydney, 230
OTWAY
Mr, 66
PAEROA
Mrs J. Nathan, 181
PARKER
George, 175
Mrs, 176
PATERSON
Anne, 265
Margaret, b.c.1801, 364
PEARCE
Elizabeth, 191
PEART
Amelia Maribel, 119, 120
Elizabeth, 119
George, 119
Jacob, 119
James, 122
James Muirhead, 120
Jane, 119
Janet, 122
John, 119
Joseph, 119, 120
Joseph Emerson, 119
Margaret, 120
Maribel, 100
Thomas, 119
PERRIAM
Charles, 73
PHILPOT
George, 31
PINK
James Thomas, 191
Rosa, 191
PLUMRIDGE
Eileen Rose, 278
POSSENISKIE, 177

Esther Isabella, 179, 180, 181
Harold Louis, 180, 181
Henry Louis, 173, 177, 178,
    179, 181
Minna Annette, 181, 183
Miss, 181
Mr, 178
Mrs. H. L., 177
Zaritta Leila, 180
POTTS
Connie, 238
PRATT
Benjamin, 368
PROPHET, 374
Ella W., 375
Euphemia, 375
Freida, 375
George L., 375
James D., 375
John R., 375
John Reid, 374, 375
William K., b.1896, 375
William, b.1863, 374, 375
REED
Mr, 128
REID
James, 355
RICHARDSON
Emma, b.1842, 347
RING, 176
Mr, 175
RITCHIE
Mrs, 96
ROBERTS
Alice, 183
Oral, 240
RODGER
K., 231
ROHRLACH
Edna Grace, 165
ROSS
Valerie, 251
ROY
Mr J. A., 232
RUSBATCH

Richard Stephen, 151
SCHOOL
  Beaumont, 53, 54, 61, 77, 89, 277
  Beaumont Presbyterian Sunday, 52
  Cornwall Park, 163
  Correspondence, 205
  Ferndale, 106
  Gibbston, 70
  Gore Convent, 231
  Gore High, 105, 106, 262, 294
  Gore Main Primary, 294
  Gore Primary, 111, 293
  Gore Public, 108
  Greenhills, 201
  Greenhills Sunday, 205
  Kaikorai Primary, 288
  Kelso, 232, 260, 262
  Kurow, 35
  Lochiel, 111
  Mimihau, 124
  Mokoreta, 259
  Oamaru South, 160
  Otago Boys' High, 288
  Queenstown District High, 135
  Southland Boys' High, 135, 298
  Southland Girls' High, 213
  Southland Technical College, 129, 135
  Tapanui District High, 124
  Waiarikiki, 74, 110
  Waikana, 90, 96, 97, 259
  Waikouaiti, 298
  Waitaki Boys' High, 40
  Winton District High, 240
  Winton Primary, 240
SCOTT
  Alex., 71
  Alexander William, 79
  James, 327
SCULLION
  Susan, 225
SHAW
  George, 15, 16, 25
SHEPHERD, 289
SHERWOOD
  Douglas Sutlej, 165
SHIP
  Athenic, 91
  Cordoba, 100
  Earnslaw, 74
  Fulwood, 157
  Helenslee, 191
  Invercargill, 144
  Jessie Readman, 353
  Lady Ann, 158
  Maori, 173
  May Queen, 16
  Mokoia, 84
  Mountaineer, 74
  New Swiftsure, 333
  Ormonde, 357
  Oxford, 17
  Paparoa, 97
  Polly, 119
  Portland, 173
  Rangitata, 133
  Tofua, 76
  Wanganella, 133
  Wennington, 191
SIM
  J., 235
SIMPSON
  William, 40
SINCLAIR
  Donald, 101
SMITH
  J., 76
SNEDDON
  Constable, 96
STEVENS
  Dr, 35
STEVENSON
  Richard Clifford, 150, 151
  Rupert, 15
STEWART
  George Vesey, 19
STOKES, 58
  Harriette Clara Eugenie, 32

Margaret Gertrude, 110, 231
William, 58
STRACHAN, 349, 357
Ann, b.c.1839, 349
Charles, 8, 9, 351
Charles, b.c.1790, 349, 350
Charles, b.c.1841, 349, 350, 353, 356, 361
Charles, b.c.1869, 350, 351
Elizabeth, 8, 9
Elizabeth Howe, b.c.1843, 350, 351, 353, 356, 363
Elizabeth Howe, b.c.1864, 350, 351, 353, 357, 363
George, b.c.1836, 349
George, b.c.1870, 350, 351, 353, 357, 363
Henrietta Cooper, b.c.1866, 350, 351, 353, 355, 357, 360, 363
Isabella Chalmers, b.c.1867, 351
James, 29
James, b.c.1872, 351, 353, 357, 363
Janet, b.c.1848, 349
John Chalmers, b.c.1874, 351
Margaret, b.c.1845, 349
Miss H.C., 9
Mr, 355
STREET
Adelaide St, Auckland, 179
Albert St, Timaru, 357
Alexander St, Firth View, Dunoon and Kilmun, Argyll, Scotland, 366
Aln St, Oamaru, 187
Angela St, Fendalton, 264
Aratonga Ave, Greenlane, Auckland, 163
Ardwick St, Gore, 303
Auchamore Rd, Dunoon, Argyll, Scotland, 366, 371
Barbadoes St, Christchurch North, 270

Beach St, Waikouaiti, 290
Cambden Rd, Invercargill, 213
Cameron St, Waitemata, 165
Castle St, Dundee, Scotland, 317, 318, 319, 321
Challis Ave, Darlinghurst, NSW, Australia, 165
Chester St, Christchurch East, 270
Clothier St, Linwood, Christchurch, 284
Clyde Place, Glasgow, Lanarkshire, Scotland, 364
Cook St, Auckland, 179
Coote Rd, Napier, 288
Coquet St, Oamaru, 160, 161
Cornwall Park, Mount Eden, 163
Coutts Rd, Gore, 295
Craighead St, Timaru, 357
Croydon Rd, Grey Lynn, 163
Cuba St, Wellington, 272
Denton St, Gore, 186
Dominion Rd, Mt Eden, Auckland, 165, 179
Durham St, Winton, 241
Elles Rd South, Invercargill, 213
Elles Rd, Invercargill, 263
Elm Row, Dunedin, 186
English St, Riccarton, 264
Fairfield Road, Grey Lynn, 163
Fox St, Invercargill, 213
Gap Rd, Winton, 251
Gay St, Cromwell, 152
Gibbston Back Rd, Gibbston, 55
Gorge Rd, Invercargill, 130
Great South Rd, Auckland, 163
Hanover St, Dunedin West, 270
Herne Bay Rd, Auckland, 277
High St, Dunedin, 186
Hillpath Rd, Forgan, Fifeshire, Scotland, 375

Hospital St, Gorbals, Glasgow,
143
Isles Lane, Hawkhill, Dundee,
Angus, Scotland, 326
Islington St, North East Valley,
Dunedin North, 249
Jackson St, St Kilda, 270
Jamaica St, Maxwelltown,
Dundee, Angus, Scotland,
335, 345
Kale St, Auckland, 179
Karangahape Rd, Central
Auckland, 165
Kensington Ave, Auckland, 179
Kilburn Tce, Forgan, Fifeshire,
Scotland, 348
Kitchener St, Gore, 303
Konini Rd, Titirangi, 253, 278
Koromiko Rd, Titirangi, 253,
278
Lambeth Rd, Dunedin North,
270
Liverpool Rd, Ashford, NSW,
Australia, 168
Love Lane, Old Machar,
Aberdeenshire, Scotland, 6, 8
Main St, Gorbals, Lanarkshire,
Glasgow, 144
Main St, Gore, 293
Market St, Manchester,
England, 182
Marsden Ave, Auckland, 179
Mary St, Dunoon, Argyll,
Scotland, 9
McQuarrie St, Invercargill, 263
Melbourne St, Invercargill, 213
Mular St, Dunedin North, 98
Murray St, Hobart, 283
Nairn St, Wellington, 274
Norwood St, Dunedin North,
187
Oakland St, St Kilda, Dunedin,
250
Omanawha Rd, Te Papa, 15
Oxford Tce, Christchurch, 271

Papanui Rd, St Albans,
Christchurch, 284
Park Rd, Grafton, Auckland,
179, 180
Plummers Row, Stepney,
Middlesex, 177
Prospect Tce, Grey Lynn, 163
Puke Rd, Paeroa, 185
Queen St, Winton, 241
Rata St, New Lynn, 253
Reimers Ave, Mount Eden, 163
Richmond Rd, Mount Eden,
163
Richmond St, Grey Lynn, 163
Shortland St, Auckland, 173
Sligo Tce, Roslyn, Dunedin,
288
St Andrew's St, Dundee,
Scotland, 318
St Andrews Rd, Roskill,
Auckland, 168
St David's Lane, Dundee,
Angus Scotland, 326
Stafford St, Timaru, 355
Stuart St, Dunedin, 120
Tainui Rd, Andersons Bay,
Dunedin, 250
Tay St, Dundee, Angus,
Scotland, 326, 327
Thomas St, Gore, 281, 291
Tillie St, Kelvin, Glasgow,
Lanarkshire, Scotland, 8,
351, 363
Town Belt, Roslyn, Dunedin,
288
Trafford St, Gore, 291
Tyne St, Oamaru, 160
Union St, East Side, Dundee,
Angus, Scotland, 345
Vanguard St, Nelson, 120
Victoria Arcade, Auckland,
177, 178
Victoria St, Auckland, 175
View Rd, Mt Eden, Auckland,
277

View St, St Marys, Auckland,
275
Violet St, Mt Albert, Auckland,
251
Warwick St, Hobart, Tasmania,
180
Washington St, Anderston,
Glasgow, Lanarkshire,
Scotland, 350
Wear St, Oamaru, 160
West St, Auckland, 179
STRINGER
George, 31
SUTHERLAND
Isabella, 120
TAYLOR
Mr W., 232
TEMPLETON
Mr J. A., 227
THOMPSON, 144
C. V., 237
THOMSON, 144
James, servant, 349
John Turnbull, 49
Mr A., 227
TIMS, 99, 278
Caroline Elizabeth, 17, 18
Eleanor Anne, 58
Eleanor Rebecca, 3, 17, 18, 157,
223
Harriette Anne, 66
Harriette Clara Eugenie, 17, 56,
58, 60, 66, 69, 231
John Chamberlin, 17
John Rolls, 17
Martha Chamberlin, 17, 58, 77
T.H., 17
Thomas Chamberlin, 17, 252
TOVEY
Edith Winifred, 273
TOWN
Aberdeen, Aberdeenshire,
Scotland, 6, 13, 278, 350,
363, 366
Adelaide, S.A., Australia, 119,
357
Alexandra, 151
Allanton, 269
Alloa, Clackmannanshire,
Scotland, 364
Arbroath, Angus, Scotland, 317,
318
Arrowtown, 36, 54, 67, 75, 130,
132, 133, 135, 136, 152, 211,
217, 223, 240
Ashburton, 185, 266
Auckland, 133, 135, 162, 168,
173, 177, 178, 185, 218, 251,
254
Balaklava, Crimean Peninsula,
173
Balclutha, 49, 265
Balfour, 106
Ballyscullion, Ireland, 225
Banbury, Oxfordshire, England,
58, 66, 278
Bedford, Bedfordshire,
England, 182, 183
Belfast, Ireland, 173
Belleville, Coromandel, 175,
176
Bluff, 198, 201, 206, 209, 303
Bristol, Gloucestershire,
England, 144, 160
Brockenhurst, Hampshire,
England, 84
Brydone, 94
Calcutta, India, 328
Cambridge, Clackmannanshire,
Scotland, 364
Chicago, Illinois, USA, 333
Christchurch, 27, 95, 146, 186,
217, 264, 265, 266, 269, 270,
284
Clinton, 232
Clyde, 146
Colombo, Sri Lanka, 357

Cornlee, Kirkpatrick-Irongray, KKB, Scotland, 120, 143, 144, 177, 182, 183
Cromwell, 54, 109, 110, 132, 142, 150, 151, 152, 153, 249
Culverden, 108
Dundee, Angus, Scotland, 5, 9, 312, 315, 317, 319, 320, 323, 324, 327, 328, 330, 331, 332, 333, 347, 348, 350, 351, 374
Dundee, Forfarshire, Scotland. *See* Dundee, Angus, Scotland
Dunedin, 55, 76, 77, 98, 110, 112, 119, 120, 145, 146, 150, 158, 162, 186, 191, 231, 238, 248, 249, 250, 290, 353, 354
Dunoon and Kilmun, Argyll, Scotland, 365
Dunoon, Argyll, Scotland, 9, 357, 364, 365, 366, 367, 373, 374
Duntroon, 25, 35, 40, 43, 50, 259
Edinburgh, Scotland, 323, 332
Eindhoven, Holland, 299
Etchells, Cheshire, England, 183
Forfar, Angus, Scotland, 312
Forgan, Fifeshire, Scotland, 374
Frankton, 298
Fremantle, W.A., Austalia, 357
Glasgow, Lanarkshire, Scotland, 8, 97, 143, 144, 323, 350, 351
Glenorchy, 133
Gore, 66, 74, 90, 94, 96, 101, 107, 109, 110, 111, 120, 122, 125, 126, 186, 218, 259, 260, 262, 269, 281, 291, 294, 298
Granby, Quebec, Canada, 333
Greenock, Scotland, 353
Hanover, Germany, 299
Harewood, 291
Hawera, 368
Heriot, 97, 225, 226, 228, 230

Hobart, Tasmania, 180, 181, 282
Hokitika, 161
Hornchurch, London, England, 91, 92
Inglewood, 183
Invercargill, 33, 109, 112, 120, 124, 128, 130, 132, 136, 191, 194, 198, 201, 206, 209, 213, 215, 216, 217, 218, 239, 241, 263, 265, 298, 303
Kincardine O'Neil, Aberdeenshire, Scotland, 8, 349, 350
Kingston, 74
Kolkata, India, 328
Kurow, 27, 30, 35, 40, 41, 66, 259
Kyle of Lochalsh, Scotland, 120
Lawrence, 50, 83, 235
Liff, Dundee, Scotland, 310, 312, 328
Liverpool, England, 157, 183
Lochee, Liff, Angus, Scotland, 333
London, England, 17, 110, 173, 182, 219, 259
Lower Hutt, 130
Lumphanan, Aberdeenshire, Scotland, 349
Maidstone, Kent, England, 191
Manchester, England, 182, 183
Mandeville, 120
Manilla, Phillipines, 299
Mataura, 74, 82, 89, 90, 94, 95, 96, 101, 106, 107, 110, 120
Melbourne, Victoria, Australia, 299, 357
Milton, 354, 355
Monikie, Angus, Scotland, 313
Montreal, Canada, 333
Montrose, Angus, Scotland, 320
Naples, Italy, 357
New York, USA, 332

Newton Mearns, Larnackshire, Scotland, 375
Newtown, New South Wales, Australia, 285
Nightcaps, 227
Oamaru, 40, 157, 160, 161, 188, 277, 298
Ohai, 109
Ohakea, 292
Osaka, Japan, 299
Paeroa, 185
Perth, Perthshire, Scotland, 314, 315, 374, 375
Port Said, Egypt, 357
Pourie, Dundee, Scotland, 312
Queenstown, 74, 132, 135, 223
Raes Junction, 49
Rattray, Perthshire, Scotland, 329
Riverton, 33, 218
Rotorua, 18, 19
Roxburgh, 49
Salford, Lancashire, England, 182
Sao Paulo, Brazil, 372
Sling Camp, Wiltshire, England, 84, 91, 99
Southampton, Hampshire, England, 133, 357
St Andrews Dysart, Fifeshire, Scotland, 157
St Cuthberts, Edinburgh, Midlothian, Scotland, 120
Sydney, NSW, Australia, 119, 130, 165, 177, 236, 299, 357
Tapanui, 225, 228, 230, 232, 236, 262
Tauranga, 9, 15, 17, 18, 19, 20, 82, 131
Timaru, 42, 355, 356, 360
Tongue, Sutherland, Scotland, 120
Tradeston, Glasgow, Clackmannanshire, Scotland, 364
Trentham Military Camp, 75, 76
Tuapeka, 158
Upper Hutt, 130
Victoria Bridge, 152
Waianiwa, 191
Waikouaiti, 72, 218, 289, 290
Warsaw, Poland, 173
Wellington, 66, 76, 84, 90, 106, 130, 133, 236, 272
Whenuapai, 292
Wigram, 291
Winton, 110, 113, 126, 135, 197, 204, 217, 236, 237, 238, 239
Wolsingham, Durham, England, 119
TURTON
H. H., 175
Mr, 175
VARCOE
J. S., 231
WATSON
A., 54
Emily, 277
Master A., 54
Noeline, 206, 217
Robert, 206, 217
WHITE
Mary, 327
WHITTEN
Betson Margaret, 165
John, 165
WILLIAMS
Mr, 122
WILLS
Inspector, 38
W., 38
WILSON
Betson, 157, 160
Bill, 123
Euphemia, 157
Julia, 375
Madge Wallace, b.1910, 373, 374

WITHEFORD
  Mr J. H., 178
WOOD

Miss, 59
Miss R., 54
R., 54

About the Author

Lorraine Berry (née Chalmers)

Lorraine is a granddaughter of John and Eleanor CHALMERS. Both had passed on before she was born. She began collecting information and items of interest from relatives in 1980. In 2004 and 2006 she travelled to England and Scotland to visit and photograph ancestral sites. Having retired from a fulltime career in education as primary school teacher and administrator, in 2007 she went to the United States to gain research skills from professional genealogists. Over three years later she returned to New Zealand and has remained as a volunteer consultant at family history centres. She is a co-author of two books on her maternal grandparents and their ancestors, one *Sunnyside :The Mitchell Family of Mimihau* and the other *Of a Very Superior Class: The Pink Family of Waianiwa.*[1]

---

[1] Lindsay Watson and Lorraine Berry, *Of a Very Superior Class: The Pink Family of Waianiwa* (Ashburton, N.Z.: Lindsay R. Watson, 2017); Lindsay Watson, Lorraine Berry and Heather Bray, *Sunnyside: The Mitchell Family of Mimihau* (Ashburton, N.Z.: Lindsay R. Watson, 2018).